1987

THE FOUNDATIONS OF
Contemporary American Education

Erwin V. Johanningmeier
UNIVERSITY OF SOUTH FLORIDA

Gorsuch Scarisbrick, Publishers
SCOTTSDALE, ARIZONA

For Christina and Elizabeth

Editor: *Wayne Schotanus*
Consulting Editor: *Alden J. Moe*
Production Manager: *Gay Orr*
Manuscript Editor: *Mary Hoff*
Cover Design: *Gordon Fong, The Omni Group*
Typesetting: *Carlisle Graphics*
Layout: *Bill Nebel, Graphic Arts Services*
Printing and Binding: *BookCrafters*

Gorsuch Scarisbrick, Publishers
8233 Via Paseo del Norte, Suite E-400
Scottsdale, Arizona 85258

10 9 8 7 6 5 4 3 2 1

ISBN 0-89787-519-2

Printed in the United States of America.

Preface

Two major convictions are the basis of this text. First is the belief that teachers must give attention not only to enhancing the quality of their students' lives but also to understanding how society uses its schools to realize social, economic, and political purposes. Second is the belief that less attention should be given to the nation's transformation from an agrarian-rural society to an industrial-urban society at the end of the nineteenth century and more attention to its transformation from an industrial to a postindustrial society. We should therefore begin with a focus on how American society has changed during and after World War II.

A major assumption of this text is that public education, like society, is suffering from something other than temporary bad times. It is experiencing the difficulties and uncertainties attendant to any period of major social, political, and economic change. The belief that criticism of public education will soon run its course should be balanced by the belief that ours is a new age and, to paraphrase English philosopher Alfred North Whitehead, a new age may call for new kinds of institutions and new ways of managing those institutions.

With the War, the technologies, issues, and problems that continue to perplex us and influence how we work, live, and school our children became part of American life. Nuclear energy has caused us to reconsider our classical notions of war and peace, as well as our assumptions about the best way to provide energy for our factories and homes. The computer and television—two ways to store, manipulate, and transmit information and images—constantly draw our attention to the "information age" and occasionally lead us to question the viability of traditional schools. The attempt to extend true equality of opportunity to all Americans began in earnest after the Supreme Court handed down its decision in the *Brown v. Topeka* case in 1954. As Diane Ravitch has shown in *The Troubled Crusade: American Education, 1945–1980,* each of these interesting developments is complicated enough for a complete book. Their implications cannot be fully explored in this text, but their importance has been considered in deciding what to include and emphasize.

This text does not claim that the precise features of the newly developing society can be predicted. Nor does it claim that the transition from one kind of society to another has been completed. The assumption is made, however, that as the transformation proceeds, our ways of living, working and educating our children will also be transformed. Indeed, by the time the process has run its course, public education may be very different from that we have known. We may need to find new ways to satisfy our needs and to maintain our basic values.

While the conceptual starting point for this text has been a consideration of post–World War II developments, the history of our schools has not been neglected for three important reasons. First, as David Hamilton of the University of Glasgow reminds me, social change is not an event but a process. It may be fast or slow but never instantaneous. While we may not have time to prevent new developments, we may be able to influence their course and decide how we want to respond to them. Second, embedded in our history are the traditions and values by which we live and those that are tested and challenged by social, economic, and political developments. History can show us how and why we value what we do. Third, history helps us to distinguish between the old and the new and between the superficial and the substantive, thereby enabling us to acquire some means, however limited, to interpret the existential predicaments in which we find ourselves.

Few, if any, texts are truly comprehensive, and this one is no exception. Choices are always necessary. In the first of four major parts, "School and Society," the state and vitality of American society are assessed. It is suggested that how we live, work, and educate our children may all be very different by the end of the twentieth century. Also examined are the criticisms of public education, which seem to have reached a new level after World War II. Such examinations enable us to see what the public values and expects of its schools. Proposals to make schools "accountable" and efforts to create alternatives to traditional forms of schooling are also considered.

Part II is entitled "The Nationalization of American Education." After World War II, the federal government began to match traditional rhetoric about the importance of public education with legislation, court decisions, and appropriations from the national treasury. During this period, new curricula were suggested and tried. What schools did and did not teach became national as well as local issues to which educators had to respond.

After the development of new curricula, the nation attempted to extend equality of educational and economic opportunity and to eliminate poverty through school-based programs. Those attempts and their evaluations have significantly influenced how we view our schools and their capabilities. Before the end of the 1970s, many persons had lost their traditional faith in the ability of public education to solve social and economic problems. Some believe we still suffer from that loss of faith.

With the exception of atomic power, nothing has had more impact on how Americans view their world than the computer and television. Part III, "The Electronic Foundations of Education," offers an account of their development and how we have thought about their uses and effects on public education. The emphasis is not on how to use these media to improve instructional efficiency but on their significance in our society. Our system of public education came about in an era when access to information was difficult, cumbersome, and even restricted. Now that access may be immediate and virtually without restriction, and information that once was available only in the schools is now readily available almost everywhere.

Part IV, "Students and Teachers," attends to the most important subjects of both the text and education. Traditional concepts regarding children and teachers have been challenged since World War II. Our view of children, their relationships to their parents and to the nation's economy, and their rights and privileges have all been the subject of discussion and reinterpretation. Special attention has been given to the needs and care of preschool children, a group for whom teachers may have to assume even greater responsibility in the future. Even if teachers do not assume this responsibility, the effects of new practices and arrangements for the care of the preschool child will eventually be felt in the classrooms of the early grades.

Older children, like smaller children, are also experiencing new challenges and difficulties. The pressure on youth to remain in school is greater than ever before. Significantly, their opportunities, especially those of minority youth, to secure meaningful and sustaining employment are diminishing.

The final two chapters examine the job of teaching, its rewards and difficulties, and new concepts in its practice. In some respects, the final chapter returns to the early parts of the text, and gives attention to the new cycle of criticism that Americans presented to their schools in the late 1970s and early 1980s.

At the end of the text is a Guide for Research. Students who either must prepare a research project or who simply want to know more about a topic can find direction to the standard references and journals in education.

In preparing this text, I have benefited immensely from the contributions and considerations of many friends, colleagues, students, and relatives. As always, Charles Weingartner remained my most faithful, persistent, and harshest critic. He should not be blamed for my failure to accept all his good advice and penetrating criticisms. Librarians always deserve special gratitude for their contributions, but Elizabeth Crahan, Director of the Los Angeles County Medical Association Library, deserves special thanks for locating government documents during a Christmas vacation. Students' questions are always helpful, but two, Carolyn Schoultz and Patricia Shoemaker, deserve special recognition. Carolyn read an early version of the manuscript and asked good, if not easy, questions, while Patricia directed my attention to literature on the media and on computers that I would probably have otherwise overlooked. Louisa Clark Bardetti carefully proofread many chapters and made many other contributions to the manuscript. Becky Cagle had the misfortune of appearing when the manuscript was near completion and had to check and recheck numerous details. Her contributions were indeed important and extremely helpful. Margaret Miller suffered through my frustrations with patience. Finally, I appreciate the help of the following reviewers who evaluated all or parts of the manuscript: Edward McClellan of Indiana University; Richard Pratte of Ohio State University; Samuel Shermes of Purdue University; Spencer J. Maxcy and Alden J. Moe of Louisiana State University; Robert Johnson of the University of North Alabama; Gerry Tucker and Jeffrey L. Haven of Lamar University; Thomas Nelson of Illinois State University; and Karl Openshaw of the University of Colorado.

Contents

PART I
School and Society

Preparation for teaching and the study of education would be much simpler if schools and their classrooms were insulated from the complex and frequently confusing "outside" world. Teaching and the administration of schools would also be simpler if teachers only had to worry about satisfying the children's interests and needs and if administrators only had to worry about providing teachers with what they require to do their jobs effectively. And if schools were controlled only, or largely, by trained professional personnel, we could confine our preparation for educational careers to study of the biological and psychological bases of human growth and development, to study about how people learn and why they frequently do not learn, and to reviews of clinical studies and practices.

For two major reasons, however, schools and teaching are shaped and directed by the major social, political, and economic environments in which they exist. First, we as citizens expect our schools to conform to our ever-changing perceptions of what is in "the national interest." Second, as parents and guardians we want schools to satisfy the current real-life interests and needs of children *and* prepare them for success in a social, economic, and political setting that may conceivably exist twenty or thirty years from now.

We can list what schools are expected to accomplish and discuss how important and complicated those expectations are; however, such discussions invariably emphasize only our uncertainty about the goals and methods our schools should formulate and follow. When our national goal was to set foot first on the lunar surface, public schools were expected to begin preparing students for such ventures. When we focused on true racial integration of our society, public schools were expected to serve as a model for all other institutions. When our economy is weakened by the import of products made less expensively in other countries, public schools are expected to teach students to be more productive workers. Soon after we let schools know that we expect them to tend to the special needs of handicapped students, we begin to complain that the average and above average students are being unduly neglected. We expect schools to identify the able students so they can be trained for scientific and professional careers, but we expect that *our* children will be among those so identified. And while we want our children to achieve at above normal rates in the traditional academic areas, we also want them to find school an enjoyable place with ample opportunities for self-expression. When we look closely at what Americans expect of their schools and at how well Americans believe their schools meet these expectations, we encounter a complex mosaic of opinions, facts, predictions, charges, and conflicting recommendations.

1

The goal of Part I, "School and Society," is to confront the reader with information about this complex and ever-evolving mosaic—our expectations—so that he or she can begin to decide what constitutes a worthy purpose for public schooling, and can identify the social, political, economic, and educational conditions necessary for realization of that purpose.

The basic assumptions of Chapter 1, "The Transformation of the American Dream," are that Americans expect their schools to contribute to the well being and prosperity of their children, that the future may be different from the past, that the nature of our society has undergone a major transformation since World War II, and that new kinds of societies require new kinds of schools. In our exploration of this assumption, we assume that the United States has indeed started down the path toward what Zbigniew Brzezinski calls the "technetronic society."

Chapter 2, "How Americans View Their Schools," shows that, since World War II, Americans have been evaluating their schools almost continuously. From the vantage point of the professional educator, it may seem that the public schools have been subject to wave after wave of criticism from a public that cannot make up its mind. But however troublesome and annoying the public's criticism of education may be to professional educators, that criticism is an index of the value the public attaches to public education. It seems unlikely that the public's attention will ever be long turned away from its schools; it is likely that the public will continue to actively participate in determining what schools do and how they do it.

Chapter 3, "From Alternatives to Accountability and Beyond," is designed to show just how diverse the public's demands on public education may be. When we think of accountability, we think of a system that is well managed, highly supervised, and tightly controlled. When we think of alternatives, we think of variety, of choices, of the possibility that all may not be required to conform to the same educational regime. That both alternatives and accountability have received so much attention in not much more than a decade clearly indicates that there has been no clear consensus on the goals and methods of our schools. These varying foci also indicate that education is a field with many possibilities. There is work to be done. We need to find ways to make schools responsive to the needs of the society and the needs of individual students. The questions before us are those Patricia Albjerg Graham recently presented:

> Why should we educate? What are the benefits that individuals legitimately should expect from education? What are the benefits that society should expect from an educated citizenry? Are these benefits in conflict or are they mutually reinforcing? How can we achieve them?[1]

Graham's comments about the purposes of education are also instructive. She reminds us that "public purposes for education change as the society perceives its needs and priorities differently."[2] If, after reading Part I, the reader is able to discuss what factors need to be considered in establishing a satisfactory educational purpose, he or she will have been successful. If the reader can offer and support alternatives to what has been presented in the text, he or she will have been more than successful and the purpose of the text will have been satisfied.

Notes

1. Patricia Albjerg Graham, "Schools: Cacophony About Practice, Silence About Purpose," *Daedalus* (Fall 1984): 29.
2. Ibid.

1
The Transformation of the American Dream

The American Dream

Americans have always believed that their circumstances could be improved through their own efforts and that the circumstances of their children would be better than their own. According to William Proefriedt, "the dream, stated minimally, was that individuals, freed from the ancient chains of caste and class, could by their own efforts and ability achieve success."[1] Paul Blumberg observed that Americans "believed that the younger generation would have it better and living standards would naturally improve almost by some divine law with each succeeding generation."[2] One generation's successes became the expected accomplishments and obligations of subsequent generations. What was received from one's parents had to be enhanced and passed on to the next generation. If parents could not improve their own situation, they worked to improve the lots of their children, usually by working to send their children to school. As a working-class parent explained to Studs Terkel:

> If you can't improve yourself, you improve your posterity . . . . I'm sure the first cave man who went over the hill to see what was on the other side —I don't think he went there wholly out of curiosity. He went there because he wanted to get his son out of the cave. Just the same way I want to send my son to college.[3]

An early and yet concise expression of the American dream is found in Hector St. John de Crèvecoeur's *Letters from an American Farmer* (1782). In these letters we are introduced to the American farmer whose father gave him an education that included not much more than "the art of reading and writing" and a good farm, the benefit of his experience, no debts, and "no kinds of difficulties to struggle with."[4] The farmer's father had built a life for his son that was clearly more prosperous than his own. The son acknowledged what had been given to him and his responsibility to maintain and nourish it:

> My father left me three hundred and seventy-one acres of land, forty-seven of which are good timothy meadow, an excellent orchard, a good house and a substantial barn. It is my duty to think how happy I am that he lived to build and to pay for all those improvements; what are the labors which I have to undergo, what are my fatigues when compared to his, who had everything to do, from the first tree he felled to the finishing of his house.[5]

As Americans moved west after the War of Independence and through the twentieth century, many developed farms, ranches, and other enterprises that they bequeathed to their

3

children. Successes somehow overshadowed failures. Sometimes towns that failed were disassembled, loaded onto wagons, and moved to a new site, thereby erasing failure. The belief in continuous progress was easy to sustain in a nation blessed with a seemingly boundless prairie, an abundance of natural resources, and an ever-increasing supply of talent and inexpensive labor from the "old country." Working for the improvement of one's family was a source of happiness and pride. The American farmer set the example for us by placing his son on the plough before him while he worked:

> Often when I plough my low ground, I place my little boy on a chair which screws to the beam of the plough. As I lean over the handle, various are the thoughts which crowd into my mind. I am now doing for him, I say, what my father did for me, may God enable him to live that he may perform the same operations for the same purposes when I am worn and old.[6]

Now it is not always practical to have our children before us while we work, but many clerks, laborers, and executives accomplish this symbolically with photographs of their sons, daughters, and spouses on their desks or above their workbenches.

Even though we may sometimes question whether the American dream is still socially, psychologically, politically, and economically viable, it persists. The American farm family believed that through hard work their children would live in a world essentially the same and yet just a bit better. Their children would have a little more and would work a little less hard. American politicians appeal to our belief in this dream when they justify their decisions with assurances that a program will make a better and safer world for our children, or warn us that another program will saddle our children with enormous debts. They can make such appeals because virtually all Americans share similar aspirations for their children. As W. Norton Grubb and Marvin Lazerson have observed, "parents across all classes, races, and income groups share much the same hope: they want their children to live comfortably, to enjoy stable, happy home lives, to have some measure of control over their own lives, not to live at the mercy of others."[7] Americans expect that their children will have a fair and equal chance at social and economic mobility, and the institution expected to ensure such opportunities is the public school.

Questions About the American Dream

Today, for a variety of complex environmental, social, and political reasons, we may not all be certain that our children will live in a world better than the one inherited by their parents. Part of our uncertainty focuses on our social institutions, and it is not the first time in our history that American institutions have been questioned. In 1914, the year that "widespread unemployment gave the anarchists in New York City an unusual opportunity for agitation,"[8] Walter Lippmann observed that the nation's institutions seemed inadequate to meet the needs and aspirations of Americans. School, church, government were all failing to satisfy the demands placed on them. As Lippmann then believed, the world of the American farmer had disappeared. In a passage that reads as though it could have been written just a few years ago, he observed:

> We are unsettled to the very roots of our being. There isn't a human relation, whether of parent and child, husband and wife, worker and employee, that doesn't move in a strange situation. We are not used to a complicated civilization, we don't know how to behave when personal contact

and eternal authority have disappeared. There are no precedents to guide us, no wisdom that wasn't made for a simpler age. We have changed our environment more quickly than we know how to change ourselves.[9]

Sociologists have long warned us about the severe lag between our technology and our ways of thinking—seemingly our value systems should guide our economic and technological innovations, and not lag weakly behind. Politicians began sensing uneasiness and discontent among their constituents and promised a restoration of old values and old ways under the banner of the "new." They offered the New Nationalism, the New Freedom, the New Deal, and even a New Frontier and a New America. They urged schools to get "back to the basics" to meet the challenges and changes before them. But what did these battle cries mean? Few politicians dare to suggest that Americans themselves may need to change, or modify their beliefs or perceptions. As Godfrey Hodgson noted in his study of post–World War II America, Americans have resisted substantive changes. According to Hodgson:

> For all its belief in innovation, American society at the beginning of the 1960s was still conservative. People wanted change; they did not want to be changed. Or, rather, they changed their clothes, their cars or their homes more easily than they changed their assumptions, their attitudes or their beliefs.[10]

As Americans faced impassioned claims that the quality of American life had deteriorated and could not be completely restored, their view of the past was also transformed. Some claimed that "we have had, all along, the wrong dream" and believed that "we have unleashed an unparalleled selfishness resulting in a divided and unequal society, attended by the envy of the poor, the mean-spiritedness of the wealthy, and the anxiety of those in between."[11] Economists who promised endless prosperity lost favor to those whom Marvin Harris describes as "a new breed of dismal economists." The new breed does not insist that "poverty is inevitable" but it does insist that "the American dream of universal prosperity will never come true."[12] Consequently, hope that social inequalities would be remedied by the abundance produced by our industries is now diminished, ironically, by the fear that equal opportunity will mean less for all. Often discussions of public education focus not on equality of educational opportunity but on quality in education, as though the two are incompatible.[13]

The growing doubts concerning the nation's ability to support its institutions and their human services programs are accompanied by the claim that Americans may, at last, have to change—they will have to learn to expect less, to reduce their ambitions and disassemble earlier plans and programs. "Those who say the dream has ended point to its dependence on the continued growth of the national world economy, a growth they see as unlikely, and to a new rigidity of class lines within the society."[14] Eric F. Goldman's prediction in the early 1960s that Americans would "continue, through extensions of the welfare state and of welfare capitalism and through a variety of other techniques, the economic and social revolutions which had marked the previous decades"[15] seemed not to materialize in the 1970s. Though during the Reagan administration Americans as a whole have experienced a revival of "national spirit," Americans nonetheless seem to accept the possibility that their future successes may be fewer than their past successes. In an address to the nation in July 1979, then President Carter noted that "We've always believed in something called progress. We've always had faith that the days of our children would be better than our own. Our people are losing faith."[16] Americans may have regained their faith in an American ideal during the 1980s, but they have retained their new, well-founded worries about the nation's institutions; according to Hodgson, "the legitimacy of virtually every institution [has] been challenged, and the validity of virtually every assumption disputed."[17] We question first and foremost the nation's abilities to sustain and support its institutions, especially schools. Even in the midst of the excellence movement in education, "two leaders of the school-finance community" warned that "public schools will have to fight in the second half of the decade just to maintain their current [1985] per pupil spending levels."[18] By the mid-1980s, it seemed very likely that federal support for public education would decrease. President Reagan was proposing either spending freezes (a freeze is only a freeze as long as there are no increases in population and no inflation; otherwise a freeze is a cut) or cuts in most elementary and secondary education programs: compensatory education, headstart, special education, bilingual education, aid for federally impacted areas, school lunch programs, job training, immunization against childhood diseases, and other programs within the jurisdiction of the National Endowment for the Humanities and the National Endowment for the Arts.[19]

Interpreting Our Past, Present, and Future

Most who have assessed the problems of the 1960s and 1970s and the prospects for the future agree that these problems are not isolated, temporary problems that can be easily resolved so that normal progress and prosperity can resume. Many believe that recent problems are signs that one historical era is, or has been, ending and that we are entering a new period of history. There is little agreement, however, about whether the new era will be better or worse—though we agree it is likely to be different from what we have known.

Christopher Lasch claims that during the twentieth century Americans lost their independence and their ability to govern themselves. Acceptance of a passive life, a life in which essential activities are directed by the corporation, the bureaucracy, and the scientific expert has resulted in a "crisis of confidence." The "crisis of confidence" characterized by the "centralization of power" and the "decline of popular participation in community life" began at the turn of the century but became "dramatically visible only in the period since World War II."[20] The development of the industrial corporation created a division of labor and a division of power that was contrary to the interests of individuals. The division between "brainwork" and "handwork" was made. Technical knowledge, knowledge about how to produce goods, was allotted to the managerial elite, the experts. Once the processes of production were organized, corporate industry proceeded to organize the mass market and created a "cultural revolution." It was, according to Lasch, a revolution designed to drive out traditional values:

> The virtues of thrift, avoidance of debt, and postponement of gratification had to give way to new habits of installment buying and immediate gratification, new standards of comfort, a new sensitivity to changes in fashion. People had to be discouraged from providing their own wants and resocialized as consumers.[21]

The division between "brainwork" and "handwork" in the nation's economy was recognized early by American educators, and before long advocates for traditional forms of liberal education were in conflict with advocates of vocational education—a conflict that has continued to thrive in recent years. In 1914 a proponent of vocational education, David Snedder, argued that "producers" needed a different education than "consumers." The aims of liberal education, usually expressed in such "vague" and "mystical" phrases as "culture," "character," "mental discipline," "self-reliance," "capacity for self-direction," and "social-efficiency," were too imprecise to prepare efficient producers. According to Snedden, the aim of vocational education—"to equip a young person for a recognized calling"—was quite precise, and, to ensure efficiency in the educational system, at age 14 children should be designated as future producers or consumers and sent to the appropriate school.[22]

Such a system, opponents declared, implied the establishment of a "permanent proletariat," a system that would fail to use talent that was evenly distributed among the social classes. William C. Bagley objected to dividing children so some could produce while others consumed, and urged postponement of differentiation for as long as possible. He maintained that separate schools for vocational education would only perpetuate existing social stratification and insisted that "the question-begging statement that such stratification already exists" was no defense for continuing it. It was, he admitted, costly "to keep the door of opportunity open at every level of the educational ladder," but that cost was necessary for the preservation of a democratic society.[23]

If we assume that, in the context of a wiser, questioning America, we may still subscribe to the American dream, and still strive for educational equality *and* educational quality, and use both traditional and vocational education to our advantage, then we are approaching a new educational vision.

Cycles and the Future

Our ability to predict, prepare, and plan for the future is limited by what we know and what we can imagine. In projecting a course for the future, we have little choice but to examine both current and past developments. Writers in the *The Futurist* have employed the work of the Russian economist Nickolai Kondratieff to construct possible future scenarios that emphasize parallels with the past. According to Kondratieff, each fifty-year economic cycle is characterized by a twenty- to twenty-five-year upward trend followed by a downward trend of the same length. In the 1930s, Kondratieff indicated that Western economies had troughs in 1790, during 1844–51 and 1890–96, and in the 1930s. Peaks, he claimed, occurred during 1810–17, 1869–73, and 1914–20. If his theory is correct, the end of this century may see greater prosperity than the decades preceding it.[24]

Dick Stoken has used the Kondratieff cycles to argue that the political and social revolution of the sixties was not "unique."[25] The prosperity and the domestic tranquillity of the early 1950s, he maintains, were similar to the qualities of the early 1900s. Each period began with "idealistic hopes that society could solve its problems." Similar to the social legislation of the 1960s was Prohibition. In each era, the social legislation designed to remedy existing social problems created new problems. Youth's attempt in the 1960s to establish a new way of life based on a new set of values was not unlike attempts in the 1920s to break away from tradition's restraints.

When economic upswings bring prosperity, many persons develop a desire to "break loose from the social constraints that groups and strict social codes impose upon them." With the belief that they actually "have control over their own destiny, with the power to solve their own and society's problems," their intolerance of social injustice increases. People seek competition and throw off regulations. As Stoken observes: "Witness the recent legislation to foster competition in the brokerage, airline, and trucking industries, to allow lawyers and doctors to advertise, to allow citizens to own gold, and to let exchange rates float—all directed at freeing markets and increasing competition."[26] In education, some favor breaking the public school monopoly so that, in the words of President Reagan, people have "greater freedom to send their children to the schools they desire without interference by . . . government."[27]

Downswings are accompanied by the adoption of cautious and conservative values, but they do not signal a complete return to earlier values and behaviors. During the Great Depression of the 1930s, "the frivolousness and open sensuality of the 1920s disappeared," but Americans did not recreate the 1890s. According to Stoken, "much of the outlandish, frenzied behavior was no longer accepted, but many of the new freedoms won by the flappers of the younger generation remained."[28] Still, during downswings, tolerance of deviant behavior seems to wane, marriage and the family are more highly prized than previously, the music slows, "and a sense of community and camaraderie takes hold." All changes during downswings are not benign, however. During the depression of the 1870s and 1880s, anti-Semitism increased greatly. Discriminatory legislation was passed in Russia and Rumania, and in Germany Adolph Stocker founded an anti-Semitic party. In the 1930s, the Nazi party built upon the foundation prepared by Stocker, and in the United States Father Charles Coughlin, an isolationist Catholic priest, conducted anti-Semitic radio broadcasts. If one places credence in the applications of the Kondratieff cycles, the expressed fears of civil rights leaders who charge that a stagnant or slowly growing economy is accompanied by attempts to take away rights and opportunities recently won by American minorities may not be without foundation. The Jim Crow laws were initiated in the 1890s.

While Stoken did not predict that America would enter a depression in the 1980s, he did offer predictions about what America would be like if one did occur. Within a decade, he claims that "most likely there will be a noticeable moderation of the recent cultural revolution. A new social mood will emerge. People will be cautious and willing to settle for less . . . . And the younger generation will be less rebellious and less scornful of marriage and family life."[29]

Ralph Hamil maintains that while "there appear to be valid reasons for pessimism regarding the West's ability to resume its former economic growth rates," a depression comparable to that of the 1930s is not inevitable. Americans have learned from the mismanagement of that era, and a number of other factors seem to preclude its repetition. Among these factors are the present controls on exchange of securities, government's long experience with Keynesian principles and its increased influence on some sectors of the economy, a decreased birthrate that will temporarily alleviate some of the pressure to create new jobs, and the position of the defense and armaments industries, which did not exist half a century ago.[30]

Jay Forrester of the Massachusetts Institute of Technology has proposed a cycle even longer than that of Kondratieff's, a 200-year cycle. He claims that the United States has reached the end of a 200-year cycle of economic growth and that the nation is somewhere between the end of its period of economic expansion and the beginning of its period of "equilibrium in both population and industrial activity."[31]

Limits

Many future scenarios emphasize that the United States, if not all of Western society, has reached some sort of limit. The notion of "limits" merits examination because some believe we have already begun to experience its effects. During the past decades, Americans have been told about many limits: the limits of social security, the limits of our capacity to feed future populations, the limits of our water supply, the limits of reason to solve our social, economic, political, and ecological problems, and so on. Renewed controversies among psychologists and educators regarding intelligence—how much it is affected by education and how much it is fixed by nature—are symptomatic of a society concerned with its limits.

The irony of the "limits" notion is that it arose from our national attempt to expand our national horizons. In 1960, John Kennedy was elected to the presidency and promised to open a new frontier. One sector of that frontier was space—seemingly unlimited. The first great excursion to the moon required encapsulation of the astronauts in vehicles that were analogous to the planet Earth. The spaceships and spacesuits supplied them all they needed for life: shelter, air, water, food, and the capacity to store waste. As the astronauts sent back pictures of Earth from space, Buckminster Fuller's term, "spaceship Earth," acquired a meaning that nearly all could comprehend. Earth was finite. It had limits. Its capacity for storing waste was limited and so were its life-supporting systems. The balance between the two was delicate and demanded careful attention. Progress and consumption of Earth's resources had their price.

The sense of limits that has developed in American society is not, however, restricted to the planet's natural resources. It applies to its inhabitants as well. Perhaps none stated the matter more succinctly than did Elliot Richardson when he left the Department of Defense. On that occasion, he remarked: "We must recognize, as we have with both foreign affairs and natural resources, that resources we once thought were boundless—human, financial, and intellectual resources—are indeed severely limited."[32] Richardson and others began to question whether the U.S. government could realize the aspirations of its people and solve the nation's social and economic problems. Even the faith, hope, and promise traditionally invested in public education was seriously questioned. The longstanding belief that the public school could be used as the mechanism to bring about social equality was undermined by the analyses and debates subsequent to the publication of the Coleman Report (1966). Historians of education—once noted for extolling the virtues, power, and successes of public education—began to document its limitations and failures.

A New Historical Era

It is possible to argue that America is not losing its power and stature but rather is merely suffering from the dislocations attendant to its entry into a truly new era—an era brought about by the continued growth of its scientific and technological capabilities. According to the historian Arthur M. Schlesinger, Jr., we have been experiencing an "increase in the velocity of history." The change we have been experiencing is so rapid that we now see more change in a week than our ancestors saw in a decade. The application of science and technology to our social and economic processes has sent us into an uncharted future. As Schlesinger observed:

Science and technology make, dissolve, rebuild and enlarge our environment every week . . . .
This has meant the disappearance of familiar landmarks and guideposts that stabilized life for

earlier generations. It has meant that children, knowing how different their own lives will be, can no longer look to parents as models and authorities. Change is always scary; uncharted, uncontrolled change can be deeply demoralizing. It is no wonder that we moderns feel forever disoriented and off balance; unsure of our ideas and institutions; unsure of our relations to others, to society and to history; unsure of our purposes and identity.[33]

The turmoil, confusion, uncertainty, and apparent decline of many established values, practices, and institutions do not necessarily signal "the inexorable decline of America." Rather, as Schlesinger suggests, they "may be less the proof of decay than the price of progress." The changes and dislocations we are experiencing may be unique to America only in that America is confronting them sooner than other nations. In fact, America has not only the opportunity to develop ways "to absorb, digest and even control the consequences of accelerated technological change" but also the opportunity to "restore American influence in the world."[34]

Schlesinger's claim that "the turmoil, the confusion, even the violence may well be the birth pains of a new epoch in the history of man" may be correct. That the future must be faced with vision, imagination, and intelligence is indeed a reasonable assertion. Human action and deliberate human choice may be more necessary now than ever before. Knowing how to act correctly and how to choose wisely is never easy, because of the temptation to apply old standards to new situations. The traditional form and content of schooling must be examined to determine their appropriateness for the future. Possibly only one or the other will need revision.

Whether the future will be different from the present or simply a facsimile of the past remains to be seen. Doubtlessly, attempts will be made to restore what was, for that is what we know best. We want certainty for ourselves and for our children and urge that our schools return to the basics without every specifying what the basics are. When we explore alternatives, we frequently regress to old ways as though an immutable set of rules exists for all situations and all purposes without interpretation and modification. At some juncture, just as has been done with industry, Americans will have to reexamine traditional school conventions and the purposes of public education to ascertain what alternatives may be considered.

Walter Lippmann argued that Americans could continue to drift toward chaos or that they could break with tradition, adopt a clear purpose, and, with the aid of science and technology, master their destinies. Some argue now that our faith in science has degenerated into a fanatic and blind faith in techniques that has rendered us numb to any sense of deliberate purpose. We look at techniques for gathering information and forget how to relate the information to our purposes. In schools, we refine, restate, and assess objectives but avoid asking how those objectives fit in with the purposes of the institution, its personnel, or the students. As Marilyn Ferguson, author of the *Age of Aquarius,* has observed, "we argue about the best methods for teaching the curriculum of public schools, yet rarely question whether the curriculum itself is appropriate."[35]

The Age of Aquarius

Ferguson is among those who agree that we have worked ourselves into a cultural crisis that reveals "the ways in which our institutions have betrayed nature."

We have equated the good life with material consumption, we have dehumanized work and made it needlessly competitive, we are uneasy about our capacities for learning and teaching . . . . Our government is complex and unresponsive, our social support system is breaking at every stress point.[36]

Nonetheless, Ferguson has not lost faith in the American dream, which, she claims, has had a variety of meanings, and, also has the potential for "renewal."

[The dream is] a chameleon; it has changed again and again. For the first immigrants, America was a continent to explore and exploit, a haven for the unwanted and the dissenters—a new beginning. Gradually the dream became an ascetic and idealized image of democracy, bespeaking the age-old hope for justice and self governance. All too quickly, that dream metamorphosed into an expansionist, materialistic, nationalistic, and even imperialistic vision of wealth and domination—paternalism, Manifest Destiny. Yet even then, there was a competing Transcendentalist vision: excellence, spiritual riches, the unfolding of the latent gifts of the individual.[37]

For one social class "the dream of tangibles" has focused "on material well-being and practical, everyday freedoms." For "the comfortable social classes," there has been another dream, "like an etheric body extending from the material dream," that "seeks psychological liberation."

Ferguson argues that both the American dream and Americans are being transformed by a movement she calls "The Aquarian Conspiracy." This movement may signal the end of one historical era and the beginning of another. Her description of it is reminiscent of Peter Gay's description of another great movement in Western civilization—the Enlightenment.

According to Gay, the enlightenment was brought about by "a loose, informal, wholly unorganized coalition of cultural critics, religious skeptics, and political reformers from Edinburgh to Naples, Paris to Berlin, Boston to Philadelphia." While "there were some discordant voices" among the eighteenth century cultural critics, they were "united on a vastly ambitious program of secularism, humanity, cosmopolitanism, and freedom, above all, freedom of trade, freedom to realize one's talents, freedom of aesthetic response, freedom in a word, of moral man to make his own way in the world."[38]

For Ferguson, the Aquarian Conspiracy is a "leaderless but powerful network" whose members "range across all levels of income and education, from the humblest to the highest." They include "school teachers and office workers, famous scientists, government officials and lawmakers, artists and millionaires, taxi drivers and celebrities, leaders in medicine, education, law, psychology."[39] They can be found in all society's institutions: "in corporations, universities and hospitals, on the faculties of public education, in factories and doctors' offices, in state and federal agencies, on city councils and the White House staff, in stage legislatures, in volunteer organizations, in virtually all areas of policy-making in the country." While the Aquarian Conspirators may "have broken with certain key elements of Western thought" and "may even have broken continuity with history," they are "without a political doctrine" and "without a manifesto." They are promoting neither revolution nor reform but a "cultural realignment," a new mind, not simply a new political, religious, or philosophical system.

The eighteenth century philosophers sought freedom; the Aquarian Conspirators seek transformation. To use Thomas Kuhn's term they are trying to establish a new paradigm that "sees humankind embedded in nature. It promotes the autonomous individual in a decentralized society. It sees us as stewards of all our resources, inner and outer. It says that we are *not* victims, not pawns, not limited by conditions or conditioning."[40]

Aquarian Conspirators do not debate whether human nature is good or bad but emphasize that it is "open to continuous transformation." They do not catalogue the ways in which people in the modern world are powerless but note that as "heirs to evolutionary riches, we are capable of imagination, invention, and experiences we have only glimpsed."[41] The possibility they glimpse in their present surroundings is "not a counterculture, not a reaction, but an emergent culture—the coalescence of a new social order."[42]

The Aquarian Mind

If the claims of the Aquarian Conspirators are correct, we can expect people in the future to think differently than we do. Not only will the objects of thought change but also the ways in which ideas and information are gathered and processed. Our values may be different and also the significance that is attached to ideas and information. The precise features of such a transformation cannot be delineated, of course, but some sense of what such a change may mean can be obtained by looking at earlier changes and differences. For example, in *The Heavenly City of the Eighteenth-Century Philosophers,* published in 1932, Carl Becker illustrated how dramatically divergent ways of thinking in different eras can be by pretending that we could bring St. Thomas Aquinas and Dante to join us in conversation. Becker urged us to ask Aquinas to define the concept of natural law, "a phrase as much used in his time as in ours." Becker then provided a passage from the *Summa Theologica* that was directly related to the question asked but also not applicable to thinking in the early 1930s. Becker then asked Dante to speak about the League of Nations and provided an appropriate passage from *De monarchia,* one that was no less obscure than that from the *Summa.* Becker concluded that Dante and Aquinas would have equal difficulty understanding us: "It is unlikely that either of them would find it strictly relevant or even understand which side of the argument we were espousing."[43]

Becker was unwilling to dismiss either Aquinas or Dante as "unintelligent." His explanation for the difficulties in communication was based on the phrase "climate of opinion," which at that time had been brought back to use by the philosopher Alfred North Whitehead. According to Becker, "What renders Dante's argument or Aquinas's definition meaningless to us is not bad logic or want of intelligence, but the medieval climate of opinion—those instinctively held preconceptions in the broad sense, that *Weltanschauung* or world pattern— which imposed upon Dante and Aquinas a peculiar use of the intelligence and special type of logic."[44] If we are to make sense of the problems our society and its schools will confront in the future, we should be mindful that from time to time "climates of opinion" change. What was once obvious and appropriate may seem strange today or in the future when the world may be governed by a "climate of opinion" quite different from our own.

Brzezinski's Technetronic Society

During the 1970s, Zbigniew Brzezinski analyzed the problems of American society and its prospects and concluded that the United States was being transformed into a "society increasingly unlike its industrial predecessor," a society he called "technetronic."[45] In the industrial society, technology is developed and applied directly to productive process, for the paramount concern is the improved efficiency of industry. Such applications have created social change, challenged and even eroded existing mores, reshaped the social structure, and altered social and personal values. But possible psychosocial consequences of such applications have been only a secondary concern, studied and accounted for after the fact, after the damage was done. The social changes resulting from the transition from the industrial to the technetronic society will not take as long to become visible as did those brought about by the transition from an agrarian to an industrial society. The lag between applications of technologies and their social consequences is radically foreshortened—so foreshortened that impact statements are sometimes completed even before a new technology is introduced. In a postindustrial society, "scientific and technical knowledge, in addition to enhancing production capabilities, quickly spills over to affect almost all aspects of life directly."[46] The economic, social, psychological and cultural consequences of new technologies, "particularly in the area of computers and communications," require immediate attention. "Accordingly," observes Brzezinski, "both the growing capacity for the instant calculation of the most complex interactions and the increasing availability of biochemical means of human control augment the potential scope of consciously chosen direction, and thereby also the pressures to direct, to choose, and to change."[47]

Brzezinski's observations are, it should be pointed out, different from either Schlesinger's or Ferguson's. While he is not pessimistic about the future, he is not as sanguine as Ferguson. He emphasizes the fundamental changes in the economy brought about by the beginning of the technetronic society and their social consequences. Ferguson's focus is on the recently developed views of the new culture that may be emerging and the new values that may accompany it. While Schlesinger notes the rapidity of change in our society, Brzezinski points out that the new society will likely entail more than an increase in the rate of change. The possibilities for direction, choice, control, and even manipulation may be greatly enhanced. With those possibilities, however, we will face an extraordinarily complex and perhaps fragile society.

The Industrial and Technetronic Societies

To indicate how different from the industrial society the technetronic society may be, Brzezinski compared the origins of the two. There are parallels, for each begins with technological developments. Brzezinski recalled that Norbert Wiener observed that the industrial revolution was based on three major fifteenth century developments: the nautical compass, gunpowder, and printing. Each of these has a twentieth century counterpart. Today's "functional equivalent of navigation is the thrust into space;" nuclear physics is today's gunpowder; and television and the capacity for quick, if not instantaneous, communication are today's printing. These twentieth century developments took place mainly after World War II and are transforming the society in which we live.

Brzezinski's comparisons of the two societies can be divided among four topics: (1) work; (2) the individual and society; (3) how we think; and (4) education. These topics are essential to any thorough discussion of the role and purpose of public education, allowing us to explore how educational requirements and practices may change between now and the beginning of the next century.

Work

Just as the industrial revolution eventually changed how people supported and sustained themselves by bringing them from their homes into the factories and from sparsely populated areas to factory towns and eventually to urban centers, so the new revolution may also change how and where people will work. Even the nature and meaning of work are likely to change: "In the technetronic society industrial employment yields to services, with automation and cybernetics replacing the operation of machines by individuals."[48] As long as most people are engaged in the actual fabrication of products and their distribution, they are required to appear at specified places at specified times to perform specified operations. Adoption of the assembly line required such regimentation of personnel. However, as our economic activities change from fabrication of products to design of products, or technology transfer, many of us may cease to be place-bound and time-bound by work.

If such is the case, the implications for typical school conventions could be quite dramatic. The American public school is in many ways an analogue to the factory with its emphasis on classes organized according to age, class periods of specified times, standardized curricula, procedures, and evaluation instruments, and adherence to a calendar comparable to a production schedule. In fact, throughout the nineteenth and the twentieth centuries, many saw fit to use the factory, the military, or the shipping metaphor to describe the process of schooling. Teachers were likened to factory workers or deck hands and students to raw materials or cargo. This should not be surprising, for the American public school was invented in the mid-nineteenth century to satisfy the requirements of a society beginning its process of industrialization. The school was to prepare its charges to participate willingly and efficiently in the developing economic order. As Christopher Lasch states the case, "the school habituates children to bureaucratic discipline and to the demands of group living, grades and sorts them by means of standardized tests, and selects some for professional and managerial careers while consigning the rest to manual labor."[49]

In the twentieth century, many schools have even looked like factories. In recent times, the transportation of students has mimicked the transportation of adults to and from work. Students from suburbs are bused into inner city schools just as their parents travel downtown to work; students from the inner city are bused to the suburban schools just as their parents travel to the suburbs to work in industrial parks or perform domestic services for the suburban dwellers.

Changes in the ways people work, as well as the possibilities offered by access to inexpensive microcomputers and interactive computer systems, may bring about a revolutionary change in public schooling. If modern communication systems allow efficient, inexpensive, and instantaneous dispatch and display of information and if most people "work" with information rather than materials, separation of the work place or school from the home may no longer be necessary. While such a possibility may be viewed as a return to a cottage-industry economy, that may be a misleading supposition. The cottages will be related to each other in ways that the old cottages were not. Communities of cottages may be defined not by their proximity but by their functions and electronic connections.

Of course, those engaged in services to people may be place-bound because services are needed at particular times and in particular places. The emphasis on services, however, is different from that on the manufacture of products. The focus is not on a specific operation, task, or product but on a person.

Schools may be required to change from emphasizing the completion of specified tasks in a timely manner to emphasizing how to interact effectively and perhaps even humanely with other people. They may have to abandon traditional class instruction and adopt new modes of individualized instruction that more closely approximate how students will be required to function when they are not in school.

In the technetronic society, schools may no longer be the primary place for the distribution of information and may become places where students attend occasionally rather than regularly. In such educational settings, token economies based on the principles of behavior modification designed to teach people to perform in prescribed ways according to inflexible schedules may no longer be relevant. The public and educators may need to reassess the custodial function the public school nominally performs. As Carl Bereiter suggested over a decade ago, it may be possible to separate child care from training and education.[50]

No less important is how these changes may also affect the content and the purpose of schooling. The consequences for just one traditional expectation of public schooling—that it prepare one for a job—should be clear. Some careers will no longer be available, while new ones, now unknown, probably will be. Traditional programs in vocational education, as well as more recently developed programs in career education, may soon be no more than curious antiquated studies. It makes little sense to urge youth to consider choices that may not even be available to them.

During periods of scarce employment opportunities, the tendency to return to the basic and secure is difficult to resist. However, attempts to train youths for jobs and to urge them to make career choices at an early age while we also provide workshops to help their parents make transitions from one career to the next do seem absurd. Educators should be encouraged to distinguish between school subjects with limited utility and applicability and those with indefinite utility. Unhappily, subjects that promise indefinite utility are often more abstract than others and are of less immediate interest to students.

In the industrial society, major concerns of employers and labor (organized employees) include just compensation for workers and the problems of employment and unemployment. The latter assume new dimensions in the technetronic society. According to Brzezinski, "in the emerging new society questions relating to the obsolescence of skills, security, vacations, leisure, and profit sharing dominate the relationship, and the psychic well-being of millions of relatively secure but potentially aimless lower-middle-class blue collar workers becomes a growing problem."[51] The new society may be able to feed, clothe, and shelter all, but the challenge of engaging them in meaningful, satisfying, and rewarding activity has yet to be met. This problem must be overcome for two reasons: (1) to avoid social unrest, social upheaval, and the social issues that arise from the neglect of large-scale personal problems and (2) to fulfill the right of all people to engage in activities that enhance rather than demean or ignore human potential. In our society, most people seek activities that enable them to support themselves and contribute to the well-being of their loved ones. To deny people that opportunity is to abandon the foundations of our society.

As society moves into its technetronic stage, economic power becomes depersonalized. In the industrial society, economic power is readily identified with individuals variously characterized as "robber barons" or "great entrepreneurs." However, as the relationships among government, scientific centers, and industry become increasingly complex and interdependent, the source of power, observes Brzezinski, "becomes more invisible and the sense of individual futility increases."[52] In the early 1950s, college students wanted to work for the largest companies and enjoy the security and comforts that would thus be afforded to them. About a decade later, many of these firms lost their appeal to youth. Students were seeking relationships that were less invisible and more personal. Recently, the trend has been toward decentralization and what Paul Hawken calls "disintermediation," which "implies small-scale appropriate technology, hands-on, self-sufficient, owner-builder activities."[53] The trend to smaller organizations is even reflected in the mass media. While such large, general purpose magazines directed to large, undifferentiated audiences as *Look, Life,* and the *Saturday Evening Post* were folding, a variety of other magazines developed that are directed to specific interest groups.

Schools will have to contend with people who have difficulty defining a confident role for themselves and finding a group with which to identify. To address such demands, however, schools may have to be transformed radically. The large school designed to serve thousands of students may give way to small schools. Some major universities are already combating impersonality by creating schools within a school, and many public school systems are giving attention to creating alternatives. Enrollments at private schools are growing because many believe they are more responsive to individuals than public schools.

The Individual and Society

Political activity in the technetronic society is not directed to either gaining the right to vote or undoing disfranchisement as it was in the industrial society but to "ensuring real participation in the decisions that seem too complex and too far removed from the average citizen."[54] For those interested in maintaining citizen participation, increased political alienation becomes a major concern. As citizens call for more participation in their own governance, they appear at the polls less frequently. There seems to be little relationship between the mechanisms for participation and the desire for participation. As access to participation becomes ever more complicated, costly, and seemingly elusive, traditional instruction about the role and the rights of citizens seems unrelated to reality. The importance of the ballot seems minimized when all can see on the nightly news telecast that a demonstration is a more effective way to gain immediate attention. The school teaches the importance of the ballot while the media show the power of knowing how to stage a media event. Patriotic rituals cease to be emotional expressions of loyalty and become little more than empty mockeries. Lasch, for example, maintains that "the disparity between the practice and the profession—between centralized bureaucratic and corporate power and the ideal of a self-governing society—remains a sensitive issue that cannot be altogether ignored so long as our political traditions retain even the lingering force of an historical myth."[55]

Just as citizens seek new ways to participate in the political process, so they give new or expanded meanings to the concepts of equality and citizenship. During the industrial era, women claimed the right to participate in politics and won the right to vote. In the new age, they claim the right to full equality and demand concrete realizations of their claim. According to Brzezinski, "In the emerging technetronic society automation threatens both males and females, intellectual talent is computable, the 'pill' encourages sexual equality, and women begin to claim complete equality."[56] As full equality is realized, new roles and new expectations are created and old expectations go unmet. Old social norms are discarded and new ones emerge. As noted in a paper from Stanford University's Institute for Research on Educational Finance and Governance, "No longer is it assumed that the proper place for a married woman is only in the home; nor as a glimpse at the pages of *Ms. Magazine* will illustrate, is a career woman assumed to be sexless."[57] In some schools, children do not wonder why their mothers work outside the home but why some do not.

As women win the right to full equality and refuse to conform to gender-specific conventions, social and personal relationships will continue to change. The traditional family structure, with specific role assignments based on gender, has been greatly eroded and is not likely to be restored. As Marvin Harris claims:

> Like it or not, the lifetime, male-dominated, two-parent, multi-child, breadwinner family has virtually ceased to exist. While it is true that most children will continue to be born into some kind of family situation, the kind of domestic units involved and the typical pattern of life experience with respect to residence, marriage, and child-bearing that Americans can look forward to as they grow up are fundamentally new additions to American culture.[58]

Traditional concepts regarding roles in the marketplace, the political arena, and the family are all being redefined. To continue to rely on and to invoke these ideas creates both personal and social difficulties. The experiences of children who begin their schooling in the 1990s will be drastically different from the experiences their teacher had as children. Traditional assumptions about how the family prepares children for school may no longer be valid.

An examination of why women have recently claimed their rights reveals how society is changing. At one level, it may be answered that women are simply claiming what has always been theirs. From this point of view, it can be argued that they have recently picked up the issues raised at the end of the eighteenth century by Mary Wollstonecraft. At another level, it can be asked what in society at this time has made the realization of the rights of women and the attendant structural changes in society either necessary or possible. According to Harris, "the timing of the feminist outburst at the end of the 1960s marks the moment of collective realization that women, married or not, would have to continue to work as a consequence of inflation." Their entry into the marketplace was, he claims, a forced entry:

> At the end of the 1960s, women were being drawn through a pneumatic tube. At one end of the tube, there was inflation squeezing them out of the home and into the job market, sucking them into a niche specifically designed for literate but inexpensive and docile workers who would accept 60 percent or less of what a man would want for the same job.[59]

As women realized they would have to continue to work at "a dull, boring, deadend job" and face "cooking, cleaning, child care, and a chauvinist male at home," they "rebelled" in order to avoid the "worst of all possible worlds."

"In part," claim Elisabeth Hansot and David Tyack, "the women's movement of the last generation can be understood as a painful realignment of cultural beliefs with actual changes that have taken place in the economy and the society."[60] Early in the nineteenth century women were allowed and even encouraged to leave, even if temporarily, their rural situations to work in the newly opened mills. By the mid-nineteenth century, women were claiming they were better suited than men to teach in the common schools. They promised to work for less if allowed to teach. Work in the mills was becoming less attractive, and women were being driven out by immigrants who would work longer hours for less pay.

Because their promise to work for less than men solved the problem of finding an inexpensive work force for the schools, women assumed the job of teaching immigrant children to conform to the ways of the expanding industrial society. Since then, teaching, clerical positions in offices, and nursing have become largely the preserve of women. Now, due to the introduction of new technologies, women are claiming their rights as they begin to experience the dislocations of the postindustrial society. Popular media descriptions of the "paperless office" may signal new opportunities to some; to others such descriptions are threats of displacement or of being rendered useless by a machine.

Women's demands for full equality may be indexes to changes in the economic and social structures of our society. They may show us the need to adopt a new social structure rather than merely making adjustments to the existing one. Schools will certainly be affected by these changes. Some will expect the schools to prepare youth for the changes associated with the women's movement, and others will want the schools to resist those changes by placing even more emphasis on traditional values. Still others will want the schools to provide different or more services to accommodate the needs of working mothers.

How We Think

Industrial societies are linear in character. Goods are made on assembly lines; desks are arranged in rows so paper can be moved efficiently and line after line can be reviewed and filed in long lines of linear containers; long linear highways move people in and out of work areas, and vertical lines (elevator shafts) move them up and down in their work areas. All the lines are arranged in logical, step-by-step, hierarchical order. Even our thought is linear in that it is structured to order and manage the ways we organize our activities. "In the industrial age," writes Brzezinski, "literacy makes for static interrelated conceptual thinking, congenial to ideological systems."[61] The advent of the industrial society destroyed the traditional agrarian society and introduced new social problems. To cope with those problems people needed to construct a world view that would make those problems understandable and manageable. Such views, or sets of social beliefs about how the world works, are called ideologies. They are beliefs about the nature of social reality and the place and power of people in that social reality.

Ideologies usually have a coherence, but they are seldom completely rational. They often degenerate into a series of set answers and oversimplified explanations to complicated situations. Curiously, while the technetronic society extends the power of rationality with its capability to collect, store, and relate information, it also heightens the disparate elements of our social reality. Brzezinski explains:

> In the technetronic society, audio-visual communications prompt more changeable, disparate views of reality, not compressible into formal systems, even as the requirements of science and the new computative techniques place a premium on mathematical logic and systematic reason-

ing. The resulting tension is felt most acutely by scientists, with the consequence that some seek to confine reason to science while expressing their emotions through politics. Moreover, the increasing ability to reduce social conflicts to quantifiable and measurable dimensions reinforces the trend toward a more pragmatic approach to social problems, while it simultaneously stimulates new concerns with preserving 'human' values.[62]

Thus, while new techniques for manipulating information enable society to resolve many social questions that were once not easily settled because of the difficulty in gathering data quickly, the very same processes frequently show how the "logical" solution is contrary to our longstanding social beliefs, values, and ideologies. They also show that our values differ in very basic ways. New techniques may assist us in specifying differences, but the resolution of these differences requires quite another process. For some, philosophical analysis and debate are needed; for others, psychological and political negotiation.

Our new computational techniques allow us to project various scenarios and impact statements. Although the consequences of social programs can sometimes be predicted with confidence, the same is not true of epiphenomenal events. Our new techniques *are* forcing us to pay more attention to values, and the faint rumblings about restoring the liberal arts to the undergraduate curriculum in college are perhaps symptomatic of this fact. Philosophers may even find that they have a province to explore other than logic and language as they begin to tend to the newly found interests in ethics, especially among colleges of medicine and business. The interest displayed by school guidance counselors and philosophers of education in values clarification may also indicate that such questions cannot be ignored indefinitely. Even the attempts of some educators to base teacher training on a foundation of humanistic rather than behavioral psychology may be a sign of this development.

As society becomes increasingly technetronic, people organize and group themselves differently to realize their interests. In the industrial society, people are unified by unions and political parties, which offer "relatively simple and somewhat ideological programs." The emphasis on literacy in the industrial society allows the molding of political allegiances "by appeals to nationalistic sentiments, communicated through the massive increase of newspapers employing, naturally, the readers' national language."[63] Innovations in communication technology provide new ways of organizing people. Brzezinski claims that

> in the technetronic society, the trend seems to be toward aggregating the individual support of millions of unorganized citizens, who are easily within the reach of magnetic and attractive personalities, and effectively exploiting the latest communication techniques to manipulate emotions and control reason. Reliance on television—and hence the tendency to replace language with imagery, which is international rather than national, and to include war coverage or scenes of hunger in places as distant as, for example, India—creates a somewhat more cosmopolitan, though highly impressionistic, involvement in global affairs.[64]

The electronic media, especially television, have considerably influenced modes of expression during the last quarter century. More people, especially young people, have more access to information than has ever been known. In addition, that access is usually on a demand basis. Learning how to gain access to such information and how to use it are not skills that are universally taught in public schools. The framework of our experience and the rationale we use for connecting the successions of image we see are elusive. Our linear way of thinking seems inadequate for interpreting what seems a simple linear succession of images. Yet, schools are still committed to print, even though the electronic media clearly constitute a new and very different form of literacy. At some point, educators will have to turn from asking how watching television affects school performance to asking how television affects how we think.

In the industrial society, status is attached to the acquisition of wealth, amounts of discretionary income, and levels of consumption. For those born into a society where goods seem abundant and easy to secure, however, use of power becomes more important than the acquisition of wealth. "In the technetronic society," Brzezinski claims, "the adaptation of science to human ends and a growing concern with the quality of life becomes possible and increasingly a moral imperative for a large number of citizens, especially the young."[65] How to increase industrial efficiency for the sake of producing more goods becomes less important than asking how life ought to be lived or exploring new technologies. That some do not have sufficient goods is often overlooked.

In a society that appears to offer many alternatives, and where many are discarding old ways and experimenting with new life-styles, fear and controversy frequently coexist with the celebration of new ways and possibilities. To the extent that schools are expected to explore the new life-styles they will be in trouble with some of the public. Historically, public schools have adhered to the three principles set down by Horace Mann in the mid-nineteenth century: (1) teach the common principles of Christianity; (2) teach the common principles of republicanism; and (3) avoid all controversial issues. In the coming decades, it may not be possible to avoid controversial issues. New concerns with morality are being pressed upon the schools, and traditional beliefs are constantly challenged. Scientific creationism as an alternative to Darwin's evolutionary theory is just one example of a fundamental issue that is receiving attention in the schools.

Education

In the postindustrial society, the nature and purposes of public education are transformed as they are in other institutions. For the social reformers of the industrial society, education was necessary for advancement and improvement. They successfully established a system of public education that was "available for limited specific periods of time." These schools were "initially concerned with overcoming illiteracy and subsequently with technical training, based largely on written, sequential reasoning." In the technetronic society, however, the role of the school is enlarged and is required to be more selective. According to Brzezinski:

> In the technetronic society not only is education universal but advanced training is available to almost all who have the basic talents, and there is far greater emphasis on quality selection. The essential problem is to discover the most effective techniques for the rational exploitation of social talent. The latest communication and calculation techniques are employed in this task. The educational process becomes a lengthier one and is increasingly reliant on audio-visual aids. In addition, the flow of new knowledge necessitates more and more frequent refresher courses.[66]

In such a society, education can no longer be properly viewed as preparation for a job or a phase of life. It becomes a process or an experience that will be available and necessary to recall throughout life, but it may not be available to all. Only those whose "social talent" can be exploited may receive it, unless society decides that the purpose of public education is to include more than preparing personnel to participate efficiently in the economy.

Exploitation of those with "social talent" began in the late 1950s and early 1960s when the nation raced to be first to the moon. That exploitation was "legitimized" and partially financed by the National Defense Education Act (1958) and subsequent federal programs. A few years later, there were protests against using the schools as "sorting machines" for the needs of the modern nation-state and demands for programs to implement full equality of educational opportunity. Since then, however, the enthusiastic belief in equality of opportunity has eroded, and the efficacy of public schooling is being questioned seriously. Many students of American education have concluded that public schools restrict rather than promote equality of opportunity. In addition to documenting past failures of the public schools, their work also shows that public schools, as we have known them, may not be capable of satisfying the requirements of a nation that has begun the transformation to a postindustrial society. Whether the public schools of the nineteenth and the first half of the twentieth century will continue into the twenty-first century seems problematical. However, American society invented new forms of schooling in the past, and there is no reason why it cannot do so again unless one believes that what is must always be.

The availability of advanced training to "all who have the basic talents" seems fair and democratic until we ask who decides who has the basic talents. Following that we must ask: Basic talents for what? Implicit in such questions are the issue of equality of educational opportunity and the issue of elites. Whether public schools can meet the expectations and interests of individuals as well as satisfy the sophisticated requirements of a technetronic society will have to be addressed. Balancing the demands for highly trained personnel with those for equal opportunity is not an easy task. Even more difficult is defining equality of opportunity: Does it mean that all should have equal access to schools or that all should enjoy equal rewards and accomplishments? Our present investigatory and evaluative techniques dramatically curtail our ability to avoid such issues.

Historical and anthropological analyses of public education show that public systems of education have been created and designed for the sake of society as opposed to the many and varied interests of individuals. That basic purpose and its attendant structure may be challenged in a society in which individuals are not only increasingly aware of their "rights" but increasingly ready to demand them as well.

The advent of the industrial society created a shift in the locus of power. Leadership positions that were mostly held by the traditional rural-aristocratic class were appropriated by the new urban-plutocratic elite. The landed gentry lost to those who successfully competed for the new wealth. In the technetronic society, knowledge becomes the basis for political power. As Brzezinski states: "In the technetronic society plutocratic pre-eminence is challenged by the political leadership, which is itself increasingly permeated by individuals possessing special skills and intellectual talents."[67] Those with command of specialized knowledge and the ability to mobilize such talent have access to power because of society's increasing reliance upon experts. If such a trend continues, issues about the purposes of education and access to it may become increasingly important and political. As knowledge becomes ever more powerful, individuals may be willing to pay more for it than they have in the past, but not in traditional ways. They may become more willing to pay for their own and their children's education but less willing to pay for that of other people's children. The growing interest in private schools may reflect this development. A society that refuses to pay for public education but is willing to pay for private education is making a statement about how important it believes equality of educational opportunity is.

Throughout the twentieth century, government has turned to "experts" at universities to help it wage war, defend the national interests, or assist in the solution of other problems to ensure domestic tranquillity. The government used chemists during World War I and physicists during World War II. When the chemists returned to their campuses, they demanded laboratories to continue their inquiries, and universities with assistance from the private sector were able to meet their demands. After World War II, the physicists also demanded laboratories, but their requirements were so great, because of the nature of modern nuclear physics, that only the federal government had the wherewithal to satisfy them. As a result, a new relationship developed between university research laboratories and the federal government.[68] The university became an instrument of the nation-state and directed many of its research programs to serve the latter's interests.

Less celebrated but perhaps equally important are the roles statisticians and social scientists have played in and for government. Psychologists, as is now widely known, developed intelligence tests for the U.S. Army during World War I. More recently, during the war on poverty and the nation's attempt to construct the Great Society, social scientists assumed important fact-gathering and policy-making duties. The discussion and controversy subsequent to James Coleman's Report, *Equality of Educational Opportunity* (1966), is but one vivid example. Another is the acceptance of testimony by the Supreme Court in the *Brown v. Topeka* case that included reports of research by psychologists Kenneth and Mamie Clark. As the importance of the university grows, other levels of the educational system are pressured, because one level is preparation for the next. Unless that pressure is recognized, it will be difficult to design schools that meet the interests of individuals—interests that may or may not coincide with those of the nation-state. To compound the problem, public schools have served another function throughout the twentieth century, providing custodial care for young people whose presence is not wanted in the labor force. Present forms of schooling may not be appropriate for a population that may be in school simply because there is no other socially sanctioned place for them to be.

Conclusion

Implicit in Crèvecoeur's early statement of the American dream is the belief that parents know what lies in store for their children and how those children should be prepared. However, as Walter Lippmann observed over half a century ago, it is now difficult for parents to know what their children will encounter or what they will need to face those encounters successfully:

> In former times you could make some effort to teach people what they needed to know. It was done badly, but at least it could be attempted. Men knew the kind of problems their children would have to face. But today education means a radically different thing. We have to prepare children to meet the unexpected, for their problems will not be the same as their fathers.[69]

The evidence is ample that many do not know what to do for our children. Parents sign up for effectiveness training and enroll in courses on how to raise a responsible child. "Responsible" usually means: "Behave the way I want you to behave—the way I was supposed to behave when I was your age." We frequently forget however, that we have placed our children in a culture significantly different from that in which we were reared and educated. We should not be so surprised that they do not always share our values and beliefs. They have been taught differently, and we have done the teaching. For example, we place our children in a culture with a variety of electronic media at their immediate disposal and then wonder why they are not committed to print. Dissatisfaction with some of our youth turns to dissatisfaction with our public schools, and the value and utility of free, compulsory, public schooling are challenged from both the right and left of the political spectrum.[70] This is a sign that the problems with the schools are social and cultural, not just matters of conservative and liberal differences.

In the early 1980s, Jean Dresden Grambs recognized a crisis in American education but also expressed hope in the future; her hope was founded on the belief that matters were so bad that they must get better:

> Despite the baffling nonresponsiveness of the system, the resistance to basic reorientation or restructuring towards a more humane or socially responsible model, one can have some modest hope for the schools. For one thing, something has to be done, if only to deal with what I believe to be a true crisis: hostile students, defeated and burned out teachers, administrators hiding behind state and federal forms, and massive shifting of undergraduates from education as a career.[71]

Gramb's claim that something had to be done proved to be so. By 1983, Lawrence C. Stedman and Marshall S. Smith were able to report that "during the last few months, several commissions have published reports proposing major reforms for our educational system." The appearance of those reports, especially *A Nation at Risk,* they claimed, "spurred the greatest national debate on education since the launching of *Sputnik* in 1957."[72] By the mid 1980s, we had once again set out to reform our schools, seemingly to restore them to what we think schools used to be like. Whether that is the direction that should have been taken is, of course, an open question.

Notes

1. William Proefriedt, "Education and Moral Purpose: The Dream Recovered," *Teachers College Record* 86 (Spring 1985): 399.
2. Paul Blumberg, *Inequality in an Age of Decline* (New York: Oxford University Press, 1980), 254.
3. Studs Terkel, *Working* (New York: Pantheon Books, 1972), 32.
4. Hector St. John de Crèvecoeur, *Letters from an American Farmer* (London: J. M. Dent & Sons, 1962), 22.
5. Ibid., 23.
6. Ibid., p. 25.
7. W. Norton Grubb and Marvin Lazerson, *Broken Promises: How Americans Fail Their Children* (New York: Basic Books, 1982), 67.
8. Walter Lippmann, *Drift and Mastery* (Englewood Cliffs, N.J.: Prentice-Hall, 1961), 15.

9. Ibid., 92.
10. Godfrey Hodgson, *America in Our Time* (New York: Vintage Books, 1960), 7.
11. Proefriedt, "Education and Moral Purpose," 399.
12. Marvin Harris, "Why It's Not the Same Old America," *Psychology Today* 15 (August 1981): 51.
13. A notable exception is Mary Anne Raywid, Charles Tesconi, and Donald Warren, *Pride and Promise: Schools of Excellence for All the People* (Westbury, N.Y.: American Educational Studies Association, 1985).
14. Proefriedt, "Education and Moral Purpose," 399.
15. Eric F. Goldman, *The Crucial Decade and After: America, 1945–1960* (New York: Vintage Books, 1960), vi.
16. Quoted in Blumberg, *Inequality in an Age of Decline,* 253.
17. Hodgson, *America in Our Time,* 12–13.
18. J. R. Sirkin, "Experts Predict Struggle Ahead to Maintain Education Funding,"*Education Week* 4 (April 24, 1985): 6.
19. James Hertling, "Administration Seeks $15.5 Billion for Education," *Education Week* 4 (February 13, 1985): 1, 12.
20. Christopher Lasch, "The Crisis of Confidence," *Democracy* 1 (January 1981): 27.
21. Ibid., 28.
22. David Snedden, "Fundamental Distinctions between Liberal and Vocational Education, I," *NEA Proceedings* (1914): 151–156.
23. William C. Bagley, "Fundamental Distinctions Between Liberal and Vocational Education, II," *NEA Proceedings* (1914): 170.
24. Ralph Hamil, "Is the Wave of the Future a Kondratieff?" *The Futurist* 13 (October 1979):381.
25. Dick Stoken, "What the Long-Term Cycle Tells Us About the 1980s," *The Futurist* 14 (February 1980):14.
26. Ibid., 16.
27. Quoted in Anne Bridgman, "Reagan Pledges Administration Focus on Choice," *Education Week,* 4 (March 5, 1985):1.
28. Stoken, "What the Long-Term Cycle Tells Us About the 1980s," 17.
29. Ibid., 19.
30. Hamil, "Is the Wave of the Future a Kondratieff?" 381.
31. Quoted in Hamil.
32. Quoted in Hodgson, *America in Our Time,* 498.
33. Arthur M. Schlesinger, Jr., "The Velocity of History," *Newsweek* 76 (July 6, 1970):35.
34. Ibid.
35. Marilyn Ferguson. *The Aquarian Conspiracy: Personal and Social Transformation in the 1980s* (Los Angeles: J. P. Tarcher, 1970), 29.
36. Ibid.
37. Ibid., 120.
38. Peter Gay. *The Enlightenment: The Rise of Modern Paganism* (New York: Alfred A. Knopf, 1966), 1.
39. Ferguson, *Aquarian Conspiracy,* 23–24.
40. Ibid., 29.
41. Ibid.
42. Ibid., 38.
43. Carl L. Becker, *The Heavenly City of the Eighteenth-Century Philosophers* (New Haven, Conn.: Yale University Press, 1932), 4.
44. Ibid., 5.

45. Zbigniew Brzezinski. *Between Two Ages: America's Role in the Technetronic* Era (New York: Viking Press, 1970), 9.
46. Ibid., 9–10.
47. Ibid., 10.
48. Ibid., 11.
49. Lasch, "Crisis of Confidence," 30.
50. Carl Bereiter, "Schools Without Education," *Harvard Educational Review,* 42 (August 1972)
51. Brzezinski, *Between Two Ages,* 11.
52. Ibid., 13.
53. Paul Hawken, "Illusory Inflation," *The CoEvolution Quarterly* 30 (Summer 1981): 35. Also see Paul Hawken, "Dis-intermediation," *The CoEvolution Quarterly* 29 (Spring 1981):6.
54. Brzezinski, *Between Two Ages,* 12.
55. Lasch, "The Crisis of Confidence," 26.
56. Brzezinski, *Between Two Ages,* 13.
57. Elisabeth Hansot and David Tyack, "The Dream Deferred: A Golden Age for Women School Administrators," Policy Paper No. 81–C2, Institute for Research on Educational Finance and Governance, School of Education, Stanford University (May 1981):33.
58. Harris, "Why It's Not the Same Old America," 36–37.
59. Ibid., 36.
60. Hansot and Tyack, "The Dream Deferred," 33.
61. Brzezinski, *Between Two Ages,* 12.
62. Ibid.
63. Ibid., 13.
64. *Ibid.*
65. Ibid., 14.
66. Ibid., 11.
67. Ibid., 11–12.
68. Daniel J. Kevles, *The Physicists: The History of a Scientific Community in Modern America* (New York: Alfred A. Knopf, 1978).
69. Lippmann, *Drift and Mastery,* 93.
70. William F. Rickenbacker, ed., *The Twelve Year Sentence: Radical Views of Compulsory Schooling* (New York: Delta, 1974).
71. Jean Dresden Grambs, "Forty Years of Education: Will the Next Forty Years Be Any Better?" *Educational Leadership* (May 1981), 654.
72. Lawrence C. Stedman and Marshall S. Smith, "Recent Reform Proposals for American Education," *Contemporary Education Review* 2 (Fall 1983): p. 85.

2
How Americans View Their Schools

A Public Ritual

Each generation of Americans seems to grow disenchanted with its public schools, complains about them, reforms or modernizes them, and then waits for the next generation to begin the process anew. In the 1830s and the 1840s, social and educational reformers convinced Americans, especially in the Northeast, to create uniform systems of public education. Almost as soon as the order and uniformity of the new system replaced the wide variety of disparate school practices that had earlier obtained, attempts were made to reform the schools and break free from standardized, oppressive, and dull classroom routines. In 1860, for example, Edward A. Sheldon, superintendent of the Oswego, New York, schools, began to dismantle "the most complete educational machine ever constructed" because "there was too much teaching by formula."[1] Sheldon's new pedagogy—known as object teaching—changed the focus of instruction from subject matter to the moral, physical, and intellectual development of the child. In place of logically ordered lessons directed toward mastery of subject matter, teachers were to offer lessons designed to appeal to the child's "activity, love of sympathy, and a desire for constant variety."[2] Children were to observe, describe, and define the objects presented to them, not according to the characteristics pointed out to them by teachers but by the characteristics they themselves could identify.

Since the days of Sheldon, the imaginary historical pendulum seems to have swung back and forth from one emphasis to another: from emphasizing academic disciplines to respecting developmental requirements; from establishing a precise and exact school routine to developing an informal and relaxed setting for students to pursue their own interests; or from using the schools to select the best and the brightest students to insure prompt realization of the national interest to turning to the schools to extend economic opportunity and prosperity to previously neglected and excluded groups. The custom has been to cast off tradition to make way for whatever conventions are suggested by the newest educational or psychological fashion.

The periodic criticism of the schools and changes in the emphases and purposes of public education may reflect not a fickle society but what Stephen R. Graubard has described as "America's 'civil religion'—its belief in itself." This civil religion is founded on the "traditional proposition that there can be raised up in each generation a new self-reliance, a new capacity to cope, a new willingness to experiment and innovate." These beliefs, or hopes, "are linked

27

to a popular faith in education, more specifically to schools that function well."[3] Periodic criticism of public schools can thus be viewed as a social celebration or civic ritual that each generation must perform as a reminder of its faith in itself.

If criticism of public education gives society a sense of reassurance or a belief that it can cope with new social predicaments, then Americans have either encountered an unprecedented number of new and puzzling social predicaments since World War II, or have developed an almost insatiable need for reassurance. In 1954, C. Winfield Scott and Clyde M. Hill reported that criticisms of public education "have mushroomed to alarming proportions." The revelation during World War II that many men and women of draft age were educationally deficient, the claims that the schools were obviously at fault, and the counterclaims that the schools "deserved much credit for the success achieved by our military forces" were, they claimed, "only a harbinger of the deluge to come."[4]

The Scott and Hill Appraisal of Educational Criticism

To ascertain the actual amount of criticism of public education, Scott and Hill examined the entries in the *Education Index*. In 1942 a new heading, "Public Schools—Criticism" was introduced. That introduction, they argued, meant "that the current wave of criticism was then a large enough ripple to attract serious attention."[5] Between 1942 and 1950, the average number of entries under the heading was nearly eight per year. The low was three in 1942 and the high was thirteen in 1949. After 1950, however, the increases were dramatic. In 1951, there were thirty-five entries, or nearly three times as many as in 1950. In 1953, there were forty-nine entries, or more than four times as many as in 1950.

The large number of complaints about the quality of public education in the popular media indicated that much of the criticism was appealing to the general public. In assembling their own collection of complaints about public schooling, Scott and Hill found significant statements in popular magazines: articles by Dorothy Thompson in the *Ladies Home Journal;* an article by Walter Biddle Saul, a senior partner in one of Philadelphia's prestigious law firms, in the *Saturday Evening Post;* an article by historian Henry Commager in the *Reader's Digest,* as well as articles in *Scientific Monthly, Life, New Republic,* the *Rotarian, Time, Parade,* the *American Legion Magazine,* the *Saturday Review of Literature,* and several other educational and lay periodicals. The volume of material found in lay magazines allowed them to "conclude that both pro and con criticism must reflect to an important extent the opinions of laymen and must represent things they try to verbalize and often try to put into action in their own circles." Editors of such magazines, they concluded, certainly would not devote so much attention to educational criticism unless it was "good grist for their mill."[6] Such grist seems to have been just what the first wave of new post–World War II parents wanted to read.

Educational criticism has continued to be good grist. In fact, in the 1980s it has taken on the form of a national media event. On 26 April 1983, a White House invitation was extended to 200 representatives of American education, business, and government to witness President Reagan receive *A Nation at Risk,* the report of the National Commission on Excellence in Education. Reagan's Secretary of Education, Terrel Bell, appointed the commission in 1981 because he was concerned about the "widespread public perception that something is seriously remiss in our educational system."[7] The commission gave him reason for his concern. It reported that "the educational foundations of our society are presently being eroded by a rising tide of mediocrity that threatens our very future as a nation and a people."[8] Five months after the presentation of the report, two of the commission's staff members were able to report that "the tumultuous reception of the report by the press and the public has yet to subside."[9] It was continuing to receive attention from both the print and the electronic media. *A Nation at Risk* was soon followed by several other "national reports" on education,[10] and two years after its publication Charles Strickland observed:

> The recent avalanche of reports on education in these United States will leave anyone aged more than fifty with a sense of *deja vu.* After nearly thirty years the schools and their problems are moving once again to the center of the nation's consciousness. Once again we hear the litany about the mediocrity of the schools, followed by demands for excellence. Once again we hear a call for a tightening of standards and a toughening of discipline. Once again, the nation's welfare and security are invoked as the justification for educational reform. Once again, the focus of concern is on the neglect of those subjects which promise technological superiority.[11]

The attention given to *A Nation at Risk* and subsequent reports indicated to millions of Americans that the public schools were facing a crisis. This was not the first time Americans had received this message. As Scott and Hill reported, the 16 October 1950 issue of *Life* warning Americans of this emergency reached nearly 24 million people over age ten. In September 1951, *McCall's* published an article, "Who's Trying to Ruin our Schools," and subsequently distributed 300,000 reprints "at cost to interested persons and groups."[12] Within five months of the publication of *A Nation at Risk,* the educational media had printed 200,000 copies and several newspapers printed portions for their readers.

By the early 1950s, nearly every aspect of education was subject to criticism. Disagreements about the aims of education were based on the many different philosophies held by the many critics. Many strenuous objections were made to the ever-present "evil"—progressive education. Many complained about how poorly reading, writing, and arithmetic were taught. The role of religion in the public schools presented a controversy that still persists. Accusations were heard that history courses were taught with a bias that failed to give objective accounts of the nation's true traditions and values. Charges that the public schools had been infected by socialistic or communistic views and materials were followed by calls for courses on the evils of communism and the virtues of democracy. As always, the schools and colleges of education were censured for not preparing teachers for their responsibilities.

Public Education's Friends and Enemies

Scott and Hill warned that the sources, nature, and meaning of the criticism of the public schools could not be ignored, even though they did not approve of all the critics. Some were able, others were not. Some were friends of public education, some were not. The critics included "scholars and professional educators, professional writers, and outright enemies of education." Among the scholars were people distinguished in their fields and credible to the public by virtue of the important positions they held in society. While they frequently had "given much serious thought to educational problems," they usually had "not had any formal training in education." Such critics included some who "have never attended nor . . . had any type of responsible, first-hand experience, or even direct acquaintance, with public schools." They usually offered "the most impressive but often grossly exaggerated criticisms." Then as now, however, such critics could not be dismissed by professional educators, because the public was listening to them. Among the professional writers, some were "thoughtful" while others presented "insights and appreciations" that were "severely limited or debatable."[13] Yet, they all had their audience, for in the United States education is controlled not by professionals and experts but by the public. Complaints by professionals have not changed that.

In addition to the friends and enemies of public education, according to Scott and Hill, were those "who honestly do not believe in the principles of public education." They believed that education was a responsibility of church rather than state and chose to send their children to church-sponsored schools. They were usually "extremely high-minded, thoroughly good citizens" who did not deserve to be "considered as enemies of public education." Other good citizens also did not believe that all children could "profit by the extended opportunities for schooling optimistically provided by our public schools."[14] They argued that ambitious attempts to provide secondary as well as elementary schooling for all children were wasteful and expensive. Then as now, however, such critics usually fail to recognize that we have no other place for children and youth than school.

What Scott and Hill overlooked was that some educators gave the public reason to believe that traditional secondary education was unsuitable for over half the population of high school age. At a meeting of vocational educators in Washington, D.C. in 1945, Charles A. Prosser summarized the views of those in attendance with what came to be known as the Prosser Resolution. The participants believed that

> with the aid of this report in final form, the vocational school of a community will be able better to prepare 20% of the youth of secondary school age for entrance upon desirable skilled occupations; and that the high school will continue to prepare another 20% for entrance to college. We do not believe that the remaining 60% of our youth of secondary school age will receive the life adjustment training they need and to which they are entitled as American citizens—unless and until the administration of public education with the assistance of the vocational education leaders formulate a similar program for this group.[15]

The Prosser Resolution was clearly stating that neither the traditional nor the vocational high school was suitable for over half the nation's youth. The majority of youth needed what some educators then called "life adjustment education"—a program specifically designed for those with little or no interest in traditional academic subjects and for those who usually came from what educators would later call "culturally deprived" or "culturally disadvantaged" families. To create new programs for such a population was, Prosser believed, "to do something that would give to all American youth their educational heritage so long denied,"[16] but not all of the public agreed. Some reacted adversely to bringing into school people who had been traditionally excluded and who were different from those who traditionally attended. The introduction of new and different programs always may cause an adverse public reaction, because people often interpret deviations from traditional patterns not as progress, or improvement, but as a decline in standards. Then (and even now) not all agreed that physical fitness classes were better for youth than classes in foreign languages or that learning to write a business letter had more value than the study of the English language and its literature. Some who believed that such activities were useful did not agree that the school was the proper or best place for their pursuit.

Scott and Hill believed that the complaints about public education could not be attributed solely to "sinister" enemies of public education. There was "a general social unrest" and concern about what was happening to the traditional American way of life. Some who saw social problems and new developments that they did not like quickly focused their attention on the schools. They assumed that schools either could have prevented the problems or caused them through some sin of commission or omission. They thought the schools could set society back on its proper traditional course by doing what they were supposed to do. In fact, Scott and Hill maintained that the "wave of criticism" could be interpreted as "an expression of a deep-seated, abiding, faith in public education. . . . Concern about the schools, even the fear of the schools on the part of the enemies of democracy," they reasoned, "is eloquent testimony of the faith they have in public education as the means through which our aspirations can be realized."[17] What many then failed to see was the disagreement regarding which "aspirations" were to be realized. While some wanted increased opportunities for achievement, others wanted to maintain the positions they enjoyed.

The Need for a New Perspective

The vocabulary of war—"friends," "enemies," "defense," and "attack"—that Scott and Hill used to assess criticism of public education had been familiar to educators for half a century, if not longer. Lawrence A. Cremin pointed out that in 1919 Ellwood Patterson Cubberley's *Public Education in the United States* presented "a picture of educational struggles which had been waged and won, and enemies which had been routed and destroyed."[18] Cubberley's history, still in use in the 1950s, was the history that showed how educators viewed the past and the future of public education in the United States. It depicted the development of public education as a series of great "battles" that had been mostly won by the beginning of the twentieth century. By then, the form and the character of American public education had been established. Only improvements and further progress seemed to be in store for public education, including larger budgets, new programs, and public support for bringing more people into the schools for longer periods of time than ever before.

While Americans were building the public school system and contending with its rapid expansion in the early twentieth century—the period when Cubberley's own views were being formed—educators and other academics frequently turned to military, or warlike, metaphors to discuss educational issues. For example, at an 1891 meeting of the NEA, J. R. Preston, State Superintendent of Public Instruction in Mississippi, reminded his audience that the "army of half a million teachers sustained by popular devotion to the cause, must in times of peace and through peaceful measures fight this continuous battle for the perpetuity of life."[19] When William James was talking to teachers in the 1890s, he counseled them that "the science of psychology and whatever science of general pedagogics may be based on it, are facts much like the science of war."[20] John Dewey also used the language of war to make his points about education. In 1896, he wrote of the necessity of having special schools that would "supply the great army of teachers with the weapons of their calling."[21] As Clarence Karrier has observed, "the Mexican War, the Civil War, the Indian Wars, and the Spanish-American War left their imprint on the rhetoric and practices of the common school."[22] That imprint, it should be emphasized, persists. In *A Nation at Risk,* the vocabulary of war and national survival was once again invoked to explain the alleged crisis in education and to incite Americans to action: "If an unfriendly foreign power had attempted to impose on America the mediocre educational performance that exists today, we might well have viewed it as an act of war."[23] Similarily, the Task Force on Education for Economic Growth warned that the nation was facing a "real emergency" and insisted that educational improvement was "crucial to our national survival."[24]

Cremin maintained that acceptance of Cubberley's historical approach explained "why the present generation of educators . . . finds itself so perplexed and disgruntled over the recent attacks on public education." By the middle of the twentieth century, a new metaphor was needed, one that would allow educators to see more clearly and accurately the nature of the relationship between school and society. They needed a new history so they could develop a new perspective. They needed a reassessment that would show that criticism of the schools was most alarming in its intensity. According to Cremin:

> Attacks on public schools and public-school people are as old as the public school itself. They were present in the early days when the fathers of the public school were beginning their work, and they have been the constant companions of the American schoolman—hounding him during some periods in guerilla action, waging full-scale warfare in others.[25]

American educators, it seemed, needed to learn that winning a battle was not tantamount to winning the war. Education was a continuous state of warfare. Rather, education was a process and an institution close to the public and an object of the public's attention whenever their circumstances seemed unsettled or threatened. Now educators recognize to a greater extent than they did a generation ago that, as Patricia Albjerg Graham has observed, "the schools are the stage on which our implicit social dramas are made explicit, and the dramas are played to audiences that are sometimes filled with hostile critics." An unsettled public finds it easier to attack schools than to attack "the most abstract social goals they are implementing."[26]

The appraisals and reappraisals of progressive education during the 1950s constituted more than a rejection of "life adjustment education." Such education may have been, as Cremin noted, "a postwar refinement of progressive education,"[27] but it was not representative of the entire progressive tradition. The progressive view held by Cubberley and many other educators—a view fashioned before World War I—was one that assigned to public education a central role in a society that was in transition from an agrarian-rural era to an urban-industrial era. The progressives expected the schools to employ the new sciences, especially psychology, to fashion innovative pedagogical methods and educational programs so that a more numerous and diverse school population could profit from schooling that would relate to the personal, civic, and vocational aspects of life in the industrial society. However, the basic assumptions of that version of progressive education were never universally accepted in American society. As Scott and Hill observed, some never believed in either the desirability or feasibility of providing public education from kindergarten through the high school for all children. Moreover, universal agreement was never reached on the progressive claim that education should be based on the characteristics of the students rather than on the logical structures of the subjects the schools were supposed to teach.

After World War II, some critics focused on what was believed to be an ever-increasing rate of social and technological change and an urgent need to defend democracy against totalitarian threats. If the challenges of the new era and its dangers were to be met successfully, more students would have to master advanced intellectual skills. The best way to accomplish that, some observers believed, was by offering students a rigorous academic curriculum, that is, by raising standards rather than diluting them through a proliferation of elective programs.

The Call for Better Standards

As early as 1949, the Reverend Barnard I. Bell argued in his *Crisis in Education* that only improved schools that tended to the cultivation of the intellect could rescue American culture from mediocrity and give it proper direction. In the same year, Mortimer Smith published *And Madly Teach,* in which he tried to warn the nation that the public schools suppressed individuality and encouraged youth to obey the herd instinct. Unless schools emphasized the cultivation of the intellect and actively encouraged the development of intellectual values, the nation would surely soon consist of little more than robots ready for political and economic exploitation by opponents of the American way of life. In 1953, Albert Lynd charged that the citizens had lost control of their schools to professional educators who had no respect for the nation's cultural heritage. The title of his work, *Quackery in the Public Schools,* left no doubt about his views on public education.

In 1955, Arthur E. Bestor, a professor of history at the University of Illinois who had earlier proposed that the nation's scholars assume responsibility for watching over the nation's public schools, reported his assessment of public schools in *Educational Wastelands*. He contended that schools had been taken over by professional educationists who lacked respect for the intellectual disciplines. He soon followed that attack with *The Restoration of Learning,* in which he called for a return to the traditional school subjects (science, mathematics, history, English, and foreign languages), which he claimed constituted the only true foundation for "contemporary life." To understand their world, students needed not "the simple minded conception of mathematics as primarily a matter of making change and figuring out how many cups of punch can be dipped from a gallon bowl" but algebra, trigonometry, and calculus. To understand developments and products they used in their daily lives students needed to know the academic disciplines. Advanced physics would enable students to understand television, which had then already entered half the nation's homes. Use of antibiotics and vitamins required knowledge of biochemistry. Use of plastics and detergents required study of chemistry.[28]

Bestor presented statistics to support his assertion that enrollments in high school mathematics and science courses had declined significantly. Between the beginning and the middle of the twentieth century, enrollment in science courses fell from 83.9 percent to 53.8 percent. The decline in mathematics courses was similar—from 85.6 percent to 54.7 percent. The decline in foreign language enrollment was even greater, from 72.2 percent to 21.8 percent.[29]

Almost thirty years after Bestor made his plea for a return to better educational days, the authors of *A Nation at Risk* also argued that the nation's educational decline had to be stopped, that students needed to return to study of the traditional school subjects, and, as

Bestor had, offered statistics to document the decline they perceived. The National Commission on Excellence warned that "the public has no patience with undemanding and superfluous high school offerings."[30] The high school curricula, it claimed, were "homogenized, diluted, and diffused to the point that they no longer have a central purpose." In the curricula smorgasbord, "the appetizers and desserts can easily be mistaken for the main course." The choices made by students from the "cafeteria-style curriculum" were reported in statistics reminiscent of Bestor's. Between 1964 and 1979 enrollment in general programs of study as opposed to vocational or college preparatory programs increased from 12 percent to 42 percent, and at least a fourth of such programs were far from the traditional course of study. "Twenty-five percent of the credits earned by general track high school students are in physical and health education, work experience outside the school, remedial English and mathematics, and personal service and development courses, such as training for adulthood and marriage."[31] Intermediate algebra is offered in virtually all high schools, but only 31 percent of students complete the course. While 60 percent of students have the opportunity to enroll in calculus, only 6 percent of the students who enroll actually finish the course. Only 13 percent complete French 1.

In the 1950s, John Gunther's *Inside Russia Today* afforded Americans an opportunity to compare their public schools to those of the Soviet Union. At that time, American children attended school five days a week, but Russian children attended six. The Soviet school year was thirty-three days longer than the American. Soviet students completed a curriculum that included ten years of mathematics, four years of chemistry, five years of physics and six years of biology. Soviet students studied English, but American students did not study Russian. Compared with Russian students, American children clearly knew very little science. Only half of the American pupils enrolled in a one year physics course, and although almost two-thirds enrolled in chemistry, it too was a one year course.

In *A Nation at Risk* the Soviet threat was not invoked as it was in the 1950s, but the fear of successful foreign competition in the world marketplace was. The Commission on Excellence reminded Americans that "the Japanese make automobiles more efficiently than Americans," that "the South Koreans recently built the world's most efficient steel mill," and that "American machine tools, once the pride of the world, are being replaced by German products." The only way for America to retain its "slim competitive edge" is through an improved educational system. "Learning," the Commission advised, "is the indispensable investment required for success in the 'information age' we are entering."[32]

The Sputnik Truce

The successful launching and orbiting of Russia's *Sputnik* in October, 1957 seemed to end the war between the "friends" and the "enemies" of public education. A formal truce seemed to be called so that action could be taken against the external enemy who had just displayed a highly visible sign of power. Debate about public education and its purposes was temporarily set aside. Russia's success in space rocketry was frequently attributed to its superior educational system, and the United States's apparent second place status in the space race was ascribed to public schools that had strayed too far from intellectual rigor and study of the academic disciplines. Nonetheless, combatants in the "great debate" worked to meet the perceived threat of the external enemy. The Russian success gave instant credibility to those who had been complaining about American education and convinced many that the time had come to improve education so the nation could take the lead in the space race.

The federal government soon adopted several measures to improve education and provided funds for their implementation. Scholars from a variety of disciplines were recruited to revise and update curricula. Educators were given a new mission by the public. They were to emphasize "excellence" in education. For almost a decade, educational discussions focused on how to implement James B. Conant's recommendations for the comprehensive high school and how to revise curricula to emphasize the structure of knowledge that Jerome S. Bruner claimed was so essential. The implication of the Prosser Resolution—that the traditional high school was inappropriate for over half the population—was not even considered.

Cremin's observation that critics have always been dogging the footsteps of educators proved to be an apt characterization of the decades after the end of World War II. Education received intense national examination after the war, for it was seen as having an importance that it did not have previously. Public education was explicitly linked to the national interest, especially defense. When defense was not at the top of the nation's agenda of priorities, education was still related to other national priorities—the elimination of poverty, the extension of equality of opportunity, and economic recovery and development. Reactions to *Sputnik* changed the character of discussions about public education and in some instances even changed a few school practices, but public education remained an important national issue.

From Space to Poverty

Even before the nation demonstrated its spatial superiority by landing a man on the moon, eradication of poverty was high on the national agenda. While educators were still attending conferences to discuss the importance and implications of the structure of knowledge for curriculum improvement and publishing new texts on curriculum that emphasized either the structure of knowledge[33] or the possibility of having both democracy and excellence in education,[34] President Kennedy was developing an interest in poverty. Soon after Kennedy's assassination, his successor Lyndon B. Johnson announced that he was declaring war on poverty in his 1964 State of the Union address. To aid him, Congress, in 1965, passed the Elementary and Secondary Education Act, which established the still popular Headstart Program. By the mid 1960s, educators had a new and perhaps impossible mission—they were to put an end to poverty.

The social planners and politicians wanted to put an end to poverty without effecting any fundamental institutional or economic changes. They wanted a better but not a different society. Consequently, the target of the new programs was children not adults. As Christopher Jencks observed:

> During the 1960s, many reformers devoted enormous efforts to equalizing opportunity. More specifically, they tried to eliminate inequalities based on skin color and to a lesser extent on economic background. They also wanted to eliminate absolute deprivation: "poverty," "ignorance," "powerlessness," and so forth. But only a handful of radicals talked about eliminating inequality per se. Almost none of the national legislation passed during the 1960s tried to reduce disparities in adult status, power, or income in any direct way.[35]

It fell upon educators to either revise or invent educational strategies and programs to qualify the poor and culturally disadvantaged peoples for jobs that would enable them to break the vicious cycle of poverty. Society directed educators to shift their emphasis from identifying talented youth for "social exploitation" and introduction to academic disciplines at an early age to assisting the poor to do well in school. It was then believed that doing well in school would lead to employment and that once the poor were employed poverty would disappear. As Harry S. Broudy observed:

> Overnight the new math and the new biology and the new physics and the new language labs were pushed into the background. The research funds began to flow into schemes in which elitist subjects and activities were "put down" so that poor children would be "turned on."[36]

Conclusion

Charles Burgess and Merle Borrowman have observed that when the nation seems to have clear and specific personpower requirements, educational ideology emphasizes "social efficiency" values. When personpower requirements are not readily identifiable, educational ideology stresses "consumatory values." At times, both the school and society, usually through the media, emphasize what students need to secure positions with significant social and economic rewards. In that way, a sufficient supply of properly trained personnel is assured to accomplish whatever is identified as being in the national interest. At other times, when there is less certainty about the kinds of skills and interests that are needed, schools emphasize how students can develop and enjoy their own interests.[37] Thus, at one time, achievement is encouraged, at the other enjoyment. Such a pattern suggests that criticism of public schools signals the beginning of one cycle and the end of another not only for public education but also for the society.

Changes required of educators are not completely unfamiliar. It *seems* that parallels can be seen between the past and the present and that modifications of earlier programs can be introduced to satisfy the demands of the new criticisms. However, the parallels between the past and the present may be but a comforting illusion. The circumstances of the present and those of the future may turn out to be quite different from those of the past. The traditional high school curriculum was established in the 1890s, before the advent of television, atomic power, and the computer.

As "friends" and "enemies' of public education offer prescriptions to fix it, an important difference between the past and the present is frequently overlooked. Up to the 1950s, when about half of the nation's youth was graduated from high school, attending school, especially high school, was viewed as an opportunity and a privilege. Then educators could easily argue that public education should be expanded so that more, if not all, youth could have the opportunity for advancement through education. Education was a growth industry with ample room for expansion. Moreover, after World War II, sufficient confidence and affluence made the expansion possible. Now, however, more than three-fourths of the nation's youth graduate from high school and over half go on to college. The K–12 market is saturated, and K–12 educators have to compete with postsecondary educators for support at a time when society seems to be moving away from its earlier willingness to maintain massive social service and social welfare programs.

Educators and supporters of public education fashioned in the public mind a strong connection between the amount of education one acquired and the likelihood of successful, rewarding, prestigious, and even enjoyable employment. Many believed, and some still do believe, that the public school's chief purpose is to prepare students for suitable jobs and thereby serve as the social mechanism for establishing a Jeffersonian meritocracy in which the most able and accomplished secure the best positions. What has been frequently overlooked, however, is that throughout the twentieth century children have become increasingly marginal to the economy. They have been needed for consumptive rather than productive purposes. Having nothing else to do with or for them, society created schools, convinced that the schools would provide the sophisticated skills needed for good jobs. If the children remained in school long enough, it was believed that they would eventually be better off than their neighbors who did not.

Once virtually all were in school, it became increasingly difficult to convince students that they were actually acquiring an economic advantage over their neighbors. If all have a high school diploma, the diploma ceases to be a distinguishing characteristic. Even its meaning to college admission officers and personnel officers is seriously eroded. Admissions officers turn to scores on standardized tests to make their selections, and employers raise their requirements. Increased educational requirements for jobs begin to reflect the availability of people with educational credentials rather than the actual requirements of a job. As Ivar Berg suggested, convincing people that they need education for jobs may be a form of robbery.[38] When the economy is not able to absorb all who are educationally qualified for jobs, so-called educational inflation develops. People cannot realize as much earning power from education as they expected or they have to settle for jobs for which they are allegedly "overqualified." At such junctures, the economic value of education is questioned, and, curiously, schools are blamed for what the economy cannot do—provide all with something rewarding and worthwhile to do. The technologies we thought would require more skilled people may instead require fewer. The few who are expert in the ways of high technology may constitute a new kind of elite, and it may be difficult to democratize their skills. Yet, educators are charged with attending to "the collosal problem of educating youngsters for jobs which do not exist and for professions which cannot be described."[39]

The conventional wisdom has maintained that highly educated people make the economy grow. Education has been seen as a good investment for society. The returns were good, for "the wealth of a nation, as Adam Smith held two centuries ago, depends in part on the skills and knowledge of its people."[40] Few considered the reverse of that proposition: that a prosperous economy allows the educational system to expand and that an efficient and highly productive economy requires schools not only as a source of "human capital" for the economy but also as an alternative to the workplace. In the coming decades, we must examine the traditional assumptions about the relationships among schooling, individual success, and the health of the nation's economy.

Notes

1. Edward A. Sheldon, "Autobiography" (1911) in *The Educating of Americans: A Documentary History,* ed. Daniel Calhoun (Boston: Houghton Mifflin, 1969), 311; and *Seventh Annual Report of the Board of Education of the City of Oswego* (1860) in Calhoun, *Educating of Americans,* 311–312.

2. Edward A. Sheldon, "Object Teaching" (1864) in *Education in the United States: A Documentary History,* ed. Sol Cohen (New York: Random House, 1974), 1782–1783.
3. Stephen R. Graubard in the preface of *Daedalus: America's Schools: Public and Private* (Summer 1911): vi.
4. Winfield Scott and Clyde M. Hill, eds., *Public Education Under Criticism* (Englewood Cliffs, N.J.: Prentice-Hall, 1954), 3.
5. Ibid.
6. Ibid., 4.
7. The National Commission on Excellence in Education, *A Nation at Risk: The Imperative for Educational Reform* (Washington, D.C.: Government Printing Office, 1983), 1.
8. Ibid., 5.
9. Milton Goldberg and James Harvey, "A Nation at Risk: The Report of the National Commission on Excellence in Education," *Phi Delta Kappan* 65 (September 1983), 14.
10. Almost all lists of the national reports include *A Nation at Risk* and the following: Ernest L. Boyer, *High School: A Report on Secondary Education in America* (New York: Harper & Row, 1983); College Board, *Academic Preparation for College: What Students Need to Know and Be Able to Do* (New York: College Entrance Examination Board, 1983); Philip A. Cusick, *The Egalitarian Ideal and the American High School* (New York: Longman, 1983); Linda Darling-Hammond, *Beyond the Commission Reports: The Coming Crisis in Teaching* (Washington, D.C.: Rand, 1984); John I. Goodland, *A Place Called School: Prospects for the Future* (New York: McGraw-Hill, 1984); Sara Lawrence Lightfoot, *The Good High School: Portraits of Character and Culture* (New York: Basic Books, 1983); The National Science Board's Commission on Precollege Education in Mathematics, Science and Technology, *Educating Americans for the Twenty-first Century* (Washington, D.C.: National Science Board, 1983); Task Force on Education for Economic Growth, *Action for Excellence: A Comprehensive Plan to Improve Our Nation's Schools* (Washington, D.C.: Education Commission of the States, 1983); Task Force on Federal Elementary and Secondary Education Policy, *Making the Grade* (New York: Twentieth Century Fund, 1983); and Theodore Sizer, *Horace's Compromise: The Dilemma of the American High School* (Boston: Houghton Mifflin, 1984). The following are also included at times in the lists of national reports: Mortimer Alder, *The Paideia Proposal: An Educational Manifesto* (New York: Macmillan, 1982) and *Paideia Problems and Possibilities: A Consideration of Questions Raised by the Paideia Proposal* (New York: Macmillan, 1983).
11. Charles Strickland, "Sputnik Reform Revisited," *Educational Studies* 16 (Spring 1985): 15.
12. Scott and Hill, *Public Education Under Criticism,* 6.
13. Ibid., 5–6, 397–398.
14. Ibid., 398.
15. Office of Education. *Life Adjustment Education for Every Youth* (Washington, D.C. Government Printing Office, n.d.) 15. Quoted in Diane Ravitch, *The Troubled Crusade: American Education, 1945–1980* (New York: Basic Books, 1983), 64–65.
16. Quoted in Ravitch, *Troubled Crusade,* 65.
17. Scott and Hill, *Public Education Under Criticism,* 199.
18. Lawrence A. Cremin, "The Curriculum Maker and His Critics: A Persistent American Problem," *Teachers College Record* 54 (February 1953): 234.
19. Reprinted in David B. Tyack (ed.), *Turning Points in American Educational History* (Lexington, Mass.: Xerox Publishing Co., 1967), 257–258.
20. William James, *Talks to Teachers* (New York: Henry Holt & Co., 1901), 9.
21. John Dewey, "Pedagogy as a University Discipline," *University of Chicago Record* 1 (September 18, 1896): 353.

22. Clarence Karrier, "Supervision in Historic Perspective," in *Supervision of Teaching: 1982 ASCD Yearbook,* ed. Thomas J. Sergiovanni (Washington, D.C.: ASCD), 6.
23. *A Nation at Risk,* 3.
24. *Action for Excellence*, 2, 9.
25. Cremin, "The Curriculum Maker" 234–235.
26. Patricia Albjerg Graham, "Whither Equality of Educational Opportunity," *Daedalus* (Summer 1981): 121.
27. Lawrence A. Cremin, *The Transformation of the School* (New York: Knopf, 1962), 333.
28. Arthur Bestor, *The Restoration of Learning* (New York: Knopf, 1956), 40–41.
29. Ibid., 42–43.
30. *A Nation at Risk,* 17.
31. Ibid., 19.
32. Ibid., 6–7.
33. For example, see Philip H. Phenix, *Realms of Meaning: A Philosophy of the Curriculum for General Education* (New York: McGraw-Hill, 1964).
34. For example, see Harry S. Broudy, B. Othanel Smith, and Joe R. Burnett, *Democracy and Excellence in American Secondary Education* (Chicago: Rand McNally, 1964). This work was an attempt to show that a theory of curriculum could be developed that would provide education for all in a mass society and also maintain excellence.
35. Christopher Jencks et. al., *Inequality: A Reassessment of the Effect of Family and Schooling in America* (New York: Colophon Books, 1973), 1.
36. Harry S. Broudy, *The Real World of the Public Schools* (New York: Harcourt Brace Jovanovich, 1972), 36.
37. Charles Burgess and Merle Borrowman, *What Doctrines to Embrace* (Glenview, Ill.: Scott, Foresman, 1969). Especially Chapter 5.
38. Ivar Berg, *Education and Jobs: The Great Training Robbery* (Boston: Beacon Press, 1971), 192.
39. B. F. Brown, *The Nongraded High School* (Englewood Cliffs, N.J.: Prentice-Hall, 1963), 14.
40. Herbert J. Walberg, "Scientific Literacy and Economic Productivity in International Perspective," *Daedalus* (Spring 1983): 2.

3
From Alternatives to Accountability and Beyond

A New Emphasis

At the beginning of the 1970 school year, James Cass, the education editor for the *Saturday Review,* wrote about the "crisis of confidence" in the schools and how the schools had resisted reform during the 1960s.[1] As Paul Woodring remarked, just one decade before, at the beginning of the 1960s, educators had been told that they were paying too little attention to academics, while at the beginning of the 1970s, they were being told "that the need is not for greater rigor or higher academic standards but rather more individual freedom and more attention to the child's social and emotional needs."[2] In a decade that included a determined civil rights movement, Lyndon Johnson's efforts toward a Great Society, and the war in Vietnam with its insistent objectors, public schools did not escape the scrutiny and even the wrath of reformers and activists of all sorts.

Just as opponents to the war in Southeast Asia detailed the atrocities committed in Vietnam, so did the critics of education in the 1960s object to what they believed was the brutal disregard for the nature of children. An early and popular effort at detailing how schools disregarded the abilities of children and taught them to fail was John Holt's *How Children Fail* (1964). Although the book was based on his observations and experiences in private schools, it was used as an indictment of public schools. It is noteworthy because it shows just how quickly fashions in education can and do sometimes change. Just seven years after *Sputnik* and one year after Admiral Hyman G. Rickover wrote in the *Ladies Home Journal* that too many "precious school hours are wasted teaching children how to make fudge, twirl batons, drive cars, budget income, handle the telephone and catch fish,"[3] Holt was arguing that if standards were raised, "our classroom will bulge with kids who can't pass the test to get into the next class."[4]

Holt was certainly not convinced that the way to effective learning was through the highly touted "new curricula." The "new math," he claimed, was the beneficiary of "a very skillful public relations job." In some places, it led to "revolutionary and constructive changes in math teaching," but in most places it was not significantly different from the old math. New texts were indeed new but not necessarily better than those they replaced. Most were "not worth all the fuss that is being made over them." Their authors attributed to children knowledge they typically did not have. An exchange of one cookbook for another was not an improvement. Children did not learn by following the recipes handed to them by adults but by

41

using the procedures that seemed suitable to them. Teachers tried to "transplant" their own highly developed cognitive structures into the minds of children. That was pointless because, Holt insisted, children "must do this structuring and building for themselves."[5]

For Holt, the most important and impressionable years of a person's life were the first three. In those years, children demonstrated a remarkable ability to learn. "Hardly an adult in a thousand, or ten thousand," he claimed, "could in any three years of his life learn as much, grow as much in his understanding of the world around him, as every infant learns and grows in this first three years."[6] Because, Holt claimed, "nobody starts off stupid" (a claim reminiscent of Rousseau's that "everything is good as it comes from the hands of the Maker of the world but degenerates once it gets into the hands of man"[7]), there had to be some way to explain why some children were more intelligent than others. The explanation was that "adults destroy most of the intellectual and creative capacity of children by the things we do to them or make them do." What was considered to be education was actually a process that destroyed children's capacities for growth and learning. It only served to make children "afraid, afraid of not doing what other people want, or not pleasing, or making mistakes, of failing, or being wrong." When adults were not using education to make children fearful, they were using the fears children already had to manipulate them into "docile, deferential children." In place of their natural love of learning, "adults taught children to work for petty and contemptible rewards—gold stars, or papers marked 100 and tacked on the wall, or A's on report cards, or honor rolls, or dean's lists, or Phi Betta Kappa keys—in short, for the ignoble satisfaction of feeling better than someone else."[8]

While scarcely any parent or teacher objected to fostering true intelligence in children, Holt's definition of intelligence was different and not readily measured in conventional ways. It was not "the ability to get a good score on a certain kind of test, or even the ability to do well in school." Intelligence was "a style of life, a way of behaving." Its test was not how much a person knew but how one reacted when one did not know precisely what to do. When confronted with a new problem, or situation, the intelligent person approached it with boldness and imagination and, above all, without fear. Failure to master a new situation did not cause shame among intelligent people. In essence, Holt's definition of intelligence was not based on the customary notions of cognitive behavior receiving so much attention from psychologists and educators but on an affective base. It was rooted not in knowledge but in feeling. The "roots" of intelligence, he claimed, "lie in a certain feeling about life, and one's self in respect to life."[9] Holt wanted schools to replace the standard fare of studies selected by adults with a generous array of athletic, artistic, creative, and intellectual activities from which children would make their own selections and follow the procedures that suited them.

In 1964, Philip Phenix warned "that the current vogue of the 'pursuit of excellence,' the growing prestige of intellectual achievement, and the mounting pressures on young people to succeed academically may eventually result in a great outcry against educational formalism, like the one that seventy-five years ago ushered in the Progressive movement."[10] The concomitant work of Holt and that of others later show that Phenix's warning was a fairly accurate prediction of what would soon be found in the literature about education in the 1960s. Indeed, as the sixties approached their end, schools were charged with what Harry S. Broudy called "unresponsiveness" to a growing list of social issues. Broudy noted that:

By the mid-sixties, the unresponsiveness of the schools was said to be toward the children of the city ghetto, then toward all poor children, and finally toward all children and youth. By the end of the sixties, the schools were alleged to be unresponsive to all social evils—poverty, racism, the war in Vietnam, and the pollution of the environment. In short, the schools at all levels were unresponsive to the Age of Aquarius.[11]

Children as Victims

In the 1960s, children were often portrayed as innocent victims of rigid bureaucratic school systems staffed by barely competent (and frequently incompetent), insensitive, and even racist teachers and administrators who mindlessly adhered to meaningless routines and policies. During the 1964–65 school year, when a number of demonstrations occurred on behalf of civil rights, Johnathan Kozol, a Harvard graduate and a Rhodes scholar, taught in a nearly all-black fourth grade class in the Boston Public Schools. During his tenure there, he kept a journal, converted it to an essay, and after being discharged from the school system (ostensibly because he taught children Langston Hughes' poem "Ballad of the Landlord"—a poem not on the approved list for fourth graders), converted the essay into a book, *Death at an Early Age.* Its subtitle, *The Destruction of the Hearts and Minds of Negro Children in the Boston Public Schools,* clearly conveyed the point he was trying to make about public schools in Boston.

Children in the Boston schools, according to Kozol, were taken to cellars and beaten with bamboo whips "for failing to show respect to the very same teachers who have been describing them as niggers."[12] Compassion for the students did not prevail among the teachers. Some spoke of the students as "animals" and the school as the "zoo." Kozol did not indicate whether those teachers considered what the animal-zoo metaphor meant when applied to the teachers. He did, however, relate that some seemed to enjoy whipping the students. He learned from other teachers that the whip had to be soaked for a night in vinegar or water to "really sting the hands." When he asked whether whipping was against the law, he was told: "Don't worry about the law. You just make damn sure that no one's watching."[13] He told of an emotionally troubled fourth grader, Stephen, described by another teacher as "not in his right mind," who was nonetheless sent to the cellar. Another child, Frederick, was hospitalized for an infection in his finger after a visit to the cellar. To Kozol's dismay, Frederick blamed himself: "When I got the stick I was scared and I must have pulled my hand a little so I got it on the knuckle instead of the finger part." When the boy's mother inquired about the injury, she was told by the teacher who had requested the whipping that she was satisfied that the teacher who had administered the punishment had "done the whipping right."[14]

Besides describing the physical brutality, Kozol recounted the practices that sapped black children of their dignity and self-respect. The text from which he was to teach reading was "a pablum out of nursery land" that had little or nothing to do with the experiences of the children in his class. Required material contained "every cliché of bad American children's literature." He speculated that even privileged suburban children would have found the stories "irrelevant and boring." To expect his students, who "had been hearing already for several years about Birmingham and Selma and tear-gas and cattle-prods and night-courts and slumlords—and Jazz," to relate to such a text was "futile."[15] Social studies materials were not only outdated but patently offensive to blacks. Materials that were not offensive to black children or materials that related to their concerns and interests were judged inappropriate for classroom use by the school's reading teacher who objected to a children's version of a biography of Martin Luther King. Such material, she explained, was suitable only for a completely segregated school. As Kozol observed: "Whether it was right or fair to the large majority of Negroes to use all white books for their regular work was a question which this otherwise observant lady teacher was not willing to ask."[16] Even in art classes children were subtly told that their talents were limited. They were not encouraged to exercise their talents but were judged according to how well they could reproduce what children from previous years had done. The teachers believed that the children then in the school were just not as good as the children used to be, and the children were taught to meet the teacher's expectations.

Kozol's book was widely noted and earned him the National Book Award. It was based on his experiences in one public school in Boston, but his description of those experiences was applied to other schools in other cities. Robert Coles wrote in the *New York Times* that the members of Congress who were investigating the causes of the riots in the nation's large cities should "read this honest and terrifying book."[17] Writing in the *Christian Science Monitor,* Henrietta Buckmaster acknowledged that Kozol wrote a "disturbing book" about Boston but agreed nonetheless that "he could be writing of the system in almost any city in the country."[18]

One reason for the wide appeal and applicability of Kozol's work was his symphathy for those who believed that educational and social change was necessary and occurring much too slowly. Kozol related that after he had been admonished by the reading teacher for introducing materials to students she judged inappropriate, she would sometimes tell him that things were changing, that she too was changing, but that "everything cannot happen just like that."[19] But, for Kozol, watching and waiting were wrong. During the wait, children were being destroyed.

Another account of the Boston Public Schools, more comprehensive and less passionate than Kozol's but just as critical, was Peter Schrag's *Village School Downtown.* While Kozol based his work on his own experiences as a substitute teacher, Schrag visited schools, churches, social centers, and the offices of protest groups, attended school committee meetings in Boston, and interviewed school officials, teachers, students, members of the clergy, and other community leaders and professionals associated with public education in Boston. Still, Schrag's account was consistent with Kozol's. It told of whippings, outdated, torn, and worn texts, too few texts, overcrowding, makeshift classrooms in cellars and auditoriums, poor instruction, teachers who were either insensitive or hostile to poor and especially black students, or burned out because they had to hold a second job to support their families adequately.

Although Schrag's primary focus was on Boston, he maintained that the same problems were present throughout the nation's great urban centers. Boston, like every other city, had its unique features, but it was "probably no more or less typical of the situation of urban education than any other metropolis." All major cities had a set of common problems: reluctance to change school practices, inability to institute change quickly, not enough money, and *de facto* segregation. All cities were adversely affected by "white flight" from the city to the suburb and seemed to be losing in an unspecified "competition" with suburban school systems. Everywhere the language of school problems was the same: "segregation, deprivation, neighborhood schools, busing, compensatory education, tracking, employment, housing, renewal, middle-class attitudes, process-centered learning, Title I, state aid, civil rights."[20]

The Boston schools, and by analogy the schools of other major cities, were failing to meet their responsibilities. While Boston schools could be portrayed in romantic, sentimental, and nostalgic terms by focusing on their distinctive architecture and on teachers who taught their classes to stand and greet visitors in unison and principals who admonished boys for forgetting their neckties, the truth was, according to Schrag, that "Boston's 4,000 teachers, its 96,000 school children, and its various programs and facilities comprise a system that bears the sociological and cultural marks of an older America: a faith in fundamental rote instruction, in character and discipline, in good order and decent manners." Not considered in Boston was the obligation of the schools to offer programs for students who would not live in a society that used to be but in one where "change is the only constant, where all 'facts' are perishable."[21] In such a society, the route to survival was education, not the traditional ways of "ward politics," "family ties," or even "character."

The "most pressing" but "least discussed" educational challenge in Boston was how to provide "relevant education to lower-middle-class kids who have only a dim and tenuous connection with the official world of success."[22] Those who most needed good schooling did most poorly in school. The number of segregated schools was not decreasing but increasing and the students who attended segregated schools did not do as well as students who attended other schools. According to Schrag:

> Following the common pattern, the Negro schools register lowest in reading scores and other tests of educational achievement—and the more Negro they are, the lower they rank—and they display the most severe signs of educational and social trauma—higher dropout rates, higher truancy figures, and, apparently, higher rates of teacher turnover.[23]

The deficiencies in the black schools were not, however, peculiar to the black schools. They were "only a reflection of the educational liabilities that plague the Boston schools generally." Those liabilities were extended not only to blacks but also to "middle-class Jews and working-class Irish." In Boston, Schrag charged, "almost every child is deprived," for the custom of the system was to look to the past rather than the future for solutions to its educational problems. The pride and the model for the system was the Boston Latin School, founded in 1636. Its graduates and students earned "virtually all its [the system's] national scholastic honors and nearly a third of its admissions to college." Its legacy to the system was a pattern of "classical rigidity" that was equated with "quality." Because the Latin School was the system's model, other schools were in the curious position of "trying to become what Latin was a century ago."[24] That was less than adequate for a system that needed to equip students for an uncertain future, a future that promised no stability.

A Political Solution

Educational reform, Schrag argued, was not enough to solve the problems in Boston. Political as well as educational revolution was needed. As a city of nearly 700,000 in the midst of a major metropolitan area of nearly 3 million, Boston was "an educational and social absurdity."

As a political entity separate from the suburbs surrounding it, it did not have the recourses to address adequately its financial, educational, and racial problems. It was neither small enough to allow "genuine citizen participation and neighborhood action" nor large enough "to provide the social and economic base that quality education requires." Both Boston and its suburbs were segregated, and both suffered from that segregation. Suburban schools were "filled with children of almost identical background" who did not have "the diversity to break down the smug ennui, the greenbelt isolation, and the privatist morality of their salubrious exclusion." Boston schools had "virtually no middle-class children" and were deprived of "the concern of middle-class parents."[25] Boston taxed itself to the limit but was only able to spend two-thirds as much as nearby suburbs spent with "ease."

Neither the city nor the suburbs could prosper without the other. Without the suburban people, who included "some of the most talented, highly trained, highly sophisticated individuals in America," Boston could be no more than "a vast ghetto." Without the central city, the suburbs could be little more than "culturally effeminate clusters of homogeneity lacking the richness that gives meaning to the metropolis." As long as the political boundaries between the two existed, complete social, economic, and racial integration of the schools was impossible. The solution to each set of problems, Schrag argued, was "a complete merger of resources and of concern."[26] In place of the Boston school district and the several suburban districts, Schrag wanted "a metropolitan Boston school district, based on a single property tax on city and suburbs." While there was "no existing model for such a district in any major city in America, no single formula that communities can adopt and implement," the concept of metropolitanism was used for other functions such as water, transportation, and parks. Boston had no choice, Schrag believed, but to adopt a metropolitan strategy, for it was "hemmed in, decimated, and deprived."[27]

A metropolitan district would allow the advantages of both centralization and decentralization. It would take power from those who did not use it on behalf of the citizens of Boston and distribute it for effective use. The metropolitan school district, governed by an elected school committee from geographical districts for six-year terms, would grant suburbanites a dominant voice and relieve Boston from the highly political and sometimes disruptive biennial school committee elections. The metropolitan district would assume responsibility for personnel, planning, construction, and maintenance of facilities, maintain liaison with other cultural and governmental agencies, and include a staff of specialists ready to assist the schools. Like other school boards, or committees, it would appoint a superintendent to administer the system. The new district would institute regional high schools large enough for 5,000 students. Some would be fourteen-year schools so they could offer specialized training as well as schooling for children with special needs.

The advantages of decentralization, Schrag maintained, would be realized by subdividing the metropolitan district into "neighborhood subdistricts each comprising some 50,000 people" or "about 10,000 school children." Each subdistrict would elect a "neighborhood school committee" that "would, in consultation with the central administration and local staff, have general authority over the local curriculum and educational policy, be empowered to conduct neighborhood programs and special educational and cultural activities, and be charged with general responsibility for supervising the operations of the local schools." Each district would receive a standard allocation of funds on a per pupil basis but "would be enabled, with the help of the central administration, to raise additional funds from individuals, foundations, business, and the state and federal governments." Schrag also urged that each district be eligible for a bonus for every student it accepted from another subdistrict. "Such an incentive would," he suggested, "help offset neighborhood fears of strange children (Negroes, poor kids, Italians) and add an inducement to make schools attractive to students from other parts of the region."[28]

Schrag admitted that adoption of the metropolitan plan would not effect complete racial and social integration of the schools. Many areas would "for the foreseeable future, remain racially and socially homogeneous." However, that homogeneity would somehow be offset by his plan, for it would "give genuine meaning to the concept of the neighborhood school." The "major voice" in determining what would be taught and how it would be taught would be the local school committees rather than the central administration or the metropolitan school committees. By placing sufficient power at the neighborhood level, the total district would benefit from the genuine participation of all citizens, the expected "academic pluralism," and "even a measure of internal competition." The neighborhood committees would have access to records and would determine how federal funds for disadvantaged students would be spent. If the neighborhood school was to remain, Schrag wanted it to be "a genuine community enterprise, not merely a political dodge for segregation."[29]

Boston and its surrounding suburbs did not unite to form a metropolitan school district. Detroit considered the idea as a means of achieving racial integration of the public schools, but the Supreme Court (*Milliken v. Bradley,* 1974) held that the Detroit suburban school districts did not have to merge with Detroit's school system. Still, in some parts of the nation, various forms of decentralization were tried for a variety of reasons. In some places, people insisted that they be allowed to exercise some level of control over their neighborhood schools, and decentralization was a way to grant such control. In some instances, it was effected to enhance communication between school personnel and parents and to augment the responsiveness of the school system to the community.

How to divide power and control, however, was and continues to be a difficult problem, chiefly because those who have power usually do not want to surrender it. After New York City effected a decentralization plan, a widely publicized controversy developed in Brooklyn. There, in what is now known as the Oceanhill-Brownsville affair, the representatives of the community wanted to decide which teachers would teach in their community's schools, but the teachers' union, the board of education, and the superintendent did not want to surrender the right to assign teachers. Some decentralization plans were adopted, not to give parents a voice in decisions, but because of the belief that smaller units can be administered more efficiently than larger ones. Some also believe that responsibility is easier to assign in smaller units and that greater accountability is thereby achieved.

As attempts at decentralization led to the desire for alternative schools either within or outside existing school systems, an old but nonetheless important question had to be addressed: Who has the right to educate? The Reverend C. Herbert Oliver from Oceanhill-Brownsville argued that the "exclusive right" to education belonged to parents and that it could not be rightfully taken away by either the state or the church.[30] Oliver's position was contrary to the conventional wisdom of educators that the state has the right to educate children to protect the interests of both. Oliver addressed only the individual benefit of public education. His position was also a challenge to professional educators who believed that their actions were based on their professional expertise and carried out in behalf of the public.

More Calls for Reform

In the latter half of the 1960s, the Carnegie Corporation of New York commissioned Charles E. Silberman to conduct a study of teacher education. Three and a half years later, he produced *Crisis in the Classroom,* a study that was about much more than teacher education. It was not possible, he explained, to indicate how to improve teacher education unless one had "some clear notion of what the schools themselves are going to be like—and what they *should* be like." To ask about the schools was, however, also to ask about "the values of the society as well as the purposes of education." It was to ask about "our concepts of the good life, the good man, and the good society."[31] The crisis he found in the nation's classrooms was "both a reflection of and a contributor to the larger crisis of American society."[32] Signs of the "larger crisis" were easy to find. They included the American involvement in Vietnam, the civil rights movement, the deaths of protestors on the Kent State University campus, the deaths of civil rights workers, and the protests such events incited. Silberman's bias was clear: "It was simply that everything now being done needs to be questioned."[33] He did not assume that everything in the schools was "necessarily wrong," but cautioned that in a time of unprecedented change it was simply not good enough to make the bad schools as good as the good ones. He was not demanding improvements of specific faults or a return to older and allegedly proven educational practices but challenging the "system" and calling for new assumptions and new practices.

Silberman's emphasis on the importance of full consideration of the purpose of education is an indication of how discussions of education had changed in just one decade. Earlier critics, such as James B. Conant and Martin Mayer, believed that discussions of educational purposes were dull and boring, but Silberman was no longer willing to agree. His earlier belief that the purpose of education was simply intellectual development was not sufficient. He no longer believed as he did in the early 1960s, that "tomorrow requires something that the world has never seen—*masses of intellectuals.*" At the beginning of the 1970s, he was convinced that society needed "not masses of intellectuals, but masses of educated men—men educated to feel and to act as well as to think."[34] To know how to think was not enough. History had shown that people with highly trained intellects could easily commit atrocities of the most horrible sort. Nor was more attention to the arts sufficient. History had shown that people who appreciated the arts were also capable of committing atrocities. Neither intellect nor feeling could be eliminated from education.

Silberman's new realization was that education was a moral enterprise. Morality, however, was not something that could be directly taught. Children learned morality not from direct instruction but from *how* they were taught. They learned more about citizenship from how they were dealt with in school, how they were promoted in school, who was promoted, and how the school distinguished among children than they did from social studies. How parents and teachers talked to children and to each other and the actions they approved and disapproved were all the subject matter of moral education.

Silberman was angry and indignant about the failures of public schools, failures that led to what Erik Erikson called "the most deadly of all possible sins . . . the mutilation of a child's spirit." Adults, Silberman believed, just did not know how bad schools were. He related that "it was not possible to spend any prolonged period visiting public school classrooms without being appalled by the mutilation visible everywhere—mutilation of spontaneity, of joy in learning, of pleasure in creating, of sense of self." To know the schools was to have an intense dislike for them. They were "grim" and "joyless" places governed by "oppressive and petty" regulations. Their atmosphere was "intellectually sterile" and "esthetically barren."[35]

Unlike others, Silberman did not attribute the dismal state of the schools to teachers and school administrators. While he did observe that they frequently failed to be civil to students and that they even "unconsciously" showed contempt for them, he also maintained that as a group they were neither evil nor stupid. Like most other Americans, however, they did suffer from the malady of "mindlessness." That was "the failure to think seriously about educational purpose, the reluctance to question established practice." "Mindlessness" pervaded all society's institutions. The task, not just for educators but for all Americans, was to determine "whether it is possible in the modern bureaucratic state to develop a sense of long-range purpose and to inquire into the meaning of the activity."[36] Silberman believed change was possible. The solution to the schools' problems and to all social problems was simply a matter of will and diligence. People needed to be continuously mindful of what they were doing. As Silberman explained:

> We must find ways of stimulating educators—public school teachers, principals, and superintendents; college professors, deans and presidents; radio, television, and film directors and producers; newspaper, magazine, and TV journalists and executives—to think about what they were doing, and why they are doing it. And we must persuade the general public to do the same.[37]

Like the good journalist he was (he was on leave from *Fortune*), Silberman surveyed the problem, catalogued the mutilations, showed how senseless it all was, and offered a simple solution that was applicable to all situations. "The preoccupation with order and control, the slavish adherence to the timetable and lesson plan, the obsession with routine qua routine, the absence of noise and movement, the joylessness and repression, the universality of the formal lecture or teacher-dominated 'discussion' in which the teacher instructs an entire class as a unity, the emphasis of the verbal and de-emphasis of the concrete, the inability of students to work on their own, the dichotomy between work and play—none of these are necessary."[38] All the routine and drudgery could be eliminated from the schools by turning to a new model. The new model did not have to be invented, but could be observed, just as Silberman observed it, "in the small cities and hamlets of North Dakota, in medium-sized cities such as Tuscon, Arizona, and Portland, Oregon, in prosperous suburbs, and in the ghettos of Philadelphia and New York."[39] If one went to England, one could find such schools in even greater abundance. The model, or what was called an "approach" to schooling, took hold in England just after World War II but did not receive much notice until 1967 when the Plowden Committee urged all England's primary schools to adopt it.

Informal Education

According to Silberman, many terms were used to describe the kind of schooling endorsed by the Plowden Committee: "free day," "integrated day," "integrated curriculum," "free school," "open school," and "informal education." His preference was "informal education." For him, the term denoted "a set of shared attitudes and convictions about the nature of childhood, learning, and schooling."[40] Some parents and educators were convinced that children should be sent to school to learn the academic disciplines and to have their intellects trained so they would be adequately prepared for competitive adult life, but Silberman and advocates of informal education were convinced that the Plowden Committee was correct when it reported that "children need to be themselves, to live with other children and with grownups, to learn from their environment, to enjoy the present, to get ready for the future, to create and to live, to learn to face adversity, to behave responsibly, in a word, to be human beings." Informal education required teachers to cherish childhood but not succumb to sentimentality. It required teachers not to bore children with what did not interest them and understand "that learning is likely to be more effective if it grows out of what interests the learner, rather than what interests the teacher."[41]

Informal education, Silberman cautioned, was different from either progressive education or "the kind of education that romantic critics like John Holt, George Dennison, and Paul Goodman now advocate."[42] In progressive education, Silberman claimed, teachers offered no direction and only responded to specific questions from students. The education advocated by the romantic critics, he claimed, likewise held that it was a violation of the child to introduce an adult opinion into the classroom. While the teachers in informal education had to be sensitive to children and their nature, Silberman observed that they were at least "very much in charge" in the schools. They not only created suitable environments for children but also knew when to help children "learn how to think, to form judgements, to discriminate."[43]

Informal education worked in England and it worked in the United States—such was the claim of its advocates. In some places in the United States where it was working, it represented "conscious adaptations and modifications of the English experience." In other places, it was "indigenous," not unlike its early development in England. If teachers in England could make it work, Silberman reasoned, so too could teachers in the United States. Both English and American primary school teachers came from similar sociological backgrounds, but American teachers were somewhat older and more experienced than their counterparts in England. Informal education did require "more alertness" from teachers so they could take advantage of whatever opportunities occurred, but it did not require a special sort of teacher. Even "ordinary, garden-variety teachers, not only superior ones" were able to do quite well in informal classrooms.[44]

Informal education had developed through necessity. During World War II, many English primary teachers found themselves with children in the countryside for the entire day—twenty-four hours. In that new relationship they began teach the children in new and different ways. They saw that children learned outside the classroom as well as in. When the children and teachers returned to the cities at the war's end, it became clearer to the teachers that it made little sense "to try to segment and compartmentalize children or learning." The diversity the teachers then encountered in their classes made improvisation necessary so that the many different children would be engaged in appropriate activities. Eventually, it was noted that the "intuitive responses" of the teachers had "strong theoretical support in the writings and works of Rousseau, Friedrich Froebel, the nineteenth-century 'inventor' of the Kindergarten, Maria Montessori, John Dewey, Rachel Macmillan, Susan Isaacs, Jerome Bruner, and most importantly, the Swiss biologist-psychologist-epistemologist, Jean Piaget."[45] Thus, those who insisted upon a theoretical base for educational practices or attitudes could choose from a wide variety of theorists. Theory followed practice.

Open Education

While Silberman urged that schooling be "informalized," other writers impressed by the Plowden Report and successful practices in British primary schools argued for "open education."[46] Its advocates were enthusiastic and frequently wrote engagingly and convincingly about the idea, but it was not adopted as the panacea for all the nation's educational and social ills. Not all were as convinced of the importance and efficacy of open education or informal education as its advocates were. For example, Amitai Etzioni agreed that "a school system is needed which exercises less control than the present" but he also wanted one that would provide "more guidance than the one Silberman advocated." Etzioni's opinion was that "the majority of the children in *our* society need more of a guiding hand, a more institutionalized school than the highly informal school that the theorists advocated."[47] Mary Jo Bane reported that while no single book challenged the idea effectively, there were signs of resistance. Some parents and school boards rejected the idea because they associated it with "lack of discipline and academic seriousness." A number of teachers found that their students responded with "hostility and destructiveness." Moreover, "some of the best practitioners in pre-school education" were able to cite "empircal evidence" to support their claims that "structured teaching is far more effective than informal programs in raising the achievement levels of disadvantaged children."[48] Some, including Joseph Featherstone, who helped to popularize the open school through a series of articles in the *New Republic,* warned that English experience and practices might not be easily transplanted to the United States.

Proponents of informal or open education were not prepared to accept that a successful approach to schooling was indicated by raising the scores made by disadvantaged students on standardized tests. To accept such a criterion was to accept, to use Silberman's language, "the false dichotomy between the 'cognitive' and the 'affective' domain" and that could "only cripple the development of thought and feeling."[49] Featherstone also refused to accept standardized scores, or quantitative data, as the principal criteria for judging educational programs. He insisted that it was "unlikely that we will find out how good schools succeed by continuing to submit relatively crude and undigested data to increasingly refined statistical manipulation." Like Silberman, he had visited schools in England. The teachers there indicated "that the quality and variety of the children's work over a period of time confirmed their instinctive feeling that there ought to be other standards besides conventional achievement and IQ tests." England's school system was a "test-ridden system." Yet, teachers and principals who were observing the excellent work performed by students were wondering whether they should "let crude quantitative test scores determine decisions concerning the education of young children."[50]

Besides calling for a different kind of education and rejecting conventional ways of judging educational success, advocates of open or informal education were trying to reform American society. As has been noted, Silberman maintained that the crisis in the classroom was but a reflection of what he saw as an even larger crisis in American society. Presumably, the right kind of education would create what he called "the just and humane society." In the late 1960s and early 1970s, however, the traditional belief that the schools could be used to reform society was being questioned and even rejected. Some even questioned whether any educational changes could be effected without appropriate changes in society. For example, Henry M. Levin attempted to demonstrate that

> the educational system corresponds to the social, economic, and political institutions of our society and that the only way we can obtain significant changes in educational functions and relations is to forge changes in the overall social, economic, and political relationships that characterize the policy. As a major corollary of this view, I maintain that no educational reforms will succeed if they violate the major tenets of our social, economic, and political system.[51]

It seemed reasonable to assume that changes in schooling were changes in how children were socialized, and proper changes in socialization would lead to changes in society, but, Levin pointed out, no "empirical support" could be found for such an assumption. Neither "the emergence of academic debates" nor "utopian visions" were powerful enough to deter the school from fulfilling its traditional role of maintaining the status quo. Schools, according to Levin, are instruments that society uses for "reproducing the social, economic, and political relationships reflected by the prevailing institutions and ideologies."[52] Etzioni agreed that schools could not change the nature of society and emphasized that "it is unfair and unrealistic" to educate students for "the educator's favorite dream world."[53] To do so was to risk preparing "a frustrated and disillusioned generation" that would "be too utopia-minded to join with other groups working for societal change, and this in turn will lead the graduates to withdraw into apathy, romantic revolutionary infantile acts, or to reject their education in favor of the world around them."[54] Even Featherstone acknowledged that it was "always silly" to believe that "schools alone can remedy the damage done to children and their families by an unjust and racist society." Yet, he argued that some change was possible as well as desirable. The effort to change the schools was worthy because the right changes "would mean a great deal for the quality of our children's lives."[55]

Alternative Schools

As dissatisfaction with public education increased and as attempts at school reform were endlessly frustrated, various sectors of the public and the profession expressed a desire to search for alternatives. While the notion of alternative schools received much attention—and still does in the form of the sustained interest in private schools—it would be difficult and even misleading to depict the experimentation with alternative schools as a single, cohesive movement. Some were motivated by the desire to escape "joyless" public schools, their drill and drudgery, and their lack of relevance to the world that students learned about from the streets and the electronic media. Others wanted to escape from what they believed was a system incapable of effectively and fairly schooling the nation's various minorities. Mortimer Smith, Executive Secretary for the Council for Basic Education and spokesperson for those who believed that the purpose of the school was "to make young people literate in word and number and in historical knowledge" reported that he saw little in the alternative school movement that was favorable to the traditional purposes of schooling. His view of those who met in New Orleans in 1972 to consider alternative schools was that they were "cultist rather than serious reformers." According to Smith:

Some of them want schools to liberate the blacks or the poor (liberators are apt to have generous traveling grants); some want schools to foster the counterculture; others are social perfectionists who can't bear to face the fact that joy and ecstasy are not constant factors in the lives of teachers and school children; still others want the schools to help overthrow the present economic order.[56]

Some tried to develop alternatives within the existing public school system. Others were convinced that alternatives could be established only outside the constraints of the existing public school systems. Kenneth Clark, who could never be described as "cultist," offered a plan not for alternative schools but for alternative public school systems. Writing in 1967, almost twenty-five years after the Supreme Court declared that deliberately segregated schools were unconstitutional, Clark noted that there was still massive resistance to school desegregation in both the North and the South. He objected to the continuation of a "bi-racial system wherein approximately 90 per cent of American children are required to attend segregated schools."[57] One system existed for the poor or underprivileged and another for the middle class. Schools for the poor and for racial minorities were just not as efficient as those attended by children of the middle class.

> This lower efficiency is expressed in terms of the fact that the schools attended by Negro and poor children have less adequate educational facilities than those attended by more privileged children. Teachers tend to resist assignments in Negro and other underprivileged schools and generally function less adequately in these schools. Their morale is generally lower; they are not adequately supervised; they tend to see their students as less capable of learning.[58]

Inefficient schools were characterized by "cumulative academic retardation" and "dropouts" who were not prepared for "a constructive role in society." They produced "a pattern of rejection and despair and hoplessness resulting in massive human wastage."[59]

The cost of the schools' inefficiency for a society that would need fewer unskilled workers and more educated workers was sure to be high. The public was paying to have the job of education done badly and would have to pay to have it done again, because the miseducated had to be reeducated. Failure to provide true equality of educational opportunity contributed "to the cycle of pathology—poor education, menial jobs or unemployment, family instability, group and personal powerlessness."[60]

The forces in the way of allowing the school to fulfill its historic function of promoting social mobility were strong and came from both white and the black sectors of the public. Besides the "more flagrant sources of opposition to any effective desegregation of American Public Schools," such as "the White Citizen's Councils in the South, parents' and taxpayers' groups in the North, and the control of boards of education by whites who identify either overtly or covertly with the more vehement opposition to change," there had developed, Clark maintained, "another formidable and insidious barrier in the way of the movement towards effective, desegregated public schools . . . in the form of the black power movement." Some blacks were so frustrated that they "asserted that there should be separate school districts organized to control the schools in all-Negro residential areas; that there should be Negro Boards of Education, Negro superintendents of schools, Negro faculty, and Negro curricula and materials."[61] While such demands were an indication "that the quality of education in *de facto* segregated Negro schools in the North and the Negro schools in the South has steadily deteriorated under the present system of white control," such demands were unacceptable to Clark.

Clark suggested that rigorous attempts to improve the quality of education for underprivileged children might help the desegregation of schools, but he was not confident that improvements could be effected even though the social, human, and financial costs of inefficient schools were high. The obvious *need* for change would not necessarily *produce* change, because the public schools were tied to tradition. "They seem to represent," he claimed, "the most rigid forms of bureaucracies which, paradoxically, are most resilient in their ability and use of devices to resist rational or irrational demands for change."[62] Public schools could resist changes easily because they were "protected public monopolies" that had only token competition from private and parochial schools. Without effective competition, the public schools would have little reason to improve. "Alternatives—realistic, aggressive, and viable competitors—to the present public school systems" were necessary.[63]

Alternatives that Clark described as "possible, realistic, and practical" included regional state schools that would be supported by the state and admit students from either side of the urban-suburban boundary; federal regional schools that would be supported from federal aid funds and would accept residential students; college- and university-related schools that would be supported by institutions of higher education "as part of their laboratories in education" and would admit students who were not the children of faculty or students; industrial demonstration schools that would be financed by the private commercial sector but would be comprehensive schools rather than vocational schools; labor union sponsored schools that would be sponsored by unions for the children of their members as well as others; and Army schools that would be able to expand upon the Defense Department's efforts of effectively educating "the casualties of our present public schools."[64]

Clark's proposals were founded on an affirmation of traditional American values. Competition worked in the private sector, so, he reasoned, it would work in public education. He was not abandoning the concept of public education but redefining it. He was arguing that

> public education need not be identified with the present system of organization of public schools. Public education can be more broadly and pragmatically defined in terms of that form of organization and functioning of an educational system which is in the public interest.[65]

He did not call for the unbridled competition of the nineteenth century but the regulated competition of the modern corporate state. Alternative public schools were not to be unregulated, because the public had an interest in how well they functioned. While they were to be "operated on a quasi-private level," they were to be subject to "quality control and professional accountability maintained and determined by Federal and State educational standards and supervision."[66]

Like many others, Clark believed that improving schools would improve society. Schools had served as "effective mobility vehicles for white American immigrants" and, if properly reformed, could do the same for the "influx of Negro and Puerto Rican youngsters into urban public schools." Inefficient schools constituted "clear threats to the viability of our cities and national stability."⁶⁷ Creation of efficient alternative systems of public education would, he maintained, free Negro children from "lives of despair and hopelessness," save white children from "cynicism, moral emptiness, and social ineptness," and save "our civilization through saving our cities."⁶⁸

Clark's plan for creating alternative systems of public education did not sweep the nation. Yet, alternatives did not disappear from either the media's reports on education or the educators discussions. Alternative schools were established within some school systems, and some received widespread attention. The attention may have been due more to their novelty than to their universality. As Donald W. Robinson, associate editor of the *Phi Delta Kappan,* wrote, "like all novelties, the alternative schools have been given publicity out of all proportion to their numbers."⁶⁹ He noted that at the time (1973), probably 15,000 students and 3,000 teachers were involved in some form of alternative school in one of 60 school districts. One highly publicized alternative school—Philadelphia's Parkway School—would only enroll about 5 percent of the city's students even if all who desired to attend were accepted.

Vernon H. Smith, a founder of the National Consortium on Options in Public Education and codirector of the Educational Alternatives Project at Indiana University, believed that the attention given to a few alternatives by the media, especially those in Chicago, Philadelphia, and Berkeley, contributed to the impression that alternatives were but "bizzare experiments." He insisted, however, that alternatives were established "to meet specific needs within their local communities." He agreed with Mario Fantini, who claimed that the alternative schools constituted "the only major movement in American education today" because the alternative schools were being developed not as an attempt by professional educators to comply with the requirements of a "national interest" but to realize the desires of people at the local level. He enthusiastically claimed that "alternatives represent the first evolutionary thrust in public education at the grass-roots level."⁷⁰

Types of Alternatives

Smith reported that eight different types of alternative schools had already been established in various communities by the early 1970s. Some alternatives were merely attempts to comply with orders to desegregate public schools. "Open schools" individualized learning activities for students and organized those activities "around interest centers within the classroom or building." "Schools without walls" were just that. Their students were directed, or allowed, to take advantage of "learning activities throughout the community." The wall-less schools encouraged "interaction between school and community" so students could learn about their world firsthand. The third type was called a "magnet school," "learning center," or educational park." It was designed to attract students from all parts of a community by concentrating special resources and opportunities in one central location. Some magnet schools were established to encourage desegregation through voluntary rather than involuntary means. "Multicultural schools," "bilingual schools," and "ethnic schools" comprised the fourth type of alternative. Such schools focused on the diversity of cultures that existed in the nation and emphasized "ethnic and racial awareness." "Street academies," "dropout centers," and "pregnancy-maternity centers" conducted programs for students whose requirements could not easily be satisfied in conventional schools. A "school-within-a-school," the "ingegration model," could be any kind of alternative "with a voluntary population that is representative in racial, ethnic, and socioeconomic class makeup of the total population of the community." The eighth type of alternative was the "free school," which, according to Smith, was a term "usually applied to non-public alternatives," even though there were very few within public school systems.[71] "Free" usually meant that teachers and students were liberated to do more of whatever they wanted to do. However, "free" did not necessarily mean an unstructured or informal classroom organized according to the current interests of students and teachers. Nor did it mean that no tuition was charged.

Allen Graubard pointed out that at least four different types of free schools existed and that the differences among them were significant. Free schools were not founded for a cross section of the population but for a particular segment. The "classical" free school usually enrolled students of all ages and was frequently modeled after A. S. Neil's Summerhill. The constituents of the school, frequently a boarding school, were typically from the white middle class. Development of the student's personality was thought to be more important than academic achievement. Accordingly, the school's program was designed to "emphasize the emotional and expressive aspects of the personality rather than the formal academic curriculum or job preparation."[72]

The "parent-teacher cooperative elementary school" again was typically a white middle class school. According to Graubard, such a school was usually founded by parents from the white middle class who were young, white, and liberal and who saw in the works of John Holt or Joseph Featherstone an alternative to the "regimentation of the normal public schools." In such schools, the "tuition is paid on a sliding scale and usually some minority students are admitted free or almost free." However, the cooperative schools had little appeal to poor minority parents and were "not intended to confront the problems of ghetto families and their children." They were also different from "the relatively new, very progressive elementary schools." The progressive schools were "well-organized, well-equipped, fairly expensive, and rather professional about staffing," while the cooperatives had "looser organizations," less equipment, and less concern about professional staff.[73]

The characteristics of the "free high school" seemed to vary according to the social class of its clientele. Some were "oriented toward the white middle class and hip youth cultures." Youth who participated in them, and especially those who provided their "initial impetus," wanted "to be involved honestly in the planning and governance of their own school." Some projected "a politically radical perspective in their rhetoric, curriculum, and other activities."[74] They focused on current political issues: the war in southeast Asia, the draft, the women's liberation movement, and the rights and problems of youth. They also participated actively in the anti-war and civil rights movements. The students in these schools were "slated for college and high career achievement." "For them," Graubard observed, "the free high school is a way to get off, for a while at least, the beaten path to college and beyond."[75]

While the "permissiveness of the free school is often congenial to progressive middle-class parents," Graubard claimed that it had "much less appeal to working-class parents who suspect that such experimental schools will not serve the needs of their children." Such parents persisted "in the hope that the American dream of working hard, getting skills and credentials, and making it in the world will somehow come true for their children."[76] Working-class parents who wanted free schools for their children were less in favor of providing opportunities for their children to be politically expressive than of having their children learn how to do well in school. Among the working-class, free high schools were the street academies—Harlem Prep is probably the most widely known—where "the pedagogy with its emphasis on skills is more conventional, and the strong commitment to getting the young people into college differs from the mood of the dominant free high school culture." These schools did, however, have an explicit political purpose in that they did "directly confront the tracking function of the public schools which 'prepare' these students for the lower rungs of the social and job hierarchy."[77] While some of these schools did focus on what it meant to be a member of the working class in America, they also focused their attention on remedial work and vocational preparation.

Just as there were free high schools for the middle class and working class so there were free elementary schools for the same two classes, with differences similar to those between the two kinds of free high schools. "Community elementary schools" were founded by low-income parents who were "wary of romantic 'freedom and spontaneity' rhetoric," and who frequently favored "the more traditional classroom approaches, including strict discipline."[78] Such schools were sometimes characterized by "pedagogical innovation" and a "libertarian atmosphere," but they were primarily interested in community control of the schools. They did not oppose change, but they did oppose any imposition of change because they had grown impatient and dissatisfied with the "system" which had been imposing changes and "failing their children for years." While such schools were closer to conventional schools in their practices than "cooperative elementary schools," they did cast off some traditional school conventions. Graubard noted that "most of these schools had an aversion to fostering individual competition by means of grades." They preferred to give "each child a sense of his or her own worth and capacities."[79]

Not for All

Advocates of both free schools and alternative schools admitted that such departures from conventional schooling were probably not suitable for all. Graubard clearly indicated that the potential effect of free schools was indeed limited, acknowledging that "they have only been able to work with a very small number—and they have not been able to 'save' all of these."[80]

Vernon Smith recognized that "the few hundred alternative public schools in operation . . . have not yet had any effects on the mainstream of public education" but he believed that they did have "significant social and educational potential." Though he did not argue, as did Kenneth Clark, that public education needed competition, he was effectively claiming that all schools need not be fashioned after the same model. He pointed out that the notion of choice was "consistent with a democratic philosophy, a pluralistic society, and a free market economy." His claim that "since the alternative school is an option within a community, it does not require consensus to justify its existence" was an admission that community consensus about public school programs was either not possible or not important. His claim that "alternatives can be developed to be responsive to the needs of minorities within the community" could be true, but it could also be a way to allow social and economic, if not racial and ethnic, segregation of schools to persist.[81] That Smith indicated that alternatives may be an option to "forced busing" is a sign of that possibility. Smith suggested that "forced busing may become unnecessary in some communities as more students and their parents are able to choose from among voluntary integration models."[82]

Graubard was not very sanguine about the future of the free school movement. His view was that "contrary to the predictions of some free education activists, this development will not mushroom into thousands of schools with hundreds of thousands of students." Besides the difficulties of maintaining them on a day-to-day basis, finding funds to support them, and the fact that most Americans were content with the idea of the traditional public school was the possibility that "free-type schools supported by the system could be used to siphon off 'malcontents,' 'troublemakers,' and activists—among students and parents—and thus ease the spreading troubles in the public schools."[83]

Depending on one's perspective, the free and alternative schools showed either how satisfied Americans were with their schools or how successful public schools were at resisting change even though many observers were telling the public it should be dissatisfied and that the schools simply had to be reformed. These movements may also be seen as the last brave attempts of the 1960s' reformers to make a difference of some sort. Smith reported that most of those who belonged to the National Consortium for Options in Public Education "were engaged in efforts to reform public education in the sixties." By the 1970s, those reformers had concluded that "educational renewal and reform in this decade will come through the development of options in public education—or they won't come at all."[84] Neither federal programs nor efforts of educators and critics seemed strong enough to change schools. Change, it seemed, would have to come one by one at the local level. So was the hope.

Accountability

A development that drew attention away from alternatives and perhaps dampened enthusiasm for them and other educational innovations was the accountability movement. Even when Vernon Smith was touting the significance and importance of alternatives in education, he reported that "accountability is the word in public education today." He suggested that the demand for accountability could be satisfied with alternatives. He cited James Moffit, who had recently proclaimed that "if we are serious about accountability, we would work it up from the people, not down to them, by replacing the present monopolistic, captive-clientele system of compulsory education with a free-choice, open-market competition of learning facilities."[85] For Smith, accountability, responsiveness, and evaluation were all packed into the notion of alternatives. The alternatives for which a community opted would tell educators how well they were responding to their interests. Alternatives were to be set out on the educational marketplace and the consumers were to select what they wanted. However, accountability did not work that way. Rather than expanding the range of options for parents, students, and educators, it restricted them. School officials became less willing to explore alternative approaches to schooling and more concerned with student performance on standardized tests. As Vito Perrone and Warren Strandbery reported:

> In our efforts at creating open classrooms we are increasingly confronted by school officials who say: "All that you advocate is fine but we have to be accountable." What they mean is that children must be at "grade-level" on various standardized achievement tests and exhibit some predetermined level of growth during the school year. Can an open classroom with an integrated

curriculum be "risked" when school officials have such concerns? Administrators do not like to discuss issues such as whether children can be trusted to initiate more of their learning, or the community becoming a major learning environment. Instead, they question whether setting such directions will cause children to produce appropriate scores on a first grade standardized reading test or a third grade achievement test in social studies, mathematics, or science.[86]

Accountability is seemingly a simple notion. It signifies the claim that the school, as a public institution, is responsible to the public that supports it and that the school has an obligation to show that it is conducting its mission responsibly by showing how well, or how poorly, students perform on tests that allow comparisons to local, state, and national norms. While few argued that public schools should not be accountable, many objected to how the measurement of the school's effectiveness was conducted. In addition, the attempts to make such measurements interfered with the ends of education and the processes schools typically employed to achieve those ends. In other words, attempts to measure school effectiveness were thought to have disruptive effects on schooling. With accountability came an ethos to which many educators objected. The authors of one critique of accountability maintained:

> The accountability movement is generating an ethos among educators that must not go unchallenged. This ethos—whose governing principles are based on a technological-economic world view—is distinguished by its frenzied insistence on the large-scale transportation of attitudes and practices from the world of business, engineering, and science to the world of education. One result of his slavish dependence on the beliefs and procedures of other fields has been to reduce the total educational endeavor to a tired litany of achievement, performance, and production characterized by the blank torpor of systems analysis, technological engineering, quality control, and replicability.[87]

For such critics, there was clearly a "myopic fixation on the means of accountability, to the systematic exclusion of any serious concern with ends."[88]

In part, the popularity of accountability was probably due to the public's dissatisfaction with education. Some sectors of the public frequently called for some sort of accountability because they believed the schools were failing to educate their children. The failures of children and their subsequent difficulties and disappointments on the marketplace seemed to indicate the schools' inability to carry out their responsibilities effectively and fairly. Some parents wanted retribution, which was frequently called accountability. In some instances, groups demanded community control of the schools. At such junctures, the results of so-called objective standardized tests often seemed a better way to satisfy demands or to answer charges of critics than testimony (no matter how sincere, detailed, or impassioned) about what schools and their teachers did on behalf of students. Joel Spring has suggested that accountability was an alternative to accepting a continuous state of "professional defensiveness" or to accepting community control—what Leon Lessinger called "populist chaos."[89]

Some were doubtlessly disturbed by and unsympathetic toward the schools' efforts (1) to make public education more joyful and (2) to develop effective programs for disadvantaged children. For those who were generally satisfied with the schools and who were concerned with ever-increasing tax rates for ever larger school budgets to pay for programs for those who did not pay taxes, accountability was an attractive notion. It meant that schools would have to show results and ask for fewer resources. It meant cutting out frills and getting back to basics.

The emphasis on basics and accountability, however, may have been motivated more by economic and political than by educational concerns.[90]

Accountability was popular and effective—effective in the sense that educators felt obliged to respond because the federal government not only supported the idea but in some instances demanded adherence to it. In fact, one of accountability's chief enthusiastic promoters was a former official from the United States Office of Education, Leon Lessinger. He was called its "high priest" and his book, *Every Kid a Winner,* its "bible." Lessinger's claims were simple. All children, regardless of their racial, ethnic, or social backgrounds, were entitled to an education that would make them productive adults. The public had a right to know how schools spent money and what results were achieved for their expenditures.

To show how public education could be made more efficient, Lessinger likened public education to a great complicated machine and educational experts to engineers. Educational engineers were to determine how the machine worked, what its difficulties and malfunctions were, and then prescribe in precise terms how the machine could be modified to effect specific results. In this system, education was defined only in behavioral terms. Educational engineers were to help specify educational outcomes in precise measurable terms, work out the technology needed for their realization, show what the cost of the objectives would be, and assist in finding external auditors who were to determine whether the established performance criteria had actually been met by the schools. The focus of the educational engineers was narrower than that of the conventional educator who typically used factors external to schooling to explain student success or failure. Advocates of accountability claimed to look only at the school and were thus charged with ignoring important social factors that influence schooling. However, to the extent that outside social factors were used as an excuse for failing to serve students fairly and effectively, Lessinger's emphasis had considerable merit.

As with any new idea in education, some observers and critics pointed out that it was not actually new.[91] One feature of accountability—payment by results—had been tried in England in the nineteenth century. There the practices of allocating school funds according to how well students scored on the school inspector's standard examinations created a narrow curriculum. Teachers taught to the test and eliminated topics not likely to be on the inspectors' examinations. It was also claimed that Lessinger's proposals were little more than a refurbishing of what Raymond E. Callahan earlier described as the "cult of efficiency" in education.[92] Earlier in the century, some educators urged that public schools be operated as though they were businesses. That meant that schools should only try to meet objectives that could be measured objectively and that they apply the principles of cost accounting to schools in order to control costs. In an earlier period, Franklin Bobbit used the steel industry as a model for schools. Later, Lessinger used the space industry.

Accountability can be viewed as an aspect of what Ernest R. House has called the technological perspective in educational innovation. Up to the mid 1960s, House reports, the strategy used for promoting change in education was "scholastic authority." Scholars from the universities developed the new materials and methods they believed appropriate and necessary and disseminated them through various publications and through workshops for school teachers. It was assumed that if given new information, teachers would use it. By the mid 1960s, that approach began to give way to a technological view of educational change that conceived of the process "as separated into functions based on rational analysis and empirical research." The new approach demanded that all assumptions be made explicit, be analyzed, and be tested empirically. This approach appeared to have worked in other sectors of society, and so, it was believed, it would also work in education. According to House:

> There were important models for this rationalization of the innovation process. Both modern industry and modern agriculture were highly successful. Space technology was occupying the front pages of newspapers. Technologized processes seemed to be related to progress. Progress was achieved by introducing new techniques into an area, and the process of modernization itself could be systematized, organized, and replicated.[93]

From the technological perspective, teaching "could be improved by the introduction of new techniques."[94] Teachers were all the same and completely fungible. Schools could be improved by enhancing the skills or knowledge of the teachers by creating better materials and methods for teachers to use. The model introducing changes into the schools was "R–D–D": *Research* would be *developed* into usable forms and then *diffused* through all educational systems. It was assumed that what worked in one place with one set of teachers would work just as well in another place with different teachers. Adoption of this perspective was not left to chance. It was vigorously supported. According to House, "more than twenty federal research and development laboratories and centers were established with this model in mind."[95] House also reported that "government funding has gone overwhelmingly into studies and projects conducted from the technological perspective."[96] Others have reported that by 1975 the federal government was spending about $100 million a year on research and development projects that were based on the technological perspective. The federal government's expenditures to evaluate programs with procedures based on the technological perspective also increased significantly after the mid 1960s. Before 1964, it has been reported, "no more than a few hundred thousand dollars were spent annually on educational program evaluation." However, by 1970, the expenditure for program evaluation was $5 million a year.[97] Thus, it is not surprising that in 1973 the U.S. Commissioner of Education, Sidney P. Marland, Jr., would attempt to explain accountability in favorable terms.

Marland acknowledged that accountability had been "a relatively fumbling, ad hoc process" but also claimed that there was reason to believe the future would be different and better. New dimensions of accountability promised "better organized and more precise methods of measurement," and, he reported, "efforts are being made to establish objectives in more systematic ways." "Management by objective" was, he related, "an important key to the smooth operation of our contemporary educational institutions."[98] He admitted that all educational considerations and goals were not easily stated in precise, measurable terms. Education was unlike product development in a research laboratory where even complex goals and processes were "relatively tangible and capable of definition." In school it was indeed difficult to tell how various events and experiences influenced students. As Marland related:

> But who is to say what happens in the heart and mind of a 10-year old when he perceives for the first time the breach, let us say, of a democratic ideal? An unintended brush off by a teacher? The academic failure or triumph of a friend? How does it affect him and his view of life, of truth, his home, his school, his community?[99]

Such concepts were indeed "vague" and "difficult to apply yardsticks to." Yet, Marland maintained that if "we establish goals such as 'the socialization of the child'," then it was necessary "to verbalize these goals in measurable terms." An alternative he did not specify but one adopted by some in response to the demand that all objectives be stated in behavioral terms was simply to abandon those educational purposes that could not be easily and simply stated and measured.

For Marland, accountability raised many "pertinent questions." They included:

> How productively are our teachers being used, and how effectively is their time and wisdom being applied to the needs of the learner? What technology is available to multiply greatly the teacher's talent? What is the full scope of the university professor's mission?[100]

Such were the crucial questions that would "become even more crucial as schools and colleges met the "economic crisis." Schools would have to become more efficient and productive. One way to give the appearance of greater efficiency and productivity, although Marland did not state so explicitly, was for the schools to eliminate all that could not be easily seen and documented.

In the systems approach employed by the advocates of accountability, Marland found a "beauty" that promised to reveal "new methods, new techniques, new materials, new ways to motivate young people, and indeed, new ways to define objectives."[101] Whether teachers found beauty in writing behavioral objectives for their classes is not known, but many teachers continue to write such objectives whether they want to or not.

Prospects for the 1980s

The prospects for public education during the remainder of the 1980s appear mixed. The appearance of so many "national reports" and the widespread attention given to them by the media have made some educators hopeful. Examination of other factors that determine how well public education will be supported in the future diminishes some of that hope. The 1982 Gallup Poll on attitudes toward the public schools indicated that Americans were "becoming increasingly concerned about the financial crunch on the public schools, and they look to the federal government to alleviate the problem 'if and when money from Washington is available'."[102] That the public is looking to Washington for additional funds for public education is not a promising prospect, for an increase in federal funds seems unlikely in an era when the fashion is to eliminate rather than expand welfare and social service programs. Moreover, the portion of funds for public schools from federal sources has only been in the range of 10 percent. While Mississippi received 24.5 percent of its funds for public schools from federal sources for the 1981–82 school year, the nation as a whole received only 8.1 percent from federal sources (49.0 percent came from the states and 42.9 percent came from local sources).[103]

While the public may be looking to the federal government for more funds for education, it is not necessarily willing to elect those who work to increase federal funding for public schools. The 1984 Gallup Poll on attitudes toward education, published about two months before the 1984 election, showed that three times as many people (66 percent) indicated that they would be "more likely" to vote for a presidential candidate "who says he would increase federal spending for education" as those (22 percent) who indicated they would be "less likely" to so vote. That same poll also showed that 42 percent perceived Walter Mondale as "more likely, as President, to improve the quality of public education in the U.S." and 34 percent so saw President Reagan.[104] Mondale did not win the election.

Michael W. Kirst has studied the recent loss of support for the nation's secondary schools and has noted that some are pessimistic about the public's confidence in education while others are optimistic. He maintains that while "there is considerable recent evidence to support both sides, an analysis of the fiscal, political, and demographic trend in the eighties favors the pessimistic view of the future."[105] The public's perception is that the school's "standards, rigor, and quality have slipped." The curriculum is not what it used to be or, in the minds of many, what it should be. Three major reasons why the curriculum has been "debased" are

> (1) an overattention to the legitimate needs of those in the bottom band of the achievement distribution, which has caused neglect of the college-bound and lowered the instructional center of gravity; (2) a preoccupation with process and technique, and with procedural accountability, finance, and governance, to the detriment of what we teach; and (3) a lack of emphasis on the usefulness and relevance of our common cultural heritage.[106]

To restore the public's confidence in education, it seems, educators need to present students with greater amounts of "challenging academic material." Just one year before the National Commission on Excellence in Education recommended that all high school students be required to complete *"Five New Basics"* (four years of English; three years of mathematics; three years of science; three years of social studies; and one-half year of computer science),[107] Gene I. Maeroff, an education writer for the *New York Times,* recommended what may be called an enlightened form of "back to basics" and urged that schools be freed from the responsibility of solving all social ills so they could focus on what they do best. It is, he claimed, necessary to distinguish between education and schooling and admit that all of education cannot be assigned to schools:

> Many pursuits in life are educational, but not all belong within the province of the schools. Let the schools be free to concentrate on the teaching of literacy in all its forms, a job that no other agency is pursuing or is as well equipped to address.[108]

Maeroff reasoned that since public confidence in the schools has declined just when so many responsibilities have been assigned to them, they would probably be better off if they could rid themselves of the additional responsibilities. For him, it is unfair to ask schools to do what parents themselves will not do. If parents are unwilling to assume responsibility for sex education or for desegregation of society, the schools should not be asked to do either. Moreover, when the school does undertake such ventures, the result is usually controversy that detracts from the school's proper and chief mission. Schools should not do what other agencies can do. For example, Maeroff recommends that driver education become the responsibility of the highway patrol rather than the public schools. Action on Maeroff's recommendations may make schools more manageable than they now are for educators. However, that would not necessarily help children whose parents cannot or do not do all they should for them.

Mortimer Adler, who established the Great Books program with the late Robert Maynard Hutchins, also agrees that public schools should do less than they have been trying to do. He organized a panel of scholars and educators to design a new approach to public education for the 1980s. Befitting his long interest in the Great Books and Great Ideas as well as the classical tradition, the panel was called the Paideia Group and their plan the Paideia Proposal. The proposal calls for equality of quality for all students by eliminating tracking, abolishing virtually all vocational educational programs, and abandoning the elective system. All students, according to the Paideia Group, should study the same twelve-year academic curriculum so they will all become good citizens and good people. Throughout their schooling, students should study in three areas called "columns." Each column is defined by its content and the teaching methods appropriate for that content. In the first column, students would acquire knowledge of history, literature, languages, mathematics, and science, which would be taught didactically—through lectures. Information would be transmitted to students, and they would be expected to receive and to retain it. In the second column, students would develop the basic intellectual skills of reading, writing, computing, and scientific method, which they would acquire through practice. In this column, teachers would not transmit knowledge directly but act as coaches. The purpose of the third column is to teach students how to think critically about ideas and values as well as to develop aesthetic appreciation through the study of art. The method proposed for the third column is the Socratic method. Besides the three columns, students would engage in physical education for twelve years and manual arts for eight years and be given one year of instruction to help them decide upon a career.[109]

Even before the publication of *A Nation at Risk*, many politicians expressed a desire for "educational eminence" and began to talk about "quality" in education. A variety of commissions and study groups began to recommend fewer electives and more study of mathematics, science, English, and foreign languages for high school and junior high school students. In California, then-Governor Jerry Brown personally delivered a resolution to the state board of education asking that all high school students be required to complete three years of mathematics, two years of science, and one-half year of computer science, as well as courses in arts and literature. Earlier he made a somewhat more rigorous proposal to the University regents by asking them to set new admissions rules that would require a fourth year of mathematics for all students seeking admission to the University of California.[110] After the appearance of *A Nation at Risk*, the Superintendent for Public Instruction for the State of California, William Honig, proclaimed that "more children than we ever expected *can* succeed in an intensive academic curriculum—not necessarily physics and calculus, but a strong common core of history, government, science and literature."[111]

Ohio State University rescinded its policy of admitting any Ohio high school graduate and announced that it planned to admit only students who have completed a traditional college preparatory program (four years of English, a foreign language, and three years of social studies, science, and mathematics). Nebraska adopted a similar policy, effective in 1986. Florida moved in a similar direction. The State College Board of Mississippi decreed that beginning in 1986 all students will have to have completed three years of science and three years of mathematics to qualify for admission to the state's colleges. Iowa's Governor Robert Ray indicated in 1982 that there was a need for more and better foreign language courses in his state's schools and colleges. Such an improvement would presumably help sell Iowa's agricultural products on foreign markets.[112]

Emphasis on stringent academic requirements may satisfy some critics of education, and more emphasis on foreign languages may eventually help some trade representatives, but such emphases are unlikely to solve all the problems confronting public education in the 1980s. As Kirst has observed, many of the problems can be addressed by educators, but some are beyond their control.[113] Moreover, "the era of unquestioned faith in schools is over."[114]

While it is true that Americans seem to have lost faith in institutions other than their schools, that does not necessarily help the schools. In fact, schools are often blamed for the actions of other institutions. Two obvious examples of programs that some do not like but which local schools are required to conduct by the federal government are bilingual education racial desegregation. When it suffers from increasing tax rates or inflation, the public finds it easy to vote against school budgets if it observes the establishment of programs it does not like. While more people were willing to support increases in taxes to support their local schools in 1984 than in 1981—41 percent as opposed to 30 percent—most were not willing to pay more for their schools in either year.[115] Ironically, the public has easier access to school budgets than to the budgets and taxing authority of other governmental agencies. Frequently, the schools suffer for what other institutions do simply because it is easier for the people to get at the schools than at other institutions.

Demographic factors will confront many school systems with difficult and unpopular decisions. The portion of the population that is of secondary school age—15 to 24 years— has declined and is expected to decline further. In 1977, it comprised 19 percent of the population but is expected to be 17 percent by 1985 and only 14 percent in 1990. However, the declining secondary school enrollment will not be evenly spread across the nation. Declines are expected to be more severe in the industrial east than in the sunbelt states. Declining enrollments eventually cause the closing of schools and, as Kirst points out,

> closing high schools causes even more political resistance than elementary schools. Class size drops initially, until schools close, and state finance formulas are adjusted. A crucial decision will be which courses are eliminated—photography, driver training, or calculus. If the advanced academic electives are eliminated because these enrollments drop the most, academic achievement and standards will decline also.[116]

Thus, as schools try to provide the courses that the majority wants and eliminate the most costly courses (those with small enrollments), they may be subjected to even more criticism for not maintaining high standards.

Further analyses of the population and the prospects for revenue for schools show that schools will have difficulties in the coming decades. The public school constituency is declining and what remains is losing its political power. Since the 1950s, the number of voters with children in school has declined from 3 in 5 to 1 in 5.[117] Sectors of the population that will be sending more children to school are "Hispanics and low-income citizens," who "have little political influence over budgets and notoriously low voter turnouts."[118] As schools continue to offer the necessary special programs for students who have not already been acculturated, voter support is likely to diminish among those who disapprove of such programs, have no children in school, and wish to object to high taxes. The number of senior citizens among the voting population will "increase dramatically," and they often have "a high tendency to vote and to resist property tax increases."[119]

While Kirst emphasizes that "the empirical evidence is *not* conclusive that the age composition of a community affects support for the public schools," he does nonetheless suggest that "the overall characteristics of U.S. senior citizens portend rough going for local school tax increases."[120] The reason for his prediction is that the more education voters have, the more likely they are to vote for school tax increases. The over-65 population is less educated than other sectors of the population, because its members grew up before the great expansion of public education. Almost half of the over-65 population has not attended high school.

Since 1960, the age structure of American society has been changing significantly and that change has not worked to the benefit of those who attend school, children. While the number of children age 15 and younger decreased by 7 percent between 1960 and 1982, the number of people age 65 or older grew by 54 percent. The expectation that such a change in the age structure would benefit children is wrong. As Samuel H. Preston has reported:

> I believe . . . that exactly the opposite has happened. Since the early 1960's the well-being of the elderly has improved greatly whereas that of they young has deteriorated. Demographic trends underlie these changes: in the family, in politics and in industry the growing number of older people and the declining number of children have worked to the advantage of the group that is increasing in size.[121]

Since 1970, the number of children under age 14 living in poverty has increased from 16 percent to 23 percent, while the number of senior citizens age 65 or older living in poverty has decreased from 24 percent to 15 percent.[122] During the 1970s, the rates of expenditure of public funds for both the elderly and for children increased at about the same rate, but children fell behind the elderly who started out with a larger share of public expenditures, about three times as great as what was being spent on children. Recently, matters have become even worse for children, for "many programs for children have been cut back while those for older people have been expanded."[123] Preston concludes that "according to several measures, including health, educational achievement and poverty status, the elderly appear to be doing better than the young."[124]

Among other factors that may interfere with traditional programs and with customary levels of funding in the schools is the changing role of women in American society and the possibility of a shortage of good teachers. Historically, mothers of children under age 6 removed themselves from the workplace, but that is no longer the case. Since the end of the 1950s, the percentage of working women with children under age 6 has increased from 19 to 42 percent. Working mothers need and will demand child care facilities for their children. Such facilities will compete with the K–12 public school programs. Some evidence for such a trend can be found in California. There, in the face of Proposition 13, some educators wanted to eliminate child care programs from the public schools in order to maintain financial support for their K–12 programs. They were not allowed to do so because the lobbyists for child care successfully included a prohibition in Proposition 13 against such a move.

As noted above, the changing role of women in American society has brought the fear that good teachers will be in very short supply. Enrollments in teacher education programs have declined as students have observed that few teaching positions are available and that salary increases for teachers have failed to keep up with inflation, especially in the mid 1970s. In addition, the traditional source for many teachers—middle-class and upper middle-class women—is diminishing as women find other career options. Good students, it seems, have been persuaded not to prepare themselves for careers as teachers. It is as though they were following the directions of the 40 percent of teachers who claim they would choose another career if they were now beginning college. As J. Myron Atkin, the Dean of the School of Education at Stanford University, observed:

> Four and five decades ago those who sought teaching positions in America's secondary schools included significant numbers of academically able people. Although it is true that teaching was one of the few fields open to many of them—even in the 1950s and 1960s, as jobs outside teaching became more plentiful—school districts that wanted them could find ample numbers of high-quality applicants. Things are different now. Today's college freshman is less likely to aim toward a career in teaching than his counterpart at any time during the last thirty years. Furthermore, the intellectual ability of those who intend to teach, as measured by standardized tests, is markedly lower than that that of college majors in every other field except ethnic studies.[125]

Whether a perceived loss of quality among teachers will prompt the public to provide additional support to improve the quality of its schools and the teachers who staff them or whether it will cause the public to refuse to support the schools is an open question.

Still another problem facing education is the disparity between the public's expressed concerns and what their representatives—school board members—perceive as the important issues facing schools. A 1980 Gallup Poll revealed that the public believes discipline to be the most important problem facing the schools (24 percent so indicated) and drug abuse to be the second most important problem (13 percent so indicated). Concerns that ranked ahead of discipline for school board members were collective bargaining (29.7 percent), cutting programs (24.9 percent), and curriculum reform (23.2 percent). Only 11 percent of the public was concerned with curriculum reform. The disparity between the concerns of the school board members and the public, according to Kirst, "portends larger decreases in public support."[126] Moreover, such a disparity gives credence to the charge that public schools use their complicated bureaucratic structures to resist effective influence on the part of the public. People are simply not likely to increase their support for an institution if the people controlling it seem unresponsive to what the public perceives to be important.

Kirst is not alone in his pessimistic outlook for public education. Stephen K. Bailey's 1981 forecast of what the future may hold for public education was as follows:

> Major signs, especially continuing inflation, current tax revolts at the state and local level, an aging population, and an increased interest in voucher schemes and federal tuition tax credits all point to a reprivatization of educational services and to fewer public resources for education generally. The logical result of these trends is unsettling, to say the least. At the end of this road may well be ghettoized schools for the urban poor, non-English language schools for Hispanics, racially pure schools for the bigoted, religious schools for the devout, and for the well-off, a wholesale reversion to the private academies of the nineteenth century.[127]

Bailey and others who fear the collapse of the nation's public school systems are concerned with more than the viability of the schools. They are also concerned about whether such a collapse and division of the population into a variety of "special interest" schools would also mean the end of "any coherent value consensus in the society at large." Since the beginning of the century, and even before, public school supporters saw the public school as the primary institution for promoting and maintaining some sense of nationhood and cultural unity among its citizens. Some believed, and some still do believe, that a strong public school system common to all people is necessary to maintain a united nation and to insure social order and domestic tranquillity.

Conclusion

Repeated accounts of declining test scores, poor academic performance, the alleged overemphasis on students with special needs at the expense of normal, nonhandicapped, and gifted students, calls for elimination of "soft electives" to make way for the "hard" academic courses, media reports about teachers' strikes and violence and vandalism in schools, claims that public education has lost is widespread support, and assertions that scientific and technical education in American public schools may be less rigorous and less extensive than that offered in the Soviet Union, Japan, or other industrialized nations may all be part of a predictable ritual of "renewal" in our society. However, the above may be something different from that. Bailey observed the parallels between past and present ciritcisms of public education and noted that "there might be no particular reason to remark on rhetorical continuities of criticism were not profound differences between the circumstances of education in the early 1950s (let alone the 1940s and the 1930s) and the early 1980s becoming increasingly, even excruciatingly manifest."[128] While the 1950s criticism was a call for higher academic standards and came at a time when schools were faced with rapidly increasingly enrollments, the 1980s criticism is carping, undirected, or "tends to deal with issues—such as lack of discipline or declining test scores—that are often manifestations of societal forces beyond the control of the schools themselves." According to Bailey, "the *fundamental* difference is found in the disintegration of the political coalitions that previously supported K–12 public education in this country."[129] After World War II, "a politics of education that traditionally had been a state and local phenomenon suddenly was on its way to becoming federal."[130] By the 1960s, advocates of federal aid to education could point to considerable success. In 1958, the federal government contributed a half billion dollars to public education. Twenty years later, its contribution had increased to $6.5 billion. However, the coalition of pro-education activitists at both the state and the federal levels began to unravel in the late 1960s.

By the 1980s, interest in public education was renewed. "Since *A Nation at Risk* was published in 1983, there have been at least 30 other national studies of education, 290 state commission and blue-ribbon task force reports, two network television documentaries, and widespread newspaper and magazine coverage of the problems of public schools."[131] However, the 1980s excellence movement seems to be for some, but not all, American students. An analysis of reports published by the National Commission on Secondary Education for Hispanics and the National Board of Inquiry into Schools conducted by Bernard Lefkowitz suggests that "the relative inattention to changes required for educating minority, low-income, female, and handicapped youngsters is a critical flaw in the current drive for educational excellence."[132] Ernest L. Boyer, president of the Carnegie Foundation for the Advancement of

Teaching, has asked: "Do we mean excellence for all, or for the privileged few?"[133] Whether the drive for excellence will become a screen behind which the poor and minority children will be "treated by school officials and policymakers as though they do not matter"[134] is a question that must not be overlooked in the coming decades.

Besides being certain that none is excluded from the excellence movement, society, and especially educators, will have to attend to the quality of life in schools as well as to the utility of schooling for both the individual and society. Trying harder to make old models more effective may prove frustrating and unsuccessful. The problems of schools are more fundamental than being more efficient, more relevant, or insuring that the high school diploma stands for whatever we believe it used to stand for. The need is not for more efficient displacements and replacements of cyclical criticism, nor is the need for responses designed to bring about either more joy or more achievement. The task facing educators may not be simply to decide whether schools should attend to the social and emotional needs of students or to the skills they need for life outside school but to determine what society can reasonably and realistically expect schools to accomplish as the society and its economy continues to evolve toward new forms.

Notes

1. James Cass, "The Crisis of Confidence—and Beyond," *Saturday Review* 53(September 19, 1970): 61–62.
2. Paul Woodring, "Retrospect and Prospect," *Saturday Review* 53(September 19, 1970): 61–62.
3. Hyman G. Rickover, "Program to Improve Our Schools," *Ladies Home Journal* 80(October 1963): 20.
4. John Holt, *How Children Fail* (New York: Pitman Publishing Co., 1964), xiii.
5. Ibid., 126–127.
6. Ibid., 167.
7. William Boyd, ed. and trans., *The Émile of Jean Jacques Rousseau* (New York: Teachers College Press, 1956), 11.
8. Holt, *How Children Fail,* 167–168.
9. Ibid., 165.
10. Philip H. Phenix, *Realms of Meaning: A Philosophy of the Curriculum for General Education* (New York: McGraw-Hill, 1964), xi.
11. Harry S. Broudy, *The Real World of the Public Schools* (New York: Harcourt Brace Jovanovich, 1972), 20–21.
12. Jonathan Kozol, *Death at an Early Age: The Destruction of the Hearts and Minds of Negro Children in the Boston Public Schools* (New York: Bantam Books, 1968), 9.
13. Ibid., 16.
14. Ibid., 12.
15. Ibid., 79.
16. Ibid., 85.
17. Robert Coles, *New York Times Book Review* (October 1, 1967): 1.
18. Henrietta Buckmaster, "The Teacher Flunked His School," *Christian Science Monitor* 59(October 5, 1967): 17.
19. Kozol, *Death at an Early Age,* 86.
20. Peter Schrag, *Village School Downtown: Boston Schools, Boston Politics* (Boston: Beacon Press, 1968), 2.

21. Ibid., 75–76.
22. Ibid., 76.
23. Ibid., 76–77.
24. Ibid., 77.
25. Ibid., 146–147.
26. Ibid., 147.
27. Ibid., 148.
28. Ibid., 148–149.
29. Ibid., 150–151.
30. C. Herbert Oliver, "Community Control of Schools" in Sheldon Marcus and Harry N. Rivlin, eds., *Conflicts in Urban Education* (New York: Basic Books, 1970), 115–116.
31. Charles E. Silberman, *Crisis in the Classroom: The Remaking of American Education* (New York: Random House, 1970), 4–5.
32. Ibid., viii.
33. Ibid., 4.
34. Ibid., 7.
35. Ibid., 10.
36. Ibid., 11.
37. Ibid.
38. Ibid., 207–208.
39. Ibid., 208.
40. Ibid.
41. Ibid., 209.
42. Ibid.
43. Ibid., 210.
44. Ibid., 266.
45. Ibid., 214–215.
46. For a discussion of five works on open education (four from the 1960s and 1970s and one from the progressive era) see Mary Jo Bane, "Open Education," *Harvard Educational Review* 42(May 1972).
47. Amitai Etzioni, Review of *Crisis in the Classroom, Harvard Educational Review* 41(February 1971): 96.
48. Bane, "Open Education," 274.
49. Silberman, *Crisis in the Classroom,* 8.
50. Joseph Featherstone, *Schools Where Children Learn* (New York: Liveright, 1971), 6–7.
51. Henry M. Levin, "Educational Reform: Its Meaning?" in Martin Carnoy and Henry M. Levin, eds., *The Limits of Educational Reform* (New York: David McKay, Co., 1976), 23–24.
52. Ibid., 24.
53. Etzioni, Review of *Crisis in the Classroom,* 97.
54. Ibid., 98.
55. Featherstone, *Schools Where Children Learn,* xi–xii.
56. Mortimer Smith, "CBE Views the Alternatives," *Phi Delta Kappan* 54(March 1973): 441.
57. Kenneth B. Clark, "Alternative Public School Systems," *Harvard Educational Review* (Winter 1968): 100.
58. Ibid., 101.
59. Ibid.
60. Ibid., 102.
61. Ibid., 103.
62. Ibid., 110–111.
63. Ibid., 111.

64. Ibid., 112–113.
65. Ibid., 111.
66. Ibid., 113.
67. Ibid., 109.
68. Ibid., 113.
69. Donald W. Robinson, "Alternative Schools: Do They Promise Reform?" *Phi Delta Kappan* 54(March 1973): 433.
70. Vernon H. Smith, "Options in Public Education: The Quiet Revolution," *Phi Delta Kappan* 54(March 1973): 434. Fantini's statement was from a speech delivered at a regional conference on options in public education at Grand Rapids, Mich., November 1, 1972.
71. Smith, "Options in Public Education," 434–435.
72. Allen Graubard, "The Free School Movement," *Harvard Educational Review* 42(August 1972): 365.
73. Ibid., 365–366.
74. Ibid., 366.
75. Ibid., 367.
76. Ibid., 366.
77. Ibid., 367.
78. Ibid., 367–368.
79. Ibid., 368.
80. Ibid., 371.
81. Smith, "Options in Public Education," 435.
82. Ibid., 436.
83. Graubard, "The Free School Movement," 372.
84. Smith, "Options in Public Education," 437.
85. Ibid.
86. Vito Perrone and Warren Strandberg, "A Perspective on Accountability," *Teachers College Record* 73(February 1972): 347–348.
87. Robert J. Nash and Russel M. Agne, "The Ethos of Accountability—A Critique," *Teachers College Record* 73(February 1972): 357.
88. Ibid., 360.
89. Joel Spring, *Educating the Worker-Citizen: The Social, Economic, and Political Foundations of Education* (New York: Longman, 1980), 201.
90. Don T. Martin, George Overholt, and Wayne J. Urban, *Accountability in American Education* (Princeton, N.J.: Princeton Book Co., 1976), 49.
91. Ibid., ch. 3.
92. Raymond E. Callahan, *Education and the Cult of Efficiency* (Chicago: University of Chicago Press, 1962).
93. Ernest R. House, "Three Perspectives on Innovation: Technological, Political, and Cultural" in Rolf Lehming and Michael Kane, eds., *Improving Schools: Using What We Know* (Beverly Hills, Calif.: Sage Publications, 1981), 21.
94. Ibid.
95. Ibid., 22.
96. Ibid., 41.
97. David K. Cohen and Michael S. Garet, "Reforming Educational Policy with Applied Social Research," *Harvard Educational Review* 45(February 1972): 339.
98. Sidney P. Marland, Jr., "Accountability in Education," *Teachers College Record* 73(February 1972): 339.
99. Ibid., 342.

100. Ibid., 344.
101. Ibid., 345.
102. Tom Migra and Eileen White, "Poll Finds Rising Concern About School Finance," *Education Week* 1(September 1982): 1.
103. "Trends in Federal, State, and Local Revenues for Public Schools," *Education Week* 1(June 9, 1982): 12.
104. George H. Gallup, "The 16th Annual Gallup Poll of the Public's Attitudes Toward the Public Schools," *Phi Delta Kappan* 66(September 1984): 28.
105. Michael W. Kirst, "Loss of Support for Public Secondary Schools: Some Causes and Solutions," *Daedalus* (Summer 1981):
106. Ibid.
107. The National Commission on Excellence in Education, *A Nation at Risk: The Imperative for Educational Reform* (Washington, D.C.: Government Printing Office, 1983), 24.
108. Gene I. Maeroff, *Don't Blame the Kids: The Trouble with America's Public Schools* (New York: McGraw-Hill, 1982), p. 12.
109. Mortimer Adler, *The Paideia Proposal: An Educational Manifesto* (New York: Macmillan, 1982), 11.
110. Chris Pipho, "States Move to Reestablish Academic Standards in Public Schools and Colleges," *Phi Delta Kappan* 64(September 1982): 5.
111. Bill Honig, "The Educational Excellence Movement: Now Comes the Hard Part," *Phi Delta Kappan* 66(June 1985): 675.
112. Pipho, "States Move to Reestablish Academic Standards," 5.
113. Kirst, "Loss of Support for Public Secondary Schools," 45.
114. Ibid., 52.
115. Gallup, "The 16th Annual Gallup Poll," 28.
116. Kirst, "Loss of Support for Public Secondary Schools," 54.
117. Ibid., 52.
118. Ibid., 54.
119. Ibid.
120. Ibid., 55.
121. Samuel H. Preston, "Children and the Elderly in the U.S.," *Scientific American* 251(December 1984), 44.
122. Ibid.
123. Ibid.
124. Ibid., 46.
125. J. Myron Atkin, "Who Will Teach in High School?" *Daedalus* (Summer 1981): 91.
126. Kirst, "Loss of Support for Public Secondary Schools," 51.
127. Stephen K. Bailey, "Political Coalitions for Public Education," *Daedalus* (Summer 1981): 38.
128. Ibid., 28.
129. Ibid.
130. Ibid., 31.
131. "Renegotiating Society's Contract with the Public Schools: The National Commission on Secondary Education for Hispanics and the National Board of Inquiry into Schools," *Carnegie Quarterly,* 29 30(Fall/Winter 1985): 2.
132. Ibid.
133. Ibid.
134. Ibid., 3.

PART II
The Nationalization
of American Education

Two dates—May 17, 1954, and October 5, 1956—stand out as the most important for public education since World War II. The events witnessed by the nation on those two days largely defined the major educational issues for an entire generation—the issues of equality of educational opportunity and excellence in education. We hop from one issue to the other as though the two are mutually exclusive; we have yet to learn how to pursue the two simultaneously.

On May 17, 1954, the Supreme Court insured active federal involvement in public education by handing down the *Brown* decision and declaring unconstitutional the doctrine of "separate but equal." Communities that maintained dual school systems in order to separate blacks from whites were to abandon such practices and integrate their schools. The practical implications of that ruling were not welcomed by all, and initial resistance quickly involved the presidency of the United States. On September 24, 1957, President Eisenhower federalized the Arkansas National Guard and dispatched troops from the 101st Airborne Division to Little Rock "to insure the carrying out of the decisions of the Federal Courts."[1] The nation had started down the long path toward school desegregation, a journey which may not yet be complete. All along that path have been federal guideposts to direct us.

On October 5, 1956, Americans learned that the Soviet Union had successfully placed in orbit the first artificial Earth satellite, *Sputnik I*. For a time, but only for a time, *Sputnik* and our reactions to it overshadowed the significance of the *Brown* decision. In January 1958, President Eisenhower asked the Congress to appropriate funds to aid public education. In the name of national defense, Congress quickly set aside all its arguments for not using federal funds to aid public education and promptly granted the president his request. Federal dollars gave many students new versions of the subjects they seemed to like least, mathematics and science. Besides providing support for the development and distribution of new curricula, the National Defense Education Act also allotted funds for loans and fellowships for students whose studies were deemed to be related to the preservation of the national interest.

Whatever one's views are about the wisdom, propriety, or even the constitutionality of federal involvement in public education, the federal government has been involved in one way or another since the late 1950s. Every president since Eisenhower has seen fit to take a stand on the importance of public education and its relationship to the federal government. For an entire generation, public education has been a national issue. The formal and legal responsibility for maintaining systems of public education remains with the individual states, but how the states exercise their rights and meet their responsibilities is now defined by national standards. Some of those standards are found in federal legislation, for example, Public Law 94–142, which mandates equal educational opportunity for the handicapped. Others are issued by the courts. Some standards are freely accepted by the states. For example, when states decide to measure their effectiveness or progress by looking at how their students rank on the SAT examinations, they are effectively accepting a national standard. When states decide that their schools, colleges, and programs should be accredited by national professional associations, they are accepting national standards.

Chapter 4, "National Defense and Curricular Reform," is devoted to how educators, scholars, and public officials responded to *Sputniks I* and *II*. In it are found an account of how educator James Bryant Conant, with the support of the Carnegie Foundation, advised Americans to organize their schools, as well as an extended discussion of how psychologists, scientists, and educators sought to establish not only new curricula for schools but new foundations and rationales for curriculum. Those who responded to the challenges symbolized by *Sputnik* were trying not only to improve public education but also to reform it. Their goal was elusive but simple. They wanted excellence in education because they believed that was the only way the nation could maintain its preeminent position in global affairs.

The principal focus of Chapter 5, "Equality, Opportunity, and Education," is on what we mean by equality of opportunity and how our notions of it were radically transformed after we read the *Coleman Report*. For two decades now, educators have been concerned not only with how people are extended opportunities but also with how well students perform. For two decades, our attention has been drawn to results. Educators have been evaluated not in terms of how hard they work but in terms of how well their students perform.

Significantly, our concern with results has prompted many to ask whether traditional forms of schooling are still the most appropriate. Some can now argue that we need new forms of schooling to realize our traditional expectations and values. In the post–World War II era, educators began to address the educational needs and aspirations of many who were frequently neglected. Their successors, those who are now preparing themselves for positions in public education, will have to ask how the educational needs and aspirations of all can be effectively realized. The ideals may remain constant but the ways we go about realizing them may have to be different. Effective educators will have to be not only informed professionals but inventive professionals.

Note

1. Quoted in Diane Rowitch. *The Troubled Crusade: American Education 1945–1980* (New York: Basic Books, 1983), p. 137.

4
National Defense and Curriculum Reform

Local Control of a National Interest

While the Constitution granted the individual states authority and responsibility for public education and while the states, especially in the early years of the nation, allowed local communities to control and support education, Americans often spoke and wrote as though the United States had *a* system of public education. Their descriptions are paradoxical in that they wrote, and still do write, as though they had both independent local systems of education and a national system.

Most state constitutions did specifically reserve authority for education for the states, but most states, especially in the early nineteenth century, paid little attention to public education. Consequently, in many instances, the local school districts—many of which existed even before the War of Independence—assumed responsibility for schools. However, how they met their responsibilities varied widely, and in the 1830s and 1840s, educational reformers led by Horace Mann and Henry Barnard worked to convince the states that they should assume more responsibility for public education. The reformers worked to create uniformity of educational opportunity in each state.

Although members of local boards of education are agents of the state and must act in accordance with state laws, they are, whether elected or appointed to their posts, responsible for the administration of education only in their local districts. As board members exercised their authority to set salary schedules, hire and fire teachers and superintendents, appoint principals, make budgets, choose textbooks and decide which courses would be taught, decide where new schools would be located, let contracts for supplies from local vendors, and approved extracurricular programs, Americans assumed that their schools were controlled locally. It was a reasonable assumption. The federal government provided no funds and issued no guidelines. State departments of education were a fraction of their current size. Funds to support schools were mostly raised by taxing local property and the decisions that affected people were mostly made locally.

While the pattern of funding and administering public schools created the impression of local control, other factors led Americans to believe they had a national system of education. As states assumed responsibility for schools, they adopted practices similar to each other—so similar that educators believed they had built a distinctively American system of education.

As Americans were preparing to celebrate the centennial of their independence, they were, according to Daniel Calhoun, "becoming confident that they had a genuine 'system' of education." The United States Bureau of Education, under the direction of William Torrey Harris, even sponsored a description of the nation's schools. Harris acknowledged the differences among states, but "the very sureness with which he described regional or other differences among schools only underscored the sureness of the system that he felt."[1]

The federal government's support for public education, especially in the nineteenth century, was indeed modest. In 1785, the Congress of the Confederation of the United States enacted a land ordinance that specified that the land northwest of the Ohio River be divided into Congressional townships six miles square and that a one-square-mile lot in each township be used for support of public schools. The Northwest Ordinance of 1787 specified how new territories and states were to be organized and included the proclamation that "religion, morality, and knowledge being necessary to good government and the happiness of mankind, schools and the means of education shall forever be encouraged." Advocates of federal support for public education and those who believed that religion should be taught in public schools used these ordinances to argue that Congress should properly support public education. However, Congress remained unconvinced, and the federal role in education was limited to the Land Grant College Act (1862), which gave the states land to support establishment of colleges that would offer instruction in agriculture and the mechanical arts, and the creation of the U.S. Department of Education in 1867. The Department of Education's purpose was limited to "collecting such statistics and facts as shall show the condition and progress of education in the several States and Territories, and of diffusing such information respecting the organization and management of schools and school systems, and methods of teaching, as shall aid the people of the United States in the establishment and maintenance of efficient school systems, and otherwise promote the cause of education throughout the country."[2] The Department, which soon became a bureau, was to manage its collection and distribution of information with a commissioner and three clerks. In 1917, Congress passed the Smith-Hughes Act for Vocational Education. It provided matching funds for the states to pay for the training and salaries of school personnel in agriculture, home economics, and trade and industrial education.

The NEA's National Influence

An important force in the creation of a national system of public education was the National Education Association (NEA). Although organized in 1870, its origins can be traced back to 1857 when forty-three people met in Philadelphia to found the National Teachers Association. Membership and attendance at annual meetings were small until 1884 when Thomas W. Bicknell organized an annual meeting in Madison, Wisconsin, that drew over 6,000 people. As its membership increased, so did its influence on American public education. Unlike today, the NEA was then dominated not by classroom teachers but by college and university presidents, professors, headmasters of private schools, and a few public school superintendents, principals, and teachers. NEA recommendations about public education were disseminated throughout the nation by those who worked on committees or participated in drafting policy statements, by those who attended annual meetings and heard platform debates and speeches, by those who read reports of the meetings in teachers' magazines, and by those who read the reports and followed the debates in professional journals.

The NEA's most well known, and perhaps most controversial report, was the Report of the Committee of Ten published in 1893. When the Committee of Ten, chaired by Harvard's president Charles W. Eliot, was appointed in 1892, high school attendance was rapidly increasing, and educators were debating whether the high school should be designed to prepare youth for college or serve as a "people's college." At the same time, many high school officials wanted colleges to effect a measure of uniformity in their entrance examinations for the various school subjects so that high school teachers would know what needed to be taught. Some educators wanted to give prospective college applicants an alternative to the classical curriculum as a means of qualifying themselves for college admission.

The Committee of Ten recommended that high schools offer four curricula: classical, Latin-scientific, modern language, and English. Each curriculum was to require four years of English, four years of a foreign language, three years of history, three years of mathematics, and three years of science—a curriculum not markedly different from that recommended in 1983 by the National Commission on Excellence in Education. Greek was required only in the classical curriculum but then only two rather than the customary three years were required. While many objected to the Committee's Report, it was widely accepted.

In 1895, the NEA appointed a Committee on College Entrance Requirements, chaired by Augustus F. Nightingale, the assistant superintendent of the Chicago Schools. In 1899, it effectively recommended that the Committee of Ten's Report become the guide for the nation's high schools. It recommended that students be required to complete "constants" as well as "electives." The recommended constants were "four units in foreign languages (no language accepted in less than two units), two units in mathematics, two in English, one in history, and one in science."[3]

The Desire for Uniformity

The desire for greater uniformity in college entrance examinations was realized in 1900. In 1899, Nicholas Murray Butler, President of Columbia University, proposed the formation of a College Entrance Examination Board to a meeting of the Association of College and Preparatory Schools of the Middle States and Maryland. In 1900, Butler presided at a meeting of a board made up of five representatives from secondary schools and eleven from colleges and universities. On June 17, 1901, the board offered examinations in English, Latin, Greek, German, French, mathematics, history, chemistry, and physics to 973 students at sixty-seven sites in the United States and at two sites in Europe. The examinations were not constructed by the NEA but by committees consisting of one representative from a secondary school and two from colleges. However, statements about what should be included did come from groups that had worked with the NEA's Committee on College Entrance Requirements. In 1942, the board adopted the now familiar "objective test" format and in 1948 the Educational Testing Service assumed administration of the tests.

The report of the NEA's Committee of Ten has endured. In 1963, the historian Richard Hofstadter remarked in his discussion of Eliot's committee that "the contemporary reader will notice the close similarity between this program and that recently recommended by James Bryant Conant, in his survey of the high schools."[4] Conant had recommended that all high school students be required to complete four years of English, one year of science, and three or four years of social studies. For "academically talented boys and girls," he recommended four years of English, four years of mathematics, three years of science, four years of a foreign language, and three or four years of history and social studies. Americans continue to discuss their high schools in terms set down by the Committee of Ten. They have argued for fewer or more constants, fewer or more electives. Attempts at changing the high school have considered whether the proposed reforms would or would not adequately prepare students for college work.

Standardization of the Elementary School

Just as the Committee of Ten's report served to standardize the nation's high schools, so did the requirements of the high schools lead to a standardization of the elementary school curriculum. High school became preparation for college and elementary school became preparation for high school. In the report of the Committee of Fifteen on Elementary Education, an 1895 NEA report, it was recommended that "the time devoted to the elementary school work should not be reduced from eight years, but . . . in the seventh and eighth years a modified form of algebra be introduced in the place of advanced arithmetic, and that in the eighth year English grammar yield place to Latin." Those modifications, it was believed, constituted "a proper transition to the studies of the secondary school and is calculated to assist the pupil materially in his preparation for that work."[5] For the Committee of Fifteen, the elementary school was to be defined, as was the high school, in terms of school subjects. Its report indicated that "language rightfully forms the centre of instruction in the elementary school" and that "side by side with language study is the study of mathematics . . . claiming the second place in importance of all studies."[6] These studies were followed by geography, history, and "other branches of instruction that may lay claim to a place in the course of study in the elementary school; for example, the various branches of natural science, vocal music, manual training, physical culture, drawing, etc."[7]

When John Dewey offered his observations on the influence of high school on elementary schooling, he noted that, as an "intermediary" between the elementary school and college, the high school "has operated to reflect back into the lower grades as much as possible of college ideal and method, thus solidifying and elevating the intellectual possessions of the public which never sees the college doors."[8] The high school had served to improve the "weakest point" in the public school system, grades 4 through 8. It effected the improvement by encouraging the elementary school to introduce new subjects in those years. The signs that indicated these significant improvements were: the introduction of geometry and algebra into the lower grades as a substitute for "the numerical contortions of the average arithmetic," "the substitution of literary masterpieces as wholes for the grind of continuing to learn to read broken off fragments after one has already known how to read for several years," the introduction of history in place of memorization of textbooks, "the extension of science work and the introduction of simple experimental and observational methods," and the introduction of foreign languages.[9]

Although educators have offered diverse statements of purpose for schools, Americans continue to think of their schools in terms of school subjects and how well one grade has prepared their children for the next. In the 1950s, federal funds for public schools were appropriated not for general aid to be used at the discretion of the states or local school boards but for specific purposes—the improvement of school subjects, especially mathematics and science, and guidance services.

The Call for Federal Aid

Early in 1918, after the entry of the United States into World War I, the NEA appointed a Commission on the Emergency in Education and the Program for Readjustment during and after the War. The Emergency Commission prepared "a program through which the outstanding defects of public education as revealed by the war might ultimately be remedied."[10] That program was converted into a legislative bill and introduced to the Senate in 1918 by Georgia's Sen. Hoke Smith and into the House in 1919 by Iowa's Rep. Horace Mann Towner. The Smith-Towner Bill called for the founding of a department of education with a secretary whose status would be equal to that of other cabinet members. Passage of the Smith-Towner Bill would also have provided "annual continuing grants" to the states: $7.5 million to Americanize immigrants; $50 million to equalize educational opportunities by improving rural schools; and $20 million for teacher education.

William C. Bagley, a member of the emergency commission who actually authored the bill, tried to allay the fears of those who believed that creation of a department of education would allow the secretary of education to assume the role of an educational dictator. The prestige of a department equal to other cabinet departments would, he admitted, give the secretary of education power, but only the power one earns for being a good leader. The bill was written so that "a good man holding this office can do a maximum of good, a weak man can do a minimum of harm."[11] While Bagley wanted "to employ the resources of the nation for the education of the nation's children," he also emphasized that he wanted to maintain "every worthy feature of local school control."[12]

Bagley and others actively campaigned for enactment of the Smith-Towner Bill. In 1920, he collaborated with John A.H. Keith to write *The Nation and the Schools,* "a study in the application of the principle of federal aid to education in the United States." In 1921, presidents of the American Federation of Labor, American Library Association, Daughters of the American Revolution, Women's Christian Temperance Union, and General Federation of Women's Clubs and the chairman of the Committee on Education of the Sunday School Council of Evangelical Denominations joined the NEA in a petition to President Harding for support of a department of education and federal aid to education. Sentiment for federal aid to public education seemed strong, but it was not strong enough. Congress demurred.

Sentiment for federal aid to education persisted, however. After the Smith-Towner Bill failed, other bills proposing a department of education but not federal aid for public education were introduced but not enacted. In 1929, President Hoover directed his secretary of interior, to whom the commissioner of education then reported, to appoint a committee to study federal relations to public education. The fifty-two member National Advisory Committee on Education endorsed general federal grants for education, but it was then 1931, and the problems of the Great Depression took attention away from the formulation of a federal policy on federal aid to education.

More Calls for Federal Aid

Several proposals to grant states aid for education were tendered during the Depression. Congress allowed the Reconstruction Finance Corporation to allocate $75 million either for loans to school systems to pay unpaid teachers' salaries or for relief payments to teachers. Congress also authorized $48 million to hire unemployed teachers and aided students through the National Youth Administration but did not allocate any funds directly to school systems. The Educational Finance Act of 1943 was debated on the Senate floor but sent back to committee when southerners withdrew their support because they objected to an amendment that required each state to provide equitable funding for segregated schools.

The large number of potential draftees rejected by the Selective Service during World War II because of illiteracy and the postwar shortage of classrooms and teachers persuaded some that federal aid to public education was imperative. As more bills for federal aid were introduced, however, the controversy over federal aid also increased. In 1945, both the NEA and the American Federation of Teachers had bills introduced to the Congress. Sen. William H. Taft of Ohio (who had earlier opposed federal aid to education) endorsed a modified version of the NEA bill. It was approved by the Senate in 1948, but the House did not act on it. Another version was passed in the Senate in the next session of Congress but was rejected by the House Committee on Education and Labor. Like other bills, it died in the midst of religious controversy.

Two acts were passed in 1950 that granted funds for the construction of schools and for operating expenses of schools in areas where federal activities affected public school enrollments. Other efforts to secure federal funds for public school construction failed, as did the attempts to allocate the federal share of tidelands oil revenues to the states for educational purposes. After the Supreme Court declared segregated schools unconstitutional in 1954, the Senate gave little attention to trying to aid public schools until the Soviet Union launched *Sputniks I* and *II* in 1956.

The Arrival of Federal Aid

When Congress appropriated funds for federal aid to public education, it justified its decision by claiming that the nation's security requirements demanded such aid. The opening paragraph of the 1958 National Defense Education Act declared:

> The Congress hereby finds and declares that the security of the Nation requires the fullest development of the mental resources and technical skills of its young men and women. The present emergency demands that additional and more adequate educational opportunities be made available. The defense of this Nation depends upon the mastery of modern techniques developed from complex scientific principles.[13]

The "present emergency" referred to the launching of the first two *Sputniks* by the Soviet Union.

The Rationale for Federal Aid

Sputniks I and *II* gave immediate credence to post–World War II education critics as well as to those who had been claiming that the federal government needed to take action to enhance the nation's scientific capability. During World War II, the nation's role in the world and the lives of its citizens were dramatically transformed. After the War, the United States enjoyed unprecedented economic, military, and political power. The nation's industries soon produced consumer goods in exceptional quantities. New technologies were rapidly developed and introduced across the nation, and a new mass culture was being formed. At the same time, a new war, the Cold War, ensued.

Some believed that readiness for war had to be a continuous process. Scientists were necessary for both domestic industries and for the nation's defenses. In earlier eras, politicians frequently proclaimed that the strength, prosperity, and security of the nation depended upon the quality of its schools, but most understood such claims to be largely rhetorical. Now such claims had a new meaning, for World War II had radically changed what scientists investigated, how their investigations were organized and conducted, and how they were funded.

The Need for Scientists

After World War II, some believed that the new relationship between the federal government and the scientific community could not and should not be disassembled. The transition in modern physics that made the building of the atomic bomb possible was also the beginning of a new kind of science. The military establishment needed scientists for weaponry development, and only the federal government, it seemed, had the resources to build and support the facilities the scientists needed for their work.

Even before Pearl Harbor, according to Daniel Kevles, some 1,700 physicists were in defense work. This group constituted about a quarter of the nation's physicists but "more than three quarters of its eminent leadership."[14] The shortage of physicists was so great that "the War and Navy departments, the U.S. Office of Education, state superintendents, and even local American Legion posts propagandized for better high-school courses and more students in physics."[15] The Westinghouse Company began a search for scientific talent and offered twenty scholarships a year to high school students who showed ability in science. Some even recommended that the federal government pay the expenses of students majoring in science and sought draft exemptions for young scientists. In late 1943 and early 1944, when the Army was preparing for D Day (the invasion of the Normandy beaches in France) and was 200,000 men short of its needed strength, Vannevar Bush, head of the Office of Scientific Research and Development (OSRD), campaigned strenuously and successfully to insure that his Reserved List of 7,500 key scientists would be protected from the draft.

"By V-J Day," according to Kevles, "from Africa to Southeast Asia and on to the Aleutians, civilian scientists were in vogue as strategic and operational advisers to a degree without precedent in the annals of American military history."[16] The end of the war, however, did not curtail the need for scientists. Rather, it was to be the beginning of the production of the new scientists that had been lost to the nation during the war. James B. Conant estimated that the war cost American science 150,000 first degree scientists and nearly 17,000 scientists with advanced degrees. In 1945, Vannevar Bush[17] predicted that by 1953 the nation would have 2000 fewer Ph.D. physicists than it needed.[17] It was also believed that if another war occurred, there would be no time to assemble the scientists for a war effort. Conant later observed that World War II showed Americans that "what was accomplished or not accomplished in school or college obviously did have a great deal to do with winning the war."[18]

World War II was a dividing line between two eras in our history. The requirements of the two World Wars were even different. As Conant noted:

> World War II, unlike World War I, called for more than courageous youth with a general education. There was a demand for technical specialists of all sorts. Most of the specialists needed mathematical training. The number of able males with particular aptitudes and skills suddenly became a matter of national interest. After the war, this interest never died. On the contrary, it was heightened, as more and more Americans came to realize we were in a cold war in a highly technical age.[19]

After World War II, the public had an interest in the education of its youth that it did not even have to consider in earlier times.

NSF and NDEA

Even before the war ended, it was recognized that the federal government would have to continue to support science. In 1944, President Roosevelt requested the director of OSRD, Vannevar Bush, to submit recommendations on how the government should support science after the war. In his report, Bush maintained that support of science was necessary to insure not only the nation's security but also the strength of the nation's economy and the health of its people. To maintain its position and prosperity, the United States would have to support basic research and secure sufficient numbers of trained scientists. Bush also recommended the establishment of an agency that would be responsible for developing plans to meet the nation's scientific needs, support "pure research," increase the number of scientists through fellowship programs, and develop programs to improve science education in the public schools. In 1945, Bush drafted a bill to satisfy those needs. Sen. Warren G. Magnuson, a freshmen New Deal Democrat from Washington, introduced Bush's plan for the establishment of the National Science Foundation (NSF) to the Senate.

Bush had proposed that NSF be governed by a board of presidentially appointed private citizens who would serve part-time but who would also appoint a director who would report directly to the board. When a version of that plan was passed by Congress and sent to President Truman in 1947, Truman vetoed it because he was unwilling to create an agency over which the president would have no direct control. That disagreement was not resolved until 1950. Then the president and Congress agreed that NSF's director would be appointed by and be responsible to the president. NSF was to fund pure research but have no jurisdiction over military research. The creation of NSF was an acknowledgment that the federal government did have an interest in supporting pure research and did give the scientific community some assurance that their work would be supported. Subsequently, and even to the present, NSF also funded programs to improve science instruction in the public schools.

In January 1958, President Eisenhower asked Congress to appropriate funds for the improvement of public education. He asked not for general aid to public education but recommended a series of measures that were directly related to the nation's defense requirements. For NSF he asked for a 500 percent increase in appropriations to continue work already begun on the development of new mathematics and science curricula. He requested funds to enable the states to develop their school guidance programs in order to identify talented students who had the aptitude to study college preparatory curricula. He asked for funds to support more foreign language instruction and funds to enable schools to purchase scientific equipment and materials for their laboratories and to hire additional science and mathematics teachers. To encourage more students to accept college teaching as a career, he asked for graduate fellowships.

Even before Eisenhower delivered his requests to Congress, the Senate Committee on Labor and Public Welfare began hearings to consider how science and education could be supported to improve the country's defense. Among those who testified to the committee was the executive secretary of the NEA, William G. Carr, who, as he had done previously, asked for general aid. He wanted Congress to allocate to each state a sum equal to $25 per child and to have that allocation increased to $100 per child by the end of a four-year period. Other than the stipulation that the funds be used for teachers' salaries, construction of new classrooms and the purchase of new equipment, Carr wanted no restrictions placed on how federal funds could be used by local school districts. He did testify that about 5 percent of the funds would be used for equipment purchase, that a third would be used for new construction, and that about two thirds would be used for teachers' salaries. Congress, however, was then predisposed to listen to scientists who complained that public schools gave too much attention to "socialization" and areas that were rightly the province of home and church. Schools needed to move away from their anti-intellectualism by placing more emphasis on the academic disciplines. Students needed to be taught how to think. The scientists who testified to the Senate committee effectively echoed the charges critics of public education had been making since the end of World War II.

In the spring of 1958, while Congress was considering President Eisenhower's proposals, *Life* magazine began to instruct its readers on the many deficiencies of American education. In the overcrowded schools, attention was given to dull students at the expense of bright students. Too much emphasis was placed on consumer education and social adjustment and too little on the academic disciplines. Many teachers were not worth what they were paid, but good teachers deserved better salaries. Public interest in the schools was quickly awakened by the public's fears of Russian scientific accomplishments. Rudolph Flesch's *Why Johnny Can't Read—and What You Can Do About It* received little notice when it first appeared in 1955 but became a best seller after *Sputnik*. Congress accepted the advice of the scientists and approved the president's proposals. It passed the National Defense Education Act (NDEA) and approved the increased appropriations for NSF. It provided no general aid for the public schools as Carr had requested.

The New Curricula

NSF had the funds to continue its earlier work in the development of a new physics curriculum. Through the NDEA, the U.S. Office of Education was empowered to introduce the new mathematics and science programs in the nation's public schools. It had funds to improve instruction in science, mathematics, and foreign languages. It had funds to enable states to introduce guidance programs and to fund programs in universities to train guidance counselors. It was able to encourage students to prepare for careers in mathematics, science, engineering, foreign languages, or teaching through a loan program. NDEA even authorized funds to encourage studies in anthropology, economics, geography, history, and political science so the United States would be able to develop intelligence about those areas of the world where it was competing with the Soviet Union for power and influence. The support NDEA offered public schools for the purchase of materials for science and mathematics curricula and for the employment of supervisors for those curricula nicely complemented work that NSF had begun to support in 1956 when it decided to sponsor the Physical Science Study Committee (PSSC).

The idea that led to PSSC originated with the Massachusetts Institute of Technology physicist Jerrold Zacharias. He and other physicists believed that a new physics course would attract more students. Improvement meant giving more attention to basic ideas and less to practical applications of physical laws. Rather than being drilled on Newton's laws and their applications, students would study nuclear and particle physics. To facilitate the introduction of the new physics into the public schools, Zacharias proposed the production of ninety twenty-minute movies as well as questions, problems, and equipment for teachers to use in conjunction with the films.

After *Sputnik* the PSSC was awarded millions of dollars annually from NSF and from private foundations to produce what students and teachers called the "new physics." The PSSC organized summer workshops to produce the new materials and even a new textbook for the new course. Other workshops were organized to train teachers to teach the new course. By 1960, new physics materials had been tested in 500 schools, and the course was declared ready for use in schools throughout the nation. With NDEA funds public schools purchased materials and equipment needed for the new course. The federal government had not dictated that the public schools teach the new course but did support a sector of the scientific community that believed that a new course was necessary and aided school systems that wanted to adopt the new approach. For many school officials it was easier to adopt the new course than to explain to parents why it was not being adopted.

The "new math," like the new physics, antedated *Sputnik*. In 1952, at the university of Illinois, Max Beberman of the College of Education and Herbert E. Vaughan of the mathematics department founded the University of Illinois Committee on School Mathematics (UICSM). The UICSM used the university's laboratory school as a site for the development and testing of a new mathematics curriculum that focused on student understanding of mathematical relationships. In place of teaching students how to use rules that produced correct sums, UICSM advocated instruction in set theory so students could learn how to relate mathematical concepts to each other. In 1957, the University of Maryland began a project to determine the best way to teach mathematics in the junior high school. The Maryland project tried to fashion a curriculum that abandoned drilling of students in rules they did not comprehend and tried to teach students how to handle mathematical abstractions. In 1959, the Commission on Mathematics that had been appointed by the College Entrance Examination Board in 1955 reported that conventional teaching of mathematics not only failed to create a liking of mathematics among students but also failed to teach an understanding of the subject.

In 1958, NSF awarded a grant to Edward G. Begle of Yale's mathematics department to organize the School Mathematics Study Group (SMSG), which was to devise a way to improve the mathematics curriculum. SMSG met in the summer of 1958 and decided that the most efficient way to improve the teaching of mathematics was to write new textbooks for grades 7 through 12. When the public schools opened in the fall of 1969, SMSG had already prepared a series of texts for grades 7 through 12 for use by over 25,000 pupils. In the spring of 1960, SMSG began its revision of the elementary school mathematics curriculum. In the early 1960s, many parents who had agreed that the schools needed to be improved complained that they were suddenly unable to assist their children with their mathematics homework. They knew how to compute but did not know how to relate mathematical concepts to each other.

SMSG was not the only group that worked on new materials for the schools in the summer of 1959. As Jerome S. Bruner noted:

A tour of the United States in the summer of 1959 would have revealed a concentration of distinguished mathematicians in Boulder, Colorado, engaged in writing new textbooks for primary, junior high, and high school grades. In Kansas City, there could be found a group of first-class biologists busily producing films on subjects such as the structure of the cell and photosynthesis for use in tenth-grade biology classes. In Urbana, Illinois, there was a flurry of work on the teaching of fundamental mathematical concepts to grade-school children, and in Palo Alto one might have found a mathematical logician at work trying out materials for teaching geometry to children in the beginning grades of school. In Cambridge, Massachusetts, work was progressing on an "ideal" physics course for high school students, engaging the efforts not only of text writers and film producers but also of men who had earned world renown in theoretical and experimental physics. At various centers throughout the country, teachers were being trained to teach this new physics course by others who had already tried it. Preliminary work was under way in Boulder on a junior high school course in biology, and a group of chemists were similarly engaged in their field in Portland, Oregon.[20]

While other groups were organized to revise the curriculum for additional school subjects, they did not command the generous support from NSF and the private foundations that the PSSC and SMSG received. In 1959, the American Institute of Biological Sciences Curriculum Study (BSCS) was founded to design a new biology curriculum. In 1960, the Chemical Educational Material Study group (CHEM Study) began work on a new text, laboratory manuals, a teacher's guide, and movies for a new chemistry course. In 1962, the American Council of Learned Societies and Educational Services tried to find a comprehensive and unified structure that would allow the creation of new courses in the humanities and social sciences that would be analogous to those in the sciences and mathematics. Their funds were meager, however, and their efforts not very successful. By the mid 1970s, there was congressional objection to *Man: A Course of Study* (MACOS) that had been supported by $2.1 million from NSF.

New Directions for Education

Some professional educators objected to specific features in NDEA. Many agreed with William G. Carr that federal aid to the public schools should be granted on a per capita basis without restrictions. However, neither Congress nor the public was then prepared to heed the advice of professional educators. Through effective use of the media, scientists and others convinced the public that the schools needed to return to academic disciplines and that distinguished scholars should decide what was to be taught and how. All the public needed was a simple blueprint of a good school. All educators needed was a theory to support the new fashion.

In February 1957, about eight months before the launching of *Sputnik I,* James Bryant Conant began to plan a study of American education that was to be supported by the Carnegie Foundation. In 1959, his first report from that study, *The American High School Today,* was published and served as the blueprint the public needed. In September 1959, at Woods Hole, Massachusetts, Jerome S. Bruner chaired a conference of scholars who were working on the improvement of the academic disciplines. By late 1960, the report from that conference, *The Process of Education,* was published and educators had a theory to support the new emphasis in schooling.

James Bryant Conant

Conant was born in a Boston suburb in 1893, the year the NEA's Committee of Ten published its report on the secondary school. In 1916, he earned a Ph.D. in chemistry from Harvard and in 1933 was named its thirty-third president. Because of his scientific accomplishments, his administrative ability, and government service in World War I, he quickly became an important figure in World War II efforts. In 1940, President Roosevelt sent him to England to work out methods for the exchange of scientific information. In 1942, when the Manhattan District of the Army Corps of Engineers was organized to administer production of the atomic bomb, he was appointed scientific advisor to its director, Maj. Gen. Leslie R. Groves. In 1953, President Eisenhower requested that he serve as high commissioner to the West German government in Bonn. When the Federal Republic of Germany was founded in 1955, he was appointed United States ambassador to the new government. In 1957, he agreed to direct a study of the nation's schools that was to be financed by the Carnegie Foundation and administered through the Educational Testing Service.

As president of Harvard, Conant tried to persuade faculty in the School of Education that the "study of education as social process—quite apart from the training of teachers—is as important as the study of law or business administration."[21] According to Arthur G. Powell, his "conception of education as a social process matured during 1939 as he grew more sensitive to threats against the American political and economic system."[22] The high school, he believed, could be used to sustain the democratic system of government. It was the one institution where all youth could be taught the principles of democracy and also given the opportunity to secure the means for their social mobility. His interest in the relationship between public education, social mobility, and social stratification continued after the war ended. He believed that public education "could unify an excessively diverse and stratified society," but he also feared that schools "were often a barrier to mobility." According to Powell, "Social science studies such as Lloyd Warner's *Who Shall Be Educated?* confirmed his suspicion that the schools were not an independent force for mobility and equality of opportunity but were entangled with the social structure as a whole."[23] More important than philosophical, curricular, or pedagogical considerations were sociological factors. The studies he conducted for the Carnegie Foundation were directed toward the creation of a uniform system of education that would serve all students regardless of their social station.

Conant's Approach

The relationship between Conant's experiences on the Manhattan Project and how he organized and conducted his study of the high school may be as important as the criticism that he and others were deliberately trying to use the high school as a mechanism for the early identification of talented students to sustain the scientific, military, industrial, and political interests of a meritocratic society.[24] The Manhattan Project demanded secrecy. A conventional way to maintain security is to rely on both the loyalty and ignorance of project operatives. Because workers cannot reveal what they do not know, they are allowed only enough information to complete their assignments. This approach to maintaining security by intelligence agencies, sometimes called compartmentalization, can also be viewed as an analogue to the principles of organization used in the industrial society. It shares many characteristics of the assembly line where tasks are specifically defined and workers often are not aware of how their tasks relate to what others are doing on the same line. Some may never even see the final product.

The Manhattan Project was compartmentalized. Work was distributed among several sites in Washington, California, New Mexico, Tennessee, Illinois, and other places, and only a limited number of workers knew about the sites and their operations. There was even some compartmentalization within each site. Although some secrets were lost, the Manhattan Project was successful. Nuclear devices were built and successfully detonated before other nations could do so.

Besides being a technique for maintaining security, compartmentalization is also used on an organizational and administrative basis. It is a way of dividing complex processes or organizations into supposedly more manageable units. Each unit, or project, is assigned goals or tasks, and a project manager coordinates and monitors progress so that the major task can be accomplished on schedule. After World War II, compartmentalization was applied to the building of nuclear submarines, bombers, and aircraft carriers, to the purposes and functions of social institutions, and eventually even to the design of teacher education programs. Administrators were taught how to divide processes and organize personnel and how to construct charts to display their goals and monitor the progress of their component units. In some instances, administrators ceased to talk about people and began to talk about personnel units just as they used personal pronouns in their discussion of machinery.

Failures, or difficulties, usually prompt studies to determine whether the system is faithfully and accurately applied but not studies of the system itself. Compartmentalization is a method that usually assumes a consensus about purpose; consequently, studies of purpose are not frequently encouraged. Besides being similar to the assembly line with which most Americans are familiar, compartmentalization is similar to outdated but still frequently accepted nineteenth-century notions of science that maintain that eventually enough bits and pieces of knowledge will be collected and assembled (like the pieces of a jigsaw puzzle) to reveal all the details of a complicated but comprehensible universe that can be controlled and managed.

If Conant's *The American High School Today: A First Report to Interested Citizens* is considered as a comprehensive statement on the American high school, it appears inadequate, incomplete, and representative of the traditional bias against the nation's great urban centers. The schools Conant and his team visited "were located for the most part outside metropolitan areas in cities with populations between 10,000 and 100,000."[25] They visited 4 school systems and 103 schools in 26 states. Except for Kentucky, Maryland, and Virginia they avoided the South. The information gathered was presented in a concise, clear, and readable form. However, it was not a report on anything that represented the great variety of American high schools; instead, it was a statement about high school for those who either lived in or aspired to live in communities like those depicted on the weekly covers of the *Saturday Evening Post.*

If, however, *The American High School* is viewed as but one member of a series of works on secondary education, then it appears that Conant, like a good project manager, was dividing the complex problem into manageable parts. In 1960, his first report was followed by *A Memorandum to School Boards: Recommendations for Education in the Junior High School Years,* which he described as "my second report to interested citizens."[26] The *Memorandum* was followed in 1961 by *Slums and Suburbs,* in which he considered the problems of inner city schools and warned the nation about the "social dynamite" that was accumulating there. In *Slums and Suburbs,* he estimated that a third of the nation's children attended school in the large metropolitan areas, but that not all of those students attended prosperous suburban schools. The schools accounted for in *The American High School Today* comprised 80 percent of the nation's school but enrolled only about a third of the nation's high school students. Even after submitting his report on the slum and suburban schools, he still believed that "the number one problem in many states is elimination of small schools by further district consolidation." He also emphasized, however, that he did not want "to attempt to match the seriousness of this problem on a national basis with the problems of big city slum schools."[27]

In the manner of a good project manager, Conant limited the focus of each work and gave clear and simple directions to the public. In the first report he even included the checklist he developed for his own survey so interested citizens could determine how good or poor their schools were. He tried to assign an unqualified yes or no answer to each of the questions at every school he visited. Presumably, citizens could visit their children's school and do the same. Subsequently, checklists became even more familiar to Americans as the voice of Shorty Powers at Mission Control in Houston announced the technicians' progress on checklists during the countdowns for the nation's early journeys into space.

Had Conant presented a work that considered all the problems of all the high schools and explained their causes, scholars and social scientists may have found it useful and interesting. A work that would have offered a variety of solutions and alternatives may have been more appropriate for a nation whose diverse population would soon be more apparent than ever before. However, such a work probably would have created more discussion and debate than action. Conant and the public he was addressing wanted action.

In *The American High School Today,* Conant simply explained that the American high school was rooted in a social, economic, and political tradition that was significantly different from European traditions, but he made no comparisons between American and European schools. He certainly did not try to sound an alarm about how the Russians were overtaking the Americans because of inferior schools. He offered no accounts of how bad the schools were and hence did not have to blame any persons or groups for the poor situation. He effectively avoided issues that could create controversy and draw attention from his recommendations. He offered a vision of a high school that could be nearly all things to nearly all people.

Conant's Directions for the High School

Conant had only one question to ask about the high school: "Can a school at one and the same time provide a good general education for *all* the pupils as future citizens of a democracy, provide elective programs for the majority to develop useful skills, and educate adequately those with a talent for handling advanced academic subjects—particularly foreign languages and advanced mathematics?"[28] He assured his readers that most communities could have such a comprehensive high school. Consolidation of schools would be necessary in some areas. However, because a school with a graduating class of 100 was large enough to offer all courses students required efficiently and economically, the move toward consolidation would not be drastic.

Conant's checklist for interested citizens included fifteen items divided into four major categories. The first division, devoted to "general education for all," was directed to the school's program in composition, literature, social studies, and American history and asked whether students were grouped according to their abilities in the required courses. The second part of the list was directed toward questions about the "non–academic elective program." An adequate non–academic program included "vocational programs for boys and commercial programs for girls," offered "opportunities for supervised work experience," and made "special provisions for very slow readers." The third part addressed the program for the "academically talented students." This program was to challenge gifted students, offer "special instruction in developing reading skills," offer summer sessions for enrichment, maintain individual programs that were characterized by an "absence of tracks or rigid programs," and included no less than seven instructional periods in the school day. The fourth section of the checklist raised questions about the adequacy of the guidance program, student morale, how homerooms were organized, and whether the school promoted "effective social interaction." Schools, Conant advised, should foster "understanding between students with widely different academic abilities and vocational goals."[29] This "understanding" was to be accomplished through "well-organized homerooms and certain student activities" and through a senior-level course in American problems or American government in which students would be "heterogeneously grouped."[30]

Conant's conversations with teachers and students, visits to classrooms, and conferences with guidance counselors and school administrators convinced him that school officials could not report with certainty what portion of the academically talented students actually enrolled in physics, mathematics, and a foreign language during their senior year. Therefore he asked twenty-two principals to make an academic inventory of the courses taken by the top 25 percent of the senior class. Those inventories showed that only eight schools were "satisfactorily fulfilling the three main objectives of a comprehensive high school."[31] Schools were not offering a sufficiently wide variety of academic courses and "the majority of the bright boys and girls were not working hard enough."[32]

The Talented

Conant advised school boards to require academically talented students to complete an eighteen-course program, consisting of four years of mathematics, four years of one foreign language, three years of science, four years of English, and three years of social studies. In addition, students were to complete three hours of homework nightly. He also urged that academically talented students be given opportunities to enroll in extra courses in foreign languages and social studies. His recommendations were designed to benefit both the individual and the nation.

> From the point of view of the individual, failure to develop talent in school may be the equivalent of locking many doors. For example, without mathematics and science in high school, it would be difficult later to enter an engineering school, to take a premedical course in college, and impossible to begin a scientific career in a university.[33]

For the nation, the neglect of "the 15 percent of the youth who are academically talented" meant either a diminution of the pool from which "the professional men and women would be selected or professionals who would not be as proficient and qualified for the social roles they would assume as they could be."[34]

Conant admitted that he strongly believed that "the academically talented youth ought to elect a full program of stiff courses in high school and ought to go to college," but he deliberately avoided describing his recommended curriculum as a "college-preparatory program."[35] The great variety of admission requirements and the diversity of courses of study available to students in the nation's many colleges and universities made it impossible to label any one program a college preparatory program.

To many parents and educators Conant's recommendations must have appeared to be yet another expression of the traditional college preparatory program. As was noted earlier, Richard Hofstadter observed that there was a "close similarity" between the program recommended by Charles W. Eliot and the Committee of Ten in 1893 and the recommendations of Conant. Conant had not recommended any radical changes. He only urged a reform, and the pattern for the reform was familiar. In 1983, without mentioning Conant, the National Commission on Excellence in Education made the same recommendation that Conant had a generation earlier.

Conant's Directions for the Junior High School

When Conant inspected the junior high school—grades 7, 8, and 9—he discovered a great diversity. Educators had many reasons for, but little agreement on, the organization of junior high schools. Because of this, Conant offered no recommendations about organization, emphasizing instead that "the place of grades 7, 8, and 9 in the organization of a school system is of less importance than the program provided for adolescent youth."[36] He acknowledged that adolescence was a time of physical, social, and emotional changes. The junior high school years constituted the time of transition from a school that emphasized the child to one that emphasized subject matter. In Conant's judgment, however, "concern for the physical, social and emotional development of boys and girls properly exists at all levels, but as they progress through the grades the role of organized knowledge becomes increasingly important."[37]

Conant's advice to school boards about the curriculum for the junior high school was consistent with the curriculum he advocated for the high school. He recommended that 60 to 70 percent of instructional time be devoted to English, social studies, mathematics, and science. Art, music, and physical education were appropriate for all children. While girls were to take home economics, boys were to study industrial arts. While instruction in basic skills that was begun in the elementary grades was appropriate as long as students would benefit, it was also necessary to allow the capable "small fraction of pupils" to begin algebra in grade 8 and study of a foreign language on a conversational basis in grade 7. "The reason for the early identification of very able pupils and the start of mathematics beyond arithmetic in grade 8," he explained, "is that at least some of these pupils can complete a four-year sequence by the end of grade 11 and be ready for college-freshman mathematics in grade 12."[38] Junior high students, like students in high school, were to have homework but less of it: one hour in grade 7 and two hours in grade 9.

Conant wanted the junior high school to prepare pupils for the senior high. Teachers for the junior high had to have the characteristics and qualifications of both elementary school and senior high school teachers. They needed "an understanding of children" and "considerable knowledge in at least one subject-matter field."[39] He advocated that the organization of the day and the instruction be more like the high school than the elementary school. Except for a block of time in grade 7, he recommended departmentalization so that students would "have specialist teachers in each of the subject-matter fields."[40] His advocacy of block-time teaching was not, however, an endorsement of "core programs" that focused on "the problems of young adolescents" and involved "considerable teacher-pupil planning."[41] His defense for limited block-time teaching was "to enable one teacher to know his pupils well" and thus be "in a position to counsel pupils who have been accustomed to the personal and solicitous attention of an elementary school teacher." It was to "effect a smooth transition for the pupil from the self-contained classroom with one teacher in the elementary school to the departmentalized situation with many teachers in the secondary school."[42] Except for guidance classes that focused on vocational opportunities for students who were likely to drop out of school in grades 9 or 10, Conant was "not enthusiastic about sequential, regularly scheduled group guidance courses as presented in some schools."[43] "Minor social crises" could be handled either by homeroom teachers or block-time teachers. Junior high schools did need guidance counselors to test and help students plan appropriate programs and to tend to the personal, social, and academic problems of students.

Like his recommendations for the high school, Conant's proposals for the junior high school called for no radical changes. As Conant himself expressed the matter in the conclusion of his report, "the recommendations in this report, like those in my first report, are purposely conservative."[44] To prepare students for senior high school, more attention had to be given to "what educators call articulation." More communication between elementary school teachers and junior high teachers was essential. To coordinate subject matter from one grade to the next, curriculum coordinators were needed. Those coordinators, Conant emphasized, "must be competent in the subject fields for which they are responsible."[45]

Responses to Conant

Conant's recommendations on the high school were widely noticed and generally received favorable endorsement from the mass media. Fred M. Hechinger wrote in the *New York Times* that Conant "successfully avoids arousing the opposition to a sham war of words" and described him as a "peaceful reformer" who was supplied with "a battery of well-aimed facts" that had "great power to improve education."[46] In a review of Conant's *The Child, the Parent and the State,* in the *Chicago Sunday Tribune,* W. H. Cornog observed that Conant had demonstrated that "the structure of American secondary education needs little in the way of major revision or reform."[47]

Jerome Bruner and the Structure of Knowledge

In September 1959, just about one month before the first anniversary of *Sputnik I,* thirty-five scientists, scholars, and educators met for ten days at Woods Hole on Cape Cod "to discuss how education in science might be improved in our primary and secondary schools."[48] The meeting was called by the Education Committee of the National Academy of Sciences and was financed by NSF, USOE, the Air Force, and the Rand Corporation. The assembled scholars believed that the many significant advances made in the various disciplines during the previous half century had not yet reached the elementary and secondary schools. They had recently begun work on new curricula to remedy that situation and were now meeting to explore ways to impart to students "a sense of the substance and method of science."[49] Something had to be done to direct attention to the structure of the disciplines because while the scholars had been making great strides in their disciplines, psychology had turned away from "its earlier concern with the nature of learning." According to the conference's chair, Jerome S. Bruner:

> The psychology of learning tended to become involved with the precise details of learning in highly simplified short-term situations and thereby lost much of its contact with the long-term educational effects of learning. For their part, educational psychologists turned their attention with great effect to the study of aptitude and achievement and to social and motivational aspects of education, but did not concern themselves directly with the intellectual structure of class activities.[50]

Bruner further explained that as high school enrollment steadily grew during the twentieth century, the proper balance "between instruction in the useful skills and in disciplined understanding" became increasingly difficult to maintain. Conant's "plea for the comprehensive high school" was, Bruner indicated, an attempt to redress the imbalance.[51] The Woods Hole Conference was an effort by many scholars and scientists to redress the imbalance by considering "anew the nature of the learning process."[52] Other educational objectives were not necessarily "less important," but it was then necessary to ask: "Are we producing enough scholars, scientists, poets, lawmakers, to meet the demands of our times?"[53]

The way to redress the imbalance and to improve the curriculum was to emphasize the *structure* of the disciplines. Bruner later observed:

> The prevailing notion was that if you understood the structure of knowledge, that understanding would then permit you to go ahead on your own; you did not need to encounter everything in nature in order to know nature, but by understanding some deep principles, you could extrapolate to the particulars as needed. Knowing was a canny strategy whereby you could know a great deal about a lot of things while keeping very little in mind.[54]

Adherents of the doctrine of "structure" believed in four important claims. The first claim was that "understanding makes a subject more comprehensible." Application of this principle dictated that students be taught that knowledge of principles would allow them to understand the significance of facts. For example, if students were taught that nations needed trade to exist, they would then understand the significance of the Triangular Trade of the colonial Americans, involving molasses, sugar cane, rum, and slaves. Similarly, if students were taught that Herman Melville was writing about the theme of good and evil in *Moby Dick* and that the number of "human plights" about which authors could write was limited, then they would understand the novel "more deeply."[55] The *second* claim was that the details of any subject were soon forgotten unless they were "placed into a structured pattern." Scientists did not commit details to memory. They did not memorize times and distances about various falling bodies but only the formula ($s = gt^2$), which allowed them to make appropriate calculations when they were needed.[56] The *third* claim related to the psychological problem of "transfer of training." It maintained that understanding something as an instance of a more general principle enabled one to develop models for understanding similar phenomena. Thus the proper understanding of the "weariness of Europe at the close of the Hundred Years' War and how it created the conditions for a workable but not ideologically absolute Treaty of Westphalia" would enhance one's ability "to think about the ideological struggle of East and West."[57] The *fourth* claim was that a constant scrutiny of the "fundamental character" of what was taught in the elementary and the secondary schools would serve to lessen the gap between the lower grades of the public schools and the discoveries of the best scholars at the universities.[58]

According to Bruner, the public school curriculum was to be organized neither by the interests of students nor by practical applications of knowledge but by "the most fundamental understanding that can be achieved of the underlying principles that give structure to that subject."[59] To insure that the "underlying structure" of a discipline was given proper attention, it was necessary "that the best minds in any particular discipline . . . be put to work on the task."[60] Experts in a field were the only ones qualified to decide what was to be taught.

Bruner's Approach

In addition to having the scholars determine the content of the school curriculum, Bruner urged that the style or attitude of the scholars be communicated to students. He suggested that there might be "certain general attitudes or approaches toward science or literature that can be taught in earlier grades that would have considerable relevance for later learning." He speculated that "the attitude that things are connected and not isolated is a case in point."[61] Somehow students were to learn how scholars thought about their work. There was a body of literature "about the forms of sensibility that make for literary taste and vigor," and historians had written about how they approached their work, gathered information, and made and defended generalizations. Mathematicians even had a name for such considerations—"heuristics."[62] The task was to determine "what attitudes or heuristic devices are most pervasive and useful" so that "rudimentary versions" could be taught to students. This seemed an appropriate approach for there was the belief among the Woods Hole participants "that there is a continuity between what a scholar does on the forefront of his discipline and what a child does in approaching it for the first time."[63]

The Woods Hole participants began with "the hypothesis that any subject can be taught effectively in some intellectually honest form to any child at any stage of development."[64]

That hypothesis allowed the scholars to propose any subject matter they wished for the curriculum. All educators needed to do was present the material in a form and manner consistent with the child's stage of development. During each grade of school, or at each developmental stage, students would study the same subject. At each stage, however, the sophistication of the subjects would be increased as students progressed from the stage of concrete operations to formal operations. Bruner explained that the criterion for selection of material was quite simple:

> We might ask, as a criterion for any subject taught in primary school, whether, when fully developed, it is worth an adult's knowing, and whether having known it as a child makes a person a better adult. If the answer to both questions is negative or ambiguous, then the material is cluttering the curriculum.[65]

Those questions were consistent with the belief that the purpose of the high school was to prepare students for college, that college was to prepare students for professional careers or graduate school, and that the purpose of elementary school was to prepare students for high school.

The Woods Hole participants assumed that students wanted to learn. To construct a successful school program, little other than the stages of intellectual development needed to be known. Even within the complex social setting of the school, which often included anti-intellectual forces, there was "the subtle attraction of the subjects in school that a child finds interesting."[66] Undoubtedly such interests could be cultivated. Belief in the student's interest was later described by Bruner as a "formula of faith." "Their motivation," he admitted, "was taken for granted."[67]

Responses to Bruner

Bruner's *The Process of Education* was widely noted, highly praised, and used to defend many educational strategies and programs. By 1971, it had been translated into twenty-one languages. The first to translate it were the Russians. Educational reformers under Premier Nikita Khrushchev apparently believed it supported their claim that students had to be led to discover the virtues of "socialist realism" rather than simply have it presented to them. In Italy, it was "used in a battle by the moderate Left, against doctrinaire Marxist educators on the one side and against traditionalists on the other who wanted to maintain a classical curriculum."[68] In the United States, Frank G. Jennings likened Bruner's endeavors at synthesizing the views of the Woods Hole participants to an "alchemist's efforts." Bruner, Jennings enthusiastically claimed, had "transmuted the inquiry of specialists into a declaration of the intellectual rights, duties, and desires of all who would teach and learn, not only in science but in the whole range of knowledge and experience."[69] Writing in *Commonweal,* G. J. Sullivan described it as "an epochal book" that gave "accurate expression to the current ferment in educational thought in the country." Sullivan suggested that it would lay "to rest the ghosts of some outmoded approaches" and offered "an exciting discussion of the direction educational theory and research should not take."[70] While Paul Goodman suggested that Bruner did not fully "appreciate the moral and ideological obstacles that are put in the way of teaching children fundamental real ideas in the study of man," he nonetheless claimed *The Process of Education* would be a classic, "comparable for its philosophical centrality and humane concreteness to some of the essays of Dewey."[71]

The NEA Seminar

After the appearance of Bruner's *The Process of Education,* educators quickly turned their attention to the disciplines, to the structure of knowledge, and to the uses of knowledge. The NEA's Project on Instruction sponsored a Seminar on the Disciplines, which "was called to facilitate study and effective use of the disciplines by (a) focusing upon those fundamental ideas and methods of inquiry from selected fields of study which should be in the mainstream of the instructional program of the public schools, and (b) exploring frontier thinking and research in the nature of knowledge and ways of knowing."[72] The NEA was sponsoring a seminar designed not to lead the nation toward a new plan for education but one designed to follow the lead that had already been provided by the scholars. The title of the seminar's report—*The Scholars Look at the Schools*—and the organization of the report clearly reflect the concern with academic disciplines that prevailed at that time. Three divisions were used to organize the seventeen subject matter areas that were considered: (1) the humanities, which included art, music, English, foreign languages, philosophy, and religion; (2) the physical and biological sciences and mathematics, which included mathematics, chemistry, biology, and physics; and (3) the social sciences,which included sociology, communication, geography, economics, history, political science, and psychology.

Joseph J. Schwab, who offered the opening presentation at the seminar, objected to the charge that the school curriculum placed too much emphasis on the learners and their social milieu. Besides wanting to maintain a proper balance among the four elements of curriculum construction—the learner, the social situation, the subject matter, and the teacher—he wanted to resist any emphasis on subject matter that assumed that the bodies of knowledge to be mastered were clearly defined and fixed. Such an emphasis incorrectly assumed that there was only "one grand genus of knowing" (he believed there were three genera) and led "to abdication of responsibility by the social scientists, the psychologist, and the educator in favor of the subject-matter specialist."[73]

Although Schwab was fearful of too much emphasis on the disciplines, he presented a position that was discipline centered. For Schwab, it was necessary to distinguish properly among "three great genera of disciplines: the investigative (natural sciences), the appreciative (arts), and the decisive (social sciences)."[74] It was also essential to note that all ideas, because of their human origins, were necessarily limited and tentative. The structures of the disciplines were always undergoing modification and correction, with some conclusions being abandoned while new ones were invented or discovered. A good curriculum was made by following three guidelines. First, the aim of education was expressed so that it encompassed "the best fruits of the disciplines." Second, the "best fruits" were taught not as immutable truths but in a manner that allowed students to understand "the extent and the sense in which they are true." Third, students had to be given "an awareness of the structure of inquiry" that produced the conclusions—the "best fruits"—so they could determine for themselves how true and durable they were.[75]

Schwab reported that he had two reactions upon contemplating the "riches of the disciplines." One was the realization that the curriculum had become "flaccid, especially for these demanding times," and the "hope that concern for the conceptual structure of the disciplines and for the rigor, precision, and thoroughness that characterizes the disciplines will repair this evil." The other reaction was the fear that the then current curriculum reforms would "take an easy and indefensible course" and procede "to ignore the learner, the teacher, and the milieu as determinants of the curriculum as, in the recent past, it tended to ignore the disciplines."[76]

To take the easy course was to risk two undesirable results. First was the possibility of setting loose a competition among the disciplines for time and prominence in the curriculum. That would result in curriculum variations from place to place that would reflect the interests of the most powerful people in those places. Second was the possibility that educators would try to create a synthesis of the disciplines to meet the many social, personal, cultural, political, and economic aspirations of the diverse school clientele. Such an attempt at a synthesis could easily violate the integrity of the disciplines, because the differences among disciplines were neither arbitrary distinctions nor historical accidents but rather reflections of the different methods scholars had developed to handle the diverse questions posed by the many disciplines. Schwab believed that educators should follow the relationships the scholars made among the disciplines but not be so presumptuous as to create the connections before the experts did.

To avoid the difficulties of the easy course, the scholars at the NEA seminar recommended that curriculum be seen as having two parts: the nuclear and the cortical. That strategy, it was argued, would allow educators to reconcile the seemingly conflicting demands of the disciplines and the requirements of society. The nuclear component would include materials selected from the disciplines "to fulfill those objectives of education which are determined primarily by the needs of the developing child and the aims imposed by our culture and society."[77] The cortical component would include representative materials from the disciplines that "would display the more important conceptual frames of each discipline, its techniques of discovery and verification, and the variety of problems to which it addresses itself."[78] When more than one discipline would meet such an objective, it would be possible to choose those which "also served present and recognized individual-social needs," provided the "criterion of representativeness of the discipline remained the paramount consideration." While the ratio of nuclear to cortical components could not be determined without detailed study, there was speculation that it would vary according to grade level. In the early grades it could "be as small as 10 percent and in the final two years of high school "it might well rise as high as 80-90 percent."[79] An advantage of the nuclear-cortical approach was that it was "followed by many colleges and capable of adaptation to the elementary and secondary schools."[80] The participants in the NEA seminar agreed that each level of schooling from top to bottom, from the elementary school to the graduate school, should reflect the organization and purposes of the one above it.

The Milwaukee Conference

Shortly after the NEA seminar the University of Wisconsin—Milwaukee School of Education used funds granted by the Uhrig Foundation to sponsor an invitational conference on "The Nature of Knowledge." The conference participants discussed the need for knowing, ways of knowing, knowledge and the structure of the disciplines, conceptions of knowledge and their significance for the curriculum, knowledge about knowledge for teachers, the structure of knowledge and the interrelationship of ideas, and the relationships among knowledge, schooling, and the preparation of teachers. The proceedings of this conference, like the report of the

NEA seminar, reveal that it is one thing to proclaim that public schools should focus their attention on the disciplines and their structures and quite another to select disciplines and identify their structures so they can be effectively organized for use in public schools.

J. Martin Klotsche, the provost of the University of Wisconsin—Milwaukee, began the conference by pointing out that while society through its schools had an obligation to create opportunities for "those so inclined by talent and desire, wherever they may stand on the social and economic ladder of society, to extend the frontiers of knowledge into new and unexplored regions," it also had an obligation to "provide understanding on the part of all of the people so that knowledge discovered by the few will in the course of events become the means of improving the quality of our entire citizenry."[81] The difficulty in satisfying such obligations was compounded by the knowledge explosion and the increased access scholars had to knowledge. Ironically, the problem was not a scarcity but a surfeit of knowledge. Scholars could neither know all there was to know nor even be certain that the utility of what they knew would endure as long as they would. In 1960, two million scientific and technical articles were published in nearly 100,000 journals in more than sixty languages. New journals were appearing daily. In 1960, the Chemical Abstract Services abstracted and indexed 150,000 articles and patents, "filling 22 issues containing as many words as the *Encyclopedia Britannica.*"[82] In just three months, the weather satellite, *Tiros I,* transmitted 22,000 pictures of the earth's cloud cover.

The capability to store and to retrieve new knowledge was truly astounding, according to Klotsche. In just half an hour the Western Reserve Center for Documentation and Communications Research could scan over 50,000 abstracts and select appropriate titles for a metallurgist who wanted to know about "the impact of forming metals at high speeds." Such capabilities underscored Margaret Mead's observation "that no one will live all of his life in the world in which he was born."[83] All changes, however, were not scientific and technical. Our relationships to other places on the planet and their relative importance had changed so much that it was necessary to question the scope and the utility of traditional courses. As Klotsche noted:

> It used to be fashionable to teach courses in Western Civilization but new knowledge has made such a focus too narrow. Peiping and Cairo are as important to us today as London and Paris. The emergence of Africa further illustrates the point. There are more people on the African continent today than in the United States. Yet only three out of one hundred persons in Africa today are of European descent. At the end of World War II only four African nations were independent. Today two-thirds of the people of that continent have independent status.[84]

Perhaps the most useful and insightful discussion of the discipline issue was Arthur W. Foshay's examination of Bruner's claim that educators should use the structure of the disciplines to shape their conceptions of subjects as well as to determine how they should be taught and learned. Foshay, the executive officer of the Horace Mann–Lincoln Institute of School Experimentation at Teachers College, Columbia University, effectively showed that by following the call of the scholars to use the structure of the disciplines as the basis of the school curriculum, they were actually trying to bring about a revolution in American pedagogy. He also showed that, to be successful in the revolutionary effort, it was necessary "to make a desirable distinction between the term *discipline* and the term *school subject.*"

Disciplines and School Subjects

For Foshay the common sense notion of a discipline as "a branch of knowledge involving research" was not as useful a notion as the one that specified that a discipline was "a way of learning, a way of knowing."[85] For a discipline to exist, several conditions had to be met. First, there had to be "agreement on the field of phenomena in question."[86] For example, physicists generally agreed on what kinds of phenomena were appropriate for study just as biologists agreed on the kinds of questions appropriate for investigation. Second, the practitioners of a discipline had to "agree upon a set of rules which are to apply to the scholar's attempt to create knowledge within the field of his inquiry." The rules of one discipline differ from those of others. Foshay indicated that "it is hard to understand that one's discipline cannot deal with all fields of human knowledge."[87] Application of one discipline's rules to another's produced either nonsense or "a kind of scholarly monstrosity." The application of the physicist's rules to poetry could lead to the conclusion that poetry was but "noise." Third, all disciplines had to have "a certain arbitrary quality which "arises in part from their histories, and in part from the nature of the agreements on domain and rules that characterize them." Each discipline had its history, which defined its domain and rules. All practitioners were obliged to adhere to the discipline's tradition. Modifications of rules did occur, but such modifications were not made by the individual scholar but "only in terms of agreements by members of the disciplines—that is, by practicing scholars."[88]

The role of educators was not to decide upon modifications in the disciplines but to "translate the disciplines into school subjects." In performing that role, they had to be aware that the practice of calling disciplines and school subjects by the same name "tended to obscure the necessary distinction between the subject and its underlying discipline."[89] "If a discipline is a way of knowing its particular body of knowledge in its appropriate way," Foshay explained, "then a school subject can be thought of as a pattern of learning activities, worked out by an educationist (a teacher, if you please) which has as its purpose the introduction of students into the discipline."[90] The purpose of a school subject was to make disciplines available to students. Foshay claimed that "if a school subject is a teacher's attempt to translate a discipline into learning activities, then the success of a school subject depends on the degree to which the students learn how knowledge is made or discovered in each of the branches of knowledge being studied."[91] Because the disciplines were defined by their distinctive modes of inquiry, school subjects had to be organized to those modes of inquiry. Such translations required new conceptions both of what was taught and of the student, for traditional school practices were indeed contrary to the new emphasis on the disciplines. As Foshay explained:

> When we try to consider school subjects as modes of inquiry, it is important that we recognize we are at war with our own tradition. Nor does the pedagogical tradition tolerate students as inquirers happily. The pedagogical tradition calls for transmittal of the "given." It is a tradition of the transmittal of certainty, not of doubt. But doubt is precisely the quality of the scholar. The scholar, taken as an intellectual is one "who makes the given problematic." Our pedagogical tradition does not deal with problematic material. If we obey our tradition, we take what is problematic and make it into sets of certainties, which we then call upon the students to "master."[92]

If school subjects were to be taught as modes of inquiry, even educators would have to break with their own traditions. Most educators, Foshay observed, were not taught to see their fields as modes of inquiry but "were educated in accordance with the pedagogical tradition that implied that knowledge is a given and taught that love of learning consists primarily of passive listening."[93]

Foshay effectively illustrated his points with examples from three disciplines: chemistry, history, and poetry. He also indicated how the teaching of their corresponding school subjects would have to be changed if they were to be used as suitable introductions to the disciplines. For example, if the objective of the chemistry course was to introduce students to how chemists think and what they try to achieve, then the student would have to spend more time in the laboratory "where he would try to learn to observe, to analyze, to predict; where he would also try to learn to formulate hypotheses, to take steps (at least) toward the development of theory and law" and less time "listening to the results of experiments, which he was to master."[94] In like manner, teachers would have to become more concerned with how well students learned to use the rules of chemistry and less concerned with how much specific content they had learned or how neatly they copied "results" into their lab manuals.

History, of course, differed from chemistry. History, Foshay related, was part art and part science. For various historians the ratio of art to science varied, and thus they agreed less on how to conduct their inquiries than did chemists. However, significant agreements existed among them. They agreed that they dealt with the chronology of events and the records of the past. Some were willing "to go very far from the immediate evidence they are dealing with" and others were not. Historians did agree on what they were trying to produce—"periodization." They tried to define and characterize historical periods, to explain why, for example, a certain period should be characterized as the "Age of Franklin" rather than the "Age of the American and the French Revolutions." When historians made such a claim, they had to state their point of view and indicate which records they used to support their claim so others could inspect and criticize their conclusions. There was also a division of labor among historians. Some were social historians, some were economic or cultural historians, and still others adopted a political, military, intellectual, or diplomatic interest. If students were to be introduced properly to the discipline of history, teachers could not be allowed to assign them lessons from standard textbooks. That approach did not afford students the opportunity "to live with the ambiguity that the historian faces and with the subjectivity of history." Better than the conventional textbook was the "documentary approach to the teaching of history." It allowed the student, like the historian, "to understand that he never reads about what happened, but rather reads someone's interpretation of the records that happen to remain from the past."[95]

The teaching of poetry undoubtedly needed to be improved. According to Foshay, "our approach to the teaching of poetry in the school is so far removed from the art itself that almost any application of the poet's approach to poetry that we would attempt would be an improvement."[96] It was difficult to state the rules of poetry or to find clear agreement about the rules, but there were, Foshay indicated, "canons of criticism, according to which at least gross distinctions can be made between good and poor poetry." It was also possible to specify that "the output of poetry as an art is *humanitas*—a deepened realization of the nature of man."[97] Meter and rhyme schemes—the focus of so many school lessons on poetry—were not unimportant to the study of poetry but they were neither its essence nor the proper focus for teaching it well. Meter and rhyme were simply elements poets used to fashion their statements about humanity. If students were to be taught to understand the discipline of poetry, teachers would have to assign them problems that could "be solved by the writing of poetry." Through comparison of their efforts with the efforts of others, students could begin to learn about the care and precision poets applied to their use of language to craft their distinctive statements.

For Foshay, a curriculum based on the disciplines was not contrary to the interests of those who believed that students should be encouraged to be creative. Creativity, he pointed out, did not occur in a "vacuum." Students had to have something with which to be creative. Proper translation of the disciplines into school subjects would proffer students "both the materials and the means of intellectual life—which is to say, creativity."[98]

The Structure of Knowledge in the Arts

In 1963, Phi Delta Kappa devoted its annual Symposium on Education Research to a consideration of how several educators viewed the relationship between the structure of knowledge and the process of schooling. While many reiterations were made of points and views offered at other meetings, some new explorations were noted.

Broudy and the Arts

Particularly significant in an era when the fashion was to construe the disciplines to mean more work in mathematics and science was Harry S. Broudy's presentation, "The Structure of Knowledge in the Arts." For Broudy, there was no question that knowledge in the arts could and should be systematically taught. Art could be taught without insisting that students become artists. There were "definitions, rules, and procedures, in art that can be identified, pointed to, and stated." That meant, Broudy explained, "that there can be systematic instruction in or, at least, about art, and that it need not be confined to apprentice training in art production."[99] It was possible to specify and classify the types of knowledge used in making statements about the content of an art work, the technique used by the artists in creating the work, and the judgments made about the work. In part, the study of art entailed the study of its history and, Broudy pointed out, there was "no insuperable difficulty in classifying the cognitive activity involved in making historical statements about art and artists, about periods, styles and developments."[100]

Art, according to Broudy, did not produce meaningful statements in the same way other disciplines did, but it did express meanings. Works of art did not make precise descriptive statements about the nature of reality that could be verified in conventional ways. However, artistic expressions were "clues from which inferences that are assertions can be made."

> While Beethoven's Ninth Symphony is not a set of statements about the exaltation of creation, the sounds are images of that complex of mood, idea, feeling, and action. Hearing it, one could infer that this is what creation feels like and that it is all very impressive and important. From the clues in some works of art one can make immediate inferences about the nature of love, of death, of war, of ideals, of every divagation of human experience, actual and possible.[101]

While the aesthetic experience needed no justification beyond itself, art nonetheless had a practical justification. As Broudy explained, "just as science is society's defense against distortions of the intellect by prejudice and special interests, so high cultivation in art is society's defense against undisciplined feeling swayed by parochial interests and limited experience."[102]

Ausubel and Psychological Structures

Also of significance was David P. Ausubel's "Some Psychological Aspects of the Structure of Knowledge," for it showed that educators were turning to new conceptions of how students learned as well as to new conceptions of what they should learn. Ausubel maintained that too little attention had been paid to the formulation and testing of "theories of learning that are relevant for the kinds of meaningful ideational learning that takes place in school and similar learning environments." While he did not challenge the concern with the disciplines, he did warn that educators needed to recognize the distinction between how subject matter was logically expressed in textbooks and how it was actually organized "in the memory structures of particular individuals."[103] If educators were to enhance students' learning of the disciplines, they had to acquire knowledge of the structure of the disciplines *and* knowledge of psychological cognitive structures. Ausubel was effectively arguing that the control of the school curriculum had to be shared by those who knew subject matter and those who purported to know how people learned.

To understand how students learned and organized what they learned, it was necessary to comprehend the principle of subsumption, that is, how information and ideas fell under comprehensive organizing principles. The structure of the human nervous system, according to Ausubel, was analogous to "a data process and storing mechanism." Its structure was such that "new ideas and information can be meaningfully learned and retained only to the extent that more inclusive and appropriately relevant conceptions are already available in cognitive structure to serve a subsuming role or to provide ideational anchorage."[4] Knowledge was not a collection of discrete and isolated facts or ideas. It was the acquisition *and* the relating of new ideas to what was already known by the learner. Students made sense of new material and experiences by relating the new to what they already knew. As students made such relationships, that is, learned, they developed hierarchical structures that comprised "the most inclusive concepts" at the top of their cognitive structures and the least inclusive at its base.

Because of the available knowledge on cognition and nervous system function, Ausubel claimed that it was possible to state how teaching should be organized and administered to facilitate learning. For the sake of organizing and integrating material, educators had to use "those unifying concepts and propositions in a given discipline that have the widest explanatory power, inclusiveness, generalizability, and relatability to the subject-matter content of that discipline" and that in the actual presentation of material to students teachers had to pay special attention to order, sequence, and the internal logic of the material they were teaching.[105]

Several principles were applicable to the design of instruction. The principle of progressive differentiation dictated that details were to be presented after the presentation of an "advanced organizer." By presenting students with a synthesis that included the general and inclusive ideas of a lesson, retention would be enhanced and rote learning would not be necessary. The principle of consolidation required that teachers present material in the proper sequence and that students master each step of a lesson progressively. Mastery was also important because it allowed one to learn how to discriminate in acquiring new material. Ausubel explained that research showed that students with "greater knowledge of Christianity" were better able to learn about Buddhism than students with "less knowledge of Christianity."[106] New material could be placed into the cognitive structure according to either its similarity or dissimilarity to existing concepts.

The principle of integrative reconciliation required explicit efforts to determine similarities and differences and "to reconcile real or apparent inconsistencies."[107] Adherence to the principle of integrative reconciliation in organizing material for instruction would, Ausubel explained, require a drastic revision in how textbooks were organized. The common practice of grouping all seemingly similar and overlapping ideas into one chapter frequently obscured "significant differences between apparently similar concepts." The practice "of compartmentalizing and segregating particular ideas or topics within their respective chapters or subchapters" so that each was presented in only one of the several possible places where inclusion was relevant and warranted was, Ausubel suggested, "perhaps logically valid, but certainly psychologically untenable."[108] Violation of this principle effectively created situations in which students had to learn without benefit of subsumable referents. In such situations learning was simply by rote.

Ausubel's emphasis on cognitive structure and the steps he outlined for educators to follow so that their instruction would be consistent with the contours of that structure was, as Arno Bellack pointed out, reminiscent of the late nineteenth century Herbartian psychology.[109] Ausubel and the Herbartians focused on a rational model of learning to determine how learning in school could be facilitated. While the Herbartians spoke of the necessity of attaching new ideas to the existing apperceptive mass, Ausubel spoke of cognitive structure. Each agreed, however, that teachers had a responsibility to determine what students knew and to relate new material to what was already known. Teachers also needed to know how students learned. The nature of the process did not assign greater importance to either subject matter or method.

Ausubel may not have subscribed to the claim that teachers had to know and tend to the needs of the "whole child," but he also did not subscribe to the claim that teachers only needed to be experts in subject matter. Subject matter was a necessary but insufficient requirement for teaching. Like other educators, he demonstrated that education was more than a collection of the right disciplines. Unlike many others, he showed that the problem of public education was more complicated than finding ways to increase the intellectual rigor of public schooling.

Implementation Problems

Some school conventions seem to survive all reformers' assaults upon them. One such convention is the prominent position that the textbook has in the instructional process. In large measure, the textbook defines the activities of both teacher and student, and, as Geraldine Joncich Clifford remarked about reforms aimed at giving the disciplines increased attention, "textbooks continued to eclipse both the laboratory inquiries and teaching machines of the latterday reformers and the discussion groups and field trips of the earlier movement—as they always had."[110]

In his reconsideration of *The Process of Education,* Bruner admitted that making new curricula was not as easy as the scholars had believed it would be. "Something a bit strained would happen," he related, "when one caused to work together a most gifted and experienced teacher and an equally gifted and experienced scientist, historian, or scholar."[111] Each side had a great deal to learn from the other. Moreover, the academic reformers learned that introduction of new materials entailed a process quite different from designing and producing them. They had not anticipated the public school bureaucracies and the complicated procedures for adopting and distributing new materials in school systems. They were also unaware of "the genuinely puzzling questions of teacher recruitment, training, and supervision."[112] They learned that public schools were something more than and different from colleges and universities.

Some educators did try to give the disciplines more attention without surrendering earlier held convictions about the necessity of relating schooling work to the world of human affairs and the interests of students. Some agreed that the disciplines were important and needed more attention but saw that the issue was more complicated than simply proclaiming that the student who was learning physics was no different from a physicist. For them, learning a new field and its rules was different from practicing or building on what one had mastered during a long period of study. Some, however, were not happy about the new curricula. They had reason to celebrate when educators were given a new direction to follow. For example, in a lecture delivered in 1970 at the meeting of the Association for Supervision and Curriculum Development—an organization which, according to Clifford, "most represents latter-day 'establishment' progressivism"[113]—Fred T. Wilhelms announced that the "silly season" of "prestigious academicians" had ended. Their emphasis on "the pure disciplines" endured only "until the facts of life caught up with them." The new "battle cry," he proclaimed, was "relevance," and it was being heard "from coast to coast." Happily, "the great humane values which have been our chief concern are once more being forced upon those who sought to ignore them."[114]

Even Bruner turned to the relevance theme. By 1970, he was explaining that in the early 1960s there was a concern for "self direction of the intellect in the use of modern knowledge," and that in the second half of the decade it seemed appropriate to ask: "Did revision of curriculum suffice, or was a more fundamental restructuring of the entire educational system in order?"[115]

Conclusion

The emphasis on and enthusiasm for the disciplines faded but did not disappear. A report ordered by President Carter and prepared by the NSF and the Department of Education claimed that the rigor of mathematics and science programs in the nation's public schools was less than that in the schools in the Soviet Union, Japan, and Germany. According to the report, "the number of young people who graduate from high school and college with only the most rudimentary notions of science, mathematics and technology portends trouble in the decades ahead." Unless "the current trend toward virtual scientific and technological illiteracy" is reversed, the report warned, many will be making important decisions in the future "on the basis of ignorance and misunderstanding."[116]

That President Carter ordered the study and that his successor's administration—the Reagan administration—also issued a report on public education are significant events. They show that, since World War II, public education has entered the arena of national politics. Public education has become a federal interest that has endured long after the *Sputnik* era. Traditional concerns about federal involvement in public education seem less important than formerly. As President Kennedy told Congress in 1963, "we can no longer afford the luxury of endless debate over all the complicated and sensitive questions raised by each new proposal on Federal participation in education."[117] The question was not whether but how much federal participation there would be.

President Carter's establishment of a Department of Education with cabinet status was still another sign that education had become a national political issue. President Reagan's support for tuition tax credits for parents who send their children to private schools and his support for master teacher plans are indications that all are not willing to end "debate over all the complicated and sensitive questions raised by each new proposal on Federal participation in education." They do, however, show that education is still a national concern.

In 1961 President Kennedy indicated to Congress that both the defense and the prosperity of the nation depended on education. Education, he concluded, was a good national investment. In his 1963 message to Congress, Kennedy emphasized that failure to invest in education was bad economic policy. Education was a good, cheap investment. It was assumed that education equipped people to secure and hold jobs. The income lost during a year of unemployment was equivalent to the cost of twelve years of schooling. The economic data made available to Kennedy showed that in the post-World War II era education accounted for approximately 40 percent of the nation's economic growth.

When President Johnson called upon the Congress to pass the Elementary and Secondary Education Act in 1965, he maintained that federal control of public education was not the issue. He indicated that his purpose was simply to strengthen state and community systems of education. He even reminded the Congress that the late Sen. Robert Taft, the conservative senator from Ohio, had agreed that "in the field of education, as in the fields of health, relief, and medical care, the Federal Government has a secondary obligation to see that there is a basic floor under those essential services for all adults and children in the United States."[118] He also reminded Congress of the cost of not providing funds for education. He pointed out that the cost of maintaining a child in a detention home was four times greater than the cost of sending a child to school ($450 a year versus $1,800 a year). The cost of maintaining a criminal in prison for a year was even greater—$3,500. The message was clear: the schoolhouse was cheaper to maintain than the jailhouse.

Notes

1. Daniel Calhoun (ed.), *The Educating of Americans: A Documentary History* (Boston: Houghton Mifflin, 1969), 295.
2. Quoted in Lloyd E. Blauch, "To Promote the Cause of Education," *School Life,* 35(May 1953): 124.
3. Reprinted in Edgar W. Knight and Clifton L. Hall (eds.), *Readings in American Educational History* (New York: Appleton-Century-Crofts, 1951), 560.
4. Richard Hofstadter, *Anti-Intellectualism in American Life* (New York: Knopf, 1963), 330.
5. Reprinted in Sol Cohen (ed.), *Education in the United States: A Documentary History* (New York: Random House, 1974), 1971.
6. Ibid., 1963, 1965.
7. Ibid., 1967.

8. John Dewey, "The Influence of the High School upon Educational Methods," *The School Review* (January 1896): 2.
9. Ibid., 6.
10. John A. H. Keith and William C. Bagley, *The Nation and the Schools* (New York: Macmillan, 1920), 129.
11. William C. Bagley, "A Federal Department of Education," *NEA Addresses and Proceedings* (1920): p. 455.
12. William C. Bagley, "Education and Our Democracy," *NEA Addresses and Proceedings* (1918): 57–58.
13. Quoted in Edward A. Krug, *Salient Dates in American Education, 1635–1964* (New York: Harper & Row, 1966), 140.
14. Daniel J. Kelves, *The Physicists: The History of a Scientific Community in Modern America* (New York: Knopf, 1978), 320.
15. Ibid.
16. Ibid.
17. Ibid., 341.
18. James Bryant Conant, *The Child, the Parent and the State* (Cambridge, Mass.: Harvard University Press, 1959), 17.
19. Ibid., 17–18.
20. Jerome S. Bruner, *The Process of Education* (Cambridge, Mass.: Harvard University Press, 1961), vii–viii.
21. Quoted in Arthur G. Powell, *The Uncertain Profession: Harvard and the Search for Educational Authority* (Cambridge, Mass.: Harvard University Press, 1980), 213.
22. Ibid.
23. Ibid., 232.
24. For such an interpretation see Joel Spring, *The Sorting Machine: National Educational Policy Since 1945* (New York: David McKay, 1967).
25. James Bryant Conant, *The American High School Today: A First Report to Interested Citizens* (New York: McGraw-Hill, 1959), 14.
26. James Bryant Conant, *A Memorandum to School Boards: Recommendations for Education in the Junior High School Years* (Princeton, N.J.: Educational Testing Service, 1960), 3.
27. James Bryant Conant, *Slums and Suburbs* (New York: McGraw-Hill, 1961), 6.
28. Conant, *The American High School,* 15.
29. Ibid., 19–20.
30. Ibid., 75.
31. Ibid., 22.
32. Ibid., 23.
33. Ibid., 59.
34. Ibid., 59–60.
35. Ibid., 60.
36. Conant, *Education in the Junior High School Years,* 12.
37. Ibid.
38. Ibid., 17.
39. Ibid., 13.
40. Ibid., 22.
41. Ibid., 23.
42. Ibid.

43. Ibid., 27.
44. Ibid., 45.
45. Ibid., 33.
46. Fred M. Hechinger, *The New York Times* (February 15, 1959), 6.
47. W. H. Cornog, *Chicago Sunday Tribune* (October 25, 1959), 6.
48. Bruner, *Process of Education,* vii.
49. Ibid.
50. Ibid., 4.
51. Ibid., 5.
52. Ibid., 2.
53. Ibid., 9.
54. Jerome S. Bruner, "*The Process of Education* Reconsidered," in Glen Hass (ed.), *Curriculum Planning: A New Approach* (Boston: Allyn & Bacon, 1977), 195.
55. Bruner, *Process of Education,* 23–24.
56. Ibid., 24.
57. Ibid., 25.
58. Ibid., 26.
59. Ibid., 31.
60. Ibid., 19.
61. Ibid., 27.
62. Ibid.
63. Ibid., 28.
64. Ibid., 33.
65. Ibid., 52.
66. Ibid., 73.
67. Bruner, "*The Process of Education* Reconsidered," 195.
68. Ibid., 198.
69. Frank G. Jennings, "A Friend of the Learning Child," *Saturday Review,* 43 (October 15, 1960): 94.
70. G. J. Sullivan, "The Natural Approach to Learning," *Commonweal,* 74 (June 23, 1961): 334.
71. Paul Goodman, *New York Herald Tribune Lively Arts* (December 25, 1960), p. 28.
72. *The Scholars Look at the Schools: A Report of the Disciplines Seminar.* (Washington, D.C.: National Education Association, 1962), 2.
73. Ibid., 3.
74. Ibid.
75. Ibid., 4.
76. Ibid., 50.
77. Ibid., 51.
78. Ibid.
79. Ibid., 52.
80. Ibid., 51.
81. J. Martin Kotsche, "The Need for Knowing," in William A. Jenkins (ed.), *The Nature of Knowledge: Implications for the Education of Teachers* (Milwaukee: University of Wisconsin—Milwaukee, 1961), 8.
82. Ibid., 9.
83. Ibid., 11.
84. Ibid., 10–11.

85. Arthur W. Foshay, "Knowledge and the Structure of the Disciplines," in Jenkins, *The Nature of Knowledge,* 28.
86. Ibid., 29.
87. Ibid., 30.
88. Ibid., 31.
89. Ibid., 29.
90. Ibid., 28–29.
91. Ibid., 32.
92. Ibid., 32–33.
93. Ibid., 35.
94. Ibid., 36.
95. Ibid., 38.
96. Ibid., 39–40.
97. Ibid., 38–39.
98. Ibid., 40.
99. Harry S. Broudy, "The Structure of Knowledge in the Arts," in Stanley Elam (ed.), *Education and the Structure of Knowledge: Fifth Annual Phi Delta Kappa Symposium on Educational Research* (Chicago: Rand McNally, 1964), 99.
100. Ibid., 105.
101. Ibid., 105–106.
102. Ibid., 104.
103. David P. Ausubel, "Some Psychological Aspects of the Structure of Knowledge," in Elam (ed.), *Education and the Structure of Knowledge,* 222.
104. Ibid., 229.
105. Ibid., 239.
106. Ibid., 242.
107. Ibid., 245.
108. Ibid., 244.
109. Arno A. Bellack, "Knowledge Structure and the Curriculum," in Elam (ed.), *Education and the Structure of Knowledge,* 277.
110. Geraldine Joncich Clifford, *The Shape of American Education* (Englewood Cliffs, N.J.: Prentice-Hall, 1975), 151.
111. Bruner, "*The Process of Education* Reconsidered," 197.
112. Ibid.
113. Clifford, *Shape of American Education,* 150.
114. Fred T. Wilhelms, "Realignments for Teacher Education: The Eleventh Charles W. Hunt Lecture," quoted in Clifford, *Shape of American Education,* 150–151.
115. Jerome S. Bruner, *The Relevance of Education* (New York: W. W. Norton, 1971), x.
116. National Science Foundation and the Department of Education, *Science and Engineering Education for the 1980s and Beyond* (Washington, D.C.: U.S. Government Printing Office, 1980), 3.
118. Reprinted in Cohen (ed.), *Education in the United States,* 3373.

5
Equality, Opportunity, and Education

Equality

Even before the federal government began to involve itself in public education with legislative appropriations immediately after *Sputnik,* the Supreme Court assured federal involvement on May 17, 1954, with its decision in the *Brown v. Topeka* case that the doctrine of "separate but equal" was unconstitutional. The federal government became active in attempts to integrate and desegrate public schools when President Eisenhower sent federal troops to Little Rock, Arkansas, in 1955 to insure desegregation of Central High.

The issue in *Brown* was equality, a critical notion ever since the founding of the United States. Everyone seems to agree that all are equal, but everyone does not agree on the extent of equality, on the standard by which its existence is to be determined, on how it should be achieved, or on how or whether the government should insure it. Some distinctions useful in clarifying its meaning are in the works of Thomas Jefferson, who started our current discussions about equality when he wrote in the Declaration of Independence that "all men are created equal."

Jefferson expressed a principle that is still central in political and educational discussions. However, his idea of equality was not a psychological notion, but a philosophical and ethical principle. He insisted that all had their rights because they were so endowed by their Creator. To claim that those rights—life, liberty, and the pursuit of happiness—are inalienable is to claim that no person, group of people, or government can deprive any other person of his or her rights. Nor is a person's freedom ever another's to give. It is, however, the responsibility of all to protect liberty, for without liberty there can be no equality.

If Jefferson had been articulating a psychological concept of equality, he would have been arguing that all have the same psychological characteristics in equal amounts. Thus, aptitude tests, interest inventories, and intelligence tests would be pointless, for everyone would score the same. There is no reason to believe, however, that Jefferson ever subscribed to psychological equality. He did believe that all were capable of learning, that all had an obligation to learn in order to protect their inalienable rights, and that experience and accomplishment were more important and valuable than inherited status and privilege. Because the mind was, to use John Locke's metaphor, a *tabula rasa,* education was fundamental and essential. Without it people had no way to protect their liberty. Whatever people knew was a consequence of their education. Through education people acquired the knowledge and skills needed to experiment, innovate, and thereby promote progress.

While governor of Virginia, Jefferson sent the state legislature the now famous "Bill for the More General Diffusion of Knowledge" (1779), in which he stated how education and freedom were related. All government, he maintained, could turn to tyranny. The best way to prevent the rise of tyranny and the attendant loss of freedom was "to illuminate, as far as practical the minds of the people at large." Through the study of history, he argued, the people would "be enabled to know ambition under all its shapes," and thus be equipped to defend themselves against forces that were inimical to liberty.[1]

By separating the Creator from nature, Jefferson was able to maintain that all were equal but that not all were equally able. The Creator had endowed all with inalienable rights, and all by virtue of that endowment were equal. However, nature had not endowed all with what Jefferson identified as "genius and virtue," certainly not in equal portions. Society had to establish procedures to identify and to select those who might benefit from a liberal education, because nature did not necessarily endow the children of the wealthy with more genius and virtue than the children of the poor. That poverty prevented many parents from properly educating their children was wasteful and prevented society from benefiting from their talents. Poor but capable children could "become useful instruments for the public." So that the best would govern rather than the worst, he recommended that capable students "should be sought for and educated at the common expense of all." Not to do so was to place the freedom of the people in the hands of the "weak and wicked." Equal opportunity had to be extended to all for the protection of freedom and the general welfare, or, as Jefferson wrote, it was necessary to insure that "the best geniuses will be raked from the rubbish annually, and be instructed, at the public expense."[2]

Even in the twentieth century, John Dewey, like Jefferson, maintained that it was necessary to distinguish between kinds of equality. While Dewey repeatedly insisted that democracy had to be a way of life and not just a form of government, he still distinguished between political and psychological equality.

> Belief in equality is an element of the democratic credo. It is not, however, belief in equality of natural endowments. Those who proclaimed the idea of equality did not suppose they were enunciating a psychological doctrine, but a legal and political one. All individuals are entitled to equality of treatment by law and in its administration. Each one is affected equally in quality if not in quantity by the institutions under which he lives and has an equal right to express his judgment, although the weight of his judgment may not be equal in amount when it enters into the pooled result of others.[3]

While Jefferson and Dewey each maintained that all were not psychologically equal and that society had to recognize the differences among people, each proposed to do something different about those differences. Jefferson wanted to exploit the gifted for the good of society. To do so, he recommended a system of public education open to all free children for three years without tuition. At the end of the three years, those boys, not girls, who demonstrated superior ability and whose parents were unable to pay for their schooling were to continue in school at the public's expense. Others could continue if they were willing and able to pay the tuition. Had Virginians accepted his plan, each year twenty scholarship students would have been graduated from grammar school. Ten of those graduates would have been awarded scholarships to allow them to continue their education at the College of William and Mary.

While Dewey recognized that "what we call intelligence may be distributed in unequal amounts," he also emphasized that such inequality was "all the more reason for establishment by law of equality of opportunity, since otherwise the former becomes a means of oppression of the less gifted." Jefferson wanted to insure a good society by selecting the best for public servants. Dewey wanted to insure a good society by insuring that the "less gifted" would not be oppressed. Even though all were not equally intelligent, Dewey maintained that each had "something to contribute whose value can be assessed only as it enters into the final pooled intelligence constituted by the contributions of all."[4] Jefferson wanted to school all, at least for three years, so they could choose good leaders. Dewey wanted to insure that "each individual shall have the opportunity to contribute whatever he is capable of contributing."[5] Jefferson used the differences to determine who would be given how much education at the public's expense. Dewey used the same differences to argue for the necessity of insuring equal opportunity for all. Neither approach has met universal acceptance in American society.

Resisting the Jeffersonian Legacy

James Bryant Conant reported that he frequently met with "something less than enthusiasm" whenever he proposed what he thought were Jeffersonian views on education. He recorded that one of the recommendations that a committee of the Seventy-eighth Congress was considering when it was reviewing ways to provide educational benefits for World War II veterans was Jeffersonian in nature. It restricted financial aid to "a limited number of exceptionally able ex-service personnel" who could demonstrate their likelihood for success in their studies as well as show that what they planned to study gave "promise of future usefulness."[6] Conant's view was that, with the exception that any student whether rich or poor might benefit from the proposal, the scheme "might be provided as a 1943 version of Jefferson's selective ideas for secondary and university education." That proposal failed. One official of the War Department (since renamed the Department of Defense) is reported to have claimed that the United States had never subscribed to any such program, that the nation had gotten on so far, and there was no need to start such a program. Those who wanted advanced or professional degrees, the official argued, should pay for it themselves. Another official, described by Conant as "an influential member of the Congressional committee," claimed that the bill smacked of "socialism." His remarks to Conant left no doubt about his opposition to the proposal: "What you are arguing for is to spend more public money on a selected student who wants to study law or medicine than on some other fellow. That is socialism, and I'm against it!"[7] The GI Bill that Congress did enact was free from any selective features. The length of time veterans could attend college as "public foundationers" was determined solely by their length of service in one of the armed forces.

Immediately after World War II the Congress was not yet prepared to use public funds to create what Jefferson called "useful instruments for the public." However, Congress did move in a Jeffersonian direction when it enacted the National Defense Education Act (NDEA) and significantly increased appropriations for the National Science Foundation (NSF). Then some selective features were allowed, for the nation needed scientists to protect its freedom from external threats. Claims that the nation has been paying too much attention to the educational needs of the disadvantaged and to the handicapped at the expense of the gifted can be construed as echoes of a Jeffersonian tradition. Rarely is there objection to providing opportunities, even equality of opportunity, to all. What that means, however, depends upon one's vision of the "good society" and one's definition of equality. Usually, there is debate about whether it means that all should have an equal chance or equal access, whether all should start from an equal condition, or whether all should be assured that they will succeed. No matter how equality is defined, however, there is the longstanding practice of denying people opportunities simply because they are different from the majority, frequently because they belong to a racial minority. That practice was declared unconstitutional in 1954, but the consequences of that practice and the attempts to deal justly with the consequences remain as relevant problems for public education in the United States.

Separate but Equal

The origin of the "separate but equal" doctrine that was used to defend and to enforce deliberate segregation of blacks until 1954 is found in the Supreme Court's decision in *Plessy v. Ferguson* (1896). Homer Plessy, who was determined to be black because he was "one-eighth black," had been arrested and convicted for violating a Louisiana law that required blacks to ride only on the "colored coaches" on trains. After Judge Ferguson denied that the law withheld his constitutional rights and effectively made him "inferior," Plessy appealed to the Supreme Court. The Supreme Court then ruled that if the facilities open to Plessy were equal to those from which he was barred, his rights had not been violated and that such a law did not affirm the inferiority of blacks. The decision was consistent with the social and political climate of the era and was handed down at a time when, as Jennings Wagoner, Jr., has noted, "most Northerners, including many who in earlier decades had been zealously involved in Southern affairs, had turned their attention away from the plight of the Southern black."[8] A year earlier, Booker T. Washington had delivered his famous "Atlanta Compromise" speech, in which he acknowledged that it would be "the extremest folly" for blacks to press for "social equality" and promised whites: "In all things that are purely social we can be a separate as the fingers, yet one as the hand in all things essential to mutual progress."[9] A few months later, Washington was invited to Harvard where he was awarded an honorary master of arts degree. As Wagoner has noted, there was "more than coincidence" in the temporal proximity of those two events.[10] After *Plessy v. Ferguson,* separate but equal was used to enforce segregation in all areas of society in all parts of the nation.

Facilities for blacks, however, were typically not equal to those established for whites. Moreover, blacks found equal facilities difficult to secure. The first petition to act on the failure of a community to prove "equal" facilities—*Cummings v. Board of Education* (1899)—was unsuccessful. When blacks from Richmond County, Georgia, informed the Court that the county did not maintain a high school for blacks as it did for whites and asked the Court to close the white school until one was provided for blacks, the Court dismissed the petition and thereby avoided making a judgment about the problem of determining how to ascertain whether facilities were in fact equal. It also avoided ruling on the legality of the separate but equal doctrine. It simply noted that closing the white school would not redress any wrong.

In practice, the operative word in "separate but equal" was "separate." When Gunnar Myrdal studied the relationship between the races in the United States in the late 1930s, he reported "that Negro schools have lately been improving faster than white schools in the South—that is, in the sense that the *percentage* of increase in expenditures may have been greater for Negro than for white schools."[11] However, the improvements were not nearly great enough to overcome the vast differences that had been established in the previous half century. The differences in funds provided for schools for the two races was "as spectacular as it is well known." For the 1935–36 school year, the average expenditure in ten Southern states was $17.04 for black students and $49.30 for white students. Mississippi and Georgia spent about $9 for every black student and about five times as much for whites. No such discrimination of expenditure existed in Delaware, Missouri, and Oklahoma, and in Washington, D.C., expenditures for black students were "only slightly smaller" than they were for whites.

The differences in expenditures affected all areas of public schooling for blacks. Black teachers' salaries were lower than those of white teachers and their classes were larger. Less was spent on transportation of black students than for whites. "Savings" were realized in black schools in all areas by maintaining a school year that was "13 percent shorter than in white schools."[12] The "financial statistics" available to Myrdal did not allow him to make the same kinds of comparisons between white and black schools in the North as those he made for the schools in the South, but he did find differences. He also found that officials in the North were unwilling to improve black schools because they feared that improvements would persuade even more blacks to move from the South to the North.

The practice of offering less than equal educational facilities and services to blacks was widespread. As late as 1954, segregated education was required in seventeen states: Alabama, Arkansas, Delaware, Florida, Georgia, Kentucky, Louisiana, Maryland, Mississippi, Missouri, North Carolina, Oklahoma, South Carolina, Tennessee, Texas, Virginia, and West Virginia. Arizona, Kansas, New Mexico, and Wyoming had laws that permitted segregation.

Challenging the Compromise

All blacks did not accept Booker T. Washington's "Atlanta Compromise." Throughout its history, the National Association for the Advancement of Colored People (NAACP), founded in 1909, sought legal remedies to the separate but equal doctrine. Beginning in the 1930s, it filed several suits to show that blacks did not have equal access to professional schools. After World War II, the NAACP filed several suits to publicize that separate but equal facilities were in fact not provided for blacks. However, by 1954, the NAACP was not content to belabor the obvious. In the *Brown* case, the attorney for the Kansas plaintiffs, Robert Carter, acknowledged that the facilities provided for blacks in Topeka were in fact equal to those used by whites. Rather than continue to attack the failure to provide equal facilities, it was decided to attack the legality of segregation by attacking the doctrine of separate but equal. Carter, Thurgood Marshall, and James Nabritt presented to the Supreme Court the argument that the quality of schooling involved more than tangible facilities. Its quality and effectiveness also depended on intangible considerations, such as the school's academic climate, the teaching standards, and prestige. To make their case they turned to the arguments of social and behavioral scientists and educators. The defendants objected to the introduction of "sociological" evidence, but the Court admitted the "extra-legal factors." Chief Justice Earl Warren cited the "academic evidence" in his decision. From that evidence, he concluded that to separate children on the basis of race creates "a feeling of inferiority" that probably could never be completely undone and thus has the effect of retarding the mental and educational progress of black children. That, the Court decided, effectively deprived them of rights specified in the Fourteenth Amendment to the Constitution.

In rendering its decision, the Court noted that it was not possible to "turn the clock back to 1868 when the Fourteenth Amendment was adopted, or even to 1896 when *Plessy v. Ferguson* was written." Public education had to be considered "in light of its full development and its present place in American life throughout the Nation." Public education had become a necessity for the welfare not only of individuals but also of the nation. Warren wrote:

> Compulsory school attendance laws and the great expenditures for education both demonstrate our recognition of the importance of education to our democratic society. It is required in the performance of our most basic public responsibilities, even service in the armed forces. It is the very foundation of good citizenship. Today it is the principal instrument in awakening the child to cultural values, in preparing him for later professional training, and in helping him to adjust normally to his environment.[13]

Justice Warren maintained that "it is doubtful that any child may reasonably be expected to succeed in life if he is denied the opportunity of an education." There was no choice but to assure all that they would be given equal opportunity for education.

Two weeks after it issued its decision in the *Brown* case, the Supreme Court issued an order giving those states with laws that either required or allowed segregation "reasonable time" to dismantle their dual systems of education to effect desegregation. The variable rates at which school systems complied with the order to desegregate schools, the refusal of some systems to comply with the order, the delaying tactics employed by some systems, the genuine difficulty some systems had in devising plans that would satisfy all community interests, and the appeals to the Court from parties who objected to the failure of some school systems to comply with the "law of the land" all served to undermine local control of education. Public education remained the responsibility of the states, but it was to some extent nationalized as the rights of the states to decide how to operate those systems—how to draw attendance zones, how to assign pupils, and eventually whether busing was required to effect desegregation—was significantly influenced by the Supreme Court. In the 1960s and 1970s when the federal government undertook its "war on poverty" and provided funds for compensatory educational programs for the disadvantaged, many local systems believed their power was further eroded because the federal government specified for whom such funds were to be expended, as well as how they were to be expended, and issued guidelines to insure compliance with the Civil Rights Acts.

Of all the issues attendant to the Supreme Court's ruling that segregation of students in the public schools on the basis of race is unconstitutional, probably none has received more publicity than mandatory busing of students to achieve racial balance in the schools. Significantly, the Court did not rule on the constitutionality of busing as a technique for segregation until it approved the busing plan in *Swann v. Charlotte-Mecklenburg Board of Education* in 1971. Of more importance for public education than the busing issue are the consequences of a provision of the 1964 Civil Rights Act that ordered what is now known as the Coleman Report.

The Coleman Report

The *Brown* decision was an important but not a decisive victory for the civil rights movement, for the Supreme Court then ruled only on the constitutionality of segregation in public schools. Racial segregation in those activities covered by the interstate commerce clause of the Constitution was not explicitly prohibited until Congress enacted the 1964 Civil Rights Act. For reasons that even James Coleman does not know, Section 402 of the Act directed the United States commissioner of education to "conduct a survey and make a report to the President and the Congress, within two years . . . concerning the lack of availability of equal education opportunities for individuals by reason of race, color, religion, or national origin in public educational institutions at all levels in the United States, its territories and possessions, and the District of Columbia."[14] In July 1966, Harold Howe II, the commissioner of education, presented the ordered report, *Equality of Educational Opportunity* (EEOR), that had been prepared under the direction of James Coleman.

Coleman and his associates examined the educational opportunities available to six racial and ethnic groups: "Negroes, American Indians, Oriental Americans, Puerto Ricans living in the continental United States, Mexican Americans, and whites other than Mexican Americans and Puerto Ricans often called 'majority' or simply 'white'."[15] They collected data to answer questions in four major areas:

1. They tried to ascertain how much segregation existed among the various racial and ethnic groups in the public schools.
2. They tried to determine whether all public schools offered equal educational opportunity by collecting information on laboratory facilities; textbooks; libraries; curricula; teacher characteristics, such as training and education, experience, salaries, attitudes, and verbal ability; and several student characteristics, such as socioeconomic status, parents' education, academic goals, and other attitudinal measures.
3. They measured student learning by examining their performances on standardized tests.
4. They tried to determine whether student achievement was related to the characteristics of the schools they attended.

The Coleman Report (EEOR) established that ten years after the Supreme Court ordered desegregation of the nation's public schools a great deal of segregation still persisted. If the measure of equality was integration, then inequality persisted. Most of the nation's children were still attending schools that had not been desegregated. Of all the minority groups studied, black children were the most segregated. Nearly two thirds of black first graders attended schools that were between 90 and 100 percent black and nearly 50 percent of black twelfth graders attended schools in which half or more of the students were black. Of all groups, white children were the most segregated—80 percent of the white students in both the first and the twelfth grades attended schools that were between 90 and 100 percent white.

That the Coleman Report documented the extent to which so many white students had successfully avoided desegregated schools may not have been surprising. What was surprising was the failure of the investigators to find significant differences between black and white schools. That the survey was ordered is an indication of the belief that the quality of black schools differed markedly from that of white schools. Even Coleman believed the study would show "striking" differences. Before the Report was completed, he predicted that

> the study will show the difference in the quality of schools that the average Negro child and the average white child are exposed to. You know yourself that the difference is going to be striking. And even though everybody knows there is a lot of difference between suburban and inner city schools, once the statistics are there in black and white, they will have a lot more impact.[16]

It was also expected, especially in the North, that Coleman's Report would "establish that Southern states systematically discriminated against the Negroes in the provision of school facilities," but "the tabulated data do not support the presumption of gross discrimination in the provision of school facilities in the South."[17] The pattern of gross discrimination that was so evident in the South before World War II had been effectively remedied.

Differences in minority schools were documented: "There are fewer physics laboratories, there are fewer books per student in libraries, texts are less often in sufficient supply, schools are less often accredited, students who fail a subject are less likely to repeat a grade, they are less often schools with intensive testing, academically related extracurricula activities are less, the curriculum less often is built around an academic program."[18] Such differences, however, were not as "striking" or as "significant" as had been expected. It was concluded that "these differences in facilities and programs must not be overemphasized," for in many instances they were "not large." Moreover, it was also determined that "regional differences between schools are usually considerably greater than minority-majority differences."[19]

What was significant was the difference in achievement between minority and majority groups. The difference between blacks and whites was found to be "progressively greater for the minority pupils at progressively higher grade levels."[20] At grade 6, the "grade level gap" in achievement was 1.6 years. By the time students entered high school, grade 9, it was 2.4 years. At the end of school, grade 12, it was up to 3.3 years. Minorities were at a disadvantage when they entered school and when they left school.

The achievement differences could not be explained by the inequalities between the schools the students attended. As Coleman noted, "it appears that variations in the facilities and curriculum of the schools account for relatively little variation in pupil achievement insofar as this is measured by standard tests."[21] It seemed clear that "whatever may be the combination of nonschool factors—poverty, community attitudes, low educational level of parents—which put minority students at a disadvantage in verbal and nonverbal skills when they enter the first grade, the fact is the schools have not overcome it."[22] Coleman's data seemed to demonstrate that differences between schools were not great enough to explain the differences in achievement. One implication was that the schools were not totally responsible for differences in achievement of the groups studied, but Coleman was not willing to relieve schools of the responsibility for effecting academic achievement.

Implications of the Coleman Report

Coleman wrote in *The Public Interest* that while it may have seemed "flat," *EEOR* was "not as uncontroversial as it appears" and suggested that "some of its findings, though cautiously presented, have sharp implications."[23] Coleman's own discussions of *EEOR* reveal not only that the implications were "sharp" but also that he was proposing a revolutionary change in the definition of equality of educational opportunity. Its "principal focus of attention was not on what resources go into education, but on what product comes out." To have equality of educational opportunity meant not just that schools were equal "in some formal sense" but that all children would leave school with the skills they needed to compete successfully either in the job market or in college, "that is, verbal and reading skills, and analytical and mathematical skills." To achieve equality of opportunity, the consistent and predictable relationship between social class and educational achievement had to be overcome. As Coleman explained, "Equality of educational opportunity implies, not merely 'equal' schools, but equally effective schools, whose influences will overcome the differences in starting point of children from different social groups."[24]

In a subsequent discussion of *EEOR,* Coleman admitted that "not just to offer, in a passive way, equal access to educational resources, but to provide an educational environment that will free a child's potentialities for learning from the inequalities imposed upon him by the accident of birth into one or another home and social environment" was "a task far more ambitious than has ever been attempted by any society."[25]

The grade level gap, which grew progressively worse as students moved from one grade to the next, was, according to Coleman, *"obviously in part a result of the school."*[26] However, the source of the problem was not in the school. "Altogether," he explained, *"the sources of inequality of educational opportunity appear to lie first in the home itself and the cultural influences immediately surrounding the home; then they lie in the school's ineffectiveness to free achievement from the impact of the home, and in the schools' cultural homogeneity which perpetuates the social influences of the home and its environs."*[27] To allocate additional resources to schools to maintain the status quo in organization and operation would not improve matters, for *"per pupil expenditures, books in the library, and a host of other facilities and curricular measures show virtually no relation to achievement if the 'social' environment of the school—the educational backgrounds of other students and teachers—is held constant."*[28] The solution was not in doing more of the same but in adopting what Coleman described as "a modest, yet radical proposal."

Coleman's "modest, yet radical proposal" did challenge conventional school practice. The first of its three major points was basically a restatement of a claim that educators and social theorists had been making since the turn of the century: the family did not have access to the resources necessary for preparing their children for the requirements of a complex technological society, and the school was the institution prepared to teach children the values, knowledge, and skills necessary for competing successfully in a complex and impersonal social order. He pointed out that traditionally the school was "a supplement to the family in bringing a child into his place in adult society" and argued that "the conditions imposed by technological change and by our post-industrial society, require a far more primary role for the school, if society's children are to be equipped for adulthood."[29] If children were to be properly equipped for adulthood in school, it was necessary to lessen the influence of the family and increase the influence of the school "by starting school at an earlier age, and by having a school which begins very early in the day and ends very late."[30] That recommendation was an endorsement of Title I of the Elementary and Secondary Education Act which Congress had recently enacted (1965)—the Act that authorized Project Head Start.

Coleman's second point effectively raised questions about attachment to the "neighborhood school" concept. Adherence to this concept insured that "the social and racial homogeneity of the school environment," which was strongly related to the differential achievement that he wanted to eliminate, would persist. For some, the way to overcome that "homogeneity" was through busing. However, Coleman opposed busing, for he believed that an "incidental effect" of busing "would be to increase the segregation within schools, through an increase in tracking."[31]

Coleman's third point was a call for "new kinds of educational institutions, with a vast increase in expenditures for education—not merely for the disadvantaged, but for all children." While he did not offer any specific suggestions for new kinds of education until he described "open schools" in 1967, he did suggest that new forms of schooling worthy of consideration "might be in the form of educational parks, or in the form of private schools paid by tuition grants (with Federal regulations to insure racial hetrogeneity), public (or publicly subsidized) boarding schools (like the North Carolina Advancement School), or still other innovations."[32] Better teaching methods had to be found so tracking could be avoided. Tracking was necessary because current methods were suited only to a narrow range of students. Better methods would allow teachers to teach a greater range of students effectively and thereby "make possible the informal learning that other students of higher educational levels can provide."[33]

Open Schools

Coleman's recommendation for open schools was a plan designed to capitalize on the effects that students had on each other in school. In *EEOR,* it was reported that

> it appears that a pupil's achievement is strongly related to the educational backgrounds and aspirations of the other students in the school. . . . Analysis indicates . . . that children from a given family background, when put in schools of different social composition, will achieve at quite different levels. This effect is again less for white pupils than for any minority group other than Orientals. Thus, if a white pupil from a home that is strongly and effectively supportive of education is put in a school where most pupils do not come from such homes, his achievement will be little different than if he were in a school composed of others like himself. But if a minority pupil from a home without much educational strength is put with schoolmates with strong educational backgrounds, his achievement is likely to increase.[34]

In his discussion of the implications of his report, Coleman simply and clearly stated that one finding of the study was that

> students do better when they are in schools where their fellow students come from backgrounds strong in educational motivation and resources. . . . This effect appears to be particularly great for students who themselves come from educationally deprived backgrounds. For example, it is about twice as great for Negroes as for whites.[35]

For Coleman, equality of educational opportunity could only be achieved through "a more intense reconstruction of the child's social environment than that provided by school integration." It could be effected in a variety of ways—"through other children, through tutorial programs, through artificial environments created by computer consoles,"—but it had to be done.[36] One way to reconstruct the social environment for the child was to open the schools. That entailed thinking of the school "not as a building into which a child vanishes in the morning and from which he emerges in the afternoon, but as a 'home base' that carries out some teaching functions but which serves principally to coordinate his activities and to perform guidance and testing functions."[37]

At the elementary school level, Coleman suggested that the teaching of reading and arithmetic—two important subjects that schools frequently failed to teach to lower class children and thereby handicapped them for life—"be opened up to entrepreneurs outside the school."[38] Entrepreneurs would have to agree to standards that would disallow discrimination on the basis of race, class, or educational level. They would be "paid on the basis of increased performance by the child on standardized tests."[39]

The high school could also be opened up to "outside entrepreneurs." There the teaching of "core subjects" would be done in many instances by "private contractors." Thus, at both the elementary and secondary levels, parents could choose to have their children attend "programs outside the school" or they could decide to leave their children in school for all subjects. The introduction of competition between the public school and the private contractors, Coleman suggested, would encourage schools to improve their programs. Moreover, schools would then be able to adopt programs and innovations that worked in the private sector.

In addition to opening schools to equalize achievement, Coleman urged that schools be opened up to address "the problem of racial and class integration." While it was "almost impossible" to integrate schools, especially those in large urban areas, it was, he maintained, possible to use schools to effect social integration. All students would have their own "home-base schools" but would have to attend other schools for some of their classes. "Thus," Coleman reasoned, "rather than having classes scheduled in the school throughout the year, some classes would be scheduled with children from other schools, sometimes in their own school, sometimes in the other—but deliberately designed to establish continuing relationships between children across racial and social class lines." Extracurricular activities could be organized and scheduled to coincide with class schedules so students "from different home base schools would not be competing against each other, but would be members of the *same* team or club." Organizations outside the school would be allowed to serve as contractors for extracurricular activities. "Community organizations," he suggested, "could design specific cultural enrichment programs or community action programs involving students from several schools of different racial or class composition, with students engaging in such programs by their own or parent's choice."[40] Students with different backgrounds would learn "to work together and to aid the community." He assumed that outside agencies would be better at conducting community improvement programs than would the public schools.

Coleman also claimed that his open school plan would settle other educational disputes. He noted that "the issue of parental control versus control by the educational bureaucracy" had always been an issue and had recently become an "intense" issue in New York City. As long as parents and students had no choices about schooling, public schooling remained a monopoly and the only way "consumers" had to express their interest in the activities of the monopoly was through "organized power." The introduction of choice through contracts with outside entrepreneurs would eliminate the need for "organized power" and presumably the strategy of confrontational politics that community groups had to employ to get the attention of their public school officials. Open schools would extend to public school users some choice comparable to that enjoyed by "those who could afford to buy education outside the public schools."[41]

Coleman was not, of course, the only one to urge that the public school monopoly be broken. As was discussed earlier, Kenneth Clark also urged that the "monopoly" be broken and replaced with a variety of alternative public school systems. Writing in 1967, as were Clark and Coleman, Fred M. Newman and Donald W. Oliver also expressed concern about the public school monopoly that "fundamentally altered the nature of childhood and adolescence in America" and "destroyed to a large extent the opportunities for random, exploratory work and play outside of a formal educational setting."[42]

Busing

As has been frequently recorded, *EEOR* devoted only 3 of its 737 pages to the possible benefits minority students would derive from attending racially mixed schools. Nonetheless the report was used to support claims that black children would benefit by being bused into predominantly white schools. Coleman, however, did not use the findings of *EEOR* to argue for "induced integration," or busing. In his first discussion of the report's implications, he indicated that equality of achievement would not be easily accomplished through busing. He then wrote that "it will not suffice merely to bus children or otherwise achieve pro forma integration."[43]

In his discussion of "open schools," Coleman argued that *"the aim of racial integration of our schools should be recognized as distinct from the aim of providing equal opportunity for educational performance."*[44] All were not, however, content to maintain the distinction Coleman wanted. As Godfrey Hodgson has reported, "Harvard's Professor Thomas Pettigrew persuaded the Civil Rights Commission to reanalyze the Coleman data to see what light they cast on the effects of desegregation, and, with David Cohen, was the main author of the resulting survey, which came out in 1967 as *Racial Isolation in the Public Schools* and gave the impression that the Coleman data supported desegregation."[45] Coleman did not deny that racial integration had positive effects on minority students, but he was unwilling to believe that mere integration would solve the problem and was therefore unwilling to endorse the recommendation of the Civil Rights Commission that Congress declare it unlawful for a school to have more than 50 percent blacks. He maintained that "the task of increasing achievement of lower-class children cannot be fully implemented by school integration, even if integration were wholly achieved—and the magnitude of racial and class concentrations in large cities indicated that it is not likely to be achieved soon." The distribution of the population, white and black, did not allow complete integration. In the nation's large cities, he related, "there are simply not enough middle class children to go around."[46] Even if it were possible to achieve complete integration, the achievement problem was unlikely to be solved. Schools as they were then constituted could not overcome the effects of family background.

> Even if the school is integrated, the heterogeneity of backgrounds with which children enter school is largely preserved in the hetrogeneity of their performance when they finish. As the Report indicates, integration provides benefits to the underprivileged. But it takes only a small step toward equality of educational opportunity.[47]

Coleman was convinced that "a more intense reconstruction of the child's social environment than that provided by school integration is necessary to remove the handicap of poor family background."[48]

Interest in busing persisted, however, as a practical and a political issue as well as an academic issue. In many instances, it appeared to be the only way to effect abolition of dual school systems, for desegregation was effectively resisted in many places and was proceeding very slowly in others. In 1968, more than a decade after the Supreme Court ordered that the schools be desegregrated, the Court ruled in *Green v. County School Board of New Kent County, Virginia* that "freedom of choice" approaches to desegregation constituted a form of tokenism that did not achieve desegregation. The Court ordered the County to devise a plan that would truly desegregate its schools by the beginning of the 1969 school year. That decision, as Hodgson has observed, "meant busing" for many school districts, especially the large ones.[49]

The Evidence on Busing

Just a year before the Supreme Court endorsed busing as a way to achieve desegregation in Charlotte-Mecklenburg, Thomas F. Pettigrew suggested to David Armor that he study project METCO, which was a plan for busing children from Boston's ghetto, Roxbury, into surrounding white suburban schools.[50] Armor acted on the suggestion and in 1972 presented "The Evidence on Busing." Besides studying the effects of busing and integration in the METCO project, he examined studies of busing in four other communities: White Plains, New York; Ann Arbor, Michigan; Riverside, California; and New Haven, Connecticut. To determine what the effects of busing were, he focused on five major possible effects: "(1) academic achievement; (2) aspirations; (3) self-concept; (4) race relations; and (5) educational opportunities."[51] He concluded that, except in the area of educational opportunities, busing students to achieve integration had no other significant effects.

In the area that Coleman emphasized—academic achievement—Armor found no significant results. He reported that "none of the studies were able to demonstrate conclusively that integration has had an effect on academic achievement as measured by standardized tests."[52] Measures of reading achievement for both elementary and secondary students in the METCO Project showed no satistically significant changes. Third and fourth grade students who were bused showed grade-equivalent gains of 0.4. Students in the control group who were not bused gained 0.3. The measures of fifth and sixth graders were similar but reversed. The bused students showed a gain of 0.5 while the control group showed a gain of 0.7. Measures of arithmetic scores showed a similar pattern.

Armor found that busing did not improve the aspirations for college or even higher occupational status. He did find, however, that "when achievement is taken into account, black students actually have higher aspirations than white students at similar levels of achievement." Studies of Ann Arbor and Riverside also showed that black students tended to have high aspirations "in both the pre- and post-integration periods."[53] However, there was some belief that black students' aspirations may have been overly high. Thus, the declines that were found in the level of aspiration could be viewed as positive in that they were brought "to more realistic levels." On the other hand, as Armor pointed out, "others would argue that any lowering of aspirations is undesirable."

To gain a measure of academic self-concept, the bused students were asked "to rate how bright they were in comparison to their classmates." The results showed that busing seemed not to raise but to lower the academic self-concept. Armor reported that the academic performance of bused students "falls considerably when they move from the black community to the white suburbs" and suggested that "in rating their intellectual ability, the bused students may simply be reflecting the harder competition in suburban schools."[54] His summary of the Ann Arbor and Riverside studies indicated that black children had lower self-esteem than white children before integration and that integration did not seem to change their self-esteem "in any clearly consistent or significant way."

It was widely assumed in the 1960s that increased "contact" or interaction between the races would decrease intolerance and improve race relations. Armor, however, found the opposite to be true. He related that "the data suggest that, under the circumstances obtaining in these studies, integration heightens racial identity and consciousness, enhances ideologies that promote racial segregation, and reduces opportunities for actual contact between the races."[55] As whites were accepting the idea of racial integration in the schools, blacks appeared to be rejecting it. Black students who were bused appeared to be developing attitudes against integration at a faster rate than the black community as a whole.

Armor had two conclusions that related directly to the busing-integration issue: (1) mandatory busing did not improve either student achievement or interracial harmony and should therefore not be used and (2) voluntary school integration programs should be encouraged and funded by both federal and state governments. His conclusions did not, however, go unchallenged. In collaboration with Elizabeth Useem, Clarence Normand, and Marshall Smith, Thomas Pettigrew, who had suggested that Armor do the study, objected to its conclusions. They claimed that Armor's findings would have been different had he not neglected to consider seven studies that offered contrary evidence, that the standards he used to evaluate the success of integration were inappropriate and too high, and that it would have been better to compare the achievement scores of blacks who were bused to other blacks rather than to whites.[56]

Armor argued that his critics opposed his recommendations against mandatory busing because they believed in "the *possibility* that under certain conditions induced school integration *might* have substantial beneficial effects on minority students."[57] His critics "missed the essential point" of his study. The issues in such a study were many, and it was, he maintained, necessary to distinguish clearly among "the findings of science, the results of policy, and the dictates of law or morality." He made the appropriate distinctions, he believed, and properly limited his focus.

> I studied the results of existing policies of induced school integration (all of which used, of necessity, varying amounts of busing). I was not studying the scientific issue of what *might* happen under various conditions (other than those in effect in the programs studied), nor the legal question of whether it *should* have happened according to various constitutional interpretations. My task was far simpler. I asked only the question: What *has* happened? Many critics have confused the *has* with the *might* and the *should*.[58]

Controversy and resistance to busing has continued into the 1980s. In a 1982 speech to the Delaware Bar Association, William Bradford Reynolds, the assistant attorney general for civil rights, related that his division would endeavor to achieve desegregation of schools through voluntary rather than mandatory means. Mandatory busing, he claimed, "had not fared well" and "resulted in 'white flight' from urban schools, erosion of tax support for city schools, and loss of parental support for public schools."[59] However, a study conducted at the Institute for Public Policy Studies at the George Peabody College for Teachers showed that mandatory busing plans were more effective than voluntary plans in reducing "racial isolation in public schools." The study covered the period 1968 to 1980 and focused on forty of the nation's largest school districts—districts with more than 30,000 students and minority enrollments that comprised between 25 and 75 percent of total enrollment. Where mandatory plans were implemented, "white flight" occurred at the time of implementation. Where voluntary plans were adopted, "the decline in white enrollment was less pronounced at the beginning, but the decline was steadier over time." However, "over time, districts with voluntary plans lost approximately the same proportion of white students as did systems in which student reassignment was compulsory."[60] Voluntary plans sometimes increased the number of schools in which minority enrollment was more than 90 percent and mandatory plans were more effective in producing schools in which the racial composition reflected the composition of the districts' populations.

The practice of moving one's residence to secure access to "better" schools for one's children was not a new social phenomenon. As Lawrence Cremin noted in 1965, "the so-called flight from the cities of today's middle class in search of better public education is no new phenomenon: fifty years ago, the middle class simply moved 'uptown' for the same reason."[61] To assume that only whites endeavor to live in areas where there is access to good schools is a wrong assumption. Joel Spring has described a suburban community in the industrial Midwest that was populated by blacks seeking better opportunities for their children. When the blacks began to move into what he calls "black suburbia" in the mid 1960s, they were, he reports, "very concerned about the quality of the educational system." However, as the blacks moved in, whites began to move out. Of significance in this instance are the income levels of those who were moving in the 1960s. The blacks "had slightly higher incomes than the whites moving out of the community."[62]

Social Science and Social Policy

EEOR and the subsequent analyses and discussions of it contributed to an awareness and examination of the role that social scientists were playing in the formation, execution, and evaluation of social policy. Through most of the twentieth century social scientists had been not only analysts of society and its problems but also advocates of various solutions to those problems. Not infrequently, their solutions entailed an increased role for public education. As Frederick Mosteller and Daniel P. Moynihan pointed out:

> Social science had come to the aid of the widest range of causes, and not least that of educational equality. A distinctive feature of *Brown v. Board of Education of Topeka* had been the introduction by the plaintiffs of social science information purporting to prove that segregated schools were inherently unequal, and that the disadvantage was sustained by the Negro children.[63]

In its *Brown* decision, the Supreme Court cited the work of Gunnar Myrdal and that of Kenneth and Mamie Clark. In the 1940s, the Clarks conducted research that demonstrated that even before reaching school age, black children, unlike their white counterparts, were less likely to prefer dolls with characteristics of their own race. Their research, Armor noted, "added a psychological dynamic to explain the operation of [Myrdal's] vicious circle."[64]

Myrdal used the "principle of cumulation" to describe the relationship between the blacks' "plane of living" and whites' prejudice toward them. Prejudice toward blacks insured that the opportunities afforded them would be insufficient to allow them to improve their way of life. Anything that would lower the blacks' plane of living would increase the prejudice against them and could even set in motion a "cumulative process" that could have "final effects quite out of proportion to the magnitude of the original push."[65] The "principle of cumulation" was, however, more than a hypothetical explanation of the relationship between white prejudice and the blacks' plane of living. It was also a hypothesis about and a design for changing the relationship, for, as Myrdal expressed it, "the vicious circle works both ways."[66]

The plane of living consisted of many elements: Negro employment, wages, housing, nutrition, clothing, health, education, stability in family relations, manners, orderliness, trustworthiness, law observance, loyalty to society at large, and absence of criminality. These elements, Myrdal maintained, were all related to each other. An effect on one would have an effect on others and ultimately an effect on the level of white prejudice.

> It is also our hypothesis that, on the whole, a rise in any single one of the Negro variables will tend to raise all the other Negro variables and thus, indirectly as well as directly, result in a cumulatively enforced effect upon white prejudice. A rise in employment will tend to increase earnings; raise standards of living; and improve health, education, manners and law observance and *vice versa;* a better education is assumed to raise the chances of a higher salaried job and *vice versa;* and so all the way through our whole system of variables. Each of the secondary changes has its effect on white prejudice.[67]

Myrdal's principle of cumulation provided a set of instructions for social scientists and policymakers who wanted to change society and also gave them reason to believe that changes could be deliberately implemented. Myrdal suggested that his principle was a complicated one and indicated that "the scientific ideal is not only to define and analyze the factors, but to give for each one of them a measure of their actual quantitative strength in influencing the other factors, as well as a measure of their ability to be influenced themselves by outside forces."[68] Some changes might produce a "backlash." Some changes also would take longer to achieve their maximum effect than others: "A rise of employment, for instance, will almost immediately raise some standards of living, but a change in the levels of education or health are slow to be achieved, and their effects back on the other factors are in turn delayed, which slows up the whole process of cumulation."[69]

Of all the variables Myrdal specified, education was the one most often chosen for a "push" by social scientists and reformers. In the 1960s, it seemed impossible to deal with the problems of poverty, race, or the urban crisis without considering the role of public education. Education's selection as the point of intervention to effect social change is partially explained by the longstanding faith Americans have expressed in its importance and power. It is also explained by political expediency. As Godfrey Hodgson has remarked about the plans to make a Great Society:

President Johnson's Great Society was to be built without alienating Congress. From the start, education was an important part of his administration's strategy for reducing poverty and racial inequality. But as other approaches, especially "community action," ran into political opposition, the Great Society's reliance on education programs grew accordingly. In the end the Johnson administration, committed up to the eyebrows to reducing inequality, was almost equally committed to education as the chief way of doing it.[70]

It has been traditionally easier to secure support for improving public education from across the political spectrum than it has for other kinds of social programs. Liberals have agreed that education is important and have been willing to invest in it to achieve social change. Conservatives have been willing to support programs for improving public education so all would have an opportunity to improve their lot through hard work and competition. Not as easy to secure has been agreement that deliberate action should be taken to change residential patterns in cities or that plans for the redistribution of income should be instituted as a means of decreasing inequality.

In the 1950s and especially in the 1960s, "social science information became increasingly central to the formulation and evaluation of social policies."[71] Opportunities for social scientists to use their skills and knowledge in "national councils" was the result of several developments. During this period, Americans became aware of their society and how it worked and became convinced that its dynamics could be altered to effect social change. For a variety of political, economic and social reasons, they wanted to do so. It was also the case, as Mosteller and Moynihan have pointed out, that many of the problems facing American society "had proved intractable in the face of 'common sense' solutions," and the social scientists with the use of their new methodologies and their access to the computer had the capability to undertake analyses that could not have been made before World War II.[72]

Delayed Implications

Ironically, *EEOR,* which was the largest social research project ever devoted to the issue of race in the United States, allowed some social scientists to argue that the power of public education to reduce inequality had been greatly overestimated. Inequality was due to the social conditions in which children were reared, and the school seemed to have very limited power to redress the inequalities visited upon children by these conditions. However, the full impact of Coleman's findings was not immediately recognized by educators and policymakers.

Moynihan was not willing to ignore *EEOR* or its implications. In the fall of 1966, he and Pettigrew, with support provided by the Carnegie Corporation, offered a seminar on equality of opportunity at Harvard. Their seminar "became the focus of an extraordinary welling up of intellectual excitement,"[73] drawing "fifty to sixty faculty members, and other interested groups."[74] "Harvard," claims Hodgson, "had seen nothing like it since the arms-control seminars of the late 1950s, at which the future strategic policies of the Kennedy administration were forged and the nucleus of the elite that was to operate them in government was brought together."[75] Christopher Jencks, who had recently begun work on a study of "The Limits of Schooling" supported by the Carnegie Corporation, joined the seminar. With the help of Theodore Sizer, dean of Harvard's Graduate School of Education, Jencks organized the Center for Educational Policy Research. The Carnegie Corporation and the federal government funded the center, and it became the site for several years of intensive study of the data Coleman had collected. In the spring of 1972, Moynihan and Mosteller published a set of papers—*On Equality of Educational Opportunity*—which had originated in the 1966 seminar. Later in the year, Jencks and his associates published a second volume of papers devoted to Coleman's data and issues—*Inequality: A Reassessment of the Effect of Family and Schooling in America*. Mosteller and Moynihan focused on inequality among groups, and Jencks and his colleagues focused on inequality among individuals. Their different foci led to different outlooks and recommendations, but each work was a forceful challenge to the traditional notion that society could use its public schools to reduce inequality in American society.

The Mosteller and Moynihan View

Mosteller and Moynihan neither contradicted nor challenged Coleman's findings. They acknowledged that his data might contain some biases and minor inaccuracies, but they discounted the possibility that refined data would alter any conclusions by pointing out that "it is the experience of statisticians that when fairly 'crude' measures are refined, the change more often than not turns out to be small."[76] They also noted that *EEOR* had effectively changed how "equality of educational opportunity" was defined:

> Stated briefly, before EEOR 'equality of educational opportunity' was measured in terms of school inputs, including racial mixture. By inputs, we mean physical facilities of schools and training of teachers; by racial mixture, the Supreme Court's emphasis on integration. With the publication of EEOR it became increasingly the practice, even the demand, that equality be measured by school outputs; that is to say, by the results of tests of academic achievement.[77]

While Mosteller and Moynihan did not deny the new definition of equality of educational opportunity and while they maintained that the dissatisfaction, disappointment, and even the "cultural despair" of some groups were understandable, they chose to emphasize how much progress had been made in satisfying the requirements of the classical notion of equality of educational opportunity. They acknowledged that at the end of the 1960s racial tensions were "higher than at any time in our history" and that the dissatisfaction with public education had reached the "point of crisis,"[78] but they nonetheless emphasized how much had been accomplished. In the middle third of the twentieth century, the nation had made "extraordinary progress:"

> There were no two areas of social policy in which progress toward a social ideal largely conceived and widely propounded was more conspicuous than those of equality of educational opportunity and equality of the races. The nation entered this period bound to the mores of caste and class. The white race was dominant. Negro Americans, Mexican Americans, Indian Americans, Oriental Americans, were all somehow subordinate, somehow something less than fully American. (Puerto Ricans had barely touched the national consciousness.) Education beyond a fairly rudimentary point was largely determined by social status. In a bare third of a century these circumstances have been extensively changed. *Changed.*[79]

Significantly, the changes were the consequences of deliberate actions. The nation had decided to eliminate inequality in two areas of society and had made progress toward doing so.

While blacks once argued that desegregation was not proceeding quickly enough, by the end of the 1960s some were charging that "the new unitary school systems continued to discriminate against blacks in various ways, that blacks still did not receive 'quality' education, and that special federal funds were not being used for educational purposes."[80] The nature of the charges—the difference between the two kinds of charges—was, according to Mosteller and Moynihan, a significant social change. That some problems had not been solved and that there were new ones were simply signs that the situation was "normal enough." There was "a long way to go," but the important point was that advances had been made. They acknowledged "the difference between the kind of equality we have and the kind we want" but they also wanted "to take stock of advances when they have occurred."[81]

No More Increases for Education

The recommendations Mosteller and Moynihan offered did call for more research "*for the purposes of improving national, state, and local educational policy,*"[82] but they did not recommend additional funds for either new or existing educational programs. They did recommend "*increased family-income and employment-training programs, together with plans for the evaluation of their long-run effects on education.*"[83] That recommendation was tantamount to tacitly suggesting that attempts ought to be made not to overcome the effects of the social environment but to change the conditions in which children are reared. That recommendation was also a tacit admission that public schools, as presently and traditionally organized, had limitations. While not rejecting the importance of schooling, they were certainly looking to alternatives to solve the problems of inequality. Thus, they recommended "*that new kinds of schools be developed and evaluated, and that in existing schools new sorts of educational policies substantially different from those of the past be tried in a research and development manner.*"[84] Their final recommendation was "optimism." They urged "*that the electorate maintain persistent pressure on its government agencies, school boards, legislatures, and executives to set specific targets, develop and revise programs, and report on progress toward local, state, and national goals in education with an attitude that optimistically expects gains, but, knowing their rarity, appreciates them when they occur.*"[85]

Shortly after the publication of *On Equality of Educational Opportunity,* Moynihan argued that increases in funding for education had been sufficient and that little was to be gained by increasing what was already enough. During the decade that had just ended, the nation had increased its expenditures for education "at a rate almost half again that of the GNP itself."[86] While the GNP was increasing at the rate of 6.8 percent, education expenditures were increasing at an annual rate of 9.7 percent.

The conclusions of a study conducted by the Rand Corporation for the President's Commission on School Finance was "devastating to whatever is left of conventional wisdom." There was a point after which additional expenditures on schools made little or no difference on achievement. The policy implications of the study were that

increasing expenditures on traditional educational practices is not likely to improve outcomes substantially. There seem to be opportunities for significant redirections and in some cases reductions in educational expenditures without deterioration in educational outcomes.[87]

The Rand researchers reported that *"research has found nothing that consistently and unambiguously makes a difference in student outcomes."*[88] Their review of "variants" of existing systems of public education also failed to find anything that was consistently related to how well students performed. Their review of compensatory educational programs was, Moynihan claimed, "wrenching." Such studies would not allow educators to argue that increased funding would enable them to make significant gains. "Production functions," or the law of diminishing returns, worked in education just as it worked in other sectors of the society. As Moynihan explained:

> Typically, in an early state increments of input have a high marginal utility which gradually diminishes until the exchange of input for output is no longer equal, and finally to the point where no additional output results. It seems to be the case that, over a considerable range of public services, we are traversing a segment of a production function which is virtually asymptotic. (The Rand report puts it with respect to education, that we are in a "flat area.")[89]

Educators had to face the prospect of no longer receiving increased funds to solve their problems. They also had to recognize the possibility that the problems they were trying to solve were not even educational problems, for the Rand report concluded that "there is good reason to ask whether our educational problems are, in fact, school problems."[90]

Any attempt to equalize expenditures for education would only raise the total cost for public education because the political system operated in a way that insured that those with less would receive more; it worked against any attempt to appropriate less for those with more. The cost of equalization would be staggering. A study conducted in Pennsylvania indicated that a 35 percent increase—$1,052,263,235—would be required to insure that all districts had funds equal to 80 percent of those expended by the districts with the highest rates of expenditures. According to Moynihan, government, whether federal, state or local, had to stop the fiscal hemorrhage.

The beneficiaries of increased expenditures for public education, Moynihan reasoned, would be teachers, not students. Teachers received about 68 percent of the operating expenditures of schools, and there was no compelling reason to increase their salaries. They were "deserving persons" but, for the most part, certainly were not "deprived." In the two decades after 1950, teacher salaries had "increased at a rate roughly twice that of wages in the private economy." Either increasing teachers' salaries or increasing the number of teachers (decreasing the student-teacher ratio) would "almost certainly increase the number of persons in higher income brackets." Increasing salaries for married women teachers—about 2 million of the 2.9 million teachers were women—would only add to the family income of those families whose incomes were already in the "top quintile of income distribution, even the top 5 percent."[91] Moynihan saw no reason to take any action that would increase income inequality.

The claim that increased expenditures for education were necessary to achieve equality was an instance of a special interest group promoting its own interest. It was, Moynihan claimed, "a way of asserting the value, and increasing the value of those services the middle class dispenses."[92] It was proper not to assume "disinterestedness" when some portion of the public sector sought increases for the services it provided, just as it was proper not to assume that the private sector was disinterested when it sought growth in the private sector of the economy. Indeed, it was proper to distinguish between facts and perceptions in such matters.

There was a perception within the "blue collar" class that "they were paying for a lot more services than they were receiving," while among the "service-dispensing classes" there was "the overwhelming perception, genuine or dissembled, . . . that the nation has not reordered its priorities and must do so."[93] What seemed to have made little impression on the service-dispensing class was the growth that had occurred in just one decade in appropriations for Great Society programs—from $1.7 billion in 1963 to $35.7 billion in 1973. There was, Moynihan hypothesized, a phenomenon at work that prevented the service-dispensing classes from seeing how greatly appropriations for their activities had actually increased.

> As government responds to a problem and the situation commences to change, those who initiated the response, and who benefit from it in one way or another, seek to ensure continued response by charging that the situation either has not improved, or has worsened, or has always been worse than originally asserted. For some, social legislation can have the effect of narcotic drugs on the addict: Ever stronger doses are required, first to achieve the remembered euphoria of the early stages of addiction, and then merely to maintain the absence of distress.[94]

Moynihan was not the only one to suggest that it would be difficult to defend increases in educational expenditures. With Mosteller, he was able to point out that a study published by the First National City Bank, *Public Education in New York,* showed that there was no positive relationship between school expenditures and achievement. The "preliminary evidence" gathered from 150 schools showed that "there is no statistical correlation between the aggregate amounts of money spent per pupil and the improvement in reading scores from one year to the next." The finding that "the race/poverty nexus appears to correlate highest with low reading levels"[95] confirmed the findings of *EEOR.*

In 1972, the economist Lester C. Thurow argued that "our reliance on education as the ultimate public policy for curing all problems, economic and social, is unwarranted at best and in all probability ineffective."[96] He reported that since World War II there had been a greater distribution of education in society but that the distribution of income did not change in any corresponding way. While the bottom fifth of the white male population had increased its share of education from 8.6 percent to 10.7 percent between 1950 and 1970, its share of the income dropped from 3.2 to 2.6 percent. The highest fifth of that same population experienced a decrease in its share of education for the same period from 31.1 percent to 29.3 percent but its share of the income increased from 44.8 percent to 46.3 percent. The conventional wisdom, or what Thurow described as "wage competition theory," held that such a redistribution of education would lead to a redistribution of income, but that clearly did not occur.

Examination of the experience of black Americans revealed a similar pattern. Thurow reported that "from 1952 to 1968, the mean education of black male workers rose from 67 percent to 87 percent of that of white male workers—yet median wage and salary incomes rose only from 58 percent to 66 percent."[97] However, that increase could be "traced to black emigration from the South, where incomes for blacks were lower than they were elsewhere. Commonly held assumptions about inequality, equality, and their causes seemed to be crumbling in the early 1970s, or as Christopher Jencks observed, "many popular explanations of economic inequality are largely wrong."[98]

The Jencks View

While Mosteller and Moynihan admitted that inequalities still persisted but chose to emphasize how much progress had been made toward effecting full equality, Jencks emphasized how
impossible it seemed to achieve equality. He questioned whether the nation wanted to eliminate inequalities, especially economic inequalities. Americans, he charged, had "no commitment to ensuring that everyone's job is equally desirable, that everyone exercises the same
amount of political power, or that everyone receives the same income."[99] Unlike others,
Jencks did not focus on the inequality among racial or ethnic groups, for that inequality was
not nearly as great as that which existed among individuals within any of the groups. It was
"quite shocking" to learn that white workers earned 50 percent more than blacks, but Jencks
was "even more disturbed by the fact that the best-paid fifth of all white workers earns 600
percent more than the worst-paid fifth." Such differences made the differences between races
seem "almost insignificant."

While many social scientists were advocates as well as analysts, Jencks, unlike many others, was very clear about what he was advocating. He explicitly indicated that "the decision to
emphasize individual rather than group differences was made on political grounds." He was
interested in achieving equality of opportunity, but he was "far more interested in a society
where the extremes of wealth and poverty are entirely eliminated than in a society where they
are merely correlated with skin color, economic origins, sex, and other such traits."[100]

Jencks challenged the widely held notion that educational reforms and the extension of
educational opportunities would eliminate poverty. The belief that middle class children rarely
wound up poor and that poor children could be made into middle class children in the public
schools was a belief without foundation. Jencks and his associates did not find any evidence to
support the belief that more or improved education would have a positive effect on the other
elements that comprised a person's life conditions. Economic and social inequalities could not
be reduced through educational reforms. Jencks reported in his conclusion:

> We have seen that educational opportunities, cognitive skills, educational credentials, occupa-
> tional status, income, and job satisfaction are all unequally distributed. We have not, however,
> been very successful in explaining most of these inequalities. The association between one vari-
> able of inequality and another is usually quite weak, which means that equalizing one thing is un-
> likely to have much effect on the degree of inequality in other areas.[101]

Conventional school reforms simply were not powerful enough to "make adults more
equal." Schools appeared not to have as much influence on children as their homes, the street,
and television. Typical reforms focused on how resources were allocated, new curricula, and
pupil assignment while what made a difference—"the way teachers and students actually treat
each other minute by minute"—was outside the control of reformers. Moreover, whatever influence a school did have on a child, it was, Jencks claimed, unlikely "to persist into adulthood."[102]

Jencks did not see much promise in conventional school reforms but he was not opposed
to educational reform. However, his was not a plan to do better what was already being done,
but a call to adopt a new conception of schooling and to assign a new purpose to schooling.
The conventional conception of the school as a factory that took in children as raw material

and processed them into "employable adults" had to be abandoned. Rather than focusing upon schools as instrumental or preparatory institutions and evaluating them in terms of their "long-term effects" on students, Jencks urged that the school be conceived not as means to ends but as ends in themselves and that they be evaluated in terms of their "immediate effects on teachers and students." To describe such schools, it was appropriate and useful to adopt "a language appropriate to a family rather than a factory."[103] Because it was generally accepted that families could be judged in a number of ways, it seemed appropriate to have a variety of ways to judge schools. That meant that schools should be characterized by diversity of purpose and procedure. The principle of uniformity disallowed the possibility of satisfying all portions of the public, but the principle of diversity would allow the public to be satisfied. There were no good reasons, he believed, not to grant people the opportunity to choose what kind of schooling they wanted for their children. For him, "the ideal system is one that provides as many varieties of schooling as its children and parents want and finds ways of matching children to schools that suit them." Whatever parents and children wanted seemed appropriate, for not even professional educators, according to Jencks, had a better understanding of the long-term effects of school than did parents. Moreover, "since the character of an individual's schooling appears to have relatively little long-term effect on his development, society as a whole rarely has a compelling interest in limiting the range of educational choices open to parents and students."[104]

Jencks clearly preferred one kind of schooling more than others but he was not willing to argue that his preference should be *the* preference for all. He did not "believe that schools should be run like mediocre summer camps" and valued "ideas and the life of the mind."[105] Others, however, preferred "discipline and competitive excellence," "high reading and math scores," "teaching children to behave properly," or something else from a "nearly endless" list of possible objectives. What was important, he maintained, was that children be allowed to feel that they were "doing something purposeful." One way to do that was to engage them in "activities that contribute to their becoming more like grownups."

Conclusion

By the mid 1970s, the national policy on equality of educational opportunity that had been assembled in the late 1950s and the early 1960s was clearly being disassembled. As David Cohen and Michael Garret have described it, this policy

> rested partly on the idea that poverty, unemployment and delinquency resulted from the absence of particular skills and attitudes—reading ability, motivation to achieve in school and the like. There was also an assumption that schools inculcated these skills and attitudes and that acquiring them would lead to economic and occupational success. In other words, this policy assumed that doing well in schools led to doing well in life. Finally, the emerging policy, which came to be called compensatory education, assumed that providing schools with more resources would enable and induce them to remedy students' deficiencies.[106]

By the mid 1970s, the studies, discussions, and controversies inspired by the Coleman Report, the Report itself, and what Cohen and Garret described as "the stream of negative Title I evaluations," all "gradually eroded the assumptions underlying compensatory policy."[107] As the climate of opinion about the effectiveness of the specific compensatory strategies changed, the support for "categorical" programs was weakened and the support for "general aid" was somewhat improved. In the political arena, however, the erosion of those assumptions made a difference when resources were allocated. As Hodgson reported:

> "The Jencks report" was freely cited by the Nixon administration's Office of Management and Budget on Capitol Hill in justification of cutting the budget for fiscal 1974. There was a widespread feeling that "Coleman and Jencks" provided a respectable rationale for giving a low priority to spending on education. [108]

The ideas of reformers and educators may have been challenged and perhaps even seriously discredited in some sectors, but the problems they were trying to address certainly did not disappear. Equality, inequality, achievement, integration, desegregation strategies, family-social background, the special problems of handicapped children, and the needs and rights of non-English-speaking Americans continued to command the attention of educators and lawmakers.

Charges that the compensatory educational programs failed were answered by arguments that they were frequently based on incorrect and unjust assumptions. During the 1960s, it was, as Ricardo L. Garcia, has observed, "popular to label students from ethnic minority or low socioeconomic backgrounds 'culturally deprived'." [109] Theories of cultural deprivation frequently maintained that the culture and language of students from outside mainstream American society were inferior or invalid because they differed from that of middle-class white students. Some compensatory programs were accordingly designed not to build upon what students knew but to replace one culture and linguistic background with another. That approach either denied or simply ignored all that educators claimed about the relevance of the structure of knowledge just a few years earlier. According to Garcia, it also "ignored the fact that ethnic minority and poor students have cultures, languages, and ethnic group heritages that cannot easily be replaced by those of another culture." [110] Such criticisms of compensatory programs are not claims that schools are necessarily ineffective. Rather, they are charges that schools have frequently violated the time-honored principle that dictates that teachers teach children in terms of what they know. If it is assumed that children know little or nothing or that what they do know is not worthwhile, often because the teachers do not know what they know, effective teaching is extraordinarily difficult, if not impossible.

Even while the effectiveness of compensatory programs was being challenged, action was being taken to insure that true equality of opportunity would be extended to all children regardless of their handicaps or their ethnic and linguistic backgrounds. In the late 1960s and early 1970s, the special problems of children from non-English-speaking families began to receive the attention they needed from educators and legislators. In 1967, Sen. Ralph Yarborough of Texas introduced bilingual educational legislation to the Congress. In January 1968, Congress enacted the Bilingual Education Act (Title VII of the Elementary and Secondary Education Act). It did not require all school districts to introduce bilingual education programs, but it did recognize that many children needed instruction in their native language as well as English if they were to progress satisfactorily in school. The Act provided funds for school districts that wanted to implement programs. However, in 1970, the Department of Health, Education and Welfare (DHEW), using the 1964 Civil Rights Act as a basis, directed all school districts with enrollments of more than 5 percent non-English-speaking children to provide language programs that would insure that all children would have the opportunity to achieve in school.

Advocates of bilingual education programs who maintained that special programs were necessary to insure that all children would have equal opportunity at academic achievement received affirmation of their position when the Supreme Court rendered its decision in *Lau v. Nichols* in 1974. The Court then agreed, unanimously, that the schools of San Francisco were not offering equal educational opportunity to Chinese-speaking students. To claim that non-English-speaking students could benefit from instructional and curricular strategies designed for English-speaking students was, the Court declared, "a mockery of public education" and a violation of the 1964 Civil Rights Act. In 1975, the Office of Civil Rights of DHEW issued a set of guidelines, generally known as the "Lau Remedies" for implementing the Lau decision. They specified that school districts have an obligation: to identify the student's primary and home language; to diagnose the students' educational needs and prescribe and implement appropriate programs to satisfy those needs; to insure that programs do not track students on the basis of English language proficiency; to insure that teachers are culturally sensitive and linguistically proficient; to prohibit ethnically identifiable schools and classes; and to notify parents of school programs in the appropriate language. Curiously, the task force that wrote the "Lau Remedies" argued against English as a Second Language (ESL) programs as an effective remedy. Yet, the basis of the Court's decision in the *Lau* case was, as Diane Ravitch has observed, "the failure of the San Francisco schools to provide ESL to all Chinese children in the system."[111] For those who do not follow the details of Court decisions and task force recommendations, it is difficult to know what has and has not been ordered by the Court. In this case, the Court ordered a remedy but did not specify any particular educational procedure.

While the Supreme Court has declared that bilingual programs be implemented and appears to have accepted a Coleman-like definition of equality of opportunity that focuses upon the opportunity to achieve academically, bilingual education remains a confusing and controversial issue. Even in the 1980s, Ravitch was able to ask rhetorically: "Was the purpose of bilingual education to provide a *transition* to the regular English-language school program or was its purpose to *maintain* the language and culture of non-English-speaking children?"[112] Some of the controversy is about the best way to teach English to non-English-speaking students—whether they should be taught to read and then to speak English or vice versa. In some measure, such controversies reflect the differences among psychologists and students of linguistics about language acquisition. However, some of the controversies have cultural and political aspects. Some argue that "maintenance models," which allow children to maintain proficiency in their native language while becoming proficient in English, are appropriate. Others argue that the emphasis should be on "transitional models," which phase out use of the native language as proficiency in English is acquired. However, the issues attendant to bilingual education are not simply questions about the best way to teach students English. The assumption that culturally different, or non-English-speaking students, needed language remediation has not helped their educational progress but has, according to Garcia, resulted in "innumerable cognitive and emotional problems."[113]

The efforts to extend equality of educational opportunity to children from racial and ethnic groups and to children from low-income families did lead to efforts to assist other children, especially handicapped children. As Erwin L. Levine and Elizabeth M. Wexler have observed:

> The problems of handicapped children, particularly related to securing an adequate education, represent a phenomenon which had its roots in the civil rights movements of the 1960s. In that decade many Blacks believed they were getting less than they were entitled to in education, employment, housing and accommodations and came together to obtain their rights. They confronted the system on executive, legislative and judicial fronts. Many of those who advocated more government aid for educating handicapped children saw themselves as part of the mainstream of politics, in the same manner as did the major civil rights groups, and set about to organize themselves in advancing the cause of the handicapped.[114]

The cause of handicapped children, which began to receive national recognition in the 1960s after President Kennedy appointed the President's Panel on Mental Retardation, achieved help from Congress in 1966 when it authorized the Office of Education to establish a Bureau of Education for the Handicapped (BEH) and created the National Advisory Committee on Education and Training of the Handicapped. Each of these organizations was expected to serve as an advocacy agency and to work for more funding and legislation to benefit the handicapped.[115] The handicapped won further benefits and rights in 1973 when Congress passed the Rehabilitation Act. Section 504 of that Act guaranteed the handicapped access to all programs in all institutions that received federal funds. Perhaps the greatest victory for the advocates of the handicapped occurred in 1975 when President Gerald Ford signed the All Handicapped Children Act into law, popularly known as Public Law 94–142. Its enactment was a clear sign that the nation had realized that more than half of the nation's eight million handicapped children were not receiving "appropriate educational services which would enable them to have full equality of opportunity" and that 1 million handicapped children were "excluded entirely from the public school systems."[116]

Since its enactment, most discussions of P. L. 94–142 have focused on the "mainstreaming" requirement—the belief that the law specified that all children, no matter what their disability, had to be placed in regular classrooms with non-handicapped children. It should, however, be noted that the law does not specifically require that all handicapped children be "mainstreamed." In fact, the law did not necessarily require the states to implement any new programs, practices, or procedures unless those states accepted federal funds to finance the cost of providing special services for handicapped children. However, once the states accepted federal funds, they were obligated to provide all handicapped children with "a free appropriate public education which emphasizes special education and related services designed to meet their unique needs." Acceptance of federal funds required states to identify handicapped children, prepare written individualized education plans (IEP's) for each handicapped child, and to provide the "least restrictive environment" for the handicapped child. For many, "least restrictive" meant the traditional classroom.

In testimony to a House Subcommittee on Select Educational Hearings, on H.R. 6692, 1977, the Council for Exceptional Children maintained that the cost of overcoming the logistical and physical problems of effecting mainstreaming should be paid just as the cost of ending racial desegration in the schools had been and was being paid. It is beneficial for all children to learn about people who are different and to learn to live and to work with them. Mainstreaming is, the Council argued, beneficial for non-handicapped children as well as for handicapped children. The Council had to so argue because by 1977, mainstreaming had become "a red flag for many, who feared that having handicapped children mixed with 'normal' children would have an ill effect on the latter."[117] The president of the Council, Harold Perry, even emphasized to the subcommittee that the Council did not advocate the mainstreaming of all handicapped children: "To say that we are going to put every retarded child, every learning disability child, every emotionally disturbed child, into a regular classroom full time is foolish, first of all; it is incorrect, most of all."[118]

If there was agreement about the definition of "appropriate education," there would be little difficulty in interpreting and implementing the provisions of Public Law 94–142, just as there would be few, if any, controversies about public education. The lack of agreement among educators, the public, and legislators about the meaning of "appropriate education" has resulted in a number of appeals to the judiciary. In some instances, the courts have ruled that Public Law 94–142 requires school districts to provide services for the handicapped even though those services are not specifically stated in the law. As Martha McCarthy has reported:

> For example, school districts have been judicially required to provide extended-year programs for severely handicapped children who would suffer substantial regression from an interruption in their educational programs (*Armstrong v. Kline*, 1980). Also, school districts have been required to support residential placements for disabled students even though the placements have been made in part for non-educational reasons (*North v. District of Columbia Board of Education*, 1979). Moreover, courts have required education agencies to provide psychotherapy (*Matter of 'A' Family*, 1979) and catheterization (*Tatro v. State of Texas*, 1980) for handicapped children who need such services in order to participate in the educational program.[119]

In 1982, the Supreme Court issued its first ruling interpreting Public Law 94–142. In the *Rowley* case, the Court declined to specify which services a school district must provide for handicapped students. In that case, the Court overturned the rulings of lower courts that a school district was obligated to provide a sign language interpreter for a student who, without such assistance, was doing above average work in school. Rather, the Court indicated that its role was not to specify what appropriate education was but only to insure that the school district observed the procedures specified in the law and to determine whether the school district did develop an IEP according to the procedures specified in the law. The Court further decreed that "the intent of the Act was more to open the door of public education to handicapped children on appropriate terms than to guarantee any particular level of education once inside."[120]

After World War II, and especially during the late 1960s and early 1970s, many attempts were made to open the door to education to many who previously faced a closed door. There may be disagreement about whether the door has been completely opened, but there can be little disagreement that the attempts to open the door to all have indeed presented many new responsibilities and challenges to schools and their teachers. Those attempts have also insured that education will continue to be a national as well as a local concern.

Notes

1. Thomas Jefferson, "A Bill for the More General Diffusion of Knowledge," reprinted in Gordon C. Lee (ed.), *Crusade Against Ignorance: Thomas Jefferson on Education* (New York: Teachers College Press, Columbia University, 1961), 83.
2. Jefferson, *Notes on the State of Virginia*, reprinted in Lee, *Crusade Against Ignorance*, 94.

3. John Dewey, "Democracy and Educational Administration," *School and Society* 45, (April 3, 1937): 458–459.
4. Ibid.
5. Ibid.
6. Quoted in James B. Conant, *Thomas Jefferson and the Development of American Public Education* (Berkeley, Calif.: University of California Press, 1962), 54–55.
7. Ibid., 55.
8. Jennings L. Wagoner, Jr., "The American Compromise: Charles W. Eliot, Black Education, and the New South," in Ronald K. Goodenow and Arthur O. White (eds.), *Education and the Rise of the New South* (Boston: G. K. Hall, 1981), 26.
9. Booker T. Washington, *Up From Slavery* (1901), in Louis Harlan (ed.), *The Booker T. Washington Papers* (Urbana: University of Illinois Press, 1972), 332–333.
10. Wagoner, "The American Compromise," 27.
11. Gunnar Myrdal, *An American Dilemma* (New York: Harper and Brothers, 1944), 32.
12. Ibid., 339–340.
13. *Brown et. al. v. Board of Education of Topeka et. al.* 347. U.S. 483 (1954), reprinted in Sol Cohen (ed.), *Education in the United States: A Documentary History* (New York: Random House, 1974, 3105.
14. James S. Coleman et al. *Equality of Educational Opportunity* (Washington, D.C.: U.S. Government Printing Office, 1966), iii.
15. Ibid.
16. Quoted in Frederick Mosteller and Daniel P. Moynihan (eds.), *On Equality of Educational Opportunity* (New York: Vintage Books, 1972), 8.
17. Ibid., 10.
18. Coleman, *Equality of Educational Opportunity,* 121–122.
19. Ibid., 122.
20. Ibid., 21.
21. Ibid., 22.
22. Ibid., 21.
23. James Coleman, "Equal Schools or Equal Students?" *The Public Interest,* No. 4 (Summer, 1966): 71.
24. Ibid., 72.
25. James Coleman, "Toward Open Schools," *The Public Interest,* No. 9 (Fall, 1967): 21.
26. Coleman, "Equal Schools," 73. Coleman's emphasis.
27. Ibid., 73–74. Coleman's emphasis.
28. Ibid., 73. Coleman's emphasis.
29. Ibid., 75.
30. Ibid., 74.
31. Ibid.
32. Ibid.
33. Ibid., 75.
34. Coleman, *Equality of Educational Opportunity,* 22.
35. Coleman, "Toward Open Schools," 21.
36. Ibid., 23.
37. Ibid., 24.
38. Ibid.
39. Ibid., 25.
40. Ibid., 26.
41. Ibid., 27.

42. Fred M. Newman and Donald W. Oliver, "Education and Community," *Harvard Educational Review* 37 (Winter 1967): 81.
43. Coleman, "Equal Schools," 74.
44. Coleman, "Toward Open Schools," 24. Coleman's emphasis.
45. Godfrey Hodgson, *America in Our Time: From World War II to Nixon* (New York: Vintage Books, 1978), 449–450.
46. Coleman, "Toward Open Schools," 22.
47. Ibid., 23.
48. Ibid.
49. Hodgson, *America in Our Time,* 454.
50. Ibid., 455.
51. David J. Armor, "The Evidence on Busing," *The Public Interest,* No. 28 (Summer 1972): 98.
52. Ibid., 101.
53. Ibid., 101.
54. Ibid., 102.
55. Ibid.
56. Thomas F. Pettigrew, Elizabeth Useem, Clarence Normand, and Marshall Smith, "Busing: A Review of 'The Evidence'," *The Public Interest,* No. 30 (Winter 1973): 88–118.
57. David J. Armor, "The Double Standard: A Reply," *The Public Interest,* No. 30 (Winter 1973): 119.
58. Ibid., 129.
59. Peggy Caldwell, "Federal Civil-Rights Chief Responds to Critics of His Integration Policies," *Education Week,* 1 (March 3, 1982): 11.
60. Peggy Caldwell, "Mandatory Busing More Effective Than Voluntary," *Education Week* 1 (March 3, 1982): 1.
61. Lawrence A. Cremin, *The Genius of American Education* (Pittsburg: University of Pittsburg Press, 1965), 69.
62. Joel Spring, *American Education: An Introduction to Social and Political Aspects* (New York: Longman, 1978), 51–52.
63. Mosteller and Moynihan, *On Equality of Educational Opportunity,* 31.
64. Armor, "The Evidence on Busing," 92.
65. Myrdal, *An American Dilemma,* 1066.
66. Ibid.
67. Ibid., 1066–1067.
68. Ibid., 1068.
69. Ibid., 1068–69.
70. Hodgson, *America in Our Time,* 447.
71. Mosteller and Moynihan, *On Equality of Educational Opportunity,* ix.
72. Ibid., 3–4.
73. Hodgson, *America in Our Time,* 449.
74. Mosteller and Moynihan, *On Equality of Educational Opportunity,* ix.
75. Hodgson, *America in Our Time,* 449.
76. Mosteller and Moynihan, *On Equality of Educational Opportunity,* 13.
77. Ibid., 6.
78. Ibid., 59.
79. Ibid., 58–59.
80. Ibid., 63.
81. Ibid., 13.
82. Ibid., 53. Emphasis in the original.

83. Ibid., 56. Emphasis in the original.
84. Ibid. Emphasis in the original.
85. Ibid., 57. Emphasis in the original.
86. Daniel P. Moynihan, "Equalizing Education: In Whose Benefit?" *The Public Interest,* No. 29 (Fall 1972): 70.
87. Ibid., 73. Moynihan's emphasis.
88. Ibid. Moynihan's emphasis.
89. Ibid., 79–80.
90. Ibid., 73.
91. Ibid., 75.
92. Ibid., 76.
93. Ibid., 79.
94. Ibid.
95. Mosteller and Moynihan, *On Equality of Educational Opportunity,* 32.
96. Lester C. Thurow, "Education and Economic Equality," *The Public Interest,* No. 28 (Summer 1972): 81.
97. Ibid., 69–70.
98. Christopher Jencks et. al. *Inequality: A Reassessment of Family and Schooling in America* (New York: Harper Colophon, 1973), 8.
99. Ibid., 3.
100. Ibid., 14.
101. Ibid., 253.
102. Ibid., 255–256.
103. Ibid., 256.
104. Ibid.
105. Ibid., 257.
106. David K. Cohen and Michael S. Garet, "Reforming Educational Policy with Applied Social Research, *Harvard Educational Review* 45 (February 1975): 21.
107. Ibid., 23.
108. Hodgson, *America in Our Time,* 461.
109. Ricardo L. Garcia, *Teaching in a Pluralistic Society: Concepts, Models, Strategies* (New York: Harper & Row, 1982), 20.
110. Ibid., 21.
111. Diane Ravitch, *The Troubled Crusade: American Education, 1945–1980* (New York: Basic Books, 1983), 275.
112. Ibid., 273.
113. Garcia, *Teaching in a Pluralistic Society,* 29.
114. Erwin L. Levine and Elizabeth M. Wexler, *PL 94–142: An Act of Congress* (New York: Macmillan, 1981, 11–12.
115. Ravitch, *Troubled Crusade,* 307.
116. P. L. 94–142 reprinted in Levine and Wexler, *PL 94–142,* 192.
117. Levine and Wexler, *PL 94–142,* 139.
118. Ibid., 140.
119. Martha M. McCarthy, "The Pennhurst and Rowely Decisions: Issues and Implications," *Exceptional Children* 49 (April 1983): 520–521.
120. Quoted in McCarthy, "The Pennhurst and Rowley Decisions," 520.

PART III
The Electronic Foundations of Education

Virtually all agree that television and the computer have great importance for education. However, television is commonly blamed for students' poor achievement and short attention spans, while at the same time educators are admonished to make better use of the medium as an instructional tool. Somehow, we must make television more educational or insure that students spend less time watching it. Poor grades are associated with excessive television viewing, but educators do not know whether one causes the other. Television is educational, but we do not always like the kind of educating it does.

Another common recommendation is for computers in every classroom. Computer literacy has become nearly as important as traditional forms of literacy, although there is no agreement on what computer literacy entails. For some, it means using the computer to monitor students' drill and practice or as a tutor so teachers may be liberated to give individualized instruction. For others, it means knowing how to use the computer, because virtually all forms of employment in the near future may require some kind of computer use. For them, it is a new kind of vocational education that will insure employment.

Television and the computer have touched all of us, especially our children. The computer has entered our lives directly and indirectly, visibly and invisibly. We daily see its use in record keeping, billing, communications, and even when making the simplest of purchases. Whether we are engaged in the exploration of space, genetic engineering, or the creation of artificial intelligence, the computer has become indispensable. Many of us have already learned to use it as a medium for interpersonal communication, creative expression, information storage, and the manipulation and retrieval of data. As Sherri Turkle has written, "it changes people's awareness of themselves, of one another, of their relationships to the world."[1]

The introduction of the computer into our daily lives seems relatively recent, but that is not the case with television. For an entire generation, virtually no American child has been without it. If we could find an American child of 6 or 7 years of age who did not know television, he or she would be an instant oddity and a prize object of study for all sorts of social and behavioral scientists. Researchers have great difficulty finding populations who do not know television, and children cannot imagine a world without it. Some adults, who still remember a world without television, persist in the belief that the medium is the major cause of many of

139

our children's problems as well as their failure to behave as we would wish. Yet, television may not be a great enemy of education. As Stephen R. Graubard has pointed out:

> In England, Scotland, and Wales, where television is less violent, less common, less pervasive, the comprehensive schools appear to be confronting a host of educational problems not significantly less serious than those experienced by many high schools in the United States. Yet, no one would argue that the BBC and ITV are quite as banal or infantilizing as NBC, ABC, and CBS manage to be on many occasions. Clearly, television cannot be the all-important variable.[2]

The major purpose of Part III, "The Electronic Foundations of Education," is to encourage the reader to entertain the possibility that neither television nor the computer is the "all-important variable" in education. While neither can be overlooked, neither is necessarily the source of the problems and disappointments we encounter in education. Nor is either likely to solve educational problems. There may be great utility however, in seeing each as something other than a friend or enemy of education. Admittedly, that may be difficult to do, for those two means of transmitting information from one place or person to another on a demand basis may indeed be "enemies" of traditional forms of schooling.

Schooling, like the computer and television, is a creation of humankind. In many respects, the three are similar contrivances. Each is a medium for transmitting information, skills, values, and ideas to people. The issue that demands our attention is not how the school can adjust to competition from seemingly more powerful and more attractive media but what is the most appropriate form of schooling for Americans in what Brzezinski calls the "technetronic society." Ultimately, we must decide what a school is and what its purposes are. That must be done before we can decide how and whether to use television and the computer in the schools.

How computers have been and can be used in the instructional process (CAI) is given attention in Chapter 6, " The Computer." In this chapter, the reader will also find a discussion of schooling as it relates to "information-poor" and "information-rich" societies. As we adopt new economies and technologies, we may need to consider new forms of schooling to maintain the values we most cherish. All people, but especially educators, must distinguish between purposes on the one hand and ways to achieve those purposes on the other. Schooling is one way to achieve our purposes.

A discussion of how television affects the most important people in the educative process—students—is included in Chapter 7, "Television." No attempt is made to deny that television influences children and youth. However, documenting how television affects the behavior and values of our children is difficult. This chapter also considers how some educators would make television an object of study in the schools. It may be possible for teachers, parents, and students to begin to understand how television exercises its influence.

Both chapters in Part III attempt to challenge the notion that the school is merely a means of transporting messages from one place to another. To understand that challenge does not necessarily mean that the reader has accepted one position or another, but it does mean that he or she understands the relationship between education and schooling.

Notes

1. Sherri Turkle, *The Second Self: Computers and the Human Spirit* (New York: Simon & Schuster, 1984), 13.
2. Stephen R. Graubard, Preface to "Values, Resources, and Politics in America's Schools," *Daedalus* (Fall 1984), ix.

6
The Computer

The End of a Revolution

Before his death in 1979, the experimental psychologist and computer scientist Christopher Evans wrote that the world was fast approaching a "Computer Revolution" that was, in terms of the changes it would introduce to the daily lives of nearly all people, comparable to the Industrial Revolution. The scope of the changes introduced by the Industrial Revolution were "immense" and transformed "all aspects of human society, affecting the individual, his family, his neighbors, his domestic and working environment, his clothes, his education, his social attitudes, his life-span, even the manner of his birth and death."[1]

The Industrial Revolution was not, however, an event that suddenly changed how people lived and worked. Rather, it was a century-long process during which a series of changes were introduced to society. The full force of the computer revolution will be felt in much less time. Evans predicted that the computer revolution would work itself out in about twenty-five years, a time shorter than the average life span. Like the Industrial Revolution, it "will have an overwhelming and comprehensive impact, affecting every human being on earth in every aspect of his or her life." However, while many were quite unaware of the Industrial Revolution, "we of the closing years of the 1970s have the gift of foresight, the ability to contemplate—if not for long—the amazing change that man is about to force upon himself."[2]

Two important reasons may be given for the "amazing change." The first is that computers are very different from machines of the industrial era. The latter were extensions of human muscle, but the computer seems to be an extension of the brain, of humankind's ability to acquire, select, store, assemble, and relate experiences. The second reason is the accessibility and portability of the computer. A generation ago, computers, like many machines in the factory, were place-bound, and people had to go to where the computers were to use them. Now, they are portable. People can take them along wherever they go, and they do.

The computer is no longer confined to businesses, laboratories, and manufacturers—it is becoming a household appliance. By the summer of 1981, about one million of the three million microcomputers sold in the United States were personal computers, and it has been predicted that by 1990, around 80 percent of American households may have computers.[3] In 1983, an estimated 18 percent of the children in California had access to computers in their homes.[4] James Eden of Micro-Marketing Consultants claims that "the microcomputer is a watershed technology" and that "like the electric light, the automobile and the telephone, it stands to change our everyday lives even more than we can know."[5]

In 1982, over 100,000 computers were available to students in schools. While they represented only one computer for every 400 students, the ratio is likely to become more favorable soon.[6] Market Data Retrieval reported that by the fall of 1983 over two thirds (68.4 percent) of the schools had personal computers available for student use.[7]

Cost seems not to be a significant factor. Patricia Marks Greenfield reported in 1984 that "in a time of limited budgets, schools have been purchasing computers like mad."[8] To provide each of the 40 million students that are expected to be in school in 1990 with thirty minutes of interactive computer use would require that the early 1980 computer inventory be increased by about 50 percent a year. The cost for such inventory expansion—including maintenance, replacement, and courseware—is estimated to be about $30 per student, or 1.2 percent of the early-1980s' instructional budget. Thus, a technology conceived in the nineteenth century but which could not be built until the twentieth century apparently has the potential for becoming as universal and as integral a part of our lives as television. Its potential for changing our lives is also as great as the effects, real and alleged, of television.

In the postindustrial society, that is, the technetronic society, the major resource is not materials but knowledge or information. The essential capability is the power to order and process that knowledge. According to Graham T. T. Molitor:

> The production, understanding, and control of knowledge have become essential, especially in the advanced nations. Knowledge and information industries are fast becoming the decisive factors in the growth of productive forces of nations. For the foreseeable future, computers will provide the largest changes. The information revolution is upon us. What steel, petroleum, and the induction motor were to the industrial revolution, computers and semiconducters will be to the post-industrial society.[10]

Molitor predicts that by the end of the century two thirds of the labor force will work in the information industry. That is three times as many people as will be working in manufacturing and thirty-three times as many as will be working in agriculture.

Origin and Development

Credit for inventing the computer is usually given to the English mathematician Charles Babbage who, in 1821, informed the Royal Astronomical Society that he could design and construct a pilot model of a "Difference Engine" that would have the capability of solving polynomial equations. The idea occurred to him while he and his friend and fellow mathematician John Herschel were checking the accuracy of logarithmic tables and decided that there had to be an alternative to such tedious work. The right machine—perhaps one driven by steam, as Babbage suggested—would relieve mathematicians of the tedium and introduce a mechanical way to eliminate human errors. The Royal Astronomical Society was impressed with the demonstration of his pilot model, as well as his paper, "Observations on the Application of Machinery to the Computation of Mathematical Tables," and awarded him the Society's first gold medal.

Babbage's plan for the "Difference Engine" was similar to calculating machines earlier designed by John Napier, Blaise Pascal, and Gottfried Leibnitz in that it consisted of cogs and wheels, but it was significantly larger than anything that had ever before been attempted. Although Babbage spent nearly £35,000 (half of which had been granted by the government), set up a shop on his estate, and employed technical assistants, the technology of his era could not produce the parts with the precision and extremely fine tolerances his plan required. Minor imperfections in the small model did not greatly interfere with its proper functioning, but in the large engine the imperfections were greatly magnified and caused the engine to shake, jam, and malfunction. Had it been possible to construct, it would have consisted of over two tons of parts.

While working on the "Difference Engine," Babbage conceived an even more complicated machine, the "Analytical Engine." Its design included most of the features found in the modern computer: a memory for 1,000 fifty-digit numbers, a "mill" to perform the four basic arithmetic functions, and a printer. Data and instructions were to be fed into the machine on punch cards that Joseph-Marie Jacquard had invented for his automatic loom in 1800. Babbage's engines were impossible to build but his principles were sound. Others pursued those principles as they were reported in Babbage's publications and the notes Ada Lovelace made of her conversations and work with Babbage.

While the demand for machines to solve and print the answers to polynomial equations was not great, by the 1880s there was a need for rapid, if not mechanical, means to process and compile large amounts of data. The U.S. Census Office decided in 1887, while still tabulating data from the 1880 census, that it needed a faster way to tabulate the data to be collected in 1890.

The office sought a solution to its problem by announcing a competition. From the many entries, three finalists were selected and invited to demonstrate their methods in a practical test in St. Louis. There Charles F. Pidgin applied his color-coded tokens to the problem and completed the task in forty-four hours. William C. Hunt used his colored cards and completed the task in fifty-five hours. Herman Hollerith used the first tabulating machine ever designed and completed the task in five and one-half hours and won the contest. Hollerith used ideas and technology of his predecessors as well as new ones. Cards into which holes were punched to represent yes-or-no answers were sorted and tabulated by the machine, which sensed the placement of the hole with an electromechanical device. Significantly, the electrical part of Hollerith's machine presented fewer difficulties than the mechanical parts. Reading the data from the cards proceeded "exceedingly fast" but it was difficult to move cards in and out of the scanner fast enough for the scanner. As Evans observed, "it was the first hint of the gulf opening up between electrical and mechanical processing systems, and an indication that the days of interlocking cogs and gears were numbered."[11] In retrospect, it can be seen as a sign that electrical, and especially electronic, systems would be qualitatively different from mechanical systems.

In the mid 1930s, Howard H. Aiken, an associate professor of mathematics at Harvard, convinced the president of IBM, Thomas J. Watson, to spend a million dollars to build an automatic sequence controlled calculator, later nicknamed Mark I. By 1944, it was operational and was the first automatic, general purpose digital computer. The U.S. Navy used it to generate calculations for ship design and ballistics, and the private sector used it to compile astronomical tables and to design lenses. It was also used by the Wright-Patterson Air Force Base and the Atomic Energy Commission. While it provided fifteen years of reliable service—operating every hour of every day, maintenance of its 500 miles of wiring and 750,000 parts contained in a stainless steel and glass cabinet (55 feet long and 8 feet high) was not easy. It contained seventy-two arithmetic registers for addition and storage of numbers, and some sixty switches for setting constants. Because Aiken used electromagnetic relays instead of vacuum tubes, operation of the machine was reported to have sounded like "a roomful of old ladies knitting away with steel needles."[12] Data was entered into Mark I either through punch cards or by setting manual switches. Answers—up to twenty-three places—came out either on punch cards or were printed by electric typewriters. Before a Mark II could be built, new developments allowed the construction of a new generation of computers that were a thousand times faster than Mark I. Still, R. Wade Cole of IBM reported that "there is hardly a computation center in the United States without at least one set of tables calculated by Mark I."[13]

About a year before Mark I was completed, John Mauchly and J. Presper Eckert of the University of Pennsylvania began plans for the construction of ENIAC (Electronic Numerical Integrator and Calculator). It was not completed until 1946 and thus was never used for its initial purpose—ballistics computations. It was, however, employed for other scientific calculations. Like Mark I, it was massive, containing nearly 18,000 vacuum tubes and 1,500 relays. It could be programmed to solve various problems, but programming required changing connections on a plugboard and sometimes took as long as a day to complete. Though not designed as a general purpose computer, "it was," according to Cole, "among the first 'electronic brains' to receive royal treatment in the Sunday supplements."[14]

The computers of the 1940s had greatly reduced the time needed to compile tables for ballistics purposes, but they were essentially single-purpose machines. New problems required new programs, and that usually meant that the computers had to be reset through a tedious manual process of changing plug-and-socket connections, rewiring, and resetting switches. Jon von Neuman, it is generally believed, suggested that the programs should be stored inside the computers in the form of numbers. With built-in programs, the computer could perform required operations faster than before. By the early 1950s, computers with built-in programs were seen to be applicable to problems in industry, commerce, science, education, social science, and other areas of government besides the Department of Defense. IBM was marketing small business machines, but as Evans observed, "it was universally assumed that computers could never play any meaningful role in the lives of ordinary people."[15] That conventional wisdom was wrong, for the cost of computers was soon to decrease significantly while their reliability increased.

In 1948, the Bell Telephone Laboratories announced that J. Bardeen, W. H. Brattain, and W. Schockley, who would later share a Nobel prize for their work, had developed the transistor, a three-layer crystal of solid material. The transistor soon introduced a measure of reliability and a decrease in computer costs that was truly revolutionary. Within ten years of its development, the transistor was clearly an economical and efficient replacement for the vacuum tube. The transistor controls electrical current just as a vacuum tube does but requires much less power because it does not need heat to work. The first transistors were about one cubic centimeter, much smaller than vacuum tubes, but attempts were made to make them even smaller almost as soon as they were developed. Those attempts were quickly successful.

To show how remarkable the reduction in size of the computer has been, Evans offered a description in terms of the human brain. If, in the early 1950s, one wanted to build a computer containing as many switches as the brain had neurons, it would have been as big as New York City and would have required more power than is used to run that city's subway system. By the early 1960s, the size would have been reduced to something about the size of the Statue of Liberty and would have needed a 10-kilowatt generator for power. While Evans was writing in the late l970s, the size had been reduced to that of a typewriter. He then predicted that it would soon be no bigger than the human brain itself and would need no more power than that provided by an ordinary portable radio battery.

The size reduction has been accompanied by a corresponding increase in the speed with which computers perform their operations. The units used to describe the elapsed time between operations have no meaningful parallels in ordinary human lives. A person can accomplish very little in a second. Yet, in that span of time, an electromechanical relay can switch itself from position to position twenty times. The vacuum tube does the same thousands of times a second. The development of the transistor and then the "chip" has allowed the manufacture of computers "whose switching potential is in the nanosecond range—that is billions of times in each tick of the clock."[16]

Another way to illustrate the dramatic revolution in the size, cost, and capability of computers is to compare their development with an imaginary but comparable development in the automobile industry. As Evans points out, had the automobile industry been as successful as the computer industry, a Rolls-Royce would cost less than $3, would travel about three million miles on a gallon of gasoline, and have enough power to propel the *Queen Elizabeth II*. Several could be garaged on the head of a pin. But automobiles are different from computers. By their nature they are restricted by time, space, and material, and their basic functions are severely limited to transporting people from one place to another and perhaps being the source of some kind of ego gratification. The computer's purpose, to maintain the analogy with the automobile, is to take information from one place to another and rearrange it. Its remarkable development has not only made it extremely portable and available to most people in the Western world but also has increased its range of their applicability. Computers may have been designed initially to perform arithmetical and mathematical functions, but of course today they are used to do much more than that.

Less than a handful of chips, each no larger than one square centimenter in surface and one millimeter in thickness, can now store the equivalent of a set or even several sets of encyclopedias. Immediate access to so much information on a demand basis will unquestionably influence public schooling. The nature of the change, however, is indeterminate. As mathematician Seymour Papert has noted, "there is a world of difference between what computers can do and what society will choose to do with them."[17] Whether they will cause any fundamental changes in schooling and the rate at which such changes may occur depends in part on how the process of schooling and its relationship to the media are conceptualized. Precise prediction of the effects of the computer is not to be found. As Edward J. Lias has written, "no society to date has ever established effective mechanisms for planning, controlling, or predicting the effects of new media."[18] Rather, as Lias points out, "we plan quite carefully for new buildings, new organizations, and new marriages, but rarely for new media."[19]

Perspectives on Schooling and the New Media

The influence of a new medium on public education can be examined by either scrutinizing (1) the ways it may alter traditional school conventions or (2) the possible consequences for teachers, students, and society as a whole. Typically, the arrival of a new medium is accompanied by two sets of responses. The first is basically an expression of fear about potential harmful effects on children.[20] That response is eventually transformed into an attitude that seeks to use the new medium to engage people in an old medium. An example of this approach is an attempt to engage children in reading by having them read about television or even television scripts. The second response proclaims that the new medium will enhance the schools' functions. A good example of this kind of response can be found in an article by William C. Norris. Writing in 1977 as chairman of the board and chief executive officer of Control Data Corporation, Norris proclaimed that "the past 30 years or so have produced a base of advancing technologies that have the power to *revolutionize* the quality, productivity, and availability of education." His notion of "revolutionize" did not suggest changes in either the means or the purposes of education but rather an application of technologies—television, radio, audio- and videotapes and discs, computers, computer conferencing, cable television, microwave and satellite transmissions, and computer-based education—to existing school purposes and conventions. "We must," he emphasized, "assemble and configure our several technologies into *a system that does what the present educational process does,* but does it with capital-intensive, productive technologies, rather than trying to drive still harder a labor-intensive process that can at best only stagger under the loads of higher needs, higher expectations, and higher and higher costs."[21]

Consideration of ways a new medium may influence society and affect its approach to schooling are rare. One instance of such a consideration has been provided by James Coleman. He reminds us that at the turn of the century most people lived in an information-poor society. Children secured most of their information from direct experiences in the family, neighborhood, and church. Their experience was "supplemented by a few windows to the outside world opened up by reading material at home or in school."[22] Levels of vicarious experience were directly related to the children's growth and their reading abilities. Those who learned to read well increased their level of vicarious experience, but for the most part, those levels "were very unevenly distributed throughout the population of children."[23]

Arrival of new media, especially electronic media, changed the ratio of vicarious to direct experience, democratized access and exposure to information, and changed the manner and rate at which children acquired information and experience. Once new media are introduced, "vicarious experience is no longer a slowly developing supplement to direct experience, but an early and large component of the child's total experience."[24]

When the ratio of vicarious experience to direct experience is increased, children enjoy unprecedented access to information. However, the phrase, "access to information," may be somewhat misleading by drawing attention away from the significant differences between information-rich and information-poor societies. "Access" suggests that people not only have the opportunity to use what is available but that they actually do so. They may or may not, however.

In an electronically rich society, the media are so pervasive that it makes more sense to consider the time the media are turned off rather than turned on, for smaller units are easier to count than larger ones. While grandparents and even parents may be able to remember when certain media were introduced into their lives—the first television set, the first color television, the first hand-sized calculator, or the video recording machine—children have no such memories. The media have always been part of their lives and "new" appliances—video games or home computers—are but attachments to existing equipment. Toddlers casually use

AURORA UNIVERSITY
CIRCULATION DESK
630-844-7583

This book has been obtained for your use through the courtesy of another library. As the borrower of this material, you are subject to the loan and fine policies of the library that has loaned this material.

If you wish to renew this item, please contact the library at least 3 days before the due date, or you may renew the item online following the directions below.

Renewing an item from the OPAC

1. Access the library's home page www.aurora.edu/library
2. Open "Illinet Online."
3. Open "Aurora University Library Catalog."
4. Open "My Account"
5. Select your home library (Aurora University)
6. Enter your library ID (2251100+your University ID number)
7. Enter your last name
8. Click on Log-in
9. When your record comes up, click in the renew box(es) to the left of the item(s) you wish to renew. If your record does not come up, contact the library at 630-844-5439.
10. Click on "renew selected items"

Patron _Jolly_

Due Date _10/14/2010_

wireless controls for television sets. Such devices are not exotic to the young, for they are readily available for trial and use just about everywhere they go.

The information available to children is not just greater than what was available to their elders; it is also distinct in kind. Information secured from media, that is, vicarious experience, differs from direct experience, affects individuals differently, and makes different demands. Direct experience requires action; the individual participates in few events over which he or she has some control. Vicarious experience requires less activity and usually is not deliberate, and the individual observes many events over which no control can be exercised. Moreover, the kind of presentation changes the nature of the information. As Coleman relates:

> Vicarious experience obtained through communication differs from direct experience in those ways that research has shown rumors to differ from reality. In rumor transmission (and more generally in any information transmission), the content is sharpened: complexities of reality are lost, the selectivity of the camera or pen impose an artificial unity of action, the intensity of the action is increased, and the participants are polarized into heroes and villains.[25]

There is general agreement that change in the ratio of vicarious to direct experience has had an effect on children, but little agreement as to what the effect is. While Coleman claims that "the vast increase in children's vicarious experience loads their cognition with attributes characterizing vicarious experience," he also reports that "social scientists do not yet know the consequences of these changes in the source of a child's cognitive world."[26] Some believe that it has led to more passive personalities, increased feelings of powerlessness, and a tendency to view the world in simple moralistic terms. There is some question about whether people are able to assimilate all the vicarious experiences they encounter.

The arrival of the new media has clearly changed the context in which schools function. In an information-poor society, the school and the family had much greater control over the child's cognitive world than either has now. The school's power in forming the child's values "arose from the selectivity the school exerted on visions of the outside world, through the alternative definitions of events it did not present."[27] Now, neither the school nor the family can counter or control the variety of information available to children. Once we could maintain secrecy and privacy. Now, with the access children have to computers, they can, as the news media reminds us, invade our privacy and secrecy.

The school has lost its monopoly and is no longer the only institution capable of teaching basic cognitive skills: languages, reading, spelling, mathematics. Now, according to Coleman, "educational television and the great number of books, toys, and games designed to help children learn to read or count provide many new learning devices for teaching children skills *outside* schools." As long as schools could maintain that they were best equipped to teach the basic skills, it was possible to hold on to the old notion of schooling: "namely, that the informational resources necessary to teach cognitive skills to the young were scarce and best provided by grouping children in a school around a teacher presumed to have such resources."[28] Now a variety of agencies—bookstores, toy stores, reading institutes, foreign language centers, and educational divisions of commercial enterprises—are all capable of doing some of what only the school could formerly do. That does not mean that children do not need tuition but the existence of those agencies creates "a further loosening of the physical constraints of location, which has necessitated grouping children together in single buildings with teachers."

To free tuition from a specific place does not mean that schools can or should be closed, "but it does make possible organizational arrangements that were impossible under the communication structures of past societies." The student and the computer terminal can be located in a variety of places, whether the student is using it to learn a basic skill or whether it is "programmed to simulate a particular physical or social environment and respond to a student who probes that environment."[29]

The changing communication structure in society led Coleman to one "inescapable conclusion." Schools, if they are to continue to be useful, must move their primary and traditional focus from the development of cognitive skills and the accumulation of factual knowledge to those functions that used to be satisfied outside the school. In earlier times, children were expected to contribute to their own and their families' welfare through some sort of productive activity. The abolition of that requirement in the "affluent society" effectively deprived many youth of the opportunity to develop this sense of responsibility. To allow children to learn to function as productive and responsible adults, schools need to adopt as a major goal the creation of opportunities for students to engage in "productive action with responsibilities that affect the welfare of others." The second goal that schools need to adopt, according to Coleman, is "the development of strategies for making use of the information richness and information-processing capabilities of the environment" so that students can learn to cope "with an information-rich and institutionally complex society." To accomplish such goals, the traditional purposes and modes of "teaching the child" must be abandoned. Students need to learn to be "contributors to a larger enterprise."[30]

While Coleman's proposals may seem revolutionary, and he does maintain that he has described "no less than a revolution in the concept and practice of educational institutions in modern society,"[31] he has abandoned neither the responsibility of the school for children's learning nor its responsibility for preparing children for adulthood. As he states the matter, his proposals do

> not mean that new educational institutions should neglect the child's learning. It means rather that a much broader conception of learning is necessary: a conception in which the roles, constraints, demands, and responsibilities of adulthood in a complex society are central; a conception in which experience once again becomes important; a conception that includes general strategies of how to make use of the environment to accomplish one's goals.[32]

Coleman analyzed the effects of communication structures on contemporary society and recommended a way to reconceptualize the school so that it can contribute to the realization of traditional values: the development of responsibility in individuals, the opportunity to engage in experiences that contribute to one's development in a wholesome way, and achievement, or the ability "to accomplish one's goals."

The Transportation Theory of Communication

Despite analyses and recommendations such as Coleman's, new media, especially the visual and the electronic media, tend to have little significant effect on how school processes are conceptualized and executed. Too many, in and out of school, subscribe to the transportation theory of communication. This theory maintains that communication is but the simple movement of a message across some distance, from one place to another, from one person to another. Subscribers to the transportation theory usually believe that people would behave properly if they had the right information. For them, all social and educational problems are communication problems. If the messenger, or the mechanical device, does indeed move the message from one point to another, then, so the theory goes, communication has occurred. The emphasis is on delivering the message. Little, if any, attention is given to either what the process of transportation does to the message or, more importantly, how the message is used once it is delivered.

The transportation theory makes the process of education seem deceptively simple. Students are receivers. Teachers are transmitters. Knowledge, information, the curriculum, perhaps the "basics," are the messages that have to be transmitted from one place to another or from one person to another. Tests are used as periodic measures of how well the message is being delivered. If it is not being received at a satisfactory level, adjustment of the transportation system is then obviously necessary. The usual working assumption is that the difficulties are in the "delivery system" and not due to student inadequacy or malfunction. It should not be surprising that the literature on teacher burnout is extensive, for as everyone knows, a malfunctioning component can be replaced more easily and cheaply than it can be repaired.

Thus, whenever there is a sign of a malfunction in the system, educators work out ways to build better delivery systems. Curriculum specialists focus on the amount, organization, and packaging of materials, while other specialists work out the best ways for teachers to deliver the messages. At times, attempts are made to satisfy the students by allowing them to choose from a wide variety of messages. At other times, students are grouped according to their ability to receive messages. At still other times, the array of messages is reduced and simplified to enhance the possibility that every receiver acquires the necessary minimum message.

While, as Papert argues, a variety of choices may be made about how the computer will be used in education, the dominant choice, at least initially, will probably be as just another technical aid to help, but not replace, the teacher. Accordingly, teachers will be assured that Computer Assisted Instruction (CAI) "is no more likely to replace classroom teachers than film-assisted instruction or book-assisted instruction."[33] Such assurances, however, can be misleading. As early as 1968, it was recognized that "some educational media have had a profound effect on how educational objectives should be stated."[34] How educational objectives are stated, especially the degree to which they must be behaviorally specific, does influence what teachers can and cannot do in the classroom. Examination of the teaching setting showed two ways to describe the design of the instructional process. To use the language of Robert M. Gagne, these were "extemporaneous design" and "pre-design." "Extemporaneous design" was used to describe instruction conducted through a human medium, the teacher, and the conditions in which the teacher made decisions about how to carry out the instructional process. In that situation, "flexible media" are emphasized rather than specific behavioral objectives or predetermined goals and procedures. However, when the human medium is replaced with a mechanical or electronic medium, the situation changes significantly. For example, Jack V. Edling has noted that:

> many nonhuman educational media, including those with electronic, mechanical, and photochemical elements, frequently employ "software" (educational materials) that must be preplanned and stored for use when required. This requirement for preplanned materials has created an ever-increasing need for a new kind of educational objective.[35]

The new kind of educational objective was, of course, the behavioral objective. Stating the objectives for a "pre-design" requires "an explicit description of the behavior of the learner in terms which make the behavior observable and measurable within the spatial and temporal context provided by the instructional situation." In such situations, it is imperative to have only objectives that can be met and "it is not sufficient to identify an aspiration, a dream, or a wish, and call it a behavioral objective."[36] In one setting, the design, the specificity, and the order of objectives are paramount. In the other, the freedom to design and execute forms of interaction with students "on the spot" is paramount.

Thomas Dwyer has described the transportation theory approach to teaching as algorithmic, "oriented toward defining predetermined goals."[37] "Outputs" must be specified in behavioral terms, and "inputs" must be selected to achieve the specified "outputs." "The algorithmic approach," he explains, "has the merit of giving structure and precision to what might otherwise be a fuzzy process, and of encapsulating that precision in a reproducible form." By creating a reproducible form with a sufficiently logical structure and sufficient detail, people or computers can be trained or programmed "to replicate the system exactly."[38] The replicative quality of the algorithmic approach appeals to many educational researchers because "much educational research is predicated on a 'pipeline' model, where the end product of that research is shipped out to users after development." Adherents of this model view "the teacher as a transmitter" of "products in reproducible form."[39] The teacher becomes no more than a passive user of techniques and materials supplied by others who have decided what is appropriate for whom.

More of the Same

The transportation theory is pervasive in most reviews of materials that describe how the computer can be used in schools. Such materials typically appeal to the values of the industrial society and use its processes as metaphors. They emphasize (1) increased rates of promptness among students who are assigned to work at terminals rather than to listening to teachers, (2) how a good program can help a teacher increase student productivity, (3) how computers hold down the rate of dropping out, and (4) how computers help students make higher scores on existing standardized tests. Many are but descriptions of how the human medium can be assisted with "new technological delivery systems."[40] Authors of such materials frequently attempt to assure teachers that they should not be threatened by the introduction of the computer. An example of this view is provided by William J. Loftus, who recommends that computer advocates "abandon their jargon-laden language for plain English." He maintains that "many teachers would be far more receptive to the pedagogical uses of the computer if only they could understand what they hear and read, if the computer were presented as a tool which could *help them to do what they already do better* and in a more efficient way."[41] To Loftus's dismay, "serious attempts are rarely made to show teachers how they can continue to teach the material they want to teach and use the books they want to use, while still taking advantage of the capabilities of the computer to assist in the learning process."[42]

Resistance to computers in the schools is usually attributed to unfamiliarity with their use. To break down this resistance, a well-designed program is needed to introduce the computer to students and teachers, but especially to teachers because, according to Barbara Townsend and Deborah Hale, faculty are among those most reluctant to use technology in the classroom:

> Their resistance stems from several sources, including lack of knowledge about the specific technology, the view that its use is inappropriate in certain disciplines such as the humanities, and the fear of being replaced by machines. Also, since some students may already be familiar with computers through their own purchase and use of them, faculty could feel threatened by their own lack of expertise in an area where students might be more knowledgeable than they.[43]

The way to dispel fears and change attitudes about computers is by increasing the teachers' knowledge. Articles related to computer use in their particular fields, slide-tape presentations, and demonstrations that include hands-on activities are recommended. Advocates claim that experience in giving a machine a command or in working through a program segment will enable faculty to see for themselves just what the machines' potential and limitations are. "In essence, they will discover that the microcomputers are neither replacements for faculty nor the solutions to all educational problems."[44]

CAI programs were first designed over two decades ago. In 1963, with funds from the Carnegie Corporation, Patrick Suppes and Richard C. Atkinson began research and development on basic skills programs for disadvantaged children at Stanford University's Institute for Mathematical Studies in the Social Sciences. Atkinson supervised the development of reading programs and Suppes supervised programs in mathematics. Subsequent funding from the National Science Foundation (NSF) and the U.S. Office of Education enabled them to develop their work further. In 1965, with funds provided through Title III of the Elementary and Secondary Education Act, they established a program that gave every elementary school student in Macomb, Mississippi, access to a computer terminal on a daily basis. Besides developing programs for disadvantaged students, the Institute developed mathematics and language arts programs for deaf students and university level courses in logic, foreign languages, and mathematics.

Descriptions of the Stanford courses indicate that they may bear a close relationship to courses conducted through a human medium. In 1965, Suppes offered a description of a mathematics program developed at the Institute for Mathematical Studies in the Social Sciences in which he indicated that "since the user may make a response only by touching the light pen to the screen, there are certain limitations on the kinds of formats that can be used." Some portions of a mathematics textbook had to be rewritten so it would "fit a multiple choice or simple keyboard format," but the material in the program did not deviate significantly from the outline of the text.[45] In 1975, he reported that the introductory courses in logic at Stanford was "one in which the students do essentially all of their work at computer terminals" and was then "the only version of introductory logic taught at Stanford."[46] There was also a course in axiomatic set theory and plans to develop courses in proof theory, the foundations of probability, and the foundations of measurement for social scientists.

Effect of Computers on Education

Many assurances are offered to teachers to allay their alleged fear of being replaced by computers. However, computers have had and will have effects on education, and all effects will not be benign. Suppes indicated that through the use of computer-based instruction he was able to change his teaching practices and increase his productivity. By ceasing to offer lecture courses and dividing his time between computer-based courses and advanced seminars, he was able to double his own teaching load. However, his account of how computer-based instruction would affect the role of the teacher was not significantly different from the projection of Fred M. Newman and Donald W. Oliver who were *not* advocating widespread use of new media in education. In 1967, they observed that new media "serve the laudable objective of communicating more fully and more effectively knowledge that the experts consider worth transmitting." While they admitted that "these new forms of communication have a significant impact on the organization of schools, on scheduling" and might "possibly" affect the teacher's role in the classroom, they also indicated "it is doubtful that they will affect in any profound way the role of the student or the way he perceives his task in school."[47]

Suppes explained that teachers would be involved with the use of computers in two ways: in "drill-and-practice systems" and in "tutorial systems." Use of drill-and-practice systems would, he predicted, affect the teachers "only slightly" by relieving them of the need to prepare and to correct practice exercises. Use of tutorial systems would, however, affect the teacher "more significantly." Where "tutorial systems" were employed, students would be introduced to new basic concepts by the computer in a variety of ways. If students needed help or had questions beyond those the computer answered, teachers would have the time necessary for the required and seemingly always desirable "personal interaction."[48]

Significantly, Suppes indicated that the use of the computer was not likely to change the content of the school curriculum. His own work, like that of most others, was chiefly directed toward the teaching of basic skills for students between the ages of six and twelve. In fact, he reported, "it was not the intent of those developing these computer-based courses to lead to changes in the content of curriculum." Rather, the intent was to develop programs for curriculum that would remain relatively unchanged for the next half century: reading, writing, and arithmetic. Use of the computer was but a means to change the style of the curriculum that would remain relatively unchanged for the next half century: reading, writing, and arithmetic. Use of the computer was but a means to change the style of the curriculum, to change its content. It was to adapt the existing curriculum to students. As Suppes explained, "the computer is being used in this case to fine tune curriculum that has been taught in one form or another since systematic education began, but to fine tune it, in a way that has not been previously possible, to the needs of individual students."[49]

As long as the use of the computer is seen as a way to increase the efficiency of traditional school conventions, the claim of Newman and Oliver that the use of the new media will not affect how students see their task in school will likely be applicable and accurate. For example, Suppes suggests that computer-based instruction could be used to provide courses for gifted students in the elementary school that would otherwise not be available. However, such options would not relieve them of standard drill-and-practice routines. Professional athletes, he explained, continue to practice their skills even after they are highly developed and so too do gifted students need to practice their skills. Both mind and body need exercise: "The kind of performance we expect of gifted students can only be obtained, in my judgment, by a continued regime of drill and practice, and such a regime is just as much a desirable aspect of their intellectual training as it is of their physical training."[50]

From Suppes's viewpoint use of the computer in education is unlikely to significantly change school practices for either students or teachers. It will allow a greater degree of individualized instruction and thereby free some students from "regimentation and moving in lockstep." All students, bright and not so bright, will be able to complete their assigned lessons at an appropriate pace. Some will not be left behind, and some will not be held back while others catch up with them. Suppes estimates that students will spend only 20 to 30 percent of their time at computer terminals.

Not all are willing to turn over practice-and-drill routines to computers. In April 1982, a Committee on Basic Skills of Education was founded to put an end to "the excessive promotion by computer manufacturers suggesting that computer literacy will solve the ills of the educational system." The Committee claims that it is not necessary to complicate the elementary school curriculum with expensive hardware because, "except for specialized computer jobs such as programming, the ability to operate computers isn't necessary for most people entering the workforce."[51] For the Committee, "direct knowledge transmission is always best."

Objections to new technologies and fears of their effects are not new. Researchers follow a pattern in determining the influence of new media on children. According to researchers at the University of Illinois: "Early in the development of a new medium research is devoted to describing media use, then attention shifts to the health effects of the new medium, and lastly, effects of media content on values, attitudes and behavior is addressed."[52] Not surprisingly, when hand-sized calculators became inexpensive enough for most pupils to own them, there was debate about their effects. Some still fear the advent of an Asimovian society in which people will not know how to perform basic arithmetical operations without the aid of an electronic device. George Steiner's prophecy that we are in the process of breeding "computer mutants" who "will be out of touch with certain springs of human identity and creativity, which belong to the full use of language rather than mathematical and symbolic codes"[53] is a legitimate fear for some but not for all.

Effectiveness of Computerized Instruction

Reviews of the effectiveness of CAI are mixed. In 1974, materials were developed for use in the instruction of reading through the University of Illinois' PLATO system, but an evaluation of PLATO's use with kindergartners and first graders failed to reveal any significant gains in achievement among pupils in the programs. The cost of developing the programs was too expensive, and the process provided too little feedback and control to satisfy teachers.[54] However, students make significant gains in reading when they use a computer-based system that provides practice on repeated lessons. Barbara Thompson conducted an exhaustive review of the use of computers in the teaching of reading and found that such programs were useful for drill and practice.[55] Donald L. Alderman found that "although empirically-based research regarding the comparative effects of CAI over conventional approaches in the teaching of reading do not universally show improvements in learning, the preponderance of evidence supports marginal improvements in English skills, in general, and to a lesser degree in reading comprehension."[56] Research at MIT's Artificial Intelligence Laboratory seems to support the contention that programs can be designed to teach first graders how to write and "string" sentences.[57] Other reports indicate that CAI is effective in teaching "topical invention" and spelling.[58]

In 1981, the EPIE Institute which publishes "the educational consumer's newsletter" examined the major commercial software programs available for microcomputers and microprocessors and discovered that 95 percent of the available programs were drill-and-practice programs for arithmetic. Most programs emphasized skill development and recall of previously learned facts. Curiously, the device designed to relieve people of the need to perform computations is being used to teach them how to do so. Significantly, EPIE found no significant materials for secondary education.[59]

Peter Kelman, editor of the Addison-Wesley Series on Computers in Education, has declared that the greatly touted computer revolution in education was announced too soon. There are few good materials and very little prospect that any will be forthcoming in the near future.

> The hardware manufacturers would seem to have very little stake in the production of quality educational materials. After all, school sales now, and in the foreseeable future, represent a small fraction of their total market. Furthermore, the creation of quality software in particular is an expensive, time-consuming proposition, requiring expertise not normally found in hardware companies. As far as they are concerned, software development is best left to the professional educators, educational publishers, and the funding agencies that have historically supported curriculum development.[60]

However, none of the traditional curriculum developers appear to be meeting the challenge of producing appropriate software. Some educators are either skeptical or hostile about the use of computers and others have neither the knowledge nor the inclination to develop materials. It may also be the case that educators would have difficulty deciding what to produce. As Harold Shane has remarked, "perhaps one of the gravest impediments to rapid development of suitable software is the lack of agreement among educators at all levels as to which methods of instruction are best and what the goals of education should be."[61] Textbook publishers have little experience in the field and some very good reasons not to develop materials. "How," Kelman asks, "does one motivate school sales reps to make the effort to sell one or two $50 disks to a school when instead, with the same effort, they could sell hundreds of copies of basal texts which are then reordered every year?"[62]

While there is "a bewildering array" of software, little of it is "any good," Kelman claims. Problems with the software include "bugs" that render programs inoperable and incorrect assumptions about children's thought processes. Most software imitates traditional approaches to schooling by employing "the very limited and limiting"[63] drill-and-practice and tutorial systems. In a review of a software program for a critical reading program, Jeff Nilson admitted that the use of the computer to teach rules of logical inference to enhance the reading comprehension skills of students is consistent with established models of reading programs, but he also emphasized that not all material read by students follows the formal rules of logic. "Puns and other forms of humor, euphemism, metaphors, professional hedge words, like appear and seem," he accurately noted, "all play with logic or distort it."[64] Whether software devoted exclusively to logical inference will in fact help students understand the variety of ways in which language is used in the materials they read is doubtful. There is, he maintains, little value in using "the computer as a page turner for a workbook."

Kelman claims that unless software producers develop better materials and begin to use the computer for "the development of curricular approaches for which the computer is uniquely suited and which could not be done effectively without the computer," the computer revolution will go the way of other educational revolutions. Computers and poorly produced software will find their place in "the classroom closets in which sit the broken 8mm film loop projectors, the video tape recorders that never quite worked when they were needed, the hopelessly boring 'teaching machines' and the snazzy rarely used slide tape apparatus, complete with 'synch' box."[65]

An Alternative to the Transportation Theory

Not all proponents of computer applications in education adhere to the transportation theory. In remarks prepared for delivery at the Second Annual Southern California Conference of Computer-Using Educators in 1982, then governor Edmund G. Brown, Jr., not only called customary attention to how computers would free teachers "of repetitive drill and practice tasks" and thereby allow them more time for "personalized assistance" but also emphasized that "the personal computer linked with telecommunication is not just a new 'tool' speeding up our present way of life, but is a fundamental change affecting the very patterns of relationships which lie at the basis of society itself."[66] For Brown, good use of computers promises to signal the beginning of an educational revolution which would be nothing less than *"a qualitative* leap in which we vastly increase the quality of public education and realize the age-old dream of empowering each person to reach the limit of his or her ability."[67]

In testimony given to a subcommittee of the U.S. House of Representative's Committee on Science and Technology, Arthur Luerhmann, Associate Director of the Lawrence Hall of Science at Berkeley, emphasized the necessity of distinguishing between the computer as "a medium of instruction" and the computer as "an object of instruction." There were, he maintained, different questions for the different foci:

> Proper questions . . . to ask about the computer as a medium of instruction are (1) whether it is better and (2) whether it is cheaper than conventional ways of managing and delivering instruction. But the appropriate questions to ask about the computer as an object of study are quite different—(1) Is it more important to learn to use a computer than to learn subjects now being taught? Can computer use be taught effectively to a broad spectrum of students?[68]

Luehrmann was pointing out that neither CAI (computer assisted instruction) nor CMI (computer managed instruction) "will teach people to use the powerful personal computers which American technology is capable of delivering to our citizenry." More important than any question about the effectiveness of CAI or CMI was the need for all students to learn to use a computer. "CAI and CMI are," he noted, "applications of technology to teaching English and teaching math, not to teaching computing itself."[69] Learning to use a computer entailed more than learning one of the computer programming languages. That was an "occupational skill," which has its "benefits," but it is not as important as teaching students "to structure their thinking so that it can be communicated to a computer; structure a problem in such a way that it can be presented to a computer for solution."[70]

To teach people to use computers in the way Luehrmann specified was to give them an additional way to think about problems. Typically, people use logic, mathematics, or their native tongue to think about problems. To be able to write a problem as a computer program, Luehrmann argued, was to have "yet another way of representing one's understanding of a problem."[71] To be able to think about a problem in a different way was the important reason for teaching people to use computers.

Because the computer could be programmed to simulate the instructional process, Luehrmann argued that students could be taught to master it or they could simply be subject to it. He preferred that they learn to master it. He urged that students be taught to use computers to locate information from a variety of existing data bases; to construct ecological systems; to use algorithms in problem solving; to secure and analyze laboratory data; to edit and rewrite materials; and to present information in graphic form. Not to learn to use the computer to perform such tasks is to remain a computer illiterate and, he asked, "how much longer will a computer illiterate be considered educated?"[72]

Seymour Papert's LOGO

Those who urge that computers should be used by educators to do something different frequently cite the work of Seymour Papert of MIT's Artificial Intelligence Laboratory. Papert developed LOGO, a computer language that employs graphics, sound, and an electronic turtle robot that responds to user's commands. When he set out to develop LOGO, he deliberately tried to build a language that would enable children as young as three years old to work at the computer and at the same time satisfy the requirements of sophisticated adults. For Papert, children are active participants in the learning process. They appropriate from their surroundings. They are not passive agents to whom teachers are to administer specified materials in prescribed ways at specified times in regulated ways.

Papert's notions about how children learn are influenced by the theories of Swiss philosopher and psychologist Jean Piaget. From Piaget, he accepted the "model of children as builders of their own intellectual structures."[73] This model focuses on how much children learn before they go to school and without formal instruction. They learn speech, intuitive geometry, which enables them to get from one place to another, "and enough of logic and rhetoric to get around parents."

Papert differs from Piaget, however, in that he explains the failure of children to learn some concepts to the scarcity of appropriate materials in the child's surroundings rather than to the child's stage of development or to the difficulty of the task. In some instances, the culture provides children with important experiences that enable them to build their cognitive structures. For example, children build an "intuitive" sense of number because they have so many experiences with pairs, (e.g., parents, shoes, and socks). In some instances, however, materials are insufficient to make a particular concept "simple and concrete." At other times, "the culture may provide materials but block their use." Thus, explains Papert, "the mathophobia endemic in contemporary culture blocks many people from learning anything they recognize as 'math,' although they may have no trouble with mathematical knowledge they do not perceive as such."[74]

Mathophobia obstructs learning, but the effects of it, Papert reports, interact with "other endemic 'cultural toxins' " such as our theories of aptitudes. Consequently, the difficulties children encounter in learning mathematics are frequently but the first stage of "an intellectual process that leads us all to define ourselves as bundles of aptitudes and ineptitudes, as being 'mathematical' or 'not mathematical,' 'artistic' or 'not artistic,' 'musical' or 'not musical,' 'profound' or 'superficial,' 'intelligent' or 'dumb.' "[75] Instead of learning to be confident and willing to explore, children learn to be insecure, fearful, and accepting of artificial and unnecessary restrictions on their ability to learn.

In developing LOGO, Papert and his associates started from a position very different from that of most educational researchers. They began with how children learn *outside* classrooms. They began not with the difficulties children encountered in learning formally prescribed and presented lessons but with how children learn how to talk. Because children learn to communicate with others without any formal lessons, Papert believed that three-year-old children could learn to communicate with computers in the same natural way. Instead of beginning with the usual strategy of programming the computer to dispense information, to tutor, or to give drill-and-practice lessons, he reversed the situation. Placed in the LOGO environment, children have the opportunity to program the computer. In the LOGO setting, the child "becomes more active and self-directed." Knowledge is not dispensed but acquired, according to Papert, "for a recognizable purpose." Knowledge becomes "a source of power and is experienced as such from the moment it begins to form in the child's mind."[76]

Having children learn to program the computer to do things for them creates a different and better approach to knowledge and learning. The process of programming the computer does not fit into an either-or view of the world. Programming teaches children to try again, to determine whether a program can be fixed, or "debugged." As Papert testified at the hearings of the Congressional Committee on Science and Technology:

> At MIT we have studied how children of elementary school ages who have learned to program computers in our LOGO computer-rich environment are able to use computer concepts to understand their own processes of learning and logic. For example, they can think about how they 'debug' a problem as a way of correcting it locally without having to demolish the whole and appreciate this programming strategy as a way to solve all kinds of problems, even those that come up far away from a computer terminal. . . . We have studied how these children are able to acquire an articulate approach to the process of learning by taking the computer as a simplified model of certain aspects of their own minds. We have seen many cases in which this process leads to very great improvements not only in 'basic skills' but in children's images of themselves as intellectual agents; and the improvement of self-image leads to improvement in learning.[77]

In his testimony to the Science and Technology Committee, Papert related that a computational revolution was undoubtedly occurring in American society, but it was a revolution "driven by industry rather than by the educational community." There was no question that it would "take place in the home whether or not the schools accept it."[78] Because other technologies had failed to fulfill their promises, there was understandable skepticism about another new technology that promised to bring about educational improvements. Yet, not to understand the unique features of the computer and the possibilities it offered was to fail to see "that its imminent mass diffusion into the home offers us the social possibility of broadening our definition of education." It was now possible to bring about "the learning society."[79]

To just wait and see how the computer could be used to transform education was to ignore the million children who dropped out of school each year and who might have been saved from "functional illiteracy" through "sensitive use of the computer presence." It was also to ignore the possibility that "the computer could release a hundred thousand physically handicapped people from a life of isolation, dependency, and cultural deprivation."[80] With access to the computer, many handicapped could have more social contacts and also the ability to develop economic independence. However, to use the computer to assist those who failed in school and the handicapped required a paradigm shift—a new way of thinking about educational phenomena and their relationships to each other. Traditional approaches usually focused on small changes in serial order without paying attention to the entirety of the enterprise. Consequently, no one change was ever great enough to make any significant difference, and the collection of innovations were usually incompatible with each other.

Papert argued that the computer was different from other forms of technology that were used in attempts to improve schooling. Computer technology "leads to a *global, holistic rethinking of education;* of how and where it happens, and of what is learned by whom." If computers were to be effectively employed, educators would have to surrender their habit of "thinking in terms of *improvements* of an existing system" and begin to think in terms of a *"holistic-global redesign* aimed at improving overall performance." Not to approach change in a holistic manner was to insure "that the computers will be used amateurishly, fadishly or under the influence of the educational software houses with the best advertising agents."[81] To do that would be tantamount to depriving children of the opportunity to learn mathematics and to learn how to write in their own language with a high degree of proficiency as easily as infants learn to speak.

Looking Ahead

The computer, especially the microcomputer, will undoubtedly be used by millions of people inside and outside the school. Discussions and speculations about the effects of computer use are no longer confined to educational and computer experts. For example, *Time* reported that in 1981 the cost of video game playing was over 75,000 person-years and over $5 billion.[82] However, the results of a study in California, show the cost in less spectacular terms. There, 80 percent of the children interviewed "spent five dollars or less per week, the price of a movie. Only 7 percent spent lunch money."[83] Nonetheless some worry and complain about the alleged effects of the games on the players, and many cities have acted to ban children from game parlors or to insure that game parlors are not located too close to schools. *Glamour* informed its readers that a symposium held at the National Academy of Sciences indicated that too much time at a video-display terminal may cause a facial rash "accompanied by itching, slight redness and a few pale pimples."[84]

In November 1982, the *Tampa Tribune* published two Associated Press articles side-by-side on its front page that suggested that video games were harmful for children but good for the elderly. The first article was an account of the warning of Surgeon General C. Everett Koop that the nation's children were becoming addicted "body and soul" to video games and that the games were having adverse mental and physical effects on adolescents.[85] The second article reported that the activity director of a nursing home in Grand Haven, Michigan,

Christy Tavener, introduced video games to help residents "develop their motor skills" as well as "to encourage creativeness, decision-making ability . . . and to strengthen self-confidence." Thus, while the surgeon general suggested that the games were bad for the mental and physical health of children, the activity director of a nursing home reported that "from what we have seen, it's totally just the opposite with the elderly."[86]

By the middle of the 1980s, the outcry about video games had faded somewhat. There are still video arcades and video games all about us but we are now less concerned about their effects on us. Like all other media, they have been absorbed into our social environment and are taken for granted. Like all other media, they have failed to either destroy us or to save us.

What remains to be determined is whether all children will have equal access to computer use. The number of computers in schools is increasing but not uniformly. A survey conducted by Market Data Retrieval revealed that while 80 percent of the nation's 2,000 largest and richest public high schools have at least one microcomputer, only 60 percent of the poorest schools have one. That difference, prompted *Time* to ask whether the rich will get smarter while the poor play video games.[87]

Daniel H. Watt, a research associate with the MIT LOGO Project, has observed that while students from affluent homes have access to computers, school is likely to be the only possible place where many students will have an opportunity to use computers. "It would be tragic," he observed, "if inner-city schools and schools in working class communities decide that they can't afford to purchase computers for their students or that the development of computer literacy is not the highest priority for use of the computers they do have." He also reported that many urban schools have employed the computer to improve students' mastery of the basics and that such use "in which the computer tells the student what to do seems ideally suited to producing 'second-class citizens' in a computer-based society."[88]

The computer literacy of teachers will in large measure determine that of their students. Some schools of education have begun to offer graduate courses and even degrees in computer education, and others have begun to consider making computer literacy a requirement for all who seek a teaching certificate. Computer literacy may be as simple as teaching *about* computers or it may entail instruction in how to use computers in the classroom.

To achieve anything other than minimal teaching about computers schools will have to make significant investments. Besides the required investments in equipment and software, considerable time will have to be allocated to teacher training. It takes a year to train a "resource teacher" capable of working effectively with other teachers, and additional time is necessary for the in-service training of other teachers. For some teachers, the move toward computer literacy may present opportunities to develop new skills and assume new responsibilities. For others, it may be a requirement to learn new ways of doing their jobs. Few teachers will likely escape the effects of the reallocation of resources that will be needed to prepare for the use or misuse of computers in schools.

Advocates of computer use in the schools for instruction will have to address the issue of the quantity and quality of available "courseware." As has been noted, many complain that available materials are often simply fancy technological turners of workbook pages. When Brown spoke to California educators, he acknowledged that many of the available materials are "still in primitive stages of development" and indicated that he wanted to make funds "available for classroom teachers, private firms or anyone else able to make innovative software programs more widely known throughout the state."[89] The director of the EPIE Institute, P. Kenneth Komoski, has complained that the practice of teaching students to do long division "with expensive 'courseware' using a device that is many times more sophisticated than the hand-held calculator that has made such paper work obsolete, seems plainly ludicrous."[90] He clearly rejects the argument that educators must continue to purchase poor materials from publishers because if they do not, the publishers will conclude that they cannot make money from "courseware," will leave the market, and never produce good materials. He urges educators to recognize that material is not necessarily new or different or better just because it is "in the chips." Rather, it is, he argues, the responsibility of educators to recognize that the lack of good materials "is a problem that educators must start solving right now (for themselves, for the publishers, and for the learners) through a consumer demand for software that lives up to—and that stretches—the capabilities of the hardware they are buying." Not to do that is, he claims, "to count the days when we are no longer the most educationally and technologically advanced country in the world."[91]

Stanley Pogrow believes that educators do not have the luxury of deciding whether they will demand or fashion new and better materials. He claims that educators have no choice but to render schools "technologically relevant" by attending to the social and economic forces created by the widespread availability and use of computers. He warns that "the increasingly critical relationship between technology and economic development will make the outcry for access to training in computer technology particularly aggressive." Before the 1980s end, "those students who acquire only minimum competences (as these are currently defined) will be functionally illiterate and unemployable in 1990 as are individuals who do not possess such competences today."[92] If educators resist the public's demand for "a technologically relevant curriculum," they will witness what Pogrow calls the "environmental collapse" of the schools. "Environmental collapse," he explains, occurs when clients cease trying to change an institution to meet their requirements and turn to "an economically compelling alternative made possible by a fundamentally new technology."[93]

The irony of the current situation is that the very technology that is beginning to create a demand for a different kind of education also provides the opportunity for an alternative to public education. Technology has the potential for allowing private schools to compete with public schools in terms of range of curricula as well as in terms of cost. More significantly, attitudes toward formal schooling could be changed by technological developments. In some cases, access to "powerful networks of technologies in U.S. homes could lead to a rejection of formal schooling in favor of home education." Parents who want the schools to continue to provide custodial care for their children while they are away from the home want different kinds of care. If children learn basic skills through use of technologies in the home, then, Pogrow suggests, "parents and the general public will then expect the schools to provide more creative and technologically relevant learning and socialization activities."[94]

Conclusion

Whether public schools will be able to meet the demands for a technologically relevant curriculum and survive challenges from private schools that are not wedded to traditional curricula and teaching methods will depend upon the willingness and ability of public schools to make schooling less labor intensive. Computers will be needed to perform routine functions so that teachers are free to work "on the more creative functions of both the traditional and new curricula." Such use of computers will entail more than a new division of labor between machines and teachers in the classroom. As Pogrow describes the change, "this move away from the present labor-intensive delivery of basic skills instruction will require new philosophies of and techniques for budgeting, fiscal management, classroom management, and teacher preparation."[95]

This would not be easily accomplished. Extensive use of computers in schools depends not only on identifying the correct technology but also on creating the appropriate organization. Schools would have to be organized to accept new systems; and there is some question about whether their current organizations are the proper ones for such technological adoptions. As Luehrmann noted:

> Information technology systems have failed often in education because they are not compatible with existing educational systems. Most information technology systems, for example, require very large initial investments in hardware, software, and courseware. . . . Schools . . . are small decentralized, diverse and independent organizations accustomed to 'cottage industry' production and development methods. They do not buy complete instructional systems; they hire teachers. A new type of organization would be needed to make use of such technology systems and the schools themselves would be threatened by such organizations.[96]

Experience gained from several decades of trying to introduce changes into schools has demonstrated that it is insufficient to design new plans and then send them on to the schools for implementation. The world view and the values of the personnel in schools are different from those who plan the changes. As Ernest R. House has noted, schools are more traditional than other sectors of the society and are not as quick to accept the modernization process. For House, "it is not surprising that schools would resist modernization pressures, particularly when these are originated from without."[97] As anthropologist Edward Spicer has explained, "almost all changes proposed as a result of extensive knowledge of science and technology originate in one subculture and, to be accepted, must be made intelligible and given value in terms of another subculture."[98] If House and Spicer are correct, effective changes will be possible only if teachers understand, support, and value those changes. Training programs and provision of extensive amounts of information may equip teachers with the techniques necessary to effect the changes but "knowing how" is not the same as understanding and accepting. If we are to have teachers who understand the possibilities before us, we will need teachers who understand what Marshall McLuhan meant when he wrote:

> The medium, or process, of our time—electronic technology—is reshaping and restructuring patterns of social interdependence and every aspect of our personal life. It is forcing us to reconsider and reevaluate practically every thought, every action, and every institution formerly taken for granted.[99]

Notes

1. Christopher Evans, *The Micro Millenium* (New York: Washington Square Press, 1979), ix.
2. Ibid., x.
3. Blake M. Cornish, "The Smart Machines: Implications for the Society of Tomorrow," *The Futurist* 15 (August 1981): 6.

4. Patricia Marks Greenfield, *Mind and Media: The Effects of Television, Video Games, and Computers* (Cambridge, Mass.: Harvard University Press, 1984), 127.
5. Cornish, "The Smart Machines," 6.
6. "Here Come the Microkids," *Time,* May 3, 1982, 53.
7. Reported in *USA Today,* June 5, 1984.
8. Greenfield, *Mind and Media,* 127.
9. Harold G. Shane, "The Silicon Age," *Phi Delta Kappan* 63 (January 1982): 304.
10. Graham T. T. Molitor, "The Path to Post-Industrial Growth," *The Futurist* 15 (April 1981): 23.
11. Evans, *Micro Millenium,* 23.
12. Ibid., 33.
13. R. Wade Cole, *Introduction to Computing* (New York: McGraw-Hill, 1969), 25.
14. Ibid., 26.
15. Evans, *Micro Millenium,* 41.
16. Ibid., 54.
17. Seymour Papert. *Mind-Storms: Children, Computers, and Powerful Ideas* (New York: Basic Books, 1980), 5.
18. Edward J. Lias, *Future Mind* (Boston: Little, Brown, 1982), 13.
19. Ibid., 14.
20. Ellen Wartella and Byron Reeves, "Recurring Issues in Research on Children and Media." Paper presented to the American Educational Research Association, New York, March 20, 1982, p. 9.
21. William C. Norris, "Via Technology to a New Era in Education," *Phi Delta Kappan* 58 (February 1977): 451. Emphasis added.
22. James S. Coleman, "Education in Modern Society," in Martin Greenberger (ed.), *Computers, Communications, and the Public Interest* (Baltimore: The Johns Hopkins Press, 1971), 116.
23. Ibid., 117.
24. Ibid., 118.
25. Ibid.
26. Ibid.
27. Ibid., 119.
28. Ibid., 120.
29. Ibid., 121.
30. Ibid., 125.
31. Ibid., 129.
32. Ibid., 125–126.
33. Lias, *Future Mind,* 116.
34. Jack V. Edling, "Educational Objectives and Educational Media," *Review of Educational Research* (April 1968): 177.
35. Ibid., 178.
36. Ibid.
37. Thomas Dwyer, "Heuristic Strategies for Using Computers to Enrich Education," in Robert P. Taylor (ed.), *The Computer in the School: Tutor, Tool, Tutee* (New York: Teachers College Press, 1980), 89.
38. Ibid., 89–90.
39. Ibid., 90.
40. Christopher Dede, "Educational, Social and Ethical Implications of Educational Technology," *Programmed Learning and Educational Technology* 18 (November 1981): 210.
41. William J. Loftus, "A User's Balance Sheet on Computer Assisted Learning," *Technological Horizons in Education Journal* 10 (September 1982): 120. Emphasis added.
42. Ibid., 121.

43. Barbara Townsend and Deborah Hale, "Coping Strategies for Resistance to Microcomputers," *Technological Horizons in Education Journal* 8 (November 1981): 49.
44. Ibid.
45. Patrick Suppes, "Computer-based Mathematics Instruction," in Taylor, *The Computer in the School,* 219.
46. Patrick Suppes, "Impact of Computers on Curriculum in the Schools and Universities," in Taylor, *The Computer in the School,* 242.
47. Fred M. Newman and Donald W. Oliver, "Education and Community," *Harvard Educational Review* 37 (Fall 1967): 29.
48. Patrick Suppes, "The Teacher and Computer-assisted Instruction," in Taylor, *The Computer in the School,* 234.
49. Suppes, "Impact of Computers on Curriculum in Schools and Universities," 238.
50. Patrick Suppes, "The Future of Computers in Education," in Taylor, *The Computer in the School,* 253.
51. "Citizens Committee Attacks Use of Computers to Teach Basic Skills," *Educational Technology* 22 (June 1982), 7.
52. Wartella and Reeves, "Recurring Issues in Research on Children and Media," 3.
53. Quoted in "Here Come the Microkids," 58.
54. David Schuelke and D. Thomas King, "New Technology in The Classroom: Computers and Communication and the Future." Paper presented to the American Educational Research Association, New York, March 20, 1982, 3.
55. Barbara J. Thompson, "Computers in Reading: A Review of Applications and Implications," *Educational Technology* 20 (August 1980).
56. Schuelke and King, "New Technology in the Classroom: Computers and Communication and the Future," 3. Also see: "Evaluations of PLATO" (Princeton, N.J.: Educational Testing Service, 1978).
57. Schuelke and King, "New Technology in the Classroom: Computers and Communication and the Future," 4.
58. Ibid. Also see: Hugh L. Burns and George Culp, "Stimulating Invention in English Composition Through Computer-Assisted Instruction," *Educational Technology* 20 (August 1980), and Patricia Nolen "Sound Reasoning in Spelling," *Reading Teacher* 33 (February 1980).
59. "Microcomputer Courseware/Microprocessor Games." EPIE Equipment Report 98/99e. (Stony Brook, N.Y.: EPIE Institute) Vol. 15, No. 1/2 (Fall/Winter, 1981).
60. Peter Kelman, "What if They Gave a Computer Revolution and Nobody Came?" *Classroom Computer News* (January/February 1982): 10.
61. Shane, "The Silicon Age," 308.
62. Kelman, "What if They Gave a Computer Revolution and Nobody Came?" 10.
63. Ibid., 54.
64. Jeff Nilson, "A Critical Look at a Critical Reading Program," *Classroom Computer News* (May/June 1982): 62.
65. Kelman, "What if They Gave a Computer Revolution and Nobody Came?" 54.
66. Edmund G. Brown, Jr., "Computers and the Schools," *Technological Horizons in Education Journal* 10 (September 1982): 99.
67. Ibid., 100.
68. *Computers and the Learning Society.* Hearings before the Subcommittee on Domestic and International Scientific Planning, Analysis and Cooperation of the Committee on Science and Technology, U.S. House of Representatives, 95th Cong. lst sess, October 4, 6, 12, 13, 18, 27, 1977 (Washington, D.C.: Government Printing Office, 1978), 313.
69. Ibid., 320.

70. Ibid., 318.
71. Ibid.
72. Arthur Luehrmann, "Should the Computer Teach the Student, or Vice-Versa?" in Taylor, *The Computer in the School,* 135.
73. Papert, *Mind-Storms,* 7.
74. Ibid., 8.
75. Ibid.
76. Ibid., 21.
77. *Computers and the Learning Society,* 267–268.
78. Ibid., 262.
79. Ibid., 264.
80. Ibid., 265.
81. Ibid., 259–260. Papert's emphasis.
82. "Games That Play People," *Time* (January 18, 1982).
83. Greenfield, *Mind and Media,* 98.
84. "Computer Rash," *Glamour* (February, 1982).
85. Peter Mattiace, "Surgeon General Says Youth Addicted 'Body and Soul'," *Tampa Tribune,* November 10, 1982.
86. Michael McKesson, "Ms. Pac Man Provides New Therapy at Nursing Home," *The Tampa Tribune,* November 10, 1982.
87. "Peering into the Poverty Gap," *Time,* November 15, 1982, 69.
88. Daniel H. Watt, "Computer Literacy: What Should Schools Do About It?" *Instructor and Teacher* (October 1981): 86.
89. Brown, "Computers and the Schools," 100.
90. P. Kenneth Komoski, "The Educational Revolution Is Not 'In the Chips,' " *Education Week* 1 (April 21, 1982): 24.
91. Ibid., 24.
92. Stanley Pogrow, "On Technological Relevance and the Survival of U.S. Public Schools," *Phi Delta Kappan* 63 (May 1982): 610.
93. Ibid., 611.
94. Ibid.
95. Ibid.
96. Arthur Luehrmann, "Technology in Science Education" in Taylor, *The Computer in the School,* 149.
97. Ernest R. House, "Three Perspectives on Innovation: Technological, Political, and Cultural," in Rolf Lehming and Michael Kane (eds.), *Improving Schools: Using What We Know* (Beverly Hills, Calif.: Sage Publications, 1981), 37.
98. Quoted in Harry F. Wolcott, "Is There Life After Technology?" *Educational Technology* (May, 1981): 25.
99. Marshall McLuhan, *The Medium Is the Message* (New York: Random House, 1967), 8.

7
Television

Development and Growth

Although the idea for television came later than for the computer, its diffusion throughout American culture has occurred much more quickly. As with the computer, full and successful development of television came after mechanical approaches and devices gave way to those which were electronically based. In 1884, the German scientist Paul Nipow was awarded a patent for a mechanical scanning device that broke down images into bits that were relayed as electronic impulses to a light source and another mechanical scanning device. In the 1920s, both the Scot John Logie Baird and the American Charles Francis Jenkins further developed mechanical scanners. By 1928, Ernst Alexanderson was conducting television tests at General Electric's experimental station.

Work on electronic television began in Russia at the St. Petersburg Institute of Technology where by 1907 Boris Rosing had already developed a television system that was more electronic than mechanical. Rosing's work ended with the Russian Revolution in 1917, but his assistant Vladimir Zworykin further developed it while working for Westinghouse in Pittsburg. In 1923, Zworykin demonstrated an all-electronic system at Westinghouse by telecasting an image of a cross. The definition of the picture was poor, however, and the contrast low, and Westinghouse decided the system was not commercially practical.

Zworykin continued to work on the development of a device that would transmit light just as a microphone transmits sound. Using the photoelectric effect noticed by Albert Einstein in 1905, Zworykin developed a camera that was appropriately called the iconoscope. For the receiving end, he developed a kinescope to replace the cathode tube he used in his 1923 demonstration. In 1929, he demonstrated both the iconoscope and the kinescope at a meeting of the Institute of Radio Engineers. Among those who saw and appreciated his demonstrations was RCA's David Sarnoff, who had urged commercial development of television in the 1920s.

Sarnoff brought Zworykin to RCA, and in 1930 NBC began experimental telecasts from the top of the Empire State Building. By 1933, Zworykin had refined his system to improve the picture resolution by producing a picture with 240 lines instead of the original 50 lines. In 1939, NBC inaugurated regular television services, beginning with the opening of the World's

Fair in New York. Franklin D. Roosevelt, the first president to appear on television, declared the Fair "open to all mankind." Many were introduced to television at the fair's RCA pavilion.

The prospect of war postponed further development of television. In May 1941, President Roosevelt declared a national emergency that required RCA to divert its materials and productive capacities to war preparation. However, on July 1, 1941, RCA did convert its experimental station (W2XBS) into a commercial station (WNBT) and presented a ten-second commercial for Bulova watches for which it received nine dollars.[1]

Television Enters the American Home

In 1948, just one year after Clarabell the Clown, Howdy Doody, Princess Summer Fall Winter Spring, and Uncle Bob Smith began entertaining children after school, there were only thirty-six television stations and about a quarter million home television sets in the United States. Now there are over 1,000 stations; 75 percent are privately owned commercial stations, and 25 percent are either public or educational stations. In 1949, less than 3 percent of American homes had television sets; five years later, over 50 percent had them. By 1975, television was as common as indoor plumbing and 97 percent of the nation's homes had at least one set. Collectively, in 1975 Americans spent the equivalent of 33 million years viewing television. Now the incidence of television in the home is greater than that of heat, indoor plumbing, or refrigerators. More than a third of the nation's homes have two or more sets.

Estimates vary, but in the average home, the television set is apparently on between five and six hours a day, and 95 percent of that time is devoted to watching commercial broadcasts. Most children begin watching television just before they reach their third month, or three to four months before they learn to sit erect without assistance. By the time they are three years old, "children begin to watch TV with systematic attention," designate some programs as their favorites, are able to sing commercials, and "are asking for products they see advertised."[2] Children between ages three and five are believed to spend over fifty hours a week watching television.

Upon entering kindergarten, children have already spent more time learning about the world and social roles and relationships from television than the time their parents spent sitting in college classrooms to earn their bachelor's degrees. Every night of the year, about three million children between ages two and eleven are watching television at 11:30 P.M. At 1:00 A.M. a fourth of that three million are still watching.[3] By the time children are graduated from high school, they will have spent between 11,000 and 12,000 hours in school and between 15,000 and 22,000 hours watching television. During that extended watch, they will have seen more than 350,000 commercials. By the time a person reaches 65, he or she will have spent about ten years watching television.

The claim that television is the babysitter for many children is not without foundation. In one study reported by Letty Cottin Pogrebin, 20 percent of the four- to six-year-old children preferred television to their mothers and 44 percent preferred it to their fathers. Another study found that junior high school students believed television more than they believed their parents, teachers, friends, books, radios, or newspapers.[4] Adults seem to like television as much as children. Nearly a third rely on television as their sole source of news and two thirds admit it is their prime source of news. Next to doctors and dentists, television is the single most important source for health information for Americans.

The Effects of Television

While the rapid growth of television is relatively easy to document, its effects are not so easy to determine precisely. As Max Lerner noted in 1957, "the psychic and cultural deposit left on young and old alike by the broadcasting arts is not likely to be resolved easily."[5] He cited the hyperbolic claims of TV columnist Harriet Van Horne, who feared that people would become less literate as they watched television, would lose the art of conversation and only tell jokes to each other, and would become by the century's end "squint-eyed, hunch-backed, and fond of the dark."[6] While the streets are not filled with "squint-eyed hunchbacks," television has unquestionably influenced and continues to influence children and adults.

One reason why so little is known about the effects of television is that some in the intellectual and academic communities have tried to ignore it. In the early 1970s, Daniel Boorstin noted that while five hundred years elapsed before the printing press democratized learning, "television conquered America in less than a generation." It "democratized experience." "It was no wonder," Boorstin concluded, "that like the printing press before it, television met a cool reception from intellectuals and academics and the other custodians of traditional avenues of experience."[7] Almost ten years later, Stephen R. Graubard asked: "What is it that keeps us from reflecting more on an age that has seen such vast changes in its communications?" There is a need to study the extent and the limits of video effects on public attitudes rather than continue to "dwell" on the medium's power. It is necessary to know, he claims, "why so many fear visual media."[8] Douglas Cater has claimed that "thinking people have difficulty coming to grips with television" because "they have yet to develop satisfactory ways to gauge the effects of this environmental phenomenon."[9] Robert Hornik argues that "the intrinsic nature of television, in particular its universal availability within the United States, makes it a difficult phenomenon to study," and "researchers have not even approached the frontier of what is investigable about its impact on schooling."[10]

Another difficulty in determining how television has influenced our society and its people is our persistence in turning to the past to give us direction for a present that is unlike anything we have ever experienced. Charles Weingartner has emphasized that "as we move into the future at supersonic speed we're not going to get much help in figuring out what it all means from looking, as Marshall McLuhan says, in the rear-view mirror."[11] McLuhan tried to teach us that most innovations in the media are typically and incorrectly seen as simple extensions of what already existed. The movie was seen as a moving book with pictures, but it turned out to function as something other than a book. Television, in turn, was also defined by what already existed: a radio with pictures. Television, however, is not just one means of communication added to what already existed at the time of its introduction. If we want to understand the effects of television, or of any new medium of communication, we should study what we typically do not study—the transactions between the individual and the total environment. As Weingartner has warned, "you never have an old environment *plus* a new element—you don't have an old Europe plus the printing press—you always have—and we seem not to have learned what this difference means yet—*a totally new environment, requiring a wholly new repertoire of survival strategies.*"[12]

Effects on Other Media

While a new medium affects people and their environment, it also affects other media. The media compete with each other for audiences and for revenues, and in the competition, they are transformed and take on new functions. Before the advent of universal television in the United States, radio was dominated by three major networks that offered a schedule of variety shows, drama, and news similar to that which the major television networks now offer. After television, radio became "a largely local medium primarily—though not exclusively—devoted to music." While its audience was once heterogeneous and local, now "each station reaches a fairly homogeneous segment of the public attracted by its particular format, so that across stations there is a diversity unknown in television."[13]

In the mid 1940s, before television was in most homes, annual movie attendance was about 82 million. By 1970, it had fallen to 19 million. As movies ceased to be the major source of inexpensive family entertainment, they began to focus on subject matter that television could not readily broadcast. As television became the medium used by people to view movies, movies were changed to suit the requirements and limitations of television.

Television also affected the print medium. After the advent of television, several general purpose magazines—*Saturday Evening Post, Life,* and *Look,* for example—lost advertising revenues and ceased publication. When they reappeared, they did so with circulations smaller than they had previously enjoyed. Television even affected comic book sales, which, according to George Comstock, "fell from 600 million in 1950 to half that in 1970."[14] While some forms of print lost their audience to television, opportunities were created for other forms. Materials related to television became popular. Books were advertised as being the story that was telecast, and *TV Guide,* which is sold to 18 million people a week, became the largest selling magazine in the United States.

The influence a new medium has on existing media should not go unnoticed. Even if we believe an earlier medium was somehow "better" and should be protected and used, it is highly unlikely that we can preserve its original status. If we attempt the return, we are likely to find, as Gertrude Stein would have said, "no there there." Moreover, television as a medium is not static. As Alan M. Rubin has noted, "as the emergence of television changed the nature of radio, so are the new technologies altering the nature of television." New technologies and variations of existing technologies—cable TV, subscription television, direct broadcast via satellites, video cassettes, video recorders, and video discs—are all changing how, when, and even why individuals use their television sets. Whether viewers will have more choices or only the illusion of choice remains to be determined, but it is possible that the television industries that now "broadcast" will be in the business of "narrowcasting."[15]

The Telecast Image of Reality

However television has affected us and our environment, there is no denying that it has given Americans access to experiences they did not previously have as well as given them those experiences in new ways. Public events of all sorts—political conventions, rallies, riots, sports, wars, artistic performances, demonstrations, protests—can all be seen and experienced "live." Watching, or experiencing the live event via television is, however, not just a simple substitution for being present at the event as an actual observer. In fact, watching the event on television may even have advantages. For many, it is an easier, better, and more economical way to view an event. Via television the viewer can see clearly without interference from other spectators. Television offers close-ups and details that cannot be seen from the balcony, the bleachers, or the street's edge. It even makes the event more comprehensible by providing commentators to explain its meaning.

Perhaps more importantly and probably more subtly, television puts an event in order for us by unifying a variety of confusing activities and scenes. The historian Daniel J. Boorstin, no stranger to how political processes work, reports that in 1956 he secured tickets to the Democratic National Convention for himself and his sons. Once admitted to their seats, they found themselves "confused by the floor events." Fortunately, the arrangements committee provided television sets for the spectators in the gallery. To make sense of what was happening on the floor, he and his sons watched those sets, which showed them "precisely the same programs we would have seen from our living room." The delegates down on the floor, he suggested, were "unlucky" and "must have been more confused than we were about what was going on."[16] Now spectators at a variety of events—football and baseball games, parades, and conventions—bring their portable television sets with them to see what they have seen, what they will see, what they failed to see, what they were supposed to see, or what they could see no place other than on television. It may be, as Boorstin observed, that "when it comes to public events, now you are often more there when you are here than when you are there!"[17]

Boorstin's discussion of the parade given in Chicago in April 1951 to honor Gen. Douglas MacArthur shows that television not only clarifies events for viewers but also transforms those events. Before the parade, local newspapers gave accounts of how spectacular it would be. While many of those who lined up along the street "complained it was hard to see what was going on" and sometimes only earned a "fleeting glimpse" of MacArthur for their hours of waiting, video viewers enjoyed a different perspective. The "actual spectators" were "doubly disappointed." They saw very little and knew that they would have seen more had they watched television at home. They went not so much to see but to be seen by their friends and perhaps even by themselves at a later time.[18]

The "Pseudo-Event"

Boorstin reports that television also creates events for viewers. He witnessed the televising (we would now say taping) of a tug of war game on the University of Chicago campus and thought the winner's victory to be "suspiciously easy" until he learned that he had been watching "a reenactment for television." On the day of the original game, "telecasting conditions were not so good."[19] In early December 1960, Mayor de Lesseps S. Morrison of New Orleans asked for a moratorium on press and television coverage of school integration protests because he believed the coverage was making the situation appear worse than it actually was. Mayor Morrison related that "in many cases, these people go to the area to get themselves on television and hurry home for the afternoon and evening telecasts to see the show." He also observed television personnel set up a scene "and then, having persuaded a group of students to respond like a 'cheering section,' had them yell and demonstrate on cue." Boorstin calls these "pseudo-events." In the pseudo-event, each person can be both actor and viewer, subject and object. In a world full of pseudo-events, many are understandably unsure about what is real and what is spontaneous.[20] As. E. B. White wrote in 1938 after witnessing a television demonstration:

> A door closing, heard over the air, a face contorted, seen in a panel of light, these will emerge as the real and the true. And when we bang the door of our own cell or look into another's face, the impression will be of mere artifice.[21]

According to Boorstin, television is only one creator of pseudo-events, although it is the latest, and perhaps most powerful, of a number of technologies that assign the print medium a secondary role and make up what he calls the "graphic revolution." The media that constitute the graphic revolution enable people "to make, preserve, transmit, and disseminate precise images—images of print, of men and landscapes and events, of the voices of men and mobs"—with unprecedented speed and efficiency.

In less than a century, actually in about just two generations, "Americans crossed the gulf from the daguerreotype to color television." In 1873, dry-plate photography was introduced and by 1941 television was "commercially important." In between those introductions, Americans witnessed the development of other media for the transmission of sounds and images: the telephone, the phonograph, easy-to-use cameras, and the radio. As more and better images could be easily created, multiplied, and distributed, "vivid image came to overshadow pale reality,"[22] that is, the image and that for which it stood became confused. Thus, "sound motion pictures in color led a whole generation of pioneering American movie-goers to think of Benjamin Disraeli as an earlier imitation of George Arliss, just as television has led later generation of television watchers to see the Western cowboy as an inferior replica of John Wayne."[23]

More recently, Wayne C. Booth has indicated that the movie *Reds* made an impression on himself and others that was certainly different from what had happened in the Russian Revolution but an impression that could not be dismissed. The movie's "visual intentions were so powerful that none of us," he has reported, "is likely to break entirely free of them, no matter how many books we may read about the historical characters." For Booth and his associates, the image became the reality: "John Reed was vividly and forever fixed as our image of Beatty; Zinoviev was forever Jerzy Kosinsky; Andre was forever Malle's Andre."[24] The image is more engrossing, demands less of us, and seems to give us more than reality. With the image we have no blanks to fill in, no wonderment, no puzzles to solve.

In the age of the graphic revolution, our attention has become more focused on the image or the recreation of reality than on reality itself. As Boorstin claims, "there is hardly a corner of our daily behavior where the multiplication of images, the products and by-products of the graphic revolution, have not befogged the simplest old everyday distinctions."[25] We no longer apply "true" or "false" to our experiences but ask whether they are "credible." Making a fact "believed" is more important than finding the fact itself. The graphic revolution "has by no means generally sharpened or clarified the visible outlines of the world" but it has "transported us into a new world of blurs." Rather than giving us clarity and precision, "the whole apparatus of the graphic revolution has put a new elusiveness, iridescence, and ambiguity into everyday truth in twentieth-century America."[26]

The use and creation of images is not, contrary to the conventional wisdom, the sole province of the commercial sectors of our society. It has become a major function of all our institutions. As Boorstin explains:

Our churches, our charities, our schools, our universities, all now seek favorable images. Their way of saying they want people to think well of them is to say they want people to have favorable images of them. Our national politics has become a competition for images or between images, rather than between ideals.[27]

We have become so accustomed to images that the "natural begins to seem contrived." We look not for indications that items have been improved or transformed but that they have not been worked over in some way. We ask for the cigarette that is "*un*filtered," the novel that is "*un*abridged," and the "*un*cut" movie.[28]

Before and After Television

To emphasize that the media, especially the graphic media, have transformed our experience is not necessarily to claim that experience was somehow better or unsullied before their arrival. A mediated experience is simply different from a direct experience. Long ago, Harold Innis, whose work inspired McLuhan, pointed out that a new technology for communication changes that which we think about, the form and character of that with which we think (the alphabet gave us new forms and the graphic revolution also gave us new forms—images), and the area in which we develop our thoughts.[29]

Even print transformed experience. As Lewis Mumford wrote in the 1930s, "more than any other device, the printed book released people from the domination of the immediate and the local." "Print," he suggested, "made a greater impression than actual events."[30] The introduction of printing changed the character of European civilization. According to Neil Postman, fifty years after the invention of the printing press, "a sharp division developed between those who could read and those who could not, the latter being restricted to a medieval sensibility and level of interest, the former being propelled into a world of new facts and perceptions."[31] Those who knew how to express their thoughts and feelings in print and who knew how to read had their area of communication enlarged and had things to consider and discuss that nonreaders did not have.

Just as civilization moved from a nonprint to a print era, it has, especially in the United States, moved into the television era. For those who began their lives in the print era but now live in the television era, the difference can be striking and even unsettling. Henry Malcolm has noted that children and adults have different conceptions of television and that their conceptions are the consequences of their early and different experiences. Writing in the early 1970s, he remarked that "every adult over the age of thirty-five has seen the entrance of the television set into the house, not as another piece of furniture but as an ultimate source of information about the world beyond the home." Children, however, "see the television set as part of the home environment—like beds, chairs, and record players."[32] For them, television is only one of many objects in a world of abundance. It is a technology that enables them to bring what the adults perceive to be the world "out there" to themselves whenever they wish. For the children—Malcolm calls them the "post-television generation"—television is not a medium that brings events to them as it does to adults. They see it quite differently.

For them, it is a window on the universe, with a "handle" (the channel changer) that gives them a world which they can create with the simple turn of the wrist. To most children, the thought that there is somebody "out there" who determines what programs, commercials, and subjects will be shown, seldom occurs. Thus, they can easily become "wrapped up" in what they are seeing, as though it were a part of their lives. It is, in a profound sense, their world which is happening.[33]

Malcolm contends that the post-television generation has developed a view toward life that is fundamentally different from that of their parents who grew up on the other side of television. With the help of television youth have had their narcissistic egos so strengthened that they believe they can make reality conform to whatever they want. The "images" they experience become the standards to which they expect the world to conform. If Malcolm's claim is accurate that youth, unlike their parents, consider the traditional pressures to conform to social reality as unwarranted and illegitimate invasions of their world, then we have been and are witnessing a new world and a new generation. If Malcolm is correct, we need to ask not just whether television causes more or less violence in society or how it influences reading scores but how television has created new criteria for the interpretation of experience and new criteria for its evaluation.

The difference between youth and their elders can be described as a generation gap, but it must be emphasized that this gap signifies more than the need for one group to catch up with the other or for one or the other group to display more patience and understanding. Weingartner also agrees that children have grown up in a world different from their parents' "mostly as a result of developments in media of communication," but maintains that it is not enough to note merely that the conflict between generations is a consequence of the youth having had grown up with "a different set of assumptions, values, perceptions, patterns of behavior from the old." Rather, he emphasizes that the media have touched the lives of all, young and old, and that we must grow used to the idea that as soon as we have a new world view and a new set of adjustments worked out, they are likely to become "irrelevant because so much has changed."[34]

Print and Television

The demands that television makes on the user are different from those made by print. Many claim that no instruction is required for television viewing. However, it is a learned ability, as is demonstrated by the confusion that the introduction of photographs and moving pictures causes among people in different and especially preindustrial cultures. Most of us do not need systematic instruction to learn how to look at photographs and to watch television, but most of us do not learn to read without systematic instruction. Compared to any form of graphic communication, print is complicated and indirect. Print requires that ideas, emotions, directions, or whatever be transformed into non-iconic symbols—countless arrangements of the alphabet's characters—and set down on a surface that can be transported to the reader who will then decode those symbols. Effective use of print also entails learning the conventions of a long and complex rhetorical tradition that "requires one to take the measure of sentences in a cautious and rigorous way, and of course, to modify meanings continuously as new elements unfold in sequence."[35]

The mastery of spelling, vocabulary, logic, and grammar that are required for reading are so complex that reading is taught in stages. Accordingly, there are preprimers, primers, graded readers, young adult books, and even adult books. Television, contrary to the desires of some critics and reformers, makes no such distinctions. While it uses language, its essence is the endless succession of images that can be perceived by all, young and old, without any prior training. Print allows us, even requires us, at times, to stop and ponder a passage, a sentence, or even a phrase. It even requires the reader to bring some aesthetic and intellectual content to the reading. Television has no such pauses and no similar requirements. It may be too fast to allow the viewer to form conceptions, but that is no matter; only perception is required.

Michael R. Winston claims that the information we receive from television's succession of images is "neither discursive nor reflective." For him, television is no match for print.

> Free of the restraints of syntax and linear discussion, television conveys a 'sense of authenticity' through the intrinsic superiority of the visual image, giving the viewer the impression that he or she has grasped a matter intellectually, when in fact only the absorption of definite visual images that *suggest* ideas and conclusions has occurred. It is simply easier for television to give the viewer the feeling that the images are accurately reflective of a complex reality than it it is to achieve the same effect with print.[36]

For many critics, television is an inferior medium but undoubtedly the most democratic. It makes few, if any, demands on the user and has no prerequisites. All are eligible and equipped to watch. Nearly all do.

Television and Schooling

The conventional wisdom holds that television is somehow responsible for the poor reading skills that children and adults display in such great abundance. Many of us believe that television interferes with what schools try to do. In 1982, *U.S. News & World Report* presented a cover story entitled "What is TV Doing to America?" It reported that the decline in SAT scores—"the broadest measure of academic ability"—began in the early 1960s when television made its way into nearly all homes. Had it not been for television, it seems, the average score on the verbal part of the SAT would not have fallen from 478 to 424 and the average score on the mathematics portion would be closer to 502 than to 466. A panel of experts appointed to study the decline noted that children spent many hours watching television and concluded that this had something to do with the decline. Television, it seemed to the panel, had, for many children, become a substitute for parents and teachers. Presumably, more time with parents and teachers and less time in front of television would increase scores.

According to Paul Copperman, president of the Institute of Reading Development in San Francisco, administration of an Adult Performance Level test to people who graduated from high school in the 1960s and 1970s showed that "20 percent of the American population was functionally incompetent, that is, could not perform the basic kinds of reading, writing, or computing tasks—such as calculating the change on a small purchase, addressing an envelope, reading a want ad or filling out a job application."[37] Although television is held responsible for the number of people who are "functionally incompetent," evidence to support those commonsense observations is not significant.

Subsequent to the *U.S. News & World Report* article, the Associated Press reported that "a growing body of research contends television has been unfairly blamed for declining reading scores among children." It further reported that a publicity agency of the television industry, the Television Information Office, had published a paper, "Television and Education: Assessing Academic Achievement," in which it was claimed that children's reading scores are more closely related to socioeconomic factors than to television watching and that "heavy television viewing" is not the cause but the result of difficulties in school.[38]

According to Hornik, most research on the relationship between schooling and television has been directed toward testing one or more hypotheses in the following areas: (1) displacement; (2) intolerance for the pace of schooling; (3) interest stimulation; (4) learning of school-equivalent content; (5) learning of new cognitive skills; and (6) learning of instrumental information.[39]

Adherents to displacement hypotheses assume that the time children spend watching television would otherwise be spent in some activity related to or supportive of school activity, such as reading, sleeping, significant interaction with one's peers, or some sort of exploratory problem-solving activity. The displacement hypotheses are supported by a large number of correlational studies that show an inverse relationship between the amount of television children watch and their level of school achievement and reading abilities. Those who watch less appear to do better at reading, mathematics, and language than those who watch more. However, when other variables, such as intelligence, parental control, motivation, and social class, are considered in such studies, the relationship between watching and achievement weakens considerably.

A major difficulty in conducting research on the effects of television on schooling, is that researchers must assume that some exposure to television, no matter how insignificant, may have an influence. In the United States, it is virtually impossible to find children who do not receive some exposure to television. To overcome that difficulty, a study in Canada compared children from two towns—one with and one without television. Results showed that children with access to television had better vocabularies than those who did not. While that advantage seemed to disappear by the time most children reached the sixth grade, it persisted for less able children. It was also found in the Canadian study that two years after the "No-tel" second and third graders acquired access to television, their advantage in reading ability was lost. Another study conducted in El Salvador with junior high school students confirmed the findings of the Canadian study. There, as students' access to television increased, the rate of growth in their reading ability decreased. Thus, Hornik has concluded that:

> Once researchers control for what the student brings to school in IQ, social background and other characteristics, the correlation between television exposure and achievement in mathematics, or in any other subject which has been measured (including science, social studies and others) is invariably zero or close to it.[40]

Still, critics of television believe a direct relationship exists between "heavy" or "excessive" viewing and poor school performance. A 1976 Gallup poll indicated that 49 percent of the respondents believed that poor education was due to too much television. Since the 1950s, researchers have found a consistent relationship between low IQ, especially for males, and heavy viewing. However, as is emphasized in the 1982 National Institute of Mental Health Study of television effects, "because the studies are correlational, it is not possible to say at this stage of the research whether those with lower IQs prefer to watch a great deal of television or whether being a heavy viewer leads to lower scores."[41]

There is no assurance that children would spend more time on homework if they did not watch television. It is also wrong to assume that before television children had nothing else to distract them. Moreover, while "homework time" is correlated with "classroom ability," researchers have yet to determine what, if any, causal relationships exist between homework time and school performance. While it is generally believed that children would read more if they watched less television, Hornik has concluded that children did not read very much before television and that they do not read very much now.

The widely held belief that children are intolerant of the pace of schooling because they have grown accustomed to the faster pace of television is supported by a number of observers. They claim that television so quickly changes the focus of attention that children have become incapable of sitting still for more than twelve minutes at a time. The Associated Press reported that New York University's professor of communications, Neil Postman, indicated that "television had probably harmed classroom performance by shortening children's attention spans and by emphasizing pictures over words."[42] No experimental evidence supports such claims, however, and there are no before-television measures to compare to after-television measures. It is simply not possible to determine the effects of thousands of hours of television watching with a simple short-term experiment. Moreover, changes in attention span can be explained by other factors. As Hornik has observed, "attended population, curriculum, and teaching method changes within the school, and a raft of sociocultural changes outside the school all are rivals (or complements) to television as causes of any in-school learning changes."[43]

Capturing children's attention is not, however, a problem confined to parents and teachers. In a discussion of educational aims used in determining how "Sesame Street" would be produced, Gerald S. Lesser, Chairman of the National Board of Advisors to the Children's Television Workshop, explained that "to teach effectively, children's attention must not only be caught and focused, but also sustained."[44] One device the designers used was humor. Another was pace. While denying charges that "Sesame Street" is "continuously frenetic," Lesser maintained that the pace of the program was an important factor in sustaining children's attention.

> The appeal of any single segment is tied closely to the contrasts provided by the episodes preceding and following it. Both fast-paced and slow-paced material will hold children's attention. . . , but a slow, peaceful episode is more appealing when surrounded by fast-moving episodes than when it follows another slow, quiet piece. Interest in any particular episode is higher if it creates a pace and mood that looks, sounds, and feels different from the one that preceded it. The principle that visual action and contrasts appeal to young children need not mean that the action must be rapid or frenetic to be effective; instead, the pace of the action should be varied.[45]

Lesser reports that the producers of "Sesame Street" did not heed the advice of educators about the attention span of children. The producers believed they needed a one-hour program to provide any "educational benefit," while "the most common misgiving of educators was that this would be too long to hold young children's attention."[46] That misgiving, Lesser believes, was proved wrong. By properly designing the segments and their sequence, "Sesame Street" has been able to hold the attention of children for the entire hour.

Some may argue that the structure of "Sesame Street" and other similarly designed programs teaches children to expect the school, like television, to provide a fast-paced episode after a slow and quiet episode. As reasonable as such an argument may seem, however, no experimental evidence supports it. Adults frequently forget that children are developing beings who have a motor side (active) as well as a mental side (cognitive) that needs training and exercise. Also, adults' opinions about what children can or cannot do may be founded on memory or beliefs about how they behaved as children. Memory is not always perfect.

Defenders of television often argue that it stimulates the interests of viewers, including children, and thereby encourages them to learn more through reading. Since 1977, the Columbia Broadcasting System's Education and Community Service Division has been conducting a script-reading program and working with educators as part of its effort to promote the use of commercial television in the classroom. CBS provides scripts for students to read, study guides for teachers, and other promotional materials. In November 1982, it telecast its thirtieth such project, "The Blue and the Gray," an eight-hour program in three parts. CBS distributed over a million copies of a 120-page abridgement of the 400-page script and 300,000 posters that included the Gettysburg Address and a picture of Gregory Peck as Abraham Lincoln. CBS also paid for 200,000 copies of a sixteen-page brochure on the program, which was distributed by the Cultural Information Service, a nonprofit organization that tries to educate people through television. The brochure included a plot outline, a brief biography of Bruce Catton upon whose history the series was based, discussion questions, and a bibliography for those who wished to learn more about the Civil War. One newspaper account of CBS's efforts to promote "The Blue and the Gray" reported that "all over the country, junior and senior high school students and some college students will be getting credit for watching the series."[47] Certainly those who believe there is no substitute for reading the book would object to awarding credit for watching a show designed to entertain the largest possible audience. Advocates could argue that such arrangements are appropriate because "television and film are more effective instructional vehicles than the other media in producing immediate gains in knowledge." Opponents, however, can cite the research of the Israeli psychologist Gavriel Salomon to argue that those gains "occur at the expense of reasoning skills that would otherwise develop as a consequence of the mental exercise imposed by the absence of cinematic qualities."[48]

Television efforts to promote books do frequently lead to increased sales and greater circulation of a book and related materials in libraries. Such promotions, however, seem not to increase reading as much as they redirect it. According to Hornik, "there is no reason to believe that total reading or quality of reading is affected by interest whetted by television."[49] Television is not a good medium for selling all kinds of books. Comstock explains that selling of books via television entails a "mutual exploitation among talk show, author, and publisher." However, because the audience to whom the sales promotions are directed is a "mass audience nonliterary in taste," the books that can be effectively sold are "largely circumscribed by boundaries of factuality, self-cultivation, titillation, and accessible prose—the how-to book, promising mastery in sex, mind, soul, and finance; the how-it-was book, usually in entertainment; and the how-it-*really*-was and is in finance, art, politics, the cosmetic business, television, and other pinnacles of glamour and notoriety."[50]

Much of what is taught and discussed in school can be viewed on television. Besides courses offered via television by universities, many programs seek to instruct as well as entertain viewers. In addition to "Sesame Street," the National Geographic specials, documentaries, regular and special news programs, and PBS programs such as "Nova," "Shock of the New," and "Connections" provide illustrations and access to materials far greater than those available to most teachers. Researchers have yet to determine how much overlap exists and how much "school content" is learned from television. Research on the effects of "Sesame Street" shows that under some conditions some children learn some things. Specification of the conditions and identification of the kinds of children who learn under those conditions presumably would permit effective use of television as an instructional medium. However, if that were to be accomplished, the setting would not be "natural" and would begin to approximate the manufactured, structured, and controlled aspects of the classroom.

The "learning of new cognitive skills hypothesis," described by Hornik as "the most intellectually intriguing of all the hypotheses," unlike the others, is directed not to the relationship between television and conventional school learning but to the learning of skills required for use of the television medium. It maintains that television, like other media, has its own set of processes, techniques, and symbols and that practice in the use of the skills needed for viewing is required for effective use and understanding of the medium. For example, the user has learned how to use the symbols and to follow the techniques used by the medium if he or she is not confused when the scene on the screen changes from a full array of activities to a detail or a close-up. Laboratory studies have shown that skills necessary for viewing can be taught, but no definitive statements can be made about how children use those skills outside the laboratory. Apparently too, not all people use all the skills that could be employed but only those they need to make sense of what is happening on the screen. If users do not use all the skills at their command, they probably will not derive as much from the "events" they view as is possible. Moreover, the skills that children develop for television viewing would not even be applicable in school, for the medium of schools is largely, if not exclusively, print.

No evidence supports any claim that television provides children with information to help them learn or understand how school works or what they must do to get through a school day successfully. Students do know about occupations that are depicted on television, and the introduction of television seems to be associated with students adopting higher educational and occupational aspirations than they had before they had access to television.

Critical Receivership Skills

While some have attempted to determine how television influences children, frequently because they want to protect children from such influences, others simply accept that it is a part of their lives and seek to make it "a positive and beneficial experience" through instructional programs. Such programs, generally known as Critical Receivership Skills (CRS), Critical Television Viewing, or Critical Viewing Skills, are based on the belief that just as children "are taught to appreciate literature, to read newspapers carefully, and so on, they need to be prepared to understand television as they view it in their homes."[51] One approach to CRS conceives of the individual as a consumer of information and is designed not to protect but to assign responsibility to the consumer. This approach assumes that "the effect of a communication can be controlled by modifying the assimilation and analytical skills of the receiver."[52]

According to one of CRS's developers, James A. Anderson, the viewer is not passive but active and therefore responsible for his or her use of television: "People do things *with* television; television does not do things *to* people."[53] CRS is an approach that accepts television, refuses to ignore it, and does not try to convince people that it is an unworthy or inferior medium. In fact, Anderson finds it necessary to specify what critical receivership skills are not:

> They are not rules of when to view, what to view, or how long to view. They are not the imposition of elitist notions of intrinsic values residing in a medium of presentation such as print or in specific content types. They are not the generation of anxiety or guilt over the uses one has for the medium and its content.[54]

People can learn to manage television's influence. The task of educators, as always, is to teach people to discern and assess the "communication messages which inform, entertain, and persuade." Such critical thinking will simply "involve the skillful collection, interpretation, testing, and application of information regardless of medium of presentation."[55]

CRS instruction teaches a kind of introspection. Children learn to become aware of and to analyze their own motives and reasons for watching television in relation to what they accept or reject and the meanings they derive. So that children can comprehend what they watch, they are taught how to identify to whom messages are directed, what the intent of a message is, and how linguistic, visual, and audio elements are used to construct and transmit a message. CRS also includes topics often found in either the language arts or the social studies curriculum. Milton E. Ploghoft even claims that "as young students work with television content, they will develop skills of observation and analysis that will be useful when they are asked to write a review of a book they have read."[56] Such skills include ability to (1) identify themes and plots, (2) discuss characters and character development, (3) distinguish among facts, values, and opinions, and (4) recognize how language can be used to create emotional effects as well as to communicate ideas or information.

Ploghoft thinks that the relationship between CRS and language development should not be ignored by educators. He maintains that "the language of television is basic, it is natural and it would be utter nonsense to hope or to expect that it would not be appealing to human beings who want to find out what is going on with other people."[57] Television employs the spoken word, nonverbal signs, and a variety of visual and sound effects. Its language is that of interpersonal communication: the medium that children encounter continuously, develop, and use to fashion skills for controlling, understanding, and evaluating the world about them. Even before children are introduced to reading, they are introduced to and use these very same modes to communicate. For Ploghoft, there is no denying that "the skills needed to deal effectively and critically with this new medium are basic language skills."[58] Poor readers typically have had inadequate language backgrounds, are deficient in listening skills, lack skill in visual discrimination, and "cannot organize into logical sequence a series of events in a story."[59] He further maintains that "in our zeal to get the youngsters to read at grade level, we have not dared to take the time to attend to the antecedent conditions that relate so closely to reading achievement."[60]

The CRS program has been implemented in several schools and in some instances even supported with federal funds. The Idaho Falls School District received Title IV-C funds to develop *The Way We See It,* a project that, according to its director, "is trying to develop high cognitive receivership levels in students by teaching them to understand, analyze and evaluate televised messages."[61] For each grade level (it is designed for children between ages three and six), instruction is given in four areas: commercials, entertainment, news, and personal uses. At Idaho Falls, parents have been included in the project. To teach parents "communication and values clarification skills" they were invited to sessions to discuss the effects of television on children and given training materials related to the curriculum for home use plus six discussion guides to help them discuss television programs with their children.

The Far West Laboratory for Educational Research and Development in San Francisco used funds from a U.S. Office of Education contract to work with Boston's public television station (WGBH) to develop materials for teaching critical television skills for high school students. The project's director reported that four viewing skills were identified:

1. Ability to evaluate and manage one's own television viewing behavior.
2. Ability to question the reality of television programs.
3. Ability to recognize the arguments employed on television and to counter argue.
4. Ability to recognize the effects of television on one's own life.[62]

To enable high school students to acquire these skills, a text, *Inside Television: A Guide to Critical Viewing,* a teacher's guide for the text, and *A Family Guide to Television* to enable families to "take a closer look at their relationship with this important 'member of the family' " were developed. The project also offered workshops to parents and educators to teach them how to teach the skills to students.[63]

Inside Television and the teacher's guide to it were designed to allow teachers to use the text's seven units either in a semester-long course or as a unit in another course. The seven units focus on the relationship between the viewer and television, explain how the television industry is organized and financed, show how television programs can be analyzed the way a work of literature can, analyze how the nature of the industry limits the kinds of programs that can be produced, explain how television is used to sell opinions and products, discuss the production of television news, compare the television world to the real world, and examine how the television industry may be changed by new developments in technologies and regulations. The text includes television scripts, interviews with members of the industry, suggestions for field visits, and the customary suggestions for debate and discussion topics and research projects. As is the case with most other such projects, all materials are designed "to encourage students to take greater responsibility for determining their own cultural environment."[64]

In New York, a PBS station, WNET/THIRTEEN, received funds from the Department of Health Education and Welfare to conduct a Critical Television Viewing Skills (CTVS) project. The WNET project taught CTVS not through television but through workshops and through the print medium. As its director, Debbie Wasserman Bilowit, reports, "We approach critical television viewing the same way a language arts teacher might approach the analysis of a novel or poem: by looking at the piece which has been set before us."[65] Students are asked to discuss, analyze, and evaluate television programs just as they would approach a book. The questions asked of students are divided into two categories, literary elements and technical elements. Literary elements include characters, setting, conflict, plot, theme, and logic; technical elements include casting, makeup and costume, music and sound effects, and special effects.

Besides receiving federal funds to conduct training sessions for teachers of teachers and community leaders, WNET was granted funds to develop training manuals for teachers and community leaders to enable them to make television "a positive viewing experience," to create *A Family Guide* designed to "help parents make more positive use of the programs which their children are already watching," and to produce a combination workbook-textbook for use in the middle school grades that would be nonjudgmental but relate "critical viewing skills to language arts skills that are already being taught in the classroom" and a teacher's edition of the text to enable them to teach CTVS with or without televisions in the classroom.[66] While the project director admitted that CTVS is not a "panacea" that will "turn everyone into incisive critical thinkers or avid readers," she does claim that it works. Children respond favorably to learning CTVS and they "actually learn generic critical television skills which can be transferred to reading or writing."[67]

The American Broadcasting Company granted funds to researchers at Yale University's Family Television Research and Consultation Center so they could design, teach, and evaluate a CTVS curriculum for third, fourth, and fifth graders. The curriculum they constructed included lessons designed to teach children the kinds of programs that are produced and aired, how they are produced, and the kinds of materials, people, and techniques that are used in their production. The lessons also showed how the employed techniques affect viewers, how to use television as a source of information, how to become aware of how one uses television, how to be more critical of television violence and "to use these lessons within a Language Arts framework so that children could gain experience in using correct grammar and spelling; writing letters; abstracting ideas; critical thinking; expressive language; oral discussion and reading."[68]

While the researchers were unable to assess their "ultimate goal of creating more discriminating television consumers," they did learn that the materials were "useful as a means of teaching vocabulary words, writing skills, mathematics, and critical thinking skills." The subjects in the experiment—the third, fourth and fifth graders—already knew that television distorted reality, but "the lessons were effective in teaching them to understand how this is done."[69] After brief preparation, teachers found the materials "easy to use." The researchers noted that the children's viewing habits and interests reflected those of their parents. Parents were reluctant to attend the workshops offered by the researchers, seemed not very interested in learning how television influenced their children, and "seemed to think that television was a problem for *other* children, especially less privileged children, rather than their own offspring."[70]

CRS is a relatively new development in education, apparently beginning in the early 1970s. While curricula for CRS have been based "mainly on a priori editorial judgments,"[71] evidence suggests that teachers do not resist teaching such material and that students not only like to learn about television but also become more aware of how television produces its effects and also of the "excesses of violence" presented on the medium.

Reports to the Surgeon General

Ever since the advent of television, there have been questions, studies, and speculations about the effects of television violence on viewers, especially children. In the late 1960s and early 1970s, several events drew national attention to the issue of television's portrayal of violence.

Besides several years of viewing civil rights demonstrations and demonstrations against American participation in the war in Vietnam, within a decade, many saw several national leaders assassinated: Pres. John F. Kennedy and the Reverend Martin Luther King in 1963, and Sen. Robert F. Kennedy in 1968. Violence seemed to breed more violence. Many saw the alleged assailant of President Kennedy shot on live television.

In the early 1960s, Sen. Thomas Dodd held hearings on the relationship between juvenile delinquency and television. In 1969, more attention was drawn to the issue by the staff report to the National Commission on the Causes and Prevention of Violence, *Mass Media and Violence.* In 1969, Senator Pastore, the chair of the Senate Subcommittee on Communications of the Senate Commerce Committee indicated to the Secretary of the Department of Health, Education and Welfare that he was "exceedingly troubled by the lack of any definitive information which would help resolve the question of whether there is a causal connection between televised crime and violence and antisocial behavior by individuals, especially children." He also requested the Secretary to order the Surgeon General to assemble a committee to "conduct a study to establish scientifically what effects these kinds of programs have on children."[72] Responsibility for the study was assigned to the National Institute of Mental Health which quickly funded a million dollars worth of research studies. By the end of 1971, the Scientific Advisory Committee on Television and Social Behavior had completed its study and submitted its report, *Television and Growing Up: The Impact of Televised Violence.* It was accompanied by five volumes of technical reports.

In the first of the five volumes, George A. Comstock reported that those who believed that television did influence viewers and that television "should contribute to social harmony will not be happy with television's portrayal of the world." If we used television to assemble a view of what the world was about and how it worked, one was likely to conclude "that life is violent, that violence often succeeds, that moral goodness and violent behavior may coincide, and that victimization is a common occurrence." From television one could learn that "nonwhites, foreigners, and persons of low socioeconomic status" were "violent to more than an average degree" and should be feared. Power and goodness, television seemed to teach, resided in white middle class males to a larger degree than in any other group.[73] The 1982 National Institute of Mental Health report, *Television and Behavior,* shows that the evidence accumulated in the 1970s "seems to support the proposition that television, in some instances, does affect the 'world view' of those who watch a great deal."[74]

Whether one believes that new roles for women and minorities must be defined and accepted or whether one believes that the alleged breakdown of traditional social roles and values must be repaired, it is easy to find cause for concern in the "social reality" that is daily transmitted by television. While the ratio of men to women seen on television is now lower than it was in the early 1970s, it is still about 3 to 1 in favor of men. Nearly all men seen on television have jobs but between a fourth and a third of women do not. The men we see on television are twice as likely to hold prestigious jobs as women. Over 90 percent of the attorneys, clergy, physicians, and proprietors are men; women tend to be secretaries, teachers, nurses, entertainers, or journalists. Even in crime there is an imbalance. On television "women are underrepresented as lawbreakers and overrepresented as victims."[75]

On television, men are dominant and more interested in their jobs than in home life. They are less emotional and more rational than women, who expect them to be the problem solvers and their source of psychological support. Men are strong and women are attractive. Beginning in the late 1970s, women have increasingly been portrayed in jobs that are difficult, daring, dangerous, or glamorous. Such jobs seem to be available only to women who are not married, however. When men and women are depicted in comparable roles or as equals, "they are apt to have a relationship involving conflict and violence."[76]

The range of intimate relationships on television is indeed narrow. Partners who work together have "close relationships," but most demonstrations of affection are confined to situation comedies. On television the ideal male is not married but the woman is. Women who are not married want to be married. Most married women do not have jobs outside the home, and "a character who is a successful working woman usually has problems with love, husband, or children." Married men, on the other hand, are just not as glamorous as single men. "When husbands and 'heroes' on Saturday morning shows were compared, the husbands came out not only as fat and quarrelsome but also as less intelligent, logical, and helpful than the heroes."[77]

The characteristics assigned to men and women on television and the roles they typically depict do make a difference in children's sex-role socialization. When children are asked to assign the proper gender to given jobs, the heavy viewers give more stereotyped answers than light viewers do. Both boys and girls find television males more attractive as role models than television females. While girls pick men as well as women from television as role models, boys always choose men. Some evidence also shows that children "learn counterstereotyped roles from some programs."[78] That suggests that the influence of television could be different from what it is.

Just as television stereotypes according to gender, it stereotypes according to age. The very young and the old are the greatest users of television but they see relatively little of their age cohorts on television. While the number of women over age 50 seen on television has increased more than threefold in the last decade, older characters are more likely to be white than black and more likely to be male than female. In subtle ways television teaches that young is better than old. The elderly are frequently depicted in a favorable but unrealistic manner. With age, people seem to acquire success and status.

In the early 1950s, few blacks were seen on television, but since the late 1960s, they have constituted about 10 percent of the television population. If knowledge of black Americans came only from television, the impression would be that black Americans are very different from white Americans. They are largely segregated from whites, and six shows "house" about 41 percent of black actors. Blacks are less likely to have jobs than whites, and the jobs they have are usually less prestigious than those that whites hold. All-white television families are likely to have fewer personal and family problems and more status than black families. While blacks frequently dominate whites in comedy shows, whites tend to dominate on crime shows. Whether blacks are portrayed as equal to whites on television may depend upon the study and its interpretation. One study found that "in shows with both black and white characters, there was no difference between blacks and whites in giving orders or giving and receiving advice."[79]

Television does affect children's race-role socialization. For many white children, television is their main source of information about minorities, and evidence shows that television can engender favorable racial attitudes. Research on the effects of three public television programs—"Sesame Street," "Carrascolendas," and "Villa Allegre"—indicates that they "have had a favorable effect on cultural pride, self-confidence and interpersonal cooperativeness of minority children."[80]

The Effects of Television Violence

Concern about the effects of television violence on children was expressed almost as soon as television became a part of American's lives. As early as 1952, the House Committee on Interstate and Foreign Commerce held hearings to determine whether television was too violent, too sexually provocative, and pernicious. According to Robert M. Liebart, opinions on the relationship of violence on television to aggressive and antisocial behavior in children "ranged from confident statements that the medium's influence is uniformly pernicious to equally glib assertions that merely watching entertainment fare can do little to shape children's social behavior."[81] However, while a sophisticated adult may easily assert that television has little or no effect on the viewer, it is not so easy to argue convincingly that children do not acquire knowledge, values, and behaviors, and a "world view" from the medium. Moreover, as is noted in the 1982 Report to the Surgeon General:

> Children are an audience qualitatively different from adults, and they may be an audience more vulnerable to television's messages. It may also be significant that there is now a generation of young adults who have grown up with television and whose children are now second generation television viewers. The effects on them probably are not the same as on previous generations who were adults when they first became acquainted with television.[82]

Children learn from observing whatever is around them, and they do not lack opportunities to watch television. Even if children's viewing were restricted to so-called children's television, they would still see a great deal of violence. In 1967 it was reported that "cartoons were more violent than any other category of program" and "in 1969, they were even more violent," increasing their lead over other types of programs.[83] The amount of violence on television during the 1970s did not change significantly. The amount is now fairly constant—8 to 10 violent incidents per hour.

In 1972, the investigators who contributed to the Report to the Surgeon General stated their belief in a relationship between television violence and aggressive behavior. Liebart, who provided an overview of the volume on *Television and Social Learning,* noted:

> *At least under some circumstances, exposure to televised aggression can lead children to accept what they have seen as a partial guide for their own actions. As a result, the present entertainment offerings of the television medium may be contributing, in some measure, to the aggressive behavior of many normal children.*[84]

Several correlational studies have shown consistent relationships between watching violence on television and various forms of aggression. The studies included children from many geographic areas and a variety of social, economic, and familial backgrounds. It was reported that "experimental studies preponderantly support the hypothesis that there is a directional, causal link between exposure to television violence and an observer's subsequent aggressive behavior." Any studies suggesting that watching violence *reduced* aggression were "rare enough to be called anomalous."[85]

The 1972 Report on Television and Adolescent Aggressiveness also indicated a positive correlation. However, there *were* studies that "rather conclusively eliminate the hypothesis that television violence is the sole, or principal cause of aggressive behavior by adolescents."[86] Investigations on the effect of viewing on adolescents revealed that "violence viewing at an earlier age is more closely associated with aggressiveness than is the adolescent's present level of violence viewing."[87]

Even after publication of the 1972 Report controversy and confusion continued about the effects of televised violence. Many behavioral scientists believed that the committee had been "too cautious and conservative," and some "blamed the tentative and somewhat ambiguous phraseology of the report on the makeup of the committee," for the television industry was given the power to veto appointments to the Surgeon General's Advisory Committee.[88] Research continued and even increased during the 1970s, and nearly 2,500 works on television and youth research were published.

The 1982 Report was less equivocal about the influence of television, indicating that the studies conducted in the 1970s definitely show that "televised violence and aggression are positively correlated in children." However, the issue has changed from whether there *is* a relation to "what processes produce the relation."[89] The four processes that have been identified for further investigation are (1) observational learning, (2) attitude changes, (3) physiological arousal, and (4) justification processes.

The observational process is perhaps the most obvious and simplest. Children, as young as age two, learn by watching their parents, siblings, playmates, and teachers. They also learn from watching television. Both laboratory and field studies show a positive relationship between watching aggressive behavior and the tendency to behave aggressively. Children who observe that certain behaviors are rewarded are likely to imitate those behaviors. Their attitudes are formed by what they watch as well as how much they watch. If they acquire an acceptance of aggressive behavior, they are inclined not only to act aggressively but also to tolerate aggression in others.[90] However, attitudes acquired from television can be controlled and modified by adult discussions of the violence children see.

While watching violent programs may cause physiological arousal, frequent viewing of violence seems to lessen the amount of arousal. Whether and how the arousal relates to aggressive behavior and whether people engage in aggressive acts to maintain a given level of arousal are as yet unknown.

The justification theory maintains that those who like violence on television are already inclined toward aggressive behavior and that they watch in order to find justification for their own behavior. Research on this theory has not been sufficient to evaluate.

Studies conducted during the 1970s not only confirmed earlier investigations but also extended their range of applicability. While earlier research focused primarily on children between ages 8 and 13, "the evidence has now been extended to include pre-schoolers at one end of the age spectrum and older adolescents at the other." Earlier studies were mostly confined to the effects experienced by boys, but more recent studies have included girls, and the new research "shows similar relationships in samples of girls as well as boys."[91] All studies done before and during the 1970s were group studies. Thus it should be noted that "as with most statistical analyses of complex phenomena, group trends do not predict individual or isolated events." To distinguish between group and individual studies is not to "minimize the significance of the findings, even though it delimits their applicability."[92] The methodological characteristics of our inquiries allow us to persist in the belief that only somebody else's children are affected.

Conclusion

Television has become a major socializer of children, and the likelihood of reducing its role as a teacher of the young is not great. The 1982 Report to the Surgeon General indicates that television changed little during the 1970s. The 3,000 books, reports, and articles completed in the 1970s offer no reason to believe that television will be significantly different in the future. Change in television is not likely to result from either audience efforts or the work of such pressure groups as the American Medical Association, the Parent-Teachers Association, the National Organization for Women, or the Action for Children's Television. As has been the case for other media, new developments in the medium itself and developments in other related media will have greater effect, although new developments will certainly be criticized for likely ill effects. In fact, the emergence and popularity of video games serve as a good example. Dr. H. James Holroyd, a "technology abuse" specialist, professor of pediatrics at the University of Southern California, and chair of the American Academy of Pediatrics Committee on Accident Prevention and Poison Control, reported that some children were so addicted to the games that they turned to truancy to keep playing them. Gamblers Anonymous reports that many adult gamblers were hooked on pinball machines in their adolescent years. The implication is clear: today's video game is yesterday's pinball machine. In what sounds like an echo of Harriet Van Horne's predictions about the possible effects of television, Patricia McCormack, the health editor for United Press International, reported that:

> Holroyd predicted hooked kids have a good chance of winding up as stunted adults. They will not be fully developed socially, intellectually, emotionally and perhaps not even physically due to trading off sports and exercise time for a long daily rendezvous with the video game.[93]

If television will be changed not so much by users and critics as by new media developments, then those who believe that effects on users, especially children, need to be monitored and controlled have four alternatives. The first may be the easiest: Forget about television and begin to study the possible effects of a new development, video games.

A second alternative is to turn away from commercial television where violence is so concentrated and toward greater use of educational and public television. As has already been noted, however, only 5 percent of viewing is now directed toward the telecasts of those stations, and whether noncommercial sectors of television would be able to find support to produce enough programming for an increased audience is problematical. A move of the audience from commercial to noncommercial television is not likely, however, for "notwithstanding arguments about who controls television, the public's evaluation of television is predominantly favorable."[94] Moreover, the public seems to have little inclination to control systematically how much television children watch. About half the public believe some programs are not appropriate for children and worry about how much sex and violence children see on television but have less concern about how much television they watch. Despite all the discussion about television, "mothers may not recognize how much their children respond to television content." Indeed, it is possible that they have been desensitized to television violence, for "children, according to their own accounts, perceive more violence than their mothers do, and mothers underreport how frightened their children are after watching scary programs."[95]

A third alternative is to invest more money and talent in the production of more and better television. In spite of programs specifically produced for children and the promise of entire channels being available for children as cable television is expanded, the concept of children's television is a curious and severely limited notion. There is no way to insure that children's viewing would be primarily restricted or even directed to children's television. Moreover, as reported in the 1982 Report to the Surgeon General, "most programs watched by children are intended for adults."[96] In fact, all television is children's television, and that fact, according to Postman, has and is causing the disappearance of childhood. Efforts at creating more and better children's television may be futile if it is designed for children who no longer exist. Producers may not be cognizant of the impact of growing up in an information-rich environment in which vicarious experience is available to all.

The fourth alternative is to take the advice of the advocates of CRS and equip students to live with and use the medium for their own purposes. While most CRS or CRS-like programs are not based on empirical studies,[97] some features should be noted. First, the program accepts the obvious: It is based on the premise that television exists, will continue to exist, and will continue to be a significant part of children's lives. Second, it proposes that people should be active, purposeful beings rather than passive recipients of whatever is directed toward them. However, CRS does try to minimize the difference between the print medium and television and even approaches the succession of images as though it were a stream of print.

Emphasis on the "receiver" in CRS may indicate that CRS is founded on the transportation theory of communication. Too much emphasis may be placed on the message and how viewers need to behave to receive the "right" message. However, in fairness to CRS proponents, it must be reported that Anderson has indicated that "the key to understanding the relation between what is presented and what results is that *content is a poor prediction* of effect."

> The fact that our research literature is full of contradictory findings can easily lead one to conclude that there are not strong consistent effects on viewing television which can be systematically associated with large segments of the viewing audience. Rather there appear to be particular effects which are associated with given motivational, attitudinal and cognitive states of the receiver. And as those states change from time to time or even moment to moment the consequences of interpretation of televised messages change.[98]

Use of the transportation theory with its emphasis on the transmitter, the message, and the receiver makes it easy to view the receiver as a passive agent or one who can be rendered passive. According to Seymour Banks, however, viewing may be an activity that involves "an active transaction between the child, the television set, and the TV viewing environment."[99] If Banks's suggestion is taken seriously, an additional variable may be added to the transportation model—the setting in which the receiver is situated. However, this element compounds matters for educators. The complexities of the viewing environment are not easily controlled, for most viewing takes place outside the school.

Whether the model for describing, analyzing, and determining the effects of television viewing has two (transmitter and receiver), three (transmitter, receiver, and message), or four (transmitter, receiver, message, and setting) elements, the basic question remains: Who does what to whom, when, where, and how? The "why" questions should not be, but usually are, ignored. The model educators use to organize their investigations not only shapes the questions that are asked but the answers that are accepted. As long as technological models and approaches are used, questions about purpose and the utility and propriety of purpose will neither be asked nor answered.

Notes

1. Laurence Bergreen, *Look Now, Pay Later: The Rise of Network Broadcasting* (New York: Mentor, 1981), 140.
2. Neil Postman, *The Disappearance of Childhood* (New York: Delacorte Press, 1982), 79.
3. Ibid.
4. Letty Cottin Pogrebin. *Growing Up Free: Raising Your Own Child in the 80's* (New York: McGraw-Hill, 1980), cited in Wayne C. Booth, "The Company We Keep: Self-Making in Imaginative Art, Old and New," *Daedalus* (Fall 1982): 58.
5. Max Lerner, *America as a Civilization: Culture and Personality* (New York: Simon and Schuster, 1961), 843.
6. Ibid., 843–844.
7. Daniel J. Boorstin, *The Americans: The Democratic Experience* (New York: Vintage Books, 1974), 397.
8. Stephen R. Graubard, "Preface to the Issue, 'Print Culture and Video Culture'," *Daedalus* (Fall 1982): v–vii.
9. Douglas Cater, "The Intellectual in Videoland," *Saturday Review* (May 31, 1975): 13.
10. Robert Hornik, "Out-of-School Television and Schooling: Hypotheses and Methods," *Review of Educational Research* 51 (Summer 1981): 193.
11. Charles Weingartner, "Communication, Education, and Change," in Harold W. Sobel and Arthur E. Salz, eds., *The Radical Papers: Readings in Education* (New York: Harper & Row, 1972), 187.
12. Ibid., 192–193. Emphasis in the original.
13. George Comstock, "Social and Cultural Impact of Mass Media," in Elie Abel, ed., *What's News: The Media in American Society* (San Francisco: Institute for Contemporary Studies, 1918), 238.
14. Ibid., 239.
15. Alan M. Rubin, "The New Media: Potential Uses and Impact of the New Technologies for Children's Learning." Paper presented at the American Educational Research Association Convention, New York, 1982, 4.
16. Daniel J. Boorstin, *The Image: A Guide to Pseudo-Events in America* (New York: Atheneum, 1977), 251.
17. Daniel J. Boorstin, *The Republic of Technology* (New York: Harper & Row, 1978), 7.
18. Boorstin, *The Image*, 27–28.
19. Ibid., 28–29.
20. Ibid., 29.
21. Quoted in Cater, "The Intellectual in Videoland," 14.

22. Ibid., 13.
23. Ibid., 13–14.
24. Booth, "The Company We Keep," 40–41.
25. Boorstin, *The Image,* 229.
26. Ibid., 213.
27. Ibid., 249.
28. Ibid., 253.
29. Postman, *Disappearance of Childhood,* 23.
30. Quoted in Postman, *Disappearance of Childhood,* 29.
31. Postman, *Disappearance of Childhood,* 28.
32. Henry Malcolm, *Generation of Narcissus* (Boston: Little Brown, 1971), 4.
33. Ibid., 146.
34. Weingartner, "Communication, Education, and Change," 193.
35. Postman, *Disappearance of Childhood,* 76–77.
36. Michael R. Winston, "Racial Consciousness and the Evolution of Mass Communications in the United States," *Daedalus* (Fall 1982): 173.
37. Quoted in "What is TV Doing to America?" *U.S. News & World Report* (August 2, 1982): 27.
38. "TV Called 'Scapegoat' for Illiteracy," *Bradenton (Fla.) Herald* (November 29, 1982).
39. Hornik, "Out-of-School Television and Schooling," 194.
40. Ibid., 199.
41. National Institute of Mental Health, *Television and Behavior: Ten Years of Scientific Progress and Implications for the Eighties,* Volume I: Summary Report (Washington, D.C.: U.S. Department of Health and Human Services, 1982), 79.
42. "TV Called 'Scapegoat' for Illiteracy."
43. Hornik, "Out-of-School Television and Schooling," 203.
44. Gerald S. Lesser, "Learning, Teaching, and Television Production for Children: The Experience of *Sesame Street,*" *Harvard Educational Review* 42 (May 1972): 258.
45. Ibid., 269.
46. Ibid.
47. Walt Belcher, "Kids Tune in Prime Time for Credit," *Tampa Tribune* (November 13, 1982).
48. Comstock, "Social and Cultural Impact of Mass Media," 244.
49. Hornik, "Out-of-School Television and Schooling," 203.
50. Comstock, "Social and Cultural Impact of Mass Media," 239.
51. *Television and Behavior,* 81. For further descriptions of CRS see: Milton E. Ploghoft and James A. Anderson, "Television Receivership Skills: The New Social Literacy," *Social Science Record* (Winter 1977): 8–13, and Milton E. Ploghoft and James A. Anderson, eds., *Education for the Television Age: The Proceedings of a National Conference on the Subject of Children and Television* (Athens, Ohio: The Cooperative Center for Social Science Education, College of Education, Ohio University, 1981).
52. James A. Anderson, "Receivership Skills: An Educated Response," in Ploghoft and Anderson, eds., *Education for the Television Age,* 24.
53. Ibid., 22.
54. Ibid., 23.
55. Ibid., 22.
56. Milton E. Ploghoft, "Critical Viewing Skills and the Basics," in Ploghoft and Anderson, eds., *Education for the Television Age,* 129.
57. Ibid., 127.
58. Ibid., 128.

59. Ibid., 127.
60. Ibid., 128.
61. N. Craig Ashton, "The Way We See It: A Program Design for Instruction of Critical Televiewing Skills," in Ploghoft and Anderson, eds., *Education for the Television Age,* 63.
62. Donna Lloyd-Kolkin, "The Critical Television Viewing Project for High School Students," in Ploghoft and Anderson, eds., *Education for the Television Age,* 93.
63. Ibid., 94.
64. Ibid.
65. Debbie Wasserman Bilowit, "Critical Television Viewing," in Ploghoft and Anderson, eds., *Education for the Television Age,* 66.
66. Ibid., 67–68.
67. Ibid., 68.
68. Dorothy G. Singer, Diana M. Zuckerman, and Jerome L. Singer, "Teaching Elementary School Children Critical Television Skills: An Evaluation," in Ploghoft and Anderson, eds., *Education for the Television Age,* 73. Also see Dorothy G. Singer, Diana M. Zuckerman, and Jerome L. Singer, "Helping Elementary School Children Learn About TV," *Journal of Communication* 30 (1980).
69. Singer, et al. "Teaching Elementary School Children Critical Television Skills," 78–79.
70. Ibid., 79.
71. *Television and Behavior,* 82.
72. Quoted in *Television and Behavior: Ten Years of Scientific Progress,* 1.
73. George A. Comstock, "New Research on Media Content and Control" in George A. Comstock and Eli A. Rubinstein, eds., *Television and Social Behavior: Reports and Papers, Volume I: Media Content and Control.* A Technical Report to the Surgeon General's Scientific Advisory Committee on Television and Social Behavior (Washington, D.C.: U.S. Department of Health, Education and Welfare, National Institute of Mental Health, June 1972), 2.
74. *Television and Behavior,* 54.
75. Ibid.
76. Ibid., 55.
77. Ibid. Also see L. Busby, "Defining the Sex Role Standard in Commercial Network Television Programs Directed Toward Children," *Journalism Quarterly* 81 (1974).
78. *Television and Behavior: Ten Years of Scientific Progress,* 56. Also see M. Miller and B. Reeves, "Dramatic TV Content and Children's Sex Role Stereotypes," *Journal of Broadcasting,* 20 (1976).
79. *Television and Behavior: Ten Years of Scientific Progress,* 58. Also see C. Banks. *A Content Analysis of the Treatment of Black Americans on Television* (ERIC Document 115 576, 1975).
80. *Television and Behavior: Ten Years of Scientific Progress,* 59. Also see R. Fillip, G. Miller, and P. Gillette, *The Sesame Mother Project: Final Report* (El Segundo, Calif.: Institute for Educational Development, 1971) and G. Va Wort, *Carrascolendas: Evaluation of a Spanish/English Educational Television Series within Region XIII,* Final Report, Evaluation Component (Educational Service Center, Region 13, 1974).
81. Robert M. Liebart, "Television and Social Learning: Some Relationships Between Viewing Violence and Behaving Aggressively," in John P. Murray, Eli A. Rubinstein, and George A. Comstock, eds., *Television and Social Behavior, Volume II: Television and Social Learning.* A Technical Report to the Surgeon General's Scientific Advisory Committee on Television and Social Behavior (Washington, D.C.: U.S. Department of Health, Education and Welfare, National Institute of Mental Health, 1972), 1.
82. *Television and Behavior,* 2–3.
83. Comstock, "New Research on Media Content and Control," 6.
84. Liebart, "Television and Social Learning," 29–30. Emphasis in the original.

85. Ibid., 29.
86. Steven H. Chaffee, "Television and Adolescent Aggressiveness," in George A. Comstock and Eli A. Rubinstein, eds., *Television and Social Behavior, Volume III: Television and Adolescent Aggressiveness.* A Technical Report to the Surgeon General's Scientific Advisory Committee on Television and Social Behavior (Washington, D.C.: U.S. Department of Health, Education and Welfare, National Institute of Mental Health, 1972), 32–33.
87. Ibid., 24.
88. *Television and Behavior,* 37.
89. Ibid., 38.
90. Ibid., 90. Also see L. K. Friedrich Cofer, A. Huston-Stein, D. Kipnis, E. J. Susman, and A. S. Clevitt, "Environmental Enhancement of Prosocial Television Content: Effects on Interpersonal Behavior, Imaginative Play, and Self-regulation in a Natural Setting," *Developmental Psychology* 15 (1979); J. L. Singer and D. G. Singer. *Television, Imagination and Aggression: A Study of Preschoolers Play* (Hillsdale, N.J.: Erlbaum, 1980); and L. D. Eron and L. R. Huesmann, "Adolescent Aggression and Television," *Annals of the New York Academy of Sciences,* 347(1980).
91. *Television and Behavior,* 90.
92. Ibid., 89.
93. Patricia McCormack, "Hazards of Video Games Debated," *Los Angeles Times* (December 21, 1982).
94. *Television and Behavior,* 75.
95. Ibid., 75. Also see J. R. Rossiter and T. S. Robertson, "Children's Television Viewing: An Examination of Parent-Child Consensus," *Sociometry* 38(1975) and J. D. Abel and M. E. Beninson, "Perceptions of TV Program Violence by Children and Mothers," *Journal of Broadcasting* 20(1976).
96. *Television and Behavior,* 56.
97. Ibid., 81. For an example of an attempt to ascertain viewing skills through research see H. Door, S. B. Graves, and E. Phelps, "Television Literacy for Young Children," *Journal of Communication* 30(1980).
98. Anderson, "Receivership Skills: An Educated Response," 4.
99. Seymour Banks, "The Effects of Critical Viewing Skills Curriculum on Advertising Forms and Strategies," in Ploghoft and Anderson, eds., *Education for the Television Age,* 160.

PART IV
Students and Teachers

Teaching can be an enormously satisfying career, but it is also enormously difficult and complex. If we were to view schools and teaching on the basis of what we read and hear in the media and from the utterances of legislators and governors interested in improving public schools, we could easily conclude that schools are places where teachers are to teach academic subject matter to students, and that students would learn more if only teachers and principals would pay more attention to school discipline and act on what we know about instruction.

Schools, however, have two sides—inside and out. Teachers do not have the luxury of contending with only how schools look from the outside. Once they accept the responsibility inside the school, it does not take long to realize that it is indeed important to know the subjects they are assigned to teach thoroughly. Indeed, many serious teachers readily admit that they never understood their subjects until they had to teach them.

Once inside the school's classroom, the teacher recognizes quickly the effects of interactive factors that originate in loci outside the school. Who the students are, the experiences they bring to the classroom, and their various psychological characteristics cannot be ignored.

Different kinds of students require different kinds of educational opportunities. Even as we prepare ourselves for teaching, we know that there are special students. Some have disabilities or handicaps; some are gifted. Even if we surrender the notion that each student is unique, we still group our students. We believe that all are educable and can profit from school, but admit that some profit more or do so more quickly than others. Rightly or wrongly, we make generalizations and create expectations based on students' socioeconomic standings in the community, their ethnic or racial origins, and even their religious backgrounds.

The purpose of Part IV, "Students and Teachers," is to explore developments in society that may affect both students and teachers greatly. Chapters 8 and 9 focus on the two ends of the school population, children and youth. Chapter 8, "Children," not only examines how our society has provided special services for children and established special agencies to monitor their welfare (the Children's Bureau, for example) but also draws attention to the day care issue. The care of preschool children is not a direct responsibility of public schools. However, it is an area of concern educators cannot ignore, for it relates directly to the most powerful of all educative institutions—the family. Some now argue that the family is in trouble. Others may claim that it is not only as important as ever but also as strong as ever. Nonetheless, many of our unquestioned assumptions about family life can no longer be supported. More than ever before, preschool children are being cared for outside the home, and the public school is not the beginning of extra-family life or the first school-like experience. Educators must be mindful that the backgrounds and experiences of the children they teach may be radically different from theirs.

Chapter 9, "Youth," focuses on what appears to be a major need of youth. More than anything else, youth want to be adults. They seek independence and something useful and interesting to do. In the simplest terms, youth want to work. For over half a century, since the Great Depression of the 1930s, there has been growing awareness that youth need more and better opportunities. They have been given but one alternative to employment—more schooling. Even during the Great Depression, when a new alternative, the Civilian Conservation Corps, was created, attempts were quickly made to attach school or school-like experiences to it. As we begin to acknowledge that youth need to make decisions about what is important for them and to assume responsibilities for their decisions, we are also realizing that they need new and different educational experiences.

Chapter 10, "Teachers and Teachings," and Chapter 11, "New Developments for Teachers," represent attempts to be honest about what teachers experience on the job and how the public values its teachers and their contributions to society. Unhappily, the public is quick to blame teachers for the social and educational problems the media bring to its attention. Even more unhappily, some teachers' qualifications and mistakes make good copy for the media. At the same time that teachers have been deprived of personal and professional satisfaction from teaching, they have also been blamed for not doing the job the public systematically does not allow them to do. Teachers are asked to make informed professional judgments about particular children but are also confined by rigid bureaucratic procedures.[1]

Happily, the public may be forced to attend more carefully to what teachers do and to their working conditions. The desire for better schools and better education may require "fundamental changes" in the structure of the profession. As Linda Hammond-Darling has written in a Rand Corporation Report:

> The many factors that discourage qualified people from entering and remaining in the teaching profession are converging at a time when teacher retirements and student enrollment trends are leading to increased demand for teachers. As a consequence, it will be necessary to hire and retain large numbers of marginally qualified people into teaching unless major changes are made in the structure of the occupation.[2]

She further warns that "if we choose to ignore the structural problems of the teaching profession, we will in a very few years face shortages of qualified teachers in virtually every subject area.[3]

There is, of course, no guarantee that the public and the profession will act to make the necessary changes in the structure of the profession. There is, however, an exciting opportunity for those entering the field in the late 1980s and early 1990s.

Notes

1. Arthur E. Wise, *Legislated Learning: The Bureaucratization of the American Classroom* (Berkeley: University of California Press, 1979).
2. Linda Hammond-Darling, *Beyond the Commission Reports: The Coming Reports* (Santa Monica, Calif.: Rand Corporation, 1984), 16.
3. Ibid., 19.

8
Children

The Need for Child Care

Children and their needs can be viewed in two ways. One view maintains that children are naturally good and that adults can allow them to unfold and develop to maturity without any adult imposition, oppression, or interference. The other view holds that adults must not only look after children but also teach them all they need to know to pursue their own interests in a manner consistent with the requirements of society. This view holds either that children are totally ignorant and helpless or that they have tendencies not befitting society.

Whichever view prevails at any given time, children cannot be totally neglected, for they are radically different from the issue of other species. They are biologically and socially dependent upon their parents, other adults, or older children for a longer period because they are less mature at birth than other species. Without adult care they have little, if any, chance for survival and full development.

Even if one believes that children are born with all they need to mature naturally, it is still necessary, as Rousseau illustrated so well in *Emile,* for the child's guardian to arrange specially constructed places for children—places where they will be free and protected from influences that would interfere with natural development. Thus, even doing nothing but allowing nature to take its course requires some deliberate effort.

How we view children, their nature, their needs, and their rights, how we define our responsibilities to them, to whom we assign those responsibilities, the kinds of circumstances we construct for them, the services we administer to them are all quite clearly subject to change. Nonetheless, the need to look after children persists. If one institution does not do it, another must.

In our society, the responsibility for looking after children resides primarily, but not exclusively, with the family. At times, the family further delegates its responsibilities to others: to relatives, to babysitters, to nurses, to day care centers, to nursery schools, to boarding schools, to both public and private schools. If the family neglects its responsibility, either private charitable institutions or public agencies step in. In our society, the state maintains that it has a special interest in children and that for the good of society it must insure that children are reared properly. It acts when children are abused, neglected, or left with no one to care for them. It sets standards for the upbringing of children, legislates the conditions and terms of employment of children, requires that they be educated, and even enforces compulsory school attendance. While educators frequently complain that parents only view them as free or inexpensive babysitters, they nonetheless typically support the claim that the family alone is incapable of doing all that needs to be done for children and that the state must therefore maintain special places and provide special services—chiefly schools and schooling—for children.

The Family and the State

In some societies, the head of the family was allowed to exercise absolute power over children. For example, in Athens, the father was empowered to decide the fate of children at their birth. With the sanction of law, he was free to "acknowledge the infant . . . or, as occasionally happened, to repudiate the child . . . or even to condemn it to death outright."[1] In ancient Rome, the doctrine of *paterfamilias* extended to fathers absolute power over children for as long as the father lived. Fathers could sell their children into slavery, determine whom they would marry and whether their children would divorce their spouses, and appropriate for their own use whatever property and wealth their children earned or secured. According to Alan Watson, the Roman "father had complete power of life and death over his children—though if he used his power arbitrarily he *might* be punished by the censors."[2] While history does show that societies have limited parental power and thereby protected children, the reasons for such limitations frequently reflect what Leon Sheleff describes as "ultimate motives." Frequently, the purpose of such laws was not to protect children but to insure that children did not become wards of the state.[3] The power enjoyed and exercised over children by parents can be thought of as a power granted them by society in exchange for the services they perform for society. As Sir William Blackstone pointed out, "The power of parents over their children is derived . . . from their duty; this authority being given, partly to enable the parent more effectively to perform his duty, and partly as a recompense for his care and trouble in the faithful discharge of it."[4]

The traditions of our society assign families primary responsibility for the care and the education of children and emphasize the importance of family to the well-being of society. Our history shows that almost as soon as Europeans began to settle the North American continent, their governments expressed an interest in how effectively families were discharging their obligations and adopted measures to insure that they did meet them. In 1642, just twelve years after the Puritans (a group firmly convinced that the family was the basic unit of society and the primary agency for the nurture of the individual) began the settlement of New England, the General Court of the Massachusetts Bay Colony enacted a measure making it the duty of parents to teach their children how to read, to obey the laws of the society, and to live by the principles of their religion. The Court recorded that in writing the law, it considered "the great neglect of many parents and masters in training up their children in learning, and labor, and other implyments which may be proffitable to the common wealth."[5] Town officials were ordered to insure that parents did raise their children properly. The Court continued to monitor the behavior of children and how well their parents or masters supervised their behavior. In 1646, it decreed that "any child above sixteen years old and of sufficient understanding who either hit or cursed his parents" could be executed "unless it can be sufficiently testified that parents have been very unchristianly negligent in the education of such children."[6] Children did have the right to protect themselves against parents who sought to maim or kill them.

In 1648, the rulers of the Bay Colony revised and strengthened the 1642 law because some parents and masters were still "too indulgent and negligent of their duty." The Court once again reminded town officials that "the good education of children is of singular behoof and benefit to any Common-wealth" and ordered that parents and masters who persisted in their negligence be fined twenty shillings for their failures.[7] The 1642 and 1648 laws show how concerned the rulers of the Colony were with the behavior of children, but the effects of those laws seemed not to satisfy the Court. In 1654, it observed that "it appears by too much experience that diverse children and servants do behave themselves too disrespectfully, disobediently, and disorderly towards their parents, masters, and governors, to the disturbance of families and discouragement of such parents and governors."[8] To remedy the situation, the Court ordered that children who were found guilty of such misbehavior be whipped, but no child was to receive more than "ten stripes" for an offense.

In seventeenth century New England, all people, not just children, were expected to be subject to the care and supervision of a good family. In 1629, the rulers of Plymouth Colony observed that the community was suffering "great inconvenience" from single people who were "not betaking themselves to live in well governed families." Accordingly, they legislated that "no single person be suffered to live of himself or in any family but such as the selectmen of the town approve of."[9] In 1672, in Watertown, Massachusetts, James Hollon had to explain why he was not living under the supervision of a family and "misspending his time by idleness." The selectmen indicated that they would find a suitable family for him if he did not find one for himself in two weeks.[10]

In the 1670s, the position of tithingman was created to help the town's selectmen and constables monitor how well the families were discharging their duties. He was ordered to report

> the names of all single persons that live from under family government, stubborn and disorderly children and servants, night-walkers, tipplers, Sabbath breakers by night or by day, and such as absent themselves from the public worship of God on the Lord's days, or whatever else course or practice of any person or persons whatsoever tending to debauchery, irreligion, profaneness, and atheism amongst us, whether by omission of family government, nurture, and religious duties, or instruction of children and servants, or idle, profligate, incivil or rude practices of any sort.[11]

Absence of family supervision was the explanation for misbehavior and proper family supervision was therefore its obvious remedy.

The belief that absence of proper family supervision is responsible for misbehavior has persisted into the twentieth century. In his classic and influential work *Poverty,* written in 1904, Robert Hunter gave clear expression to that notion. Then, to make that point, he quoted from testimony that Dr. Elisha Harris gave to a New York Legislative Committee in 1866. In his discussion of the 1863 riot in New York, Dr. Harris told the legislators that "by far the largest part, 80 percent at least of crimes against property and against the person, are perpetrated by individuals who have either lost connection with homelife, or never had any, or whose homes have ceased to be sufficiently separate, decent, and desirable to afford what was regarded as ordinary wholesome influences of home and family."[12]

The laws that the early New England settlers enacted to require that children be educated were passed neither to benefit children nor to relieve families of their responsibilities. Rather, they were passed to further the interest of the state. As an historian of early education in Massachusetts reported:

> The child is to be educated, not to advance his personal interests, *but because the State will suffer if he is not educated.* The State does not provide schools to relieve the parent, not because it can educate better than the parent can, but because it can thereby better enforce the obligation which it imposes.[13]

The Family in the Industrial Society

As the nation was clearly being transformed from a rural-agrarian society to an urban-industrial society in the 1890s, the school was often viewed as the institution that could do what families could not do in an increasingly complicated social order. The school, as Herbert M. Kliebard has observed,

> became a mediating institution between the family and an increasingly distant and impersonal social order, an institution through which the norms and ways of surviving in the new industrial society would be conveyed. Traditional family life was in decline, but even when it remained stable, it was no longer sufficient to initiate the young into a complex and technological world.[14]

Even John Dewey insisted upon the necessity of taking "the broader or social, view" in educational discussions.[15] In a series of lectures delivered to the parents and friends of the University of Chicago Elementary School in April 1899, he explained that it was "inconceivable" that the industrial revolution that was changing commerce, manufacturing, political boundaries, how and where people lived, and even how they practiced their religion would "not affect education in some other than a formal and superficial fashion."[16] To continue to think of education as an individualistic process that involved only the student and the teacher, or the parent and the teacher, was clearly inadequate. It made as much sense as conceiving of "the locomotive or the telegraph as personal devices." The social and the individualistic had to be combined. As Dewey so eloquently and convincingly stated the matter, "What the best and the wisest parent wants for his own child, that must the community want for all of its children."[17] To accept anything less was to accept what was "narrow and unlovely." It was also to accept that which could destroy our democracy. All the possibilities open to both the individual and to the society could be realized through the school, and only through the school. As Dewey explained:

> All that society has accomplished for itself is put, through the agency of the school, at the disposal of its future members. All its better thoughts of itself it hopes to realize through the new possibilities thus opened to its future self.[18]

By the beginning of the twentieth century, discussions about the rights of parents to educate their children were almost beside the point, for access to what society had to offer and the path to success both began at the school's doorstep. At the same time, social problems were being reconceptualized. Even the traditional belief that poverty was a personal problem and was best addressed by private charitable organizations was being eroded. Hunter argued that poverty and all the social problems associated with it were socially created and therefore must be solved through social action. Among the problems he addressed were those of children in the new industrial order. He explained that before the industrial revolution "the children received practically their entire education either in the home or in the adjoining fields." Children, like their parents, worked daily but they were never out of their parents' sight. As they worked together, the parents instructed their children in myriad ways. "In a word," Hunter explained, "the home was the centre of the moral, educational, industrial, and social life."[19] Then it did not matter that formal schooling was restricted to reading, writing, and arithmetic.

Industrialization brought children to cities. They were separated from their parents for most of the day and had no place to spend their time but the streets, where they usually fell into some form of delinquency. The consequences of these changes required "new agencies for the care of the child and a series of important readjustments of the social and educational institutions." Some institutions had changed, but unfortunately "the distinctly educational institutions," Hunter noted, "have been slow to change."[20] For Hunter, "the problems of child life" had become "social problems." It was untenable to allow the school to "ignore this larger work of education and remain a sort of dispensary of learning—an inflexible missionary of the three R's." Teachers had to become surrogate parents because parents had to work. Neither teachers nor city officials, however, realized "that the home is passing away and that, unless the school takes the child, he is left to the street."[21] Teachers and city officials looked upon the problems of children as the result of "parental selfishness" and "parental neglect," but Hunter contended that "the charge of neglect must rest upon the community and the school, and not, in most cases, upon the parent."[22] Parents were not totally responsible for the problems of the child or their solution. It was the duty of teachers "to be familiar with some of the social and industrial conditions out of which the child comes to receive his education in school and into which he must return when his education is finished."[23]

Besides insisting that educators know more about the social conditions of their students, Hunter wanted them to assume responsibility for more children for more time. Children who were working—about 1.7 million children were in the fields, factories, mines, and shops—belonged in school. Child labor before the industrial revolution "was not an evil," for "the labor of the children in the days of the craftsman and artisan was educative, and the process of learning how to weave, spin, and brew, to do the work in the fields or home, was not such as to overburden and break down little workers." However, after the industrial revolution, when steam and electricity rendered the power of little hands "insignificant," the employment of children became "an evil,—superfluous and wicked,—a shame to our civilization and an inexpiable crime against humanity."[24] In a previous age, work was a "blessing" for children but in the new urban industrial order it had become a "curse."

Because the home had been transformed by the industrial order and was no longer an educative institution, the only suitable place for children was school. To Hunter's dismay, however, schools were not always available to children. He found, for example, that "the schools of New York City, the most important and vital instruments for advancing the social welfare, are closed from one-half to two-third of the time between eight in the morning and ten at night." He wanted to open schools to provide nurseries for infants whose mothers had to work and to provide supervised play for older children. "It is," he argued, "absolutely necessary for the social losses of the home to be replaced by the school if the children are to be saved from the worst evils of city and street life."[25]

Federal Protection for Children

The view that children were the private property of parents was further eroded by social reformers, who insisted that children were the nation's most valuable natural resource. Because they were, the nation had to look after their welfare. As Rochelle Beck has noted, once the metaphor of the child as a natural resource was accepted, "the discussion of policy governing child welfare was shifted to the public domain."[26] That meant that the federal government had an interest in and an obligation to look after the welfare of all children, not just those who were abused, neglected, or abandoned. According to this new conception, how, where, and when children were employed and how they were prepared for employment were not only private concerns of the family but also legitimate public concerns. The new view was neither easily nor immediately accepted, however.

Regulation of Child Labor

In 1903, Florence Kelley proposed legislation to regulate child labor and published a legislative proposal in *The Annals of the American Academy of Political and Social Science*. When the National Child Labor Committee was organized the following year, it adopted Kelley's recommendations. In his 1904 annual message to Congress, Pres. Theodore Roosevelt urged Congress to investigate "the horrors incident to the employment of young children in factories or at work anywhere."[27] He repeated his recommendation in 1905 and again in 1906. In 1907, Congress directed the Secretary of Commerce and Labor "to investigate and report on the industrial, social, moral, educational and physical condition of women and child workers in the United States wherever employed, with special reference to their age, hours of labor, terms of employment, health, illiteracy, sanitary and other conditions surrounding their occupation, and the means employed for the protection of their health, person and morals."[28] In 1910, the first volume of what turned out to be a nineteen-volume report appeared; the final volume was issued in 1913.

In 1906, Indiana's Sen. Albert J. Beveridge introduced "A Bill to Prevent the Employment of Children in Factories and Mines" (S. 6562) in the Senate and New York's Rep. Herbert Parsons introduced it (H.R. 21404) in the House. Each congressional house sent the bill to the appropriate committee where it was promptly pigeonholed. Subsequently, Beveridge tried to place his bill before his colleagues by offering it as an amendment to a bill designed to regulate child labor in the District of Columbia. He argued that Congress had to act to stop the unnecessary deaths of thousands of children who were killed while at work, that the states were not acting, and it was not a matter to be left to the states because "the ruin of citizens in any one State, the murder of the innocents in any one Commonwealth, affects the entire Republic as much as it affects that State."²⁹ He failed to secure support for his bill, however. Even the National Child Labor Committee decided not to endorse the bill; the Committee found a difference of opinion on the bill among its membership and decided to address its efforts to promoting state legislation rather than allow the difference of opinion to split the Committee.

In 1914, A. Mitchell Palmer, a congressman from Pennsylvania who would later serve as U.S. Attorney General, introduced H.R. 122292. Sen. Robert L. Owen of Oklahoma introduced the companion bill, S. 4751. The basis of the Palmer-Owen legislation was a bill that had been earlier drafted by the National Child Labor Committee. Members of Congress, the Children's Bureau, and constitutional lawyers also assisted in its drafting. Its purpose was to prohibit employment of children under age fourteen in factories and to limit the workday of all children under age sixteen to eight hours. Hearings were held, but the bill was not enacted. It was reintroduced as the Keating-Owen bill in the first session of the Sixty-fourth Congress and enacted on September 1, 1916, to become effective on September 1, 1917. Some believed enactment of the bill into law constituted a significant advance for children. However, Owen R. Lovejoy wrote in the *New Republic* that it only affected 150,000 of 2 million children. The 1.85 million remained as wards of the individual states where they did not benefit from the federal law. They were "the young hawkers of news and chewing-gum on our city streets, the truck-garden conscripts of Pennsylvania, New Jersey, Ohio, Colorado and Maryland; the sweating cotton-pickers of Mississippi, Oklahoma and Texas; the 90,000 domestic servants under 16 years of age in our American homes; the cash-girls in our department stores." According to Lovejoy, "street trading in our large cities is the primary department in the school of vice," and, he urged, "that school must be closed." However, the federal law did not apply to those activities and only one state enacted a law to regulate them.³⁰

The Keating-Owen Act remained in effect for only 275 days. Even before the law took effect, attempts were under way to repeal it. In August 1917, Roland H. Dagenhart, the father of two sons—John, aged 12, and Reuben, aged 14, who both worked in North Carolina cotton mills—asked the Federal District Court to issue an injunction to restrain enforcement of the law. Dagenhart's counsel argued that if the law were allowed to take effect, his sons' employer would probably dismiss the boys rather than risk government prosecution. That would effectively deprive the father of his sons' earnings and the sons of the right to pursue their chosen life's work. Federal Judge James E. Boyd agreed and prohibited enforcement of the law in the Western District of Carolina. The federal government appealed his decision to the Supreme Court, which heard the case in April 1918. On June 3, 1918, the Supreme Court, by a 5 to 4 vote, upheld Judge Boyd's decision and declared the Keating-Owen Act unconstitutional. Children were still free to work.

The Court's decision in the Dagenhart case did not deter social reformers from trying to eliminate, or at least regulate, child labor. As would later reformers, they sought to implement their programs through regulations if they could not do so with laws. They also sought constitutional remedies, with some success but even more failure.

In 1918, the War Labor Policies Board directed that all federal war contracts include the following clause: "The Contractor shall not directly or indirectly employ in the performance of this contract any minor under the age of 14 years, or permit any minor between the ages of

14 and 16 years to work more than 8 hours in any one day, more than six days in any one week, or before 6 A.M. or after 7 P.M."[31] However, the efforts of reformers and the declarations of federal officials notwithstanding, children continued to work. In the fall of 1918, the *New York Times* reported that all across the nation children were working rather than attending school. In New York City, the requests for work permits from children between ages 14 and 16 had increased by 10 percent and it was not known how many were "working without legal papers." In Massachusetts, where 50,000 children had "been sucked up into the industries," school attendance was down by 14 percent. In Philadelphia, the Bureau of Compulsory Education raided several establishments "in order to bring back to school 2,000 school delinquents who were found working without necessary papers." In Lexington, Kentucky, school officials openly advertised that it would assist in the employment of children. There the *Lexington Leader* published the following announcement:

> If business men and others who want to employ boys within the provisions of the child labor law will send their needs in writing to Attendance Officer J. Sherman Porter, McClelland Building, he will recommend boys for such places. All boys who want to work this year who are under 16 years of age and over 14, and through the fifth year of the public schools, will be given certificates if they ask for them.[32]

In the fall of 1918, the Dallas superintendent of schools suspended enforcement of the compulsory education law until January 1, 1919, "on account of war conditions and because more children were needed for work in the Fall months than in the Winter months."

Opponents to child labor believed they could eliminate it through taxation. In December 1918, the Senate amended the War Revenue Bill to levy a 10 percent tax on the net profits of products sold across state lines and by establishments that employed children. The following February the House approved what the Senate had enacted, but the Supreme Court declared the tax unconstitutional on May 15, 1922. Almost immediately, a campaign was waged to amend the constitution to give Congress the power to regulate employment of all people under age 18. While Congress was considering the amendment, the Woman Patriot Publishing Company submitted a petition to Congress in which it was claimed that the "benign-looking amendment" was "a straight Socialist measure" that was "promoted under direct orders from Moscow" and "drawn and promoted principally by an American Socialist leader (Mrs. Florence Kelley, translator of Karl Marx and friend of Friedrich Engels, who instructed her how to introduce socialism 'into the flesh and blood' of Americans)." It was further argued that the amendment would force poor children "to work underground," where they would be deprived of the protection of existing laws. Adoption of the amendment, it was claimed, would produce "swarms of bureaucrats from Washington with inquisitorial powers" who would invade the nation's homes in search of working children. Moreover, there was no reason to believe, Congress was warned, that the "salaried professional humanitarians" would be as concerned with the welfare of children "as the mothers who bore them or the communities in which they live."[33]

Congress did not acquiesce to the warnings and objections of the amendment's opponents and proposed it to the states in June 1924. Opponents urged states not to ratify the amendment, warning them that the federal government, if the amendment were passed, would interfere with the parents' rights and even take control of education—an obligation that was believed to belong exclusively to localities. In the *Manufacturers' Record* (September 4, 1924), it was claimed that it had been "fathered by Socialists, Communists and Bolshevists" who saw the amendment as an opportunity "to nationalize the children of the land and bring about in this country the exact conditions which prevail in Russia." To prevent its adoption was to do nothing less than "to save the young people of all future generations from moral and physical decay under the domination of the devil himself."[34] To deny children the right to work was to render them idle and to enlarge the devil's workshop. The *Record* (September 11, 1924) also warned parents that the proposed amendment "takes entirely from the parents the right to have their children, sons or daughters, do any work of any kind so long as they are under 18 years of age." It would even be illegal for a mother "to teacher her daughter to do any housework whatsoever, whether it be the sweeping of floors or the washing of dishes."[35] In 1924, the legislatures of Georgia and Louisiana voted against the amendment, and it was defeated in a referendum in Massachusetts. By 1926, New York and Ohio had refused to ratify it, and the prospects of securing approval by the required three-fourths of the states then seemed unlikely.

In 1933, when the time allowed for the amendment's ratification had expired, only six states had approved it. Schooling and the right of children to work were free from federal control and interference until Congress passed the Fair Labor Standards Act of 1938. Then "oppressive child labor" was prohibited by law. The law prohibited children under age 18 from working at hazardous occupations and children under age 16 from working in manufacturing establishments. However, Congress did not prohibit all child labor:

> The Secretary of Labor shall provide by regulation or by order that the employment of employees between the ages of fourteen and sixteen years in occupations other than manufacturing and mining shall not be deemed to constitute oppressive child labor if and to the extent that the Secretary of Labor determines that such employment is confined to periods which will not interfere with their health and well-being.[36]

In 1941, the Supreme Court upheld the constitutionality of the law and it was strengthened in 1949.

The early efforts of social reformers who focused on the problems and value of children were not completely unsuccessful, but they did manage to bring the problems of children to the public's attention. They saw their efforts result in not only the enactment of child labor laws at the state level and better enforcement of truancy laws but also the beginning of a series of national conferences on children and youth and the establishment of the Children's Bureau in 1912.

The Children's Bureau

The time that elapsed between the proposal for the Children's Bureau and its creation (as well as its limited mission, the controversy about its mission, and its modest budget) all show how difficult it is to effect social legislation that even hints at reassigning responsibility for a basic social function. The arguments for the necessity of the Bureau also show the faith that many reformers had in the efficacy of collecting and disseminating information. The idea for the Bureau first came from a leader in the settlement house movement, Lillian Wald of New

York's Henry Street Settlement. Wald, Florence Kelley, and Edward Devine proposed the idea to Pres. Theodore Roosevelt and worked to gain support for it from other reform-minded leaders.

The purpose of the Bureau, according to its advocates, was to provide necessary and useful information to those who needed it—information that the public needed but was not getting from existing federal agencies. Florence Kelley, for example, had complained in 1906 that the "so-called Department of Education" offered information that was "so inconclusive and so belated that it is the laughingstock of Europeans interested in our educational institutions" and "worthless for our own uses in obtaining improved legislation in this country." The data offered by the Department of Education, like that offered by the Department of Labor, were as "remote from the life of the working children of Georgia and Pennsylvania" as were the "hieroglyphics on the pyramid of Cheops."[37] When Lillian Wald recorded her reasons for advocating a Children's Bureau, she explained that "the birth rate, preventable blindness, congenital and preventable disease, infant mortality, physical degeneracy, orphanage, desertion, juvenile delinquency, dangerous occupations and accidents, crimes against children, are questions of enormous national importance concerning some of which reliable information is wholly lacking."Settlement house workers, judges and others had been receiving inquiries about children which could not be answered with any scientific precision but only "out of our own experience or from fragmentary and incomplete data."[38]

As was the case with legislation to regulate child labor, it was easier to have legislation introduced than enacted. On January 10, 1906, Massachusetts' Sen. Winthrop M. Crane introduced S. 2962 which had been drafted by the National Child Labor Committee. S. 2962 called for the creation of a Children's Bureau in the Department of the Interior, which was responsible for looking after the nation's natural resources. Its companion bill, H.R. 19115, was introduced by New Jersey's Rep. John J. Gardner. Each bill was sent to committee, where it remained. In 1909, Senator Crane and Rep. Herbert Parsons of New York reintroduced the bill to Congress. During the 1909 Conference on Dependent Children, the House and the Senate heard favorable testimony at hearings held on the bill. In February, President Roosevelt sent a special message to Congress in which he expressed his belief that "the National Government not only has the unquestioned right of research in such vital matters [the welfare of children and the nature of child life], but is the only agency which can effectively conduct such general inquiries as are needed for the benefit of all our citizens."[39]

The House Committee on Expenditures for the Interior Department reported favorably on the bill, but its vote was not unanimous. The majority explained that the information the Bureau would collect and publish would "multiply many fold the value of the work" that was being undertaken in behalf of children in the states. All "would be stimulated to better efforts" by access to what others were doing and that, the majority claimed, would "result in enlightened legislation and the betterment of the conditions surrounding many of the poor and afflicted children, and in the end we would have better men and women." The committee's minority explained that it opposed the bill because it believed it would only duplicate efforts already under way by other governmental agencies and that "the bill goes into the domain of the health and character of its citizens, a field not belonging to the States but one with which the States are better qualified to deal, for the reason that they can follow up the work of investigation with necessary legislation."[40] The minority view prevailed and the bill failed to reach the House floor.

In April 1911, Idaho's Senator Borah introduced a bill (S. 252) that proposed establishment of a Children's Bureau in the Department of Commerce and Labor. Opponents claimed that the bill was an unwise and unnecessary effort to meddle in the affairs of the family. Senator Borah's fellow senator from Idaho, Senator Heyburn, admitted that to speak against a measure in behalf of children was tantamount to being against "the eternal salvation of mankind" but argued it was still his duty to speak against the bill. "No one can be more sympathetic than I am with the needs, the welfare, and the comfort of the children of the country," he told the Senate, "but I am not willing to substitute any other control for that of the parent."[41] The federal government did not need to assume jurisdiction over the family. History and nature had provided suitable guides that should not be ignored. According to Senator Heyburn:

> The jurisdiction established over the children of mankind in the beginning of the human race has worked out very well. It is in accord with the rules of nature. It is based not upon duty but upon the human instinct that establishes the principle upon which all duties rest. The mother needs no admonition to care for the child, nor does the father. The exceptions to the rule are such as those to the rule against the taking of human life. We have laws providing for the punishment of those who destroy human life, but as compared with the family the instances in which it is necessary to invoke them are rare.[42]

Heyburn also argued that the bill to establish a Children's Bureau belonged to a class of measures already before Congress that sought to interfere "with the control of a parent over the child," such as the bills seeking to prevent the employment of children under age sixteen. Such acts, he asserted, "would result in the necessity of aged or infirm parents going to the public almshouse, notwithstanding there were strong, hustling sons 14 and 15 years of age."[43] Congress had no right to interfere with the rights of parents to control and to profit from their children. Moreover, those who urged him to support the bill, he insisted, were interested in more than collecting information. "They wanted to become substitutes for the parents." The ancient Greeks, he warned, had allowed the state to become the children's nursery and they even allowed the idea to be extended. That eventually "resulted in the depreciation of the sentiment of the family among those people; and one day their eyes opened and they realized that what they lacked in Greece was the home tie, and that without it they could have no concerted patriotism."[44]

Opposition to the Children's Bureau came from many quarters. Elmer E. Brown, the U.S. Commissioner of Education, supported the Bureau, but when P. P. Claxton succeeded him in 1911, the Bureau no longer had the support of the Commissioner's Office. Claxton argued that the work of the proposed Bureau could be done more effectively and efficiently by the Bureau of Education. The latter had working relationships with agencies across the nation from which the Children's Bureau would have to solicit information. He informed the Secretary of the Interior, Walter L. Fisher, that creation of the Bureau would create a senseless division of responsibility for children. Children's conditions did not change as they moved from home to school. "The same individual cannot be a healthy child in school," Claxton argued, "and a sick, diseased or uncared for child out of school."[45] Educators had to have not less but more responsibility for children. Moreover, "to unite in the Bureau of Education all things which pertain to the welfare of children would aid much in giving to the people the right conception of education, which is too often supposed to be merely the results of formal lessons in school."[46]

Despite the many sources of opposition, the bill introduced by Senator Borah was enacted into law when Pres. William Howard Taft signed it on April 9, 1912. Upon passage of the bill, Jane Addams and Julius Rosenwald recommended that Julia Lathrop, who had worked at Chicago's Hull House with Jane Addams, be appointed head of the Bureau. Their recommendation was accepted and Julia Lathrop became the first woman to be appointed by a president and confirmed by the Senate as chief administrative officer of a statutory federal bureau.[47] In March 1913, the Children's Bureau was placed under the aegis of the newly formed Department of Labor.

Enactment of Senator Borah's bill did not end opposition to the Bureau. Its appropriations were held at $25,000 a year, and it had to defend itself against charges it was not cooperating with other agencies and that it was needlessly duplicating the work of other agencies. By 1914, friends of the Bureau were complaining that while Congress was refusing to grant the Bureau an additional $165,000 to conduct studies and add personnel, it was appropriating $600,000 to reduce hog cholera, $375,000 to find ways to reduce the damage inflicted by the cotton boll weevil, and $400,000 to free southern cattle from the tick.

By 1917, the charges against the Bureau were so intense that Lathrop prepared a memorandum that Senator Kenyon of Iowa had read into the *Congressional Record*. She related that as soon as she assumed office, she visited the Public Health Service to discuss the Bureau's plan to study "the social and economic factors surrounding infant mortality" and to indicate that the Bureau also "proposed publishing a series of popular pamphlets upon the care of children, beginning with one on prenatal care." The next year she "learned by chance" that the Public Health Service was about ready to begin distribution of a pamphlet on infant care. That was, she explained in her memorandum, not the impression she was given during her visit. Then, it was indicated to her that the Service did not intend to undertake any projects similar to hers and even offered advice on the Bureau's pamphlet on prenatal care. She proceeded with the publication of the Bureau's pamphlet because it "was then well under way, was much fuller than that of the Public Health Service, differed in presentation, and formed part of a series originally discussed with the Public Health Service." Any duplication was insignificant, for she explained, "the call for this type of literature is so great that the Children's Bureau publications, and those of the Public Health Service jointly, are not sufficient to meet the demand."[48]

According to Lathrop, the Bureau was only doing what it "was especially assigned to it by law" and was cooperating with other agencies. It supplied child care materials to the Department of Agriculture for distribution by its county agents and worked with the Census Bureau to encourage "better birth registration." It also worked with both the Bureau of Education and the Public Health Service, as well as with Delaware education officials "in a study of feeble-minded in Delaware." In that cooperative work, the Bureau did not attempt "to establish a service of medical experts upon feeble-mindedness" but only conducted "the social and family studies of the feeble-minded."[49]

Nearly two decades after its creation, the Bureau still had to be defended. Other agencies still wanted responsibility for the aspects of childhood that friends of the Bureau believed belonged in the Bureau. In 1930, Lillian Wald warned that Pres. Herbert Hoover might order a governmental reorganization "in which federal activities in public health might possibly taken away from the various services and bureaus to which they are now delegated and grouped under an assistant secretary." For Wald, there was no good reason to "dismember the child" and every reason to maintain the Bureau's habit of "considering the child as a whole and very human being, not merely as an actual or potential victim of malaria or hookworm, or of the many other adverse social conditions which can be considered *en masse.*"[50] The Bureau did maintain its focus on the child, and, to effect a "unified approach to the problems of childhood," employed teams of experts to study the problems of childhood—doctors, lawyers, psychologists, scientists, and statisticians. That division of labor apparently did not lead to any dismembering of the child.

Rochelle Beck has observed that the Bureau confined its work to infant and maternal death and the health of children in order "not to threaten various interest groups."[51] These concerns were thoroughly consistent with the notion that the child was the nation's most precious natural resource. As has been noted, the Bureau worked with the Census Bureau to campaign for better birth registration practices. According to Lathrop's successor, Grace Abbott, the Bureau's first study was on infant mortality "because it was of fundamental social importance and of popular interest, and could be made in small units and the conclusions given to the public as each unit was completed."[52]

As the Bureau ascertained what practices for prenatal, infant, and child care were effective, it published and distributed the appropriate information. In 1923, Abbott reported that 600,000 bulletins had been distributed during the previous year. A half century later, Mary Jo Bane reported that fifty-nine million copies of the Bureau's *Infant and Child Care* had been distributed since its publication in 1916—a number sufficiently great to support the claim that a copy had been sold "for almost *every* first child born to an American family during the relevant time period."[53] The only other book for which a comparable claim can be made is Benjamin Spock's *Baby and Child Care.* Forty years after its initial publication in 1946, Spock had sold thirty million copies of his work.

In *Infant Care,* Mrs. Max West instructed mothers that immediate formation of good habits would save "time and patience" for both mother and child. The paramount habit for which mothers were to strive was a regular system for the baby's care. Accordingly, Mrs. West provided a schedule to indicate when the infant should be nursed, set down for naps, taken out for air, and bathed. In addition, times were given when the family should have its breakfast, when other children should be sent off to school, and when and how it was permissible to play with the baby. "The rule that parents should not play with the baby may seem hard," Mrs. West admitted, "but it is without doubt a safe one." She further explained:

> A young, delicate, or nervous baby especially needs rest and quiet, and however robust the child, much of the play that is indulged in is more or less harmful. It is a great pleasure to hear the baby laugh and crow in apparent delight, but often the means used to produce the laughter, such as tickling, punching, or tossing makes him irritable and restless.[54]

Fathers had no choice but to stay away from their babies. That fathers had only a few minutes in the evening to play with their children and that such play "may result in nervous disturbance of the baby and upset his regular habits" could only be described as "regrettable." While mothers were not to kiss their babies on the mouth to avoid spreading germs and while they were to avoid placing their babies "in constant motion," they were told by Mrs. West that babies did need "mothering." When babies were awake they were "to be taken up and held quietly in the mother's arms, in a variety of positions, so that no one set of muscles may become overtired." If older children were not taught to sit alone while they were awake, they would soon "make too great demands upon the mother's strength."[55]

The information on child care the Bureau distributed to mothers through its publication and through working with social workers and public health nurses seemed to contribute to a decline in the incidence of infant mortality but did not solve the problem. The infant death rate between 1915 and 1921 declined in areas of the nation where births were registered, but five other countries had lower rates. Moreover, "a study of vital statistics showed that little progress was being made in reducing the deaths in early infancy, including deaths caused by premature birth, congenital debility, and injuries at birth, which all have maternal causes." In fact, the maternal death rate had increased in the United States and in 1921 was "the highest among all the nations for which recent statistics are available."[56]

In the early 1920s, when the nation was losing nearly 200,000 infants and 20,000 mothers annually, Congress acted on earlier recommendations of Lathrop and approved the Sheppard-Towner Act, which authorized the annual expenditure of $1.2 million for the improvement of the welfare and hygiene of infants and mothers. The Children's Bureau administered the act, but development and administration of the program were, according to the terms of the act, state responsibilities. With the Surgeon General of the U.S. Public Health Service and the Commissioner of Education, the Bureau served on the Federal Board of Maternity and Infant Hygiene, which approved or disapproved the proposals submitted by the states. By 1923, the Supreme Court had refused a request from Massachusetts to declare the act unconstitutional and forty of the forty-eight states had enacted the required legislation to qualify them for a $5,000 grant as well as additional matching grants.

By the early 1920s, the Bureau had established six divisions that reflected its interests and work: a maternity and infancy division; a division of social service that investigated matters related to dependent, neglected, and delinquent children and children with special needs; an industrial division; a recreation division; a statistical division; and an editorial division. In its first studies on infant death, it departed from the traditional methodology and adopted one that would enable it to see what sustained life. Instead of beginning with death records, the Bureau decided to "begin with birth records and follow each child through the first year of his life, or such part of the first year as he lived."[57] In studies conducted in ten "industrial towns" and in twelve rural communities in the South, West, and Middle West, it was determined that the problem of infant death was not peculiar to any one part of the nation but was related to "low earnings, poor housing, the employment of the mother outside the home, and large families."[58] The Bureau even studied the way New Zealanders cared for their children, because New Zealand had "the enviable record of the lowest infant-mortality rate."

The Bureau also collected and published statistics on child labor, including the street trades and the importation and exportation of children, the work of the juvenile courts, illegitimate children, sexual abuse of children, and aid to mothers with dependent children. However, the chief function of the Bureau was neither to care for children nor to compel others to care for children in specific ways, for the public was not willing to allow the federal government to interfere with the privacy, rights, and responsibilities of the family. Rather, the Bureau's chief function was to collect and disseminate information in order to draw attention to the need for better care of the nation's most precious resources.

To draw attention to the problems of children and to educate the public about how those needs could be satisfied, the Bureau built on its efforts to improve birth registration practices.

In 1916, it began work with the General Federation of Women's Clubs to organize a National Baby Week to educate the public about the care of infants. Over 2,000 Baby Weeks were celebrated across the nation, and no state failed to join in. In 1917, after the United States entered World War 1, the Bureau worked with other agencies and committees to organize a longer period of education—the Children's Year. The Bureau emphasized a program for child care that focused on "public protection of maternity and infancy; mother's care for older children; enforcement of all child-labor laws and full schooling for all children of school age; and recreation."[59] In order to involve people in the program and gain data that would be useful for further studies and follow-up work, a program for the weighing and measuring of school children was organized. Initially, 500,000 cards were printed for recording the data, but 5.5 million more were needed for the 11 million women who served on 17,000 committees in 16,500 cities, towns, and villages.

By the eve of the Great Depression, more attention was being paid to the welfare of children than before the founding of the Bureau. As early as 1923, Grace Abbott reported that in a period of just ten years forty-five states had established a division to deal with child health and that forty states had instituted some form of aid for dependent children and their mothers. Over half the states had formed agencies to attend to the problems of delinquent, dependent, and neglected children. More than half had also appointed "commissions to make comprehensive inquiries into all aspects of child welfare, with a view to recodification of existing laws and such improvements in law and administration as are found to be needed to bring the State's care of children up to standard."[60] Moreover, those concerned with the care and welfare of children had abandoned their earlier narrow approaches to their work and adopted more comprehensive approaches. Physicians were paying more attention to "the social and economic aspects of child health" and social workers had learned about "the importance of a physical diagnosis before determining social treatment."

During the Depression of the 1930s, Congress rejected suggestions that the Bureau administer relief programs for children. However, the Bureau was allowed to monitor the needs of children and in 1938 assumed responsibility for administering sections of the Fair Labor Standards Act. In 1934, when Grace Abbott submitted her last annual report as chief of the Bureau, she emphasized that there were many services children still "greatly needed." Many were suffering the consequences of "faulty hygiene" and were not sufficiently protected from communicable diseases. Too little was being done for dependent and delinquent children or to maintain the family in order to prevent delinquency and dependency. As late as 1956, Martha Eliot, then preparing to retire as the Bureau's chief, wrote to Pres. Dwight D. Eisenhower that if the nation's goal was "the optimum development of every child," then "the needs of children must receive much higher priority in our public, and personal budgeting of time, thought, and money than they now receive."[61]

The White House Conferences

By 1909, the National Child Labor Committee and leaders of the settlement house movement, especially Jane Addams and Lillian Wald, persuaded Pres. Theodore Roosevelt to call a White House Conference on the Care of Dependent Children. Since then other conferences have been held to draw attention to the need for child welfare standards, the problems of child health and protection, and issues related to children in a democratic society.

At the first White House Conference, organized by Addams and Wald, those interested in solving the problems of dependent children believed that the same approaches used to render the nation's industrial process more efficient and productive could be applied to human and social problems. Accordingly, as Beck has reported, "200 experts from the fields of medicine, education, data collection, and social work were invited to set an agenda for a Children's Bureau."[62] The 200 participants at the second conference also reflected the values and procedures of the commercial and industrial sectors of society and established standards of quality control for the proper welfare of children. For example, in the standards recommended for school health, the Bureau, besides advising that schools provide health instruction, ample playground space, and open-air classes for tubercular and pretubercular children, specified the proper ratio of nurses and physicians to students (one full-time doctor and two nurses for 4,000 children). The medical experts were to give each child a complete physical examination annually, maintain their health records, control the spread of communicable diseases, and recommend "treatment for all remediable defects, diseases, deformities, and cases of malnutrition."[63]

In 1930, the White House Conference addressed a much broader agenda. The 3,000 participants included leaders in the medical, educational, and social fields.[64] As Beck has observed, "education, mobility, labor, vocational training, the family, and recreation were included as well as concerns about health, the handicapped, and child growth and development."[65] The child was seen as a commodity that had to be processed by experts, an object that no longer belonged to the family but to the community. As Dr. Ray Lyman Wilbur, the Secretary of the Interior and chair of the conference expressed it, "every child is *now* our child."

> We have injected so many artificial conditions into our industrial civilization that the old normal relationships of mother and child, child and family, family and neighborhood have been changed. There is now a much less direct struggle with nature and her immediate forces than has ever been the situation before in our country. We have softened this struggle for man by all forms of protection—better houses, better clothing, more and better food supplies, and by preventive medicine and better medicine and sanitation in general. All of this has called for a delegation of functions, once performed by the individual in the home, to all sorts of outside dependencies.[66]

Wilbur accepted the "artificial conditions" and simply tried to explain that the changes in society were such that the family was neither solely responsible nor even capable of tending to all that children required. A great number of experts and institutions had been inserted between the child and the family.

> If we compare the mother of the past who nursed her own child to the one who must now rely on prepared foods, we find that between the mother and the child we have a whole series of persons and forces upon which the safety of the child depends. . . . Beyond babyhood we have substituted another whole series of organized services between the mother and her child and have replaced much of the home training of the child with these activities . . . kindergartens, playgrounds and schools under government or private auspices. . . . We face the absolute necessity of making good in all of this through expert service. It is probably true that it is beyond the capacity of the individual parent to train her child to fit into the intricate, interwoven, and interdependent social and economic system we have developed.[67]

Society could not afford to rely on maternal instincts to protect and nurture children.

Expressions of the importance of the family and home life for children were heard at the 1930 conference, but it was generally accepted that "the conditions of production and consumption are tending to remove from the home certain functions formerly considered inherent in family life."[68] Because parent education was the means whereby "all the problems facing family life are brought into conscious consideration, traditions are evaluated in the light of present-day living, and new techniques and methods of adjustment are evolved,"[69] the conference recommended that all schools and colleges offer instruction in "courtship, marriage, and parenthood."[70]

While a good home was important for children, the traditional home was no longer necessary. Louise Stanley indicated that "unquestionably, too much significance has been attached to keeping in the home some of the traditional activities." Some women, she explained, could work outside the home and earn enough to pay "for the goods or services she would produce in the home." She agreed that the practice of giving children chores in the home did "develop independence, cooperation, and a feeling of accomplishment" but also indicated her belief that "the extent to which activities need to be kept in the home for this purpose is a matter which may be seriously considered."[71]

Except in rural areas, the American family seemed to be adjusting to new social conditions. In fact, the difference between urban and rural families was greater than the difference between white and Negro families in urban areas. Immigrant families from urban areas adjusted to American urban society more readily than did those from rural areas. The rural family seemed particularly resistant to change and was depicted as "disinterested in money matters, antagonistic to social change, and staunch in the maintenance of older ideals of family life, or religion, morality, and ethics." Its adherence to tradition led Stanley to suggest that "the apparent discrepancy between the picture of the 'stable' family presented by rural culture and the poorer adjustment of rural children seems to warrant a conjecture that there are aspects of the older family pattern which not only could but should be changed."[72]

The view of the child as public property or as a precious resource that had to be cultivated and protected by experts achieved even fuller expression at the 1940 conference—a conference held when the nation knew it was probably about to be involved in another world war. Then the family's responsibility was limited to "giving the child food, shelter, and material security."[73] Other needs would be satisfied by the experts, especially those who ran the public schools. Children had to be protected and properly nurtured so that democracy would prevail over its enemies.

Children and the New Deal

When Franklin D. Roosevelt won the presidential election in 1932, 13 million people were unemployed. When he took office in March 1933, 15 million were unemployed. Many were not only out of work but out of money, out of clothes, out of shoes, and even out of their homes. As William E. Leuchtenburg has noted, "many lived in the primitive conditions of a preindustrial society stricken by famine."[74] Children were barefoot and hungry, and as the Commissioner of Charity in Salt Lake City reported, many were not attending school because the schools had closed.[75] Over 80 percent of the children who attended schools in white rural Alabama were home because their schools had closed during the 1932–33 school year. In Georgia, more than a thousand schools were closed, and over 170,000 children had no school to attend.

In the winter of 1933, the schools in Dayton were open only three days a week. In Chicago, the schools were open, but the teachers went without pay for months and sometimes collapsed from hunger in their classrooms.[76]

During his campaign, Roosevelt promised a New Deal to Americans. Part of that New Deal included the Civilian Conservation Corps (CCC), a program that reflected Roosevelt's conviction that young men from the city would benefit from a stay in the country, that the nation's forests needed attention, and that all should serve their country in some manner. After the election, his advisors—Secretary of Labor Frances Perkins, Harry Hopkins, Colorado Sen. Edward Costigan, and Wisconsin Sen. Robert La Follette, Jr.—persuaded him to ask Congress for relief funds as well as for the CCC. Congress complied with his requests, and on March 29, the CCC was approved.

Soon several new alphabetical agencies were created to assist children and youth. On May 12, Congress agreed to appropriate half a billion dollars for relief, and Harry Hopkins was appointed head of the Federal Emergency Relief Administration (FERA). Hopkins soon secured Roosevelt's authorization to establish the Civil Works Administration (CWA), an agency that enabled Hopkins to bypass the states and localities and to place unemployed workers on the federal payroll.

The CWA was short-lived. It operated for less than a year, but had 4.2 million people on its payroll by January 1934. While it was not specifically created to assist children, children were the beneficiaries of some of its efforts. Besides working on 500,000 miles of roads and 1,000 airports, CWA workers either built or repaired 40,000 schools and 3,500 playgrounds and athletic fields. Included in the 50,000 people hired by CWA were all the unemployed teachers in Boston. CWA teachers taught adult education classes and also taught in rural schools that otherwise would have been closed.

Soon after the CWA's dissolution, the Works Progress Administration (renamed the Works Projects Administration (WPA) in 1937) was established under Hopkins's direction. Like the CWA, the WPA employed artists, writers, scientists, and teachers. It constructed public facilities, including 5,900 schools and nearly 13,000 playgrounds. Like the FERA and the CWA, the WPA hired unemployed teachers to organize and operate nursery schools.

Nursery Schools Before the New Deal

Day nurseries for children whose mothers had to work began to appear as the nation began its transition from a predominantly rural-agrarian to an urban-industrial society. The first such nursery apparently opened at the Children's Hospital in New York in 1854. Similar ones followed in Troy, New York (1858), and Philadelphia (1863). By the turn of the century, there were about 175 such nurseries, usually located in settlement houses. At the National Conference on Charities and Corrections in 1912, Mrs. Arthur M. Dodge tried to persuade her audience that new social conditions required a new conception of the nursery school. She explained that "the basic rule of assistance for deserted women or widows obliged to work underlies all day nursery work, but industrial conditions have changed to such an extent that exceptions must be made and there are now cases where both father and mother are working."[77] Moreover, some women had to work because of the low wages paid to their husbands. In some instances, women could find work when and where men could not. Then, it seemed, children were not to be under their father's supervision but in a nursery. However, the view that mothers belonged with their children, that both belonged at home, and that day care was a temporary measure persisted. Nurseries were acceptable during World War I to enable mothers to work but "as soon as the war ended, progressive reformers proposed mother's pensions and other measures designed to enable mothers to stay at home," and the federal government "continued its hands-off policy toward day care, as if any move to protect the quality would be viewed as an endorsement of mothers working."[78]

New Deal Nursery Schools

When the federal government began to support nurseries in a significant way, it "was careful to underline day care's temporary status."[79] It did so to benefit adults, not children. As Mary Elizabeth Pidgeon later explained in a government publication, the nursery schools established by the federal government during the Roosevelt administration "enabled many children to attend nursery schools whose families otherwise could not have given them this experience even though the primary objective had been to give useful work to unemployed persons and though these services had to be fitted in among other projects."[80] In the early years of the New Deal, federally supported nursery schools were established only in those communities that had submitted a request through their state's Director of Emergency Education and were located only in buildings that were owned by or loaned to the local public school systems. The federal government wanted to avoid even an appearance of entering the area of education or child care.

The WPA reported that during 1934–35 it supported 1,900 nurseries that served 75,000 children. In 1936, Edna Ewing Kelley, a supervisor of nursery schools for the Texas Department of Education a supporter of the new development, reported that between 1934 and 1936, 65,000 children between ages two and four found "understanding and happiness" in the 2,000 federally funded nursery schools that had been opened in Puerto Rico and 47 of the 48 states.[81] In 1938, the WPA reported that it was serving over 44,000 children in nearly 1,500 schools and had already served 200,000 children from low income families. When Grace Langdon, a specialist in family life education for the WPA, addressed a conference called by the Children's Bureau in the summer of 1941 to discuss the coordination of day care programs, she reported that the WPA was then supporting about 1,500 schools in each of the states as well as in the Virgin Islands.[82]

Langdon reported that the WPA nurseries had "always been limited to service the low-income groups,"[83] but it appears that others found ways to enroll their children. Kelley analyzed 10,000 records and found that "the vast majority of the children who attended the free nurseries had American-born parents; a third of the parents had some high school training; more than seven percent had at least one year of college."[84] Because the federally supported nurseries were established as an emergency relief measure, the government was committed to closing them as economic conditions improved. Yet, those whose children attended the schools and the agency workers wanted them to continue. The alternatives were clear: either the agency workers had to find new clients who satisfied the eligibility requirements or the requirements had to be modified. As Langdon reported: "The economic level of many of our families has changed now and we need sometimes to move the nursery schools or to change the personnel of the group being served within the limits of our own regulations."[85] The nation's requirements for national defense, however, provided a new rationale for maintaining the schools. In the summer of 1941, even though Congress had reduced its appropriations, the WPA was planning to continue its support of nursery schools "because the administration considered the care of children an important contribution to defense."[86]

Once the nation entered World War II, there was a clear justification for continuing nurseries. As was recorded in the WPA's Final Report: "A special usefulness was found for them in the war period, and the program was expanded in the fiscal year 1942 so as to include the children of working mothers, of men in the armed forces, and of workers engaged in war production, whether or not they were low-income groups."[87] In 1943, Congress appropriated $6 million for WPA nursery schools. The need for workers in war plants allowed agency workers, educators, and social workers to abandon their traditional claim that the best place for children was at home with their mothers. Because the nation had to rely on women to work in war plants, day care was not only justified but also necessary. As Kathryn Close observed in 1943:

> It is also being realized that care must be provided for the children of these working mothers not only for the children's sake, but also in order to maintain top efficiency on the assembly line. For though some mothers seem irresponsible, the majority either will not report to work or function properly if their plans for their children have broken down.[88]

Good day care reduced absenteeism and increased plant productivity.

Undoubtedly nursery schools were popular among many parents, and they were definitely needed. In the summer of 1941, Langdon reported that the WPA was receiving more requests for child services than it could possibly satisfy. Requests came from a wide variety of sources—from the "dislocated population" to the chambers of commerce and mayors of cities where large numbers of women were beginning to work in the war plants. Many women who worked had no one to care for their children. "We have," Langdon reported, "many instances cited, such as 800 women going to work in a factory one morning and 40 children being found locked in parked automobiles." Such instances were "common" and represented the practices of those who cared about their children. They locked them up "so that they will be sure to know where they are."[89] There were reports that in Rhode Island it was "customary for parents working on alternate shifts to leave the children in the care of the one remaining at home, even though he may be sleeping."[90] In Seattle, a young couple who worked in war plants unknowingly left their nine-month-old baby with an "unbalanced woman" and her "impatience" resulted in the baby's death. Too frequently children were "left at home with only the casual supervision of a neighbor,"[91] and older children ran the streets after school with no adult supervision. Such practices, it was believed, "would certainly lead to juvenile delinquency."

Children placed in WPA nurseries were not given formal education, but they *were* given more than custodial care. The WPA tried to provide a staff of three—a head teacher, an assistant teacher, and a nurse or dietician—to give "a sense of security, opportunity for wholesome play, social contacts, and good habits," as well as "food properly prepared and rest under favorable conditions."[92] During their morning play period, children were given a glass of fruit juice and, in the winter months, a spoon of cod liver oil. In the afternoon, they were given a glass of milk and sometimes bread. At lunch they learned social skills by taking turns at assuming the role of host or hostess.

The nurseries also attended to the health and cleanliness of children. Upon entering school, children were inspected and sometimes given a bath or a shampoo before being allowed to begin their play. If they showed signs of illness, they were separated from other children and, if ill enough, taken home so mothers could be given assistance in finding a doctor. They were periodically weighed and measured so school nurses would know when to consult with their mothers about their diets. They were tested for tuberculosis and given immunizations against smallpox, diphtheria, and typhoid.

Conditions were not always perfect in the nurseries. The need for professional staff was greater than the supply. To compensate for the shortage, the WPA invited parents—mothers *and* fathers—to help on a voluntary basis, used National Youth Administration (NYA) workers, and allowed students from high school and college home economics classes to use the schools as laboratories. In areas where the WPA could not open a school, it sent its "family-life education leader" to teach parents how to organize and maintain a cooperative nursery. At times, community groups, such as PTA's, Rotary Clubs, the American Legion, and other civic organizations, assisted the nursery schools. In some areas, private industry either maintained schools or contributed to public ones so their workers would have a place for their children.

After World War II began, the WPA nursery school program was transferred to the Federal Works Agency (FWA), administered by the Office of Defense, Health and Welfare Services, and supported with funds made available by the passage of the Lanham Act. However, neither the transfer nor the administration of the nursery school program was as orderly as many would have liked. Some children's advocates were disappointed that "the Children's Bureau was again relegated to the sidelines of federally subsidized programs."[93] Various federal officials complained that the FWA spent more energy in trying to maintain former WPA nurseries, which were originally planned as relief projects and not always strategically located for the convenience of war workers, than it did on "over-all community projects planned to meet the needs of working mothers." Officials in federal agencies such as the Children's Bureau, the U.S. Office of Education, and the Office of Community War Services charged that the new administrative arrangements provided "no assurance of proper supervision of day care facilities . . . that necessary health and welfare items, such as counseling, foster day care and homemaker services are deleted from all projects before they are approved, that the federal agencies longest experienced and best equipped for setting up standards for safeguarding children have little say in this emergency service."[94] Children's advocates and state officials noted that there was virtually no supervision of the nursery schools, but the Lanham Act allowed only quarterly audits and did not provide for supervision of the schools. Both state and federal officials reported that in some instances communities received funds for programs without the prior knowledge of the state and federal agencies (state departments of education, state welfare agencies, the Children's Bureau, and the U.S. Office of Education) that were supposed to review, process, and approve the applications for program funding. Communities sometimes objected to the requirement that they match the funds provided by the federal government. Charges were even made that the programs had grown like Topsy, "without any congressional parents," and that "few if any legislators had day care in mind when they voted for the Lanham Community Facilities Act."[95]

The Lanham Act provided for fewer funds than the children's advocates wanted. The FWA could only use its funds "for the group care and activities of children" and thus could not fund "other types of child care or auxiliary services that could constitute a more complete program."[96] Children's advocates were interested in the long-term welfare of children, but the government was primarily interested in providing mothers a place for their children while they worked in the war plants. From the government's viewpoint, the nursery schools were needed only for the duration of the war. Once the war ended, federal funds were promptly discontinued. Pidgeon later concluded that the program, despite its limitations and difficulties, was not without its accomplishments. More children—between 550,000 and 600,000—had received either day care or after-school care than ever before. Both the public agencies and the public had acquired an understanding "of the working mother's problems and the community's responsibilities in assisting with them." Some states provided funds to continue the schools, but most were closed. The program also gave educators and welfare workers an opportunity to understand "each other's policies and objectives, and created a more general knowledge of the standards recommended by educational and welfare agencies."[97] Testimony from employers that "the nurseries had great value in reducing absenteeism and turnover in their plants" allowed the government to conclude that the program was successful and that placing control of the program in an agency not primarily concerned with child welfare was perhaps justified.

After the New Deal

Neither attitudes toward day care or nursery schools nor the federal government's ways of administering its nursery-school programs changed significantly after the war's end. The federal government reentered the area of day care in 1962 when Congress approved Title IV-B of the 1962 amendments to the Social Security Act—an amendment that allowed appropriation of federal funds to enable state welfare agencies to provide day care services. During the 1960s and 1970s, when the federal government was waging war on poverty, its commitment increased, and by the late 1970s, its appropriations for day care had reached $2 billion. However, as Edward Zigler, the former Director of the Office of Child Development in the Department of Health, Education and Welfare (HEW), and David Cohen, his special assistant, observed in 1977, "Despite the increasing federal government involvement in day care, the federal government has been reluctant to enforce standards for day care quality." The government's investment in day care has not been supervised by one agency such as the Children's Bureau or the Office of Child Development (created in 1969) but by "at least twelve different federal agencies, ranging from the Department of Agriculture to the Small Business Administration."[98]

The largest federal day care program, funded under Title XX of the Social Security Act (1975), was placed in the Community Services Administration of HEW. While personnel in the Children's Bureau were assigned responsibility for "guaranteeing the quality of Title XX day care," they did "not have the power to make such review meaningful."[99] Moreover, Congress directed that day care facilities funded with Title XX funds not be subject to the 1969 Federal Interagency Day Care Requirements because a 1973 audit by HEW showed that "four-fifths of the 552 facilities sampled did not meet federal requirements even in basic health and safety areas."[100] The largest federal day care program was required to comply only with state licensing laws. The federal government was not able to meet the standards it had set for itself.

Placement of the largest federal day care program in the Community Services Administration is an effective reminder of why such programs are usually funded. Typically, day care is not seen as a benefit to children but rather as a way to free mothers so some other social purpose can be realized. As Karen Authier has concluded: "The practical needs of the child get lost in the demand for day care so that adults can move toward their own lofty goals of winning a war, reducing unemployment, or decreasing the amount of funds allocated for welfare."[101] To advocate day care as a benefit for children still seems impractical. As Cohen and Zigler so aptly observed:

> It is remarkable that, even with the advent of large numbers of working mothers and substantial public funding, this conception of day care as a social welfare tool has endured. Day care has remained suspect—at worst, family-undermining; at best, an inferior alternative to mothers staying at home. Thus, politicians rarely advocate day care simply for the sake of children; rather they feel compelled to justify day care as a device to achieve some other social goals, such as freeing women to join the mobilization for war, or helping to reduce public welfare rolls.[102]

Such views persist, even though "there is no convincing evidence that day care helps welfare parents become working parents."[103] Proponents still frequently defend day care as a means of supporting the family and point out that "there is every indication that the provision of good services in no way affects the number of women who enter the labor force."[104] Clearly, the strongly held belief that women do not belong in the job market persists. However, that belief and the belief that day care is only a concern for welfare mothers is being challenged in the 1980s. For example, a state child-care advisor in California stated in a 1984 *Newsweek* article: "Ten years ago, when you talked about day care, you were talking about welfare mothers. Today you're talking about everybody."[105]

Claims that children are the responsibility of their families, that the family's right to exercise its responsibilities must be protected and even assisted, and that children belong in the home with their mothers are all still maintained. Such views were clearly expressed at the 1960 White House Conference on Children and Youth. While the Conference agreed to recommend that the federal government increase its support for day care facilities for children of working mothers, it also recommended that "to maintain the important relationship of infant and mother, children under 3 remain in their own homes unless there are pressing social or economic reasons for care away from home." It was also recommended that "counseling services be available . . . to help parents decide wisely whether her [the mother's] employment will contribute more to family welfare than her presence in the home."[106] At a 1960 conference on day care sponsored by the Department of Labor's Women's Bureau and the Children's Bureau, Mrs. Randolph Guggenheimer, president of the National Committee for the Day Care of Children, read a letter from then president-elect John F. Kennedy in which he wrote: "The suggestion of a program of research and development to serve the children of working mothers and of parents who for one reason and another cannot provide adequate care during the day deserves our full support."[107]

Child Care After World War II

It was expected that married women who had been working during World War II would quit their jobs and return to their homes to assume traditional homemaker roles. It was also expected that other women would do the same once they were married and began to bear children. Many did, but many did not. Since then, the number of women, married and unmarried, who have children and either choose to work or must work has continued to increase.

By 1974, more than 40 percent of the nation's children had mothers who worked. There were eighteen million children between the ages of six and fourteen who had working mothers. There were also 6.5 million children under age six whose mothers worked, or 17 percent more than at the beginning of the decade. Almost a third of married women with children under age three worked, as did almost half of unmarried women with children under age three.[108]

By 1979, slightly over half of all women and 43 percent of those with children under age six were working. These rates are likely to continue increasing, because "the fastest-growing group of mothers coming into the labor force have children under three, and 70 percent of these work full time."[109] By the mid 1980s, slightly over 60 percent of mothers with children under age eighteen were employed. Nearly half of those with children under age three and slightly over half of those with children between ages three and five were working. Many children will continue to be cared for by someone other than a parent either inside or outside their homes or perhaps even left alone. Evidence of this trend is seen in the size of the day care centers and the age of the children who are placed in them. Elizabeth Jones and Elizabeth Prescott have reported that day care centers are getting bigger and the children they serve younger. "A decade ago, few served children under two, and many states forbade group care of children so young. Now both custom and law have changed, and infants and toddlers appear in group care in rapidly increasing numbers."[110] They also reported that by 1990, an estimated 10.5 million of the 23.3 million preschoolers will have working mothers, "an increase of more than 50 percent over 1978."[111]

As the number of working mothers increases, it will be difficult to ascertain where and how all their children are cared for. The Children's Bureau reported that by 1965 there were more than twelve million children under fourteen years of age with working mothers, but only about 10 percent of those children were cared for by an agency or people outside their families. About 1 percent (81,000) were in group care homes with more than six children; about 2 percent (265,000) were in day care facilities; and 7 percent (979,000) were in either a relative's or a nonrelative's home. About a million were cared for either by siblings under age sixteen or relatives over age sixty-five. At least a million were without any care, "including about 7,000 children under age six."[112] A 1968 survey determined that 47 percent of preschool children whose mothers worked were cared for in their own homes (29 percent by a relative and 18 percent by a nonrelative) and 37 percent of the preschoolers were cared for in another's home (about half in a relative's home and the other half in a nonrelative's). Less than 8 percent were in group care centers, and 7 percent were watched by their mothers while they worked. Less than 1 percent of the preschoolers were left to care for themselves.[113]

In 1970, Dr. Marsden G. Wagner testified to the House Committee on Education and Labor that over one million children under age ten were being left without supervision while their mothers were at work. Many of them also looked after younger brothers and sisters.[114] In 1978, HEW reported that 1.5 million children under age six were in nursery schools and preschools; 2.9 million in a family day care setting, and 1.8 million in some kind of in-home arrangement.[115]

Privately operated day care facilities that are subject to inspection and therefore required to maintain some set of minimum standards are much easier to find than publicly supported facilities that meet those standards. The Child Welfare League reported in the late 1960s that "96 percent (23,085) of the family day care homes, and 70 percent (7,280) of the day care centers" were privately operated. Among the licensed facilities, only 12 percent (4,335) received community support. Most of those receiving community support were conducted under "voluntary auspices" (26 percent, or 2,704, of the day care centers and 2 percent, or 486, of the family day care homes). Under "public auspices" were 2 percent (729) of the family day care homes and 4 percent (416) of the day care centers.[116]

Private facilities are more costly to the parents than publicly subsidized facilities, and some parents simply cannot afford them. The Wage and Labor Standards Administration reported that in 1968 nearly a third of all households headed by women lived in poverty and that many other such households were very near the poverty level.[117] Consequently, many children are in unlicensed and unsupervised settings. Many parents are forced to make arrangements outside the system of licensed and professionally operated centers.

> Nonmaternal care in the homes of children between the ages of 6 and 14 increased from 66 percent in 1965 to 78 percent in 1970 (these figures did not include situations in which children cared for themselves). Care in the home of a nonrelative for children under 6 increased from approximately 13 to 19 percent between 1958 and 1970 while remaining relatively stable at 5 percent for children between 6 and 14. Day care centers accounted for the smallest percentage (2 to 10 percent) of child care arrangements.[118]

Evidence shows that the nonmaternal care children receive in either their own or others' homes is frequently far less than adequate. Sometimes older children are sent to school only on alternate days so they can take turns watching their younger siblings. Some are left "with very elderly, disabled, or infirm caretakers" and even "sedated during the day" so they will be less troublesome. A study conducted in Baltimore in the 1960s determined "that only 5 percent of the children of working mothers were enrolled in day care centers" and that "18 percent of the care mothers had arranged for their children was 'totally adequate'."[119] Yet, some studies have "indicated that most parents were satisfied with their current child care arrangements, which were usually in unlicensed facilities."[120] The scarcity of affordable services probably influences what many parents consider satisfactory.

Adequate Care

What constitutes good, or even adequate, care depends on what one believes the ultimate justification of day care is. As yet, however, agreement is not universal as to why day care should be provided, for whom it should be provided, or who should pay for it. In the simplest terms, the division of opinion is between (1) those who believe it is an acceptable, or the least objectionable, way to free parents from their children so they may realize some social or even personal objective and (2) those "at the other extreme . . . who have grandiose notions about child care programs playing fairy godmother to children who are neglected or abused in their own homes."[121] Yet, Karen Authier claims that no matter what end of the spectrum characterizes one's view, four basic purposes of day care may be specified: "(1) as substitute care while parents work or participate in training or educational programs, (2) as substitute care for parents who are physically or mentally disabled, (3) as a provider of enriching, stimulating, and developmental activities for children from less than adequate home environments, and (4) as an alternative to institutionalization for children living in dangerous home situations."[122]

Even though the purposes served by day care are "not mutually exclusive," and even though it is easy to distinguish between "care that protects a child from bodily harm, insures a clean and safe environment, and perhaps even provides nutritious meals and care that provides these features as well as opportunities for emotional, physical, and intellectual growth,"[123] it is still difficult for those with an interest in day care to agree upon which purposes should be emphasized and supported. In large measure, the quality and scope of services depends on how much users are willing to pay. If one believes that both custodial care and developmental-educational programs should be available to all children at public expense, then one is effectively arguing that the public should establish an institution comparable to the public school or that the public should extend its responsibilities and services downwards. In either case, the cost would be significant. If one wants to limit the cost as much as possible, provision of only custodial care for the children of the poor may be satisfactory, though not very generous.

Some may still want to claim that the state has no right to provide any child care and that any attempt to do so is contrary not only to sound economic principles but also the best interests of children. For example, the nationally syndicated columnist Nicholas Von Hoffman has written that the best way to increase the number of "unhappy, neglected and abused children" is to increase support of federally financed day care centers. Unless one believes "that the state, not the parents, ought to shape the character and the values of children," there is no reason, he asserts, to continue support of day care services. It would be, in his judgment, better for children and cheaper for the government to increase payments given to poor mothers with dependent children. Those who support day care, he charges, are "the cursed American Federation of Teachers and other groups with a misplaced confidence in their own ability to replace mothers with machines and licensed professionals," and are doing so when even the Soviet "collectivist countries are having serious thoughts about bureaucratic child rearing."[124]

Cohen and Zigler argue that the nature and the quality of day care programs, even when directed to the same or a very similar population, may vary significantly "if the commitment to day care is based on some other social goal than the welfare of children, and if the fiscal power is distributed accordingly." To support their claim, they compare two programs—Title XX day care and the day care component of Headstart—that were each assigned responsibility for the care of economically disadvantaged children. For them, Headstart is "viewed as a quality program" that "represents an oasis of concern about children." Its "education and health components" were "specifically designed to meet the needs of the children it serves," and "it has served as a national model of developmental programming for children." Compared to Headstart, they claim, "the quality of Title XX day care varies considerably."

The differences between the programs are reflections of the agencies responsible for them. In the case of Headstart, "the fiscal as well as theoretical jurisdiction" was in the Office of Child Development, an agency primarily concerned with child welfare.[125] In the case of Title XX, as previously noted, responsibility was placed in HEW's Community Services Administration and the process of establishing day care programs was a political process, for Title XX funds were appropriated not only for day care but for a variety of social services, including programs for the aged and the handicapped. The amount and type of day care provided in each of the states were frequently the result of the lobbying process in the several states.

Whenever there is competition for limited funds, the criteria for their distribution may be based on how many will be served and how effectively the applicants articulate their requests in the political process rather than on who most needs the programs and how good the services will be. Children cannot lobby for themselves.

There is agreement that all day care programs should comply with a set of standards and some agreement that the adoption of federal standards would eliminate the difficulties caused by the differences found among state standards and even between communities within a state. It is difficult, however, to specify what those standards should be once the discussion moves beyond the obvious points of protecting children from unsanitary conditions, from the possibility of fire, and from caretakers who may have communicable diseases. In part, determination of standards is a function of the purpose of the care. Standards for custodial care, which attempts only to provide a safe place to satisfy a child's basic physical and psychological needs, would certainly be different from the standards for comprehensive programs designed to satisfy all of a child's social, psychological, developmental, and educational needs. Even if there were agreement on the standards, it would be difficult to determine how well agencies complied with them. As Authier notes: "Checklists work well to make sure that the water is sufficiently hot for dishwashing and that the fire extinguishers are in place, but it is difficult to monitor warmth, understanding, patience, and enjoyment of children by means of a checklist that can be administered by a licensing representative."[126]

Determination, administration, and enforcement of standards depend on who is to control the delivery of day care services. However, there is disagreement about whether day care should be controlled by parents or professionals. Authier reports that "parents who have been involved with parent-planned and controlled programs have discovered the difficulties inherent in applying the democratic process to day care decision-making but seem to prefer those difficulties to the problems of dealing with decisions imposed by administrators."[127] Most professionals agree that some form and level of parent involvement is necessary, and many standards recommend that parents be used as employees, volunteers, or advisors.[128] The Federal Interagency Day Care Requirements (1968) specify that each program serving forty or more children have a policy advisory council and that at least 50 percent of the council's membership consist of parents or their representatives.[129]

Even when it is agreed that professionals should control day care, there is frequently disagreement about which interested and qualified professionals should assume the responsibility. Authier records that "professionals in education, social work, child development, and health may all agree that the expertise of each discipline is essential but disagree about which profession should captain the ship, which should navigate, and which should have scullery duty."[130] Some, but certainly not all, "advocates feel that the public school system, with its history of administrative and educational sophistication, could best guarantee the delivery of quality day care under the supervision of local boards of education." However, "others feel that the school system is already overburdened, often educationally unsuccessful, and too insulated from community forces to be entrusted with day care."[131] Some even question the motives of educators who are interested in day care.

At its 1975 convention, the American Federation of Teachers (AFT) agreed upon a program called Educare as a national priority. Educare, a cradle-to-grave program for education, included a proposal for expanded preschool programs. The AFT also recommended that Congress assign responsibility for all early childhood, or preschool education, to public schools.

As Joel Spring has remarked, many saw that as a proposal "designed to protect the interests of public schools, which represented the basis of their membership."[132] AFT was opposed by the Day Care and Child Development Council of America and the Children's Defense Funds, and, as late as 1979, educators were "criticized for focusing more on the need unemployed teachers have for jobs than on the needs of children."[133]

Still another difficulty in determining adequate standards for day care is the "paucity of experimentally-controlled, rigorous data to guide social policy concerning children."[134] That lack of data is particularly frustrating for policymakers when they are confronted with departures from traditional beliefs and practices. For example, since World War II, the general belief has been that children under age three do not profit from group day care arrangements. Yet, the mothers of this age group are entering the labor force at the fastest growing rate. These data point in different directions and do not indicate a course for policymakers. Cohen and Zigler relate that:

> While we are far from sanguine about this increase, there is no clear evidence that infant day care, or adequate quality, harms children. Outstanding psychologists have concluded that infant day care is not associated with any marked deleterious consequences. While other studies report possible negative effects, they are perhaps too subtle to guide the policymaker.[135]

Without adequate data for guiding policy, child care workers must, they claim, use what knowledge and experience they have and be directed by the "medical dictum, 'first of all, do no harm'."[136]

The Effects of Day Care

Little research has been done on the effects of day care on children. However, as the number of mothers working outside the home has increased, so has the interest in the effects of non-maternal care. Harriet D. Watkins and Marilyn R. Bradbard reported in 1982 that they had found sufficient material on the effects of day care on children's socialization to enable them to make suggestions about four areas of concern: "(1) mother-child attachment; (2) curiosity and play; (3) peer relationships and influences; and (4) sex-typing and sex-role development."[137] Like other reviews, however, their review of the literature shows that the research is not absolutely conclusive.

Mother-Child Attachment

Researchers are concerned with the effects of day care on the affectional tie between mother and child because studies of institutionalized children, conducted in the late 1940s and early 1950s, suggested that early and prolonged separation of the child from the mother adversely affected the "child's emotional security and overall development." More recently, a study conducted in a "high quality, university-based program" on children from low-income families who entered the program at or near age one showed that "full-time care does not necessarily prevent children from developing normal and secure attachments to their mothers."[138] A subsequent study that compared the reactions of two groups of two- and three-year-old children—a day care group and a home care group—to repeated separations from the parent and introductions to a stranger (the strange situation technique) showed different results. "The day care group interacted less with their mothers before separation and displayed more oral behavior and avoidance of the stranger." From that study, it was concluded that "many repetitions of minor separations *may* have effects similar in form, although not in severity, to major ones."[139] Other studies failed to show similar findings and still another found that "the home-reared children were the ones who displayed more symptomatic distress upon separation from the mother."[140]

Variations of attachment studies have tried to determine whether separation from the mother causes children to develop stronger affectional ties with the caregiver than those developed with the mother. A laboratory study of twenty-three black children between the ages of nine and twenty-three months who had been placed in day care showed that "a strong mother-child attachment bond had been formed despite the fact that all of the infants had spent approximately six hours per day in group care since two or three months of age." Similar studies have shown that while children do develop strong attachments to caregivers and even show distinct preference for "stable" as opposed to "non-stable" caregivers, "such relationships are still subordinate to the one with the mother."[141] After conducting an extensive review of the research literature, Claire Etaugh reported that "the bulk of evidence indicates that non-maternal care starting in the first two years of life does not impair the child's attachment to the mother" and that "nonmaternal care starting after the first two years of life does not necessarily impair the child's attachment to the mother."[142]

Michael Rutter of the Institute of Psychiatry in London has also reviewed the attachment literature. He reports that "the evidence is inconclusive but it seems that, although most young children do not become overtly insecure and anxious as a result of day care, it is possible nevertheless that more subtle ill effects occur in some children."[143] Watkins and Bradbard emphasize that most of the studies "have been conducted in *high-quality, university-based centers that are staffed with highly trained personnel and equipped with an abundance of learning aids to enhance all aspects of a child's development.*" Consequently, nothing definitive can be said about "the effects that privately-owned local centers and franchises have on the mother-child attachment bond."[144] They do suggest, however, that children's adjustment to day care can be facilitated by appointing and furnishing the center with some of the characteristics of the home. It appears to be beneficial to allow children to leave favorite toys at the center, to paste family pictures to their lockers, to invite parents to join the children for lunch when possible, and even to use some items from the children's homes in the center.

Curiosity and Play

The assumption has generally been made that infants and children who have been reared by their mothers and who have therefore developed a strong attachment to their mothers have the security and the confidence to move from their mothers to play and explore because they have the feeling that their mothers will be there when they decide to return to them. One study of six-month-old infants found that those who had been under the care of their mothers were more likely to engage in exploratory behavior than those who received nonmaternal care and that the "mothers were significantly more responsible and stimulating toward their infants than were caregivers."[145] Evidence shows, however, that the responsiveness of caregivers to children in their charge is directly related to the length of time they have known them. Once children and caregivers develop rapport, the children may develop the confidence they need for exploratory behavior. As might be expected, however, another study found that "toddlers in community-based day care exhibited a significantly higher developmental level of play when compared with their home-reared counterparts." Significantly, "day care children explored more unique properties of toys and objects while the home-reared group engaged in more non-specific manipulation." Thus, it has been concluded that peer interaction among toddlers seems to increase their "competence with inanimate objects."[146]

Evidence is not strong that nonmaternal care damages the cognitive development of children. Etaugh's review of the literature indicates that "good-quality, nonmaternal care does not appear to have either adverse or beneficial effects on the intellectual and cognitive functioning of middle-class children." However, it does indicate that "high-quality, educationally oriented day-care programs often have been shown to prevent the decline in intellectual performance frequently found in home-reared children from lower-class families."[147] Perhaps more important than whether the child is placed in a day care setting is the nature of the setting in which they develop. Settings in which the caregiver, maternal or otherwise, pays attention to what stimulates or overstimulates children and to what objects they need to develop their exploratory inclinations and skills are obviously better than those in which no consideration is given to developmental requirements.

Still, some object to separating children from their homes and parents during their early years. For example, Burton White has written: "I don't believe full-time substitute care during the first years of life would be in my own child's self interest; therefore I can't recommend it to other parents, except in extraordinary circumstances."[148] On the other hand, Christine Anderson has concluded that children's normal personality development is probably more a function of the kind of time children spend with parents than the amount of time.[149] Anita Farel hypothesizes that the mother's attitude toward working may have more of an effect on children than whether the mother actually works outside the home. She claims that some evidence indicates that the children of mothers who want to work and do work and the children of mothers who do not want to work and do not work perform better on certain measures of achievement and adjustment to school (the Classroom Behavior Inventor, the Preschool and Primary Scale of Intelligence, and the Tests of Basic Experience) than children of mothers who work but desire to stay home and children of mothers who remain home but want to work. Children whose mothers remained home and believed that their working would not be good for their children scored the highest on the administered measures while children whose mothers did not work but believed that working outside the home would be good for their children scored lowest of four groups.[150] Mothers whose attitudes and behavior are congruent will, according to the terms of this hypothesis, have children who adjust to and perform better in school than children whose mothers have incongruent attitudes and behaviors.[151]

Peer Relationships and Influences

Peer relationships are of particular interest and importance to educators for many reasons. First, a great amount of our learning is social in nature. We learn by watching and imitating others. Second, it is through the approval, disapproval, rejection, acceptance, and recognition experienced in group interactions that one learns social skills, practices newly developed skills, and acquires a sense of values, that is, of what is important, what is praiseworthy, what is rewarded, or what is punished. Third, we develop a sense of self through interaction with others. We first need a sense of others before we can develop a sense of self as an independent being. Fourth, modern life is such that people must work and live in proximity and cooperate to achieve even some small measure of success. Finally, some believe that both the individual and society can and will achieve more through cooperation than through competition. The ability to work and play effectively with peers is an ability that most of society values highly.

Recent studies show that infants and toddlers as well as young children engage in peer interaction, that children who have more experience with and spend more time with their peers are more likely "to be more peer-oriented than their home-reared counterparts." Watkins and Bradbard also report that some studies suggest that "early peer exposure in a day care setting might actually facilitate the acquisition of more forms of social behavior."[152] It may seem curious and perhaps even contradictory that children's advocates can be concerned about the strength of the affectional tie between children and their mothers and still be concerned with the ability of the child to act independently. Rather, their concern merely reflects our adherence to both psychological and philosophical principles in determining how children should be nurtured and educated. From psychological studies of children we have learned that they do need a sense of security and that that sense of security is enhanced and developed by a strong and consistent relationship with a responsive and nurturing caregiver. Philosophically, we frequently profess our belief that nothing is more important than the value of the individual even while we maintain the importance of learning how to work well with others. We want our children to function effectively with their peers and to have opportunities to do so, but at the same time we are concerned that the peer group not exercise so much influence that our children do not have opportunities to express their unique qualities. Watkins and Bradbard remind childcare workers that

> the literature on peer relations implies that a day care setting provides ample opportunity for the development and maintenance of peer relationships, which encourage infant/child autonomy and separation from adult caregivers. Moreover, studies exist that document the subtle but pervasive influence that the peer group exerts on its members. Consequently, it is vital that caregivers recognize the fact that, even among preschoolers, peers have a dramatic impact on children's social development.[153]

One's evaluation of the peer influences on a child in a day care setting probably reflects the degree to which one believes the child's development should be primarily guided by adults. Those who believe children require significant adult supervision are probably more sensitive to the subtle influences of the peer group than those who believe more in the natural development of children.

The influence of peers in a day care setting is difficult to predict, for "children do vary in their degree of susceptibility to the influences of peer modeling and reinforcement."[154] It has been reported that "children who begin day care early (before the age 2 years) are more likely than later-entering children to interact with peers both in positive and in negative ways." However, that difference may simply indicate that children with more experience in an activity are more likely to engage in it than those with less experience. As Etaugh points out, it may also "be related to the finding that activity level generally is higher among children who enter day care before the age of 2."[155]

Attempts to determine how day care influences interactions with adults have not shown "any consistent differences" between day-care and home-care children, although some studies suggest that "home-reared children have been found to interact more and to verbalize more with their caretakers, whereas day-care children have been found to interact more with an unfamiliar adult."[156] Long-term influence of day care cannot be assessed because only one study has been made of the effects of day care through adolescence. That study showed that day-care boys, but not day-care girls, were more likely to disagree with their parents at age seven than were their home-reared counterparts. At age fifteen, the differences were still evident, and the day-care males were less responsive to punishment than were their home-reared counterparts.[157]

Sex-Typing and Sex-Role Development

There is probably more interest and speculation about how educators, parents, and caregivers can modify how children acquire gender identity than there is knowledge about how day care influences traditional notions of masculinity and femininity. The interest comes from those who believe that traditional conceptions of masculine and feminine sex roles are being challenged, reevaluated, and even revised and also from those who believe that society and individuals would benefit from more androgynous individuals, that is, those who are more flexible and capable of functioning in a broader variety of activities because they possess "a balanced combination of both masculine and feminine characteristics."[158]

Because the number of children in day care is increasing, it is not surprising that "the recent sex-role clamor has led to speculation that early day care experience might be a mediating factor in narrowing sex differences in young children and producing more androgynous individuals."[159] Although few studies are devoted to this topic, some indication has been noted that "early exposure to day care might reduce sex differences in young children." Specifically, "proximity-seeking dependency" behaviors of day care girls are less than those of home care girls. Traditionally, boys have been somewhat less dependent on their mothers and have displayed less "proximity-seeking dependency" than girls. However, some studies show that day care girls are as independent of their mothers as day care boys. Thus, for some, day care is a way to reduce sex differences "by fostering independence from the mother and encouraging the formation of peer relationships that support exploration and play."[160] It is unlikely, however, that day care will automatically create a generation of androgynous individuals.

Watkins and Bradbard suggest that those caregivers who wish to reduce sex differences and promote the development of androgynous individuals should "consider assuming a 'bicultural' atmosphere where the language of both sex-role cultures is spoken." They further urge that "in a bicultural environment the caregiver's sex-role expectations should encourage expression of academic and play preferences, interests, and behaviors which represent a blending of traditional sex-role patterns."[161] Obviously, the separation of boys from girls in day care would promote traditional sex roles. However, even the placement of traditional activities can influence what children will do and learn. If the toys and territories traditionally assigned to children on the basis of gender are adjacent to rather than removed from each other, girls show as much interest in playing with blocks as boys and boys shows as much interest in playing in the "family center" as girls. The most effective way to influence the behaviors and the values children acquire is through the caregivers who serve as effective models, for children do learn their roles through observation and imitation.

New Attitudes Toward Day Care

Those who believe that nonmaternal care is as acceptable as maternal care can find more support for their beliefs than they could a generation ago. By the early 1960s our views toward the family, children, and the role of women were recognizably changing. The argument then arose that day care should be seen as something other than an instrument of welfare. For example, at the conference jointly sponsored by the Women's Bureau and the Children's Bureau, Mrs. Randolph Guggenheimer indicated that

> ambivalence is widespread in our society about the woman's role. So much of the way we live invites women to seek employment outside the home. . . . Day care should be used to strengthen family life and its acceptance should not be based on economic need. The latter should be important only in determining the fee paid by parents.[162]

Significantly, she also expressed the belief that "in many cases, a mother who works is a better mother during the hours she is at home than one who feels she is frustrated by being 'nothing more exciting than a housewife'."[163]

By the end of the 1960s, Florence A. Ruderman, who directed a series of studies on day care, reported that "the working mother today is the focus of a great deal of attention, much of it well meant, but often reflecting ignorance or bias." It was, she claimed, time to stop thinking of working mothers as a symptom of a social pathology.

> It should be possible to say that in American society today mothers frequently work because they want to; they enjoy it; they are ambitious for their families and themselves; they have, or want, interests and activities beyond their homes and domestic circle. (And this is frequently true of mothers in low income brackets, too.) It should be possible to say that in the future this may become even more commonplace and, rather than something to be deplored or half-heartedly accepted, this may actually be socially and psychologically good.[164]

A case can be made that the concern with the rights of women and the rights of children is an ideological diversion to draw our attention away from an economy that requires more effort for fewer rewards. At the end of World War II the middle-class ideal was that one person could support two adults and 2.2 children. Now we need two adults to support two adults and .9 children, and many women work out of economic necessity. In any case, by 1972 the National Council of Jewish Women noted that day care was needed and desired by all social and economic levels of society and recommended that "comprehensive developmental child care services should be available to all families who wish their children to benefit from them."[165] The Council further recommended that all day care centers "be integrated racially, ethnically, and with respect to socio-economic groupings" and, like Guggenheimer, urged that economic need be considered only in determining who should pay and how much.

Perhaps the clearest indication that attitudes toward day care have changed significantly since World War II are the results that Etaugh reported after examining the views expressed toward working mothers in child care books and leading women's magazines (*McCall's, Ladies' Home Journal, Good Housekeeping, Redbook, Cosmopolitan, Parents' Magazine,* and *Mademoiselle*) between 1956 and 1976. She found that "a major trend discernible both in magazine articles and in child-care books between the 1960s and 1970s is a shift in the direction of a more favorable view of working mothers and nonmaternal care."[166] During the 1950s and 1960s, nearly all works on child care, including the two most popular—the Children's Bureau's pamphlet, "Infant Care," and Benjamin Spock's *Baby and Child Care*—expressed strong disapproval of working mothers and nonmaternal care. Until they were revised in the 1970s, such topics were only considered under the heading, "special problems." Each of the popular works urged that mothers remain with their children and emphasized that if children under age three could not be cared for by their mothers, they should not be placed in group care. Spock even warned that the neglected children of working mothers would likely grow up to be maladjusted. Even as late as 1967, Spock questioned why mothers would pay someone else to do what they certainly could do better. For example, in the 1976 edition of *Baby and Child Care,* Spock—still maintaining that children under age three should not be placed in group care—nonetheless admitted his earlier prejudice toward working mothers and no longer treated the topic as a "special problem." In moving away from his earlier views, he acknowledged the legitimacy of new life-styles and assigned new rights and responsibilities to fathers. He indicated that "both parents have an equal right to a career if they want one . . . and an equal obligation to share in the care of their child."[167] If mothers have neither guilt feelings nor doubts about whether they should work, then it is likely, Spock related, that their children will accept it and even be proud of them and their jobs. Other writers, like Spock, have begun to discuss the importance of the father in the caring and rearing of children but some "appear merely to have paid lip service to the father's role as caretaker of his young children."[168]

Examination of the popular press also shows that attitudes toward nonmaternal care have changed. Perhaps an important sign of the beginning of the change in those attitudes is a series of six articles on day care published in the *Ladies Home Journal* in 1966. That series, according to Etaugh, was a "campaign promoting day care as a 'new family birthright'."[169] In those articles, parents, and especially mothers, were instructed that even nonworking mothers may not be able to supply their children with all the care and experiences they need for proper development.

Our attitudes toward what we do to and with our children are possibly as important as what we do. As our beliefs about what is appropriate and necessary for children change, so too do the research questions we ask about the effect on children of various arrangements and practices. Even though some literature based on carefully conducted research indicates that nonmaternal care of children is not necessarily harmful and may even be beneficial, the literature is based on a very small spectrum of the wide variety of arrangements that have been created for children. Most facilities to which researchers have easy and complete access are the best and are usually professionally operated centers that try to do more than provide safe custodial care for children.

Conclusion

Children are frequently viewed as either the victims of our misdeeds and omissions or the beneficiaries of our actions. Sometimes they have benefited from action taken on their behalf, and sometimes they have benefited from actions taken to realize some other social goal. As

Howard Cohen has observed, for at least three centuries "children have been the objects of adult protection."[170] As such objects, they have been seen as "the most vulnerable and power-less people in our society."[171] Indeed, as Cohen so accurately states:

> The dominant thrust of concern for the treatment of children in contemporary America has been for more "care taking." In response to a perceived need for more structure in adult-child rela-tionships, those with the caretaker outlook have sought new ways to protect children from real and potential abuses. Caretakers have been responsible for institutionalizing compulsory educa-tion, limitations on child labor, laws prohibiting child abuse and neglect, aid to families with de-pendent children, school lunch programs, infant health programs, some public support for day care and so on.[172]

Critics of the caretaker notion insist that children deserve more than care. Even though the state has traditionally acted to provide protection and care for children when parents have not, the care has not always been in the best interest of children. In fact, according to the crit-ics of the caretaker notion, no matter who assumes the responsibility for care, "there is no ef-fort to diminish the vulnerability and powerlessness of children."[173] The nature of the relationship between children and adults remains unchanged.

Critics of the caretaker notion, or advocates of children's rights, want not just to provide more protection for children but "see the standard, normal, socially acceptable treatment of children as part of the problem." They are attacking not how poorly children are protected but the "very institution of American childhood." They are not content to improve the state of childhood. They want to "restructure" the relationships between adults and children. They claim that we have recognized other systematic modes of abuse in our society and that we must do the same for our children. As Cohen explains:

> As a society we have come to understand that there is not only personal bigotry, but institutional racism; not only male chauvinism, but economic and social discrimination against women. We are now being asked to acknowledge that there is not only child abuse, but systematic mistreat-ment of children.[174]

Advocates of children's rights claim that adults do not necessarily know what is in the best interests of the child and that adults typically overlook the conflicts of interest that exist be-tween children and adults. They challenge the belief that the only way to improve the well-being of children is to continue to pass control over them from adult to adult.[175] Children, they maintain, should have effective control over their own lives. For example, John Holt proposes "that the rights, privileges, duties, responsibilities, of adult citizens be made *avail-able* to any young person, of whatever age, who wants to make use of them."[176] Moreover, Holt leaves no room for any question about what those rights are. They include:

1. The right to equal treatment at the hands of the law—i.e., the right in any situation, to be treat-ed no worse than an adult would be.
2. The right to vote and take full part in political affairs.
3. The right to be legally responsible for one's life.
4. The right to work, for money.

5. The right to privacy.
6. The right to financial independence and responsibility—i.e., the right to own, buy, and sell property, to borrow money, establish credit, sign contracts, etc.
7. The right to direct and manage one's own education.
8. The right to travel, to live away from home, to choose or make one's own home.
9. The right to receive from the state whatever minimum income it may guarantee to adult citizens.
10. The right to make and enter into, on a basis of mutual consent, quasi-familial relationships outside one's immediate family—i.e., the right to seek and choose guardians other than one's own parents and to be legally dependent on them.
11. The right to do, in general, what any adult may legally do.[177]

In part, the children's rights movement is an attempt to extend more privileges and opportunities to children as well as an attempt to improve their well-being. It is also much more than that. For some, it is based on a reexamination and even a new conceptualization of the nature of the relationship between children and adults. Leon Sheleff, for example, maintains that generational hostility flows not in one direction but in two. He further maintains that the traditional use of the Oedipus complex to explain tensions and difficulties between adults and children creates imbalanced perspectives. To correct the imbalance and to provide a theory to account for crimes committed against children by adults as well as the hostility of parents toward their children, he proposes a complex to complement the Oedipus complex—the Rustum complex.

Sheleff finds the basis for his complementary complex in the Persian story of Sohrab and Rustum—the story that served as the basis for Matthew Arnold's epic poem "Sohrab and Rustum." In the Persian tale there is a chance meeting of father and son, Rustum and Sohrab, on a battlefield where each has been chosen to represent his army. Only after the face-to-face combat has been concluded and only when the son is at the edge of death, does Rustum learn that he has mortally wounded his son whom he had not until that moment ever known. Because the tale includes a scene in which the son has the advantage over the father and even offers a truce that Rustum clearly refuses, Sheleff suggests "that parents have a built-in antagonism toward their progeny, that their attitude toward them may range from ignorance and indifference, through denial and contempt, to open attack and ultimate destruction."[178] The Rustum complex enables Sheleff to explain what is either an increasing rate of child abuse or a newly found awareness of its extent. He also suggests that our view of children would be different if we considered their perspective as well as our own.

Sheleff urges adults to learn to appreciate children's "legitimate aspirations," "their growing capacities and maturity," and "their rights with the prudence befitting those who have a stake in the present and the future of society." Children, he argues, have the right to more control over how they live, their jobs, and their schooling. They should even have at least "a partial vote equal to a fraction of the adult vote."[179] Clearly, Sheleff wants children to participate in more, not fewer, "adult activities."

To advocate a bill of rights for children that would grant them equal status to adults may be to contribute to what Neil Postman describes as the "disappearance of childhood."[180] Postman's analysis, based on a study of how the mass media have influenced children and our conception of childhood, shows that the nature of media in modern society is such that adults can no longer regulate what children know. The inability of adults to censor what children learn destroys the distinction between childhood and adulthood because childhood is maintained by keeping secrets from children. With universal access to the media by all regardless of age, there are no secrets and thus no children. If Postman is correct, then those who advocate children's rights, or children's liberation, may be doing little more than setting down guidelines for what is already upon us.

Some, such as Postman, may regret the loss of childhood but not all are convinced that childhood is necessarily so good that it must be preserved. Holt, for example, claims that children know that childhood is not all that adults make it out to be.

> "A child's world." "To experience childhood." "To be allowed to be a child." Such words seem to say that childhood is a time and an experience very different from the rest of life and that it is, or ought to be, the best part of our lives. It is not, and no one knows it better than children. *Children want to grow up.* While they are growing up, they want, some of the time, to be around the kind of adults who like being grown-up and who think of growing up as an exploration and adventure, not the process of being chased out of some Garden of Eden.[181]

Whether one wants to maintain or to destroy childhood, whether or not one sees it as an ideal Garden of Eden, most children are insulated from the adult world—or so it has been. In part, advocates of children's rights are questioning the propriety of maintaining age segregation in a society that has recognized the effects and the injustice of racial, ethnic, and even sexual segregation.

Any extension of the range of choice and responsibility that children and youth are allowed to enjoy will certainly meet with some objection. Those who claim that children need not more responsibility but more protection and nurture are likely to be called paternalistic and charged with being overprotective and unfair. More important than determining how much responsibility and choice children should have and more important than determining who is obligated to provide children with the effective means to exercise those choices is the existence of the questions. The questions themselves serve as effective reminders that children have ethical claims on adults even though the children may be powerless, vulnerable, and incapable of expressing those claims. Because the questions exist, children have those claims, and adults cannot deny them.

Children's rights, however conceived, cannot relieve adults of their responsibilities to children. How those rights are conceived does, however, determine how adults meet their responsibilities. As our conceptions of gender rights, roles, and responsibilities are being challenged and transformed and as our conceptions of the family are being redefined so is our conception of children. Our conceptions of teaching and of schooling are not likely to escape those challenges and transformations. Teachers will have to understand conceptions of childhood that differ from those that obtained when they were children if they are to meet their professional and ethical responsibilities to students effectively and justly.

Notes

1. Charles A. Savage, *The Athenian Family: A Sociological and Legal Study* (Baltimore, 1967), 89. Quoted in Leon Sheleff, *Generations Apart: Adult Hostility to Youth* (New York: McGraw-Hill, 1981), 195.

2. Alan Watson, *The Law of the Ancient Romans* (Dallas: Southern Methodist University Press, 1970), 38. Emphasis added.
3. Sheleff, *Generations Apart,* 195.
4. Quoted in Sheleff, *Generations Apart,* 195.
5. "Massachusetts School Law of 1642," reproduced in Sol Cohen, ed., *Education in the United States: A Documentary History* (New York: Random House, 1974), 393.
6. "Instructions for the Punishment of Incorrigible Children in Massachusetts," reproduced in Cohen, ed. *Education in the United States,* 379.
7. "Massachusetts School Law of 1648," reproduced in Cohen, ed., *Education in the United States,* 394–395.
8. Reprinted in Robert G. Bremner et al., eds., *Children and Youth in America: A Documentary History,* vol. 1 (Cambridge, Mass.: Harvard University Press, 1970), 39.
9. Ibid., 49.
10. Ibid.
11. Ibid., 42.
12. Robert Hunter, *Poverty* (New York: Harper Torchbook, 1965), 195.
13. George H. Martin, *The Evolution of the Massachusetts Public School System* (New York, 1894), quoted in Ellwood P. Cubberley, *Public Education in the United States* (Boston: Houghton Mifflin, 1934), 19.
14. Herbert M. Kliebard, "Education at the Turn of the Century: A Crucible for Curriculum Change," *Educational Researcher* (January, 1982): 16.
15. John Dewey, *The School and Society* (Chicago: University of Chicago Press, 1963), 7.
16. Ibid., 9.
17. Ibid., 7.
18. Ibid.
19. Hunter, *Poverty,* 200–210.
20. Ibid., 205.
21. Ibid., 209.
22. Ibid., 210.
23. Ibid., 212.
24. Ibid., 225–226.
25. Ibid., 208.
26. Rochelle Beck, "The White House Conferences on Children: An Historical Perspective," *Harvard Educational Review,* 43 (November 1973): 654.
27. Theodore Roosevelt, "Sixth Annual Message, December 3, 1906," reprinted in Robert Bremner et al., eds., *Children and Youth in America: A Documentary History,* vol. 2 (Cambridge, Mass.: Harvard University Press, 1971), 687.
28. *U.S. Statutes at Large, 59 Congress, 2nd Session* (1907), reprinted in Bremner, ed., *Children and Youth,* vol. 2, 689.
29. *Congressional Record, 59 Congress, 2nd Session* (1907), reprinted in Bremner, ed., *Children and Youth,* vol. 2, 692.
30. Owen R. Lovejoy, "What Remains of Child Labor," *New Republic* 9 (November 11, 1916): 39.
31. Reprinted in Bremner, ed., *Children and Youth,* vol. 2, 718.
32. Ibid., 719–720.
33. Ibid., 735.
34. Ibid., 737.
35. Ibid., 737.
36. Reprinted in Robert Bremner et al., eds., *Children and Youth in America: A Documentary History,* vol. 3 (Cambridge, Mass.: Harvard University Press, 1974), 342.

37. Florence Kelley, "The Federal Government and the Working Children," *The Annals of the American Academy of Political and Social Sciences* 27 (1906), reprinted in Bremner, ed., *Children and Youth,* vol. 2, 758.
38. Lillian Wald, *The House on Henry Street* (New York: Holt, Rinehart & Winston, 1915), reprinted in Bremner, ed., *Children and Youth,* vol. 2, 757.
39. Reprinted in Bremner, ed., *Children and Youth,* vol. 2, 762.
40. Ibid., 762–765.
41. Ibid., 766.
42. Ibid., 765.
43. Ibid.
44. Ibid., 766.
45. Ibid., 770.
46. Ibid., 771.
47. Ibid., 775.
48. Ibid., 780.
49. Ibid., p. 781.
50. Lillian Wald, "Shall We Dismember the Child," *Survey* 62 (1929–1930), reprinted in Bremner, ed., *Children and Youth,* vol. 2, 787.
51. Beck, "The White House Conferences on Children," 656.
52. Grace Abbott, *Ten Years Work for Children* (Washington, D.C., 1923), reprinted in Bremner, ed., *Children and Youth,* vol. 2, 781.
53. Mary Jo Bane, "A Review of Child Care Books," *Harvard Educational Review* 43 (November 1973): 669.
54. Reprinted in Cohen, ed., *Education in the United States,* 2359.
55. Ibid.
56. Abbott, *Ten Years Work for Children,* reprinted in Bremner, ed., *Children and Youth,* vol. 2, 782.
57. Ibid., 781.
58. Ibid., 782.
59. Ibid., 784.
60. Ibid., 785.
61. Quoted in Bremner, ed., *Children and Youth,* vol. 3, xi.
62. Beck, "The White House Conferences on Children," 655.
63. *Standards of Child Welfare, A Report of the Children's Bureau Conferences May and June, 1919,* reprinted in Cohen, ed., *Education in the United States,* 2360.
64. *White House Conference, 1930: Addresses and Abstracts of Committee Reports* (New York: Century, 1930), v.
65. Beck, "The White House Conferences on Children," 656.
66. *White House Conference, 1930,* 16.
67. Ibid., 17.
68. Ibid., 134.
69. Ibid., 149.
70. Ibid., 151.
71. Ibid., 146–147.
72. Ibid., 142–143.
73. *White House Conference on Children in a Democracy, 1940,* quoted in Beck, "The White House Conferences on Children," 659.
74. William E. Leuchtenburg, *Franklin D. Roosevelt and the New Deal* (New York: Harper Torchbook, 1963), 1.
75. Ibid., 3.

76. Ibid., 21.
77. Quoted in Mary-Elizabeth Pidgeon, *Employed Mothers and Child Care,* Bulletin of the Women's Bureau No. 246 (Washington, D.C., 1935), reprinted in Bremner, ed., *Children and Youth,* vol. 3, 678.
78. Donald J. Cohen and Edward Zigler, "Federal Day Care Standards: Rationale and Recommendations," *American Journal of Orthopsychiatry* 47 (July 1977): 457.
79. Ibid.
80. Pidgeon, *Employed Mothers and Child Care,* reprinted in *Bremner,* ed., *Children and Youth,* vol. 3, 678.
81. Edna Ewing Kelley, "Uncle Sam's Nursery Schools," *Parents Magazine* (March 1936), reprinted in Bremner, ed., *Children and Youth,* vol. 3, 679.
82. Grace Langdon, "The Program of the Works Progress Administration in U.S. Children's Bureau," *Proceedings of the Conference on Day Care of Children of Working Mothers,* Publication No. 281 (Washington, D.C., 1942), reprinted in Bremner, ed., *Children and Youth,* vol. 3, 681.
83. Ibid., 682.
84. Kelley, "Uncle Sam's Nursery Schools," in Bremner, ed., *Children and Youth,* vol. 3, 679.
85. Langdon, "The Program of the Works Progress Administration in U.S. Children's Bureau," reprinted in Bremner, ed., *Children and Youth,* vol. 3, 683.
86. Ibid., 682.
87. U.S. Federal Works Agency, *Final Report on the WPA Program, 1935–1943* (Washington, D.C., 1947), reprinted in Bremner, ed., *Children and Youth,* vol. 3, 681.
88. Kathryn Close, "Day Care Up to Now," *Survey Midmonthly* 74 (July 1943), reprinted in Bremner, ed., *Children and Youth,* vol. 3, 684.
89. Langdon, "The Program of the Works Progress Administration in U.S. Children's Bureau," reprinted in Bremner, ed., *Children and Youth,* vol. 3, 682.
90. Close, "Day Care Up to Now," reprinted in Bremner, ed., *Children and Youth,* vol. 3, 688.
91. Ibid., 684.
92. Kelley, "Uncle Sam's Nursery Schools," reprinted in Bremner, ed., *Children and Youth,* vol. 3, 680.
93. Cohen and Zigler, "Federal Day Care Standards," 457.
94. Close, "Day Care Up to Now," reprinted in Bremner, ed., *Children and Youth,* vol. 3, 686.
95. Ibid., 690.
96. Pidgeon, *Employed Mothers and Child Care,* reprinted in Bremner, ed., *Children and Youth,* vol. 3, 692.
97. Ibid.
98. Cohen and Zigler, "Federal Day Care Standards," 457.
99. Ibid., 458.
100. Ibid.
101. Karen Authier, "Defining the Care in Child Care," *Social Work* 24 (November 1979): 502.
102. Cohen and Zigler, "Federal Day Care Standards," 457.
103. Ibid., 458.
104. Ibid.
105. R. Watson, "What Price Day Care?" *Newsweek,* (September 10, 1984).
106. Golden Anniversary White House Conference on Children and Youth. *Conference Proceedings* (Washington, D.C.: Golden Anniversary White House Conference on Children and Youth, 1960), reprinted in Bremner, ed., *Children and Youth,* vol. 3, 704.
107. Gertrude L. Hoffman, comp., *Day Care Services: Form and Substance, A Report of a Conference,* November 17–18, 1960, U.S. Children's Bureau Publication No. 393 (Washington, D.C., 1961), reprinted in Bremner, ed., *Children and Youth,* vol. 3, 706.

108. Authier, "Defining the Care in Child Care," 502.
109. Elizabeth Jones and Elizabeth Prescott, "Day Care: Short- or Long-Term Solution?" *American Academy of Political and Social Sciences Annals* (May 1982): 92.
110. Ibid., 92–93.
111. Ibid., 92.
112. Reported in Child Welfare League of America, *Standards for Day Care Service* (New York: Child Welfare League of America, 1973), 3.
113. Reported in Claire Etaugh, "Effects of Nonmaternal Care on Children: Research Evidence and Popular Views," *American Psychologist* 35 (April 1980): 310.
114. Reported in R. B. Zamoff, *Guide to the Assessment of Day Care Services and Needs at the Community Level* (Washington, D.C.: The Urban Institute, 1971), 3.
115. Laurence D. Steinberg and Cindy Green, "What Parents Seek in Day Care," *Human Ecology Forum* 10 (1979): p. 13.
116. Child Welfare League of America, *Standards for Day Care Service,* 3.
117. Zamoff, *Guide to the Assessment of Day Care Services and Needs at the Community Level,* 3–4.
118. Authier, "Defining the Care in Child Care," 502.
119. Zamoff, *Guide to the Assessment of Day Care Services and Needs at the Community Level,* 4.
120. Authier, "Defining the Care in Child Care," 502.
121. Ibid., 502–503.
122. Ibid., 503.
123. Ibid.
124. Nicholas Von Hoffman, "Child Caretaking Not State Function," *St. Petersburg Florida Independent,* December 30, 1976.
125. Cohen and Zigler, "Federal Day Care Standards," 458.
126. Authier, "Defining the Care in Child Care," 504.
127. Ibid., 503.
128. Child Welfare League of America, *Standards for Day Care Service,* 11.
129. Cohen and Zigler, "Federal Day Care Standards," 461.
130. Authier, "Defining the Care in Child Care," 503.
131. Cohen and Zigler, "Federal Day Care Standards," 463.
132. Joel Spring. *American Education: An Introduction to Social and Political Aspects* (New York: Longman, 1978), 184.
133. Authier, "Defining the Care in Child Care," 503.
134. Cohen and Zigler, "Federal Day Care Standards," 459.
135. Ibid., 462.
136. Ibid., 459.
137. Harriet D. Watkins and Marilyn R. Bradbard, "The Social Development of Young Children in Day Care: What Practitioners Should Know," *Child Care Quarterly* 11 (Fall 1982): 170.
138. Ibid.
139. Ibid., 171.
140. Ibid.
141. Ibid., 172.
142. Etaugh, "Effects of Nonmaternal Care on Children," 311.
143. Michael Rutter, "Social-Emotional Consequences of Day Care for Preschool Children," *American Journal of Orthopsychiatry* 51 (January 1981): p. 9.
144. Watkins and Bradbard, "The Social Development of Young Children in Day Care," 173. Emphasis in the original.
145. Ibid., 174.
146. Ibid., 175.

147. Ibid., 179.
148. Burton L. White, "Should You Stay at Home With Your Baby?" *Educational Horizons* 59 (Fall 1980): 20.
149. Christine W. Anderson, "Attachment in Daily Separations: Reconceptualizing Day Care and Maternal Employment Issues," *Child Development* 51 (March 1980): 242.
150. Anita M. Farel, "Effects of Preferred Maternal Roles, Maternal Employment, and Socioeconomic Status on School Adjustment and Competence," *Child Development* 51 (December 1980): 1183.
151. Ibid., 1181.
152. Watkins and Bradbard, "The Social Development of Young Children in Day Care," 182.
153. Ibid., 180.
154. Ibid.
155. Etaugh, "Effects of Nonmaternal Care on Children," 312.
156. Ibid.
157. Ibid.
158. Watkins and Bradbard, "The Social Development of Young Children in Day Care," 182.
159. Ibid.
160. Ibid., 182–183.
161. Ibid., 183.
162. Hoffman, comp., *Day Care Services,* reprinted in Bremner, ed., *Children and Youth,* vol. 3, 705.
163. Ibid.
164. Florence A. Ruderman, *Child Care and Working Mothers: A Study of Arrangements Made for Daytime Care of Children* (New York: Child Welfare League of America, 1968), reprinted in Bremner, ed., *Children and Youth,* vol. 3, 711–712.
165. Mary Dublin Keyserling, *Windows on Day Care: A Report on the Findings of the National Council of Jewish Women on Day Care Needs and Services in Their Communities* (1972), reprinted in Bremner, ed., *Children and Youth,* vol. 3, 720.
166. Etaugh, "Effects of Nonmaternal Care on Children," 314.
167. Quoted in Etaugh, "Effects of Nonmaternal Care on Children," 315. Also see Benjamin Spock and Michael B. Rothenberg, *Baby and Child Care* (New York: A Wallaby Book, 1985), 42.
168. Etaugh, "Effects of Nonmaternal Care on Children," 315.
169. Ibid.
170. Howard Cohen, *Equal Rights for Children* (Totowa, N.J.: Littlefield Adams and Co., 1980), vii.
171. Ibid., 1.
172. Ibid., 5.
173. Ibid., 7.
174. Ibid., 9.
175. Victor L. Worsfold, "A Philosophical Justification for Children's Rights," *Harvard Educational Review* 44 (February 1974): 142–143.
176. John Holt, "Why Not a Bill of Rights for Children?", in Beatrice Gross and Roland Gross, eds., *The Children's Rights Movement* (New York: Anchor Press/Doubleday, 1977), 319.
177. Ibid., 324–325. For another "bill of rights" for children see Richard Farson, "Birthrights," in Gross and Gross, eds., *The Children's Rights Movement,* 325–328.
178. Sheleff, *Generations Apart,* 37.
179. Ibid., 235.
180. Neil Postman, *The Disappearance of Childhood* (New York: Delacorte Press, 1982), Part 2.
181. Holt, "Why Not a Bill of Rights for Children?" in Gross and Gross, eds., *The Children's Rights Movement,* 320.

9
Youth

Between Childhood and Adulthood

Between the end of childhood and the beginning of adulthood is a transitional stage. At one time, it coincided nicely with the stage that psychologists call adolescence and began with the onset of puberty. While discussions of puberty and adolescence are often conducted in terms of chronological age, psychologists frequently remind us that we must distinguish between chronological and physiological age. At puberty, children experience changes in voice, height, weight, body proportions, metabolic rates, blood pressure, and strength but do so at different times and at different rates. The norms for these processes include a wide range of different growth curves. Thus, puberty typically, but not necessarily, begins between the ages of twelve and fifteen. For girls, it may begin as early as age nine or as late as age seventeen. For boys, it usually begins a year or two later than it does for girls. Menarche is accepted as the signal of its beginning for girls. For boys, there is no comparable event but most seem to begin puberty at age thirteen.

The beginning of adolescence is a biological process, but is not totally independent of social and environmental conditions. In highly developed nations in the Western world, the average age of menarche has been steadily declining. Since the middle of the nineteenth century, it has been occurring about a half year earlier each decade. The decline appears to be related to living conditions, especially diet and medical care. Evidence suggests that differences among peoples from different parts of the world are neither racial nor genetic.

Historically, our treatment of children and adolescents has reflected our understanding of their developmental processes. As they enter their teens, they are sent to a different kind of school, a high school. When we recognized that puberty was beginning somewhat earlier, we developed junior high schools. More recently, some school systems have created middle schools to help children make the transition from childhood to adolescence.

Child labor laws and compulsory education laws reflected what was believed to be the beginning of adulthood, or the end of adolescence. Accordingly, children have been required to attend school until age sixteen and child labor laws typically specified that children between the ages of fourteen and sixteen needed permission to work and could work for only limited amounts of time, at specified times, and only in approved places or occupations. At age sixteen, they were allowed greater choice and opportunity but still could not work in mines or operate machinery until age eighteen. The beginning of adulthood was marked by the age at which people were granted the right to vote, the right to drink liquor, and the right to marry without parental consent.

Now, however, our social, economic, and cultural circumstances seem to require states and categories that are not as closely related to biological stages as they once were. Either end of the transitional stage seems to be changing. As our attitudes toward the desirability of child labor has changed and the availability of work for young people has declined significantly, we have become somewhat less willing to accept that adolescence begins when children enter some form of high school and ends when they are graduated from high school and secure a job.

While there is agreement that the beginning of the transitional stage is occurring earlier for both boys and girls, there is no clear agreement as to how long it actually lasts. Some maintain that the transition is as much a socially imposed stage as a physiological one and that it extends beyond what we have traditionally thought of as adolescence. During the last several decades, especially since the 1960s, it has been customary to focus attention on the problems and needs of "youth." The increasing frequency in the use of the term suggests that the transitional stage has acquired new characteristics to which educators need to attend.

The Beginning of Adolescence

In large measure, our conception of adolescence has been fashioned by the work of an early and probably one of the most controversial founders and practitioners of modern psychology, G. Stanley Hall. Unlike many of his contemporaries in psychology at the turn of the century, Hall was not content to limit himself to nicely defined and limited experimental studies. Rather, he wanted to get outside the laboratory and "construct a psychology that would rival religion and philosophy by addressing itself to cosmic questions about human nature and destiny."[1] In the construction of his psychology, Hall adopted the theory of psychic recapitulation. The recapitulation theory, which had been used in various forms by Rousseau, Goethe, Hegel, Pestalozzi, and others, maintained that the individual's growth and development—from infancy to adulthood—reflected, or retraced, the cultural-historical evolution of humanity.

In developing his notions on adolescence, Hall used the recapitulation theory to revive "an important notion set forth in *Émile*" that was ignored by other followers of Rousseau. Like Rousseau, Hall observed "an abrupt and fundamental alteration in the character of the pupil with the onset of puberty."[2] The change was so great that it clearly marked the great difference between the "savage" child and the "civilized" adolescent. Puberty was nothing less than a "new birth," a time of great "storm and stress" comparable to significant upheavals in the development of the race. During adolescence, Hall wrote, "development is less gradual and more saltatory, suggestive of some ancient period of storm and stress when old moorings were broken and a higher level achieved."[3]

In children between the ages of eight and twelve, Hall saw little savages who represented the ways of our prehistoric ancestors. Outside school, the little savages were to be granted as much freedom as possible—freedom to fight, run, and hunt and freedom to visit nature's fields, forests, hills, and shores—so they could work their way up to the next developmental stage. Inside school, they were to be strictly disciplined. Proper teaching methods for children between ages five and eight were "mechanical, repetitive, authoritative, dogmatic."[4] Adolescents, however, required and deserved something quite different. Hall waxed romantic, if not eloquent:

> These years are the best decade of life. No age is so responsive to all the best and wisest adult endeavor. In no psychic soil, too, does seed, bad as well as good, strike such deep root, grow so rankly, or bear fruit so surely. To love and feel for and with the young can alone make the teacher love his calling and respect it as supreme.[5]

For adolescents, teachers could safely abandon the drill and regimentation administered to children and emphasize content rather than form. Adolescents were sensitive, idealistic, and ready to respond sympathetically and properly to the requirements of the adult world. In adolescents, Hall found all the noble qualities which, if properly nurtured and protected from the corrupt influences of the modern world, would save humanity. The adolescent sought "more knowledge of body and mind," was "more objective than subjective," and was interested "in adult life and in vocations."[6] Adolescence was nothing less than "a marvelous new birth, and those who believe that nothing is so worthy of love, reverence, and service as the body and soul of youth, and who hold that the best test of every human institution is how much it contributes to bring youth to the ever fullest possible development, may well review themselves and the civilization in which we live to see how far it satisfied this supreme test."[7] Unfortunately, the nature and form of modern society were absorbing youth and robbing it of its best energies and causing society to neglect what youth needed most. Hall warned:

> We are conquering nature, achieving a magnificent material civilization, leading the world in the applications though not in the creation of science, coming to lead in energy and intense industrial and other activities; our vast and complex business organization that has long since outgrown the comprehension of professional economists, absorbs ever more and earlier the best talent and muscle of youth and now dominates health, time, society, politics, and law-giving, and sets new and ever more pervading fashions in manners, morals, education, and religion; but we are progressively forgetting that for the complete apprenticeship to life, youth needs repose, leisure, art, legends, idealization, and in a word humanism.[8]

Unlike many of his contemporaries, Hall was willing to broach "the relations between sex and psychology at a time when Victorian structures on the subject had not yet given way to the relative freedom of discussion that marked the 1920s."[9] He advocated deliberate and systematic sex instruction for students. While he advocated that the boys and girls be separated from each other for sex instruction, he also indicated that "where it is not practical this should not prevent teaching the subject, even to mixed classes just before puberty."[10] For girls, "the chief need" was for "hygienic instruction concerning their monthly regimen at an age when folly and ignorance are most dangerous."[11] Boys needed more instruction than girls. They needed "to know the harmfulness of self-abuse, which is very grave, although it has been the fashion to exaggerate it," and "some plain talk about the dangers of infection, both by the black plague and gonorrhea and the enormous evils of the latter, which are only lately adequately understood." They also needed to be "disabused of their morbid fears of being lost because of the spontaneous nocturnal experiences which quacks know so well how to prey upon."[12]

In sex instruction, a proper balance was imperative. The responsibility of educators was to promote and encourage whatever would "sublimate, spiritualize and normalize sex."[13] The best way to normalize sexual curiosity and sexual desires, Hall maintained, was through the strenuous life, not through denial of the body but through its proper development.

The Influence of Hall's *Adolescence*

Hall's two volume work—*Adolescence: Its Psychology, and Its Relations to Physiology, Anthropology, Sociology, Sex, Crime, Religion, and Education*—was the first major work on the subject. As its full title indicates, its treatment of the topic was indeed comprehensive. E. G. Boring reported that it "had tremendous vogue," for it appeared "at the time when psychology was supposed to be about to unlock the door to scientific education."[14] As the discipline of psychology was developed, however, psychologists saw "fit to ignore his theory of recapitulation" and "to repudiate the saltatory concept of emergent adolescence,"[15] but they have not been able to escape entirely from his influence.[16] Hall's work still strikes responsive chords. Many still share the same values and the same view of the world.

Hall's fear of the evils of an urban industrial society and his romantic invocations of the worthiness of nature may seem quaint only because of his romantic expression. His notions are not unlike those of many Americans who came after him. Pres. Franklin D. Roosevelt recommended the founding of the Civilian Conservation Corps (CCC) during the depression in part because he believed young men would benefit from a stay in the country. During the 1960s, many Headstart teachers made special efforts to plan visits to the country for children from inner cities, and yearly thousands of middle-class Americans send their children to summer camps in the country because they, like Hall, believe that children benefit from being near nature and in the great outdoors.

The continuing concern about the sexuality of teenagers, teenage pregnancy, and whether and how teenagers should receive sex education persists. In 1983, David Fink reported in a national newspaper that the people of Mankato, Minnesota, were about to receive three half-hour television programs on sex education that the federal government spent $13.5 million to produce. The programs' "message," he reported, was that "parents need to discuss sex with kids, and telling them how to say 'no' should be part of the discussion."[17] In 1908, seventy-five years earlier, Hall wrote that "all girls before leaving the secondary schools should be told of the commonest wiles and arguments used for their betrayal and some think as to risks, dangers and degrees of permissible liberty."[18]

Parents and teachers still casually explain the behavior of children and adolescents they cannot successfully suppress or control as simply symptoms of a stage that time will cure. When we fail to control behavior, we still wait for children to "outgrow" whatever stage they seem to be in. We still search for ways to allow youth to exercise their idealism and energy constructively. Competitive athletic programs continue to receive parental and community support because it is believed such programs provide youth a worthy and constructive way to channel energies that would otherwise be used to get into trouble.

Youth's Energy and Idealism

While a student at Columbia University in 1912, Randolph S. Bourne wrote of youth in a way that was consistent with Hall's saltatory notion of adolescence. For Bourne, youth was clearly a period between childhood and adulthood that was markedly different from either. It was a time of "contradictions and anomalies," but it was also a "great, rich rush and flood of energy."

> It is as if the store of life had been accumulating through the slow placid years of childhood, and suddenly the dam had broken and the waters rushed out, furious and uncontrolled, before settling down in the quieter channels of middle life. The youth is suddenly seized with a poignant consciousness of being alive. . . . He finds himself overpoweringly urged toward self-expression.[19]

Bourne held that the finest quality of youth—its eagerness to experiment—was the cause of its conflict with its elders. The older generation's adherence to established ways was the chief torment of youth. "There is," he claimed, "no scorn so fierce as that of youth for the inertia of older men." That inertia was not wisdom but an attempt to "excuse the older generation for the mistakes and failures which it has made."[20] The power the older generation held over society effectively caused society to be forever behind the times. "Very few people," he observed, "get any really new experience after they are twenty-five, unless there is real change of environment." Consequently:

> Press, pulpit, and bar teem with the radicalism of thirty years ago. The dead hand of opinions formed in their college days clutches our leaders and directs their activities in this new and strangely altered physical and spiritual environment. Hence grievous friction, maladjustment, social war. And the faster society moves, the more terrific is the divergence between what is actually going on and what public opinion thinks is actually going on.[21]

Only the young knew what was "actually going on," for they were the only ones "who have to constantly face new situations, to react constantly to new aspects of life, who are getting the whole beauty and terror and cruelty of the world in its fresh and undiluted purity."[22] They were without prejudice and had a truer vision and fairer interpretation of events than did their elders. Youth had, Bourne maintained, a responsibility to conserve its resources "and keep its flame of imagination and daring bright" in order to improve the social order.

Just as the progressive social reformers viewed children as the nation's most precious resource so they viewed youth as a source of energy that could be directed toward social reform. The passion, or what Jane Addams called "youthful ardor," was a "divine fire" that could be either fed or smothered. For her, it needed to be fed. She complained that society did "little or nothing with this splendid youth ardor and creative enthusiasm" and therefore allowed it to "turn upon itself" and create "youths who so bitterly arraign our present industrial order." She did not want "to permit these young people to separate themselves from the contemporaneous efforts of ameliorating society and to turn their vague hopes solely toward an ideal commonwealth of the future." Rather, she wanted to enlist youth in the work of making society more humane by having them work toward the realization of "the most conservative of present social efforts"—"protective legislation for women and children in industry."[23]

The recognition of youth's energy and the desire to use it for social amelioration was peculiar to neither any age group nor any racial group. In 1925, Alain Locke, a professor at Howard University, indicated that there was a Negro Renaissance in America to which black youth was bringing "its gifts." Youth was the harbinger of tomorrow. In that Renaissance were "Negro youth, with arresting visions and vibrant prophecies; forecasting in the mirror of art what we must see and recognize in the streets of reality tomorrow."[24] In 1923, at age 20, Countee

Cullen reported that there was a world-wide youth movement, and the "young American Negro is having his Youth Movement also." Throughout the world, he claimed, youth "is undergoing a spiritual and intellectual awakening, is looking with new eyes at old customs and institutions, and is finding for them interpretations which its parents passed over."[25] In both the North and the South, "the elder generations of both Caucasian and colored Americans have not come to the best mutual understanding."[26] Youth's task was to increase that understanding by showing a willingness and courage to meet the other halfway.

In 1910, William James proposed that youth could be used to effect "a moral equivalent of war." He proposed that "military conscription" be replaced by "a conscription of the whole youthful population to form for a certain number of years a part of the army enlisted against *Nature.*" He argued that universal national service for young men would eventually transform the world and quality of life for all and create better relations among people, especially rich and poor peoples. Once in place, universal national service would "preserve in the midst of a pacific civilization the manly virtues which the military party is so afraid of seeing disappear in peace." By helping to make the world a better place to live in and by seeing the differences between the rich and the poor, youth would be materially improved, especially those from the "luxurious classes." After having paid their "blood-tax," James predicted that youth "would tread the earth more proudly, the women would value them more highly, they would be better fathers and teachers of the following generation."[27]

James's recommendation for a program of universal national service was not adopted, but forms of the idea have appeared throughout our history. The CCC was a voluntary form of national service. In the 1960s, the Peace Corps was founded not only as a means to aid developing nations but also as a way to allow American youth an opportunity to use their energies and ideals in fulfilling and constructive endeavors.

Youth and the New Deal

As was earlier noted, thirteen million people were out of work when Franklin D. Roosevelt won the presidential election in 1932, and an additional two million were out of work when he assumed office in March 1933. Unemployment affected youth both directly and indirectly. Many were then obliged, as many still are, to support themselves, and many were obliged, as many still are, to contribute to the support of their families. In the 1930s, job opportunities for youth were fewer than ever before. Even in 1930, before people were completely aware of the employment-unemployment problem, at least a million youth were looking for work. As the economy deteriorated, the situation for youth grew worse. In 1930, 27.5 percent of the unemployed consisted of youth between ages fifteen and twenty-four. By 1937, it had increased to 36 percent. For young women and for minorities of both sexes, the situation was even more adverse.[28] Throughout the depression, youth were the last hired and the first fired.

Youth not only suffered from the effects of the depression but also were victims of the efforts to aid the nation's recovery. Even President Roosevelt acknowledged that

> certain provisions of the N.R.A. codes increased the difficulty of the problem. Most industries had abolished employment of persons under 16 years of age, a condition which resulted in the immediate discharge of 1,500,000 employed youth. The adoption of minimum wages served also

to keep out of employment vast numbers of young people otherwise eligible, because employers who had to pay a definite minimum naturally selected their employees from the vast number of unemployed adults rather than young persons. The result was to swell the number of the hopeless young people looking for jobs, or just "hanging around" on the street corners or aimless wandering around the country.[29]

To alleviate some of the problems of some of the nation's youth, the federal government established the CCC and the National Youth Administration (NYA).

The CCC

During his campaign for the presidency, Roosevelt promised a New Deal to Americans. As we have noted, part of it included the CCC, a program that reflected his beliefs that young men from the city would benefit from a stay in the country, that the nation's forests needed repair, and that all should serve their country in some manner. Enacted during Roosevelt's first month in office (March 29, 1933), the CCC was one of the earliest and eventually one of the most popular of the New Deal "alphabet soup" agencies. It accepted single, unemployed males between ages seventeen and twenty-three as well as a limited number of World War I veterans. During its first six months, its enrollment was just over 300,000. By 1934, it reached 360,000. After August 1935, when enrollment reached its high of 520,000, the number ranged between 240,000 and 300,000. When it was disbanded in 1942, all CCC enrollees were working on projects "devoted entirely to construction work at military reservations and protection and development of natural resources."[30] In 1940, the American Youth Commission of the American Council on Education reported that "a larger number of boys enter the CCC each year than the number who enter the colleges and universities of this country as freshmen."[31]

By the CCC's third anniversary, Roosevelt was convinced that it had shown that "young men can be put to work in our forests, parks, and fields on projects which benefit both the Nation's youth and conservation generally."[32] Participation in the CCC improved not only the nation's natural resources but also the minds and bodies of its members. According to Roosevelt, the CCC's "greatest and most worthwhile achievement . . . was the help given to the young men." Besides giving them employment and a safe and wholesome place to live, they had educational opportunities "and a chance to help support their families."[33] By the end of the CCC's fourth year, it had given work to nearly two million people (about 1.5 million youth and over 135,000 World War I veterans), and its enrollees had sent home $350 million to help support their families.

The CCC was popular, but it did not satisfy all youth's needs. Roosevelt issued executive orders to authorize the enrollment of Indians and work on Indian reservations, but women were excluded and racial quotas and segregation were imposed in the program. After Roy Wilkins, then National Secretary of the National Association for the Advancement of Colored People (NAACP), complained to Robert Fechner, director of the CCC, that instructors in the CCC camp at East Barre, Vermont, "not only are holding separate classes for whites and colored campers, but are restricting certain courses to whites only,"[34] Fechner replied: "You know, of course, that from the beginning of Emergency Conservation work it was felt desirable to segregate white enrollees, negro enrollees and war veterans in separate camps."[35] He further indicated that he had conferred with "a number of representative negro leaders" and "they were in hearty accord with the policy." Segregation was not enforced at a few sites, but "the general policy was against this practice." Luther C. Wandall reported in 1935 that when he arrived at Camp Dix, New Jersey, for CCC training, "the separation of the colored from the whites was complete and rigidly maintained."[36]

While there were about 11 million males between ages seventeen and twenty-three in the nation in 1942, the CCC was enrolling about a quarter of a million a year, or slightly more than 2 percent. Even at its peak, the CCC was enrolling only about 5 percent of the nation's male youth, and after the number of male youth in school or at work were subtracted from the 11 million, between 1.5 and 2 million still were neither in school nor at work. Thus, the CCC was enrolling between 12 and 16 percent of those who were out of school and out of work. Some did not know about the CCC. Others were not interested in "camp life," and still others were ineligible. Besides meeting age, marital, and "non-employment" requirements, applicants had to be citizens of the United States, in good health, and "preferably with families to whom they were willing to allot a portion of their earnings."[37] Those who were on parole, or probation or had been convicted of an offense for which they had received a jail term of more than a year were not eligible for CCC membership. When the program began, strong preference was given to applicants whose families were receiving or who needed public relief. That "restriction" was eliminated after 1937.

As the economy improved, the CCC moved its focus from providing relief for youth and families in need to preparing youth to meet the requirements of the marketplace. By 1939, it became an agency designed to train youth for work. The guide given to CCC selection agents in 1941 emphasized that "industry wants *the best trained men it can find,* whereas the CCC wants the *best youth it can find to train.* "[38] It was even claimed that the CCC had prepared young men for service in the Army. At the 1942 Senate hearings on the termination of the CCC, it was proclaimed "that the vast majority of the men who have enlisted in the Army from the C.C.C. could not pass the Army physical examination had it not been for their Corps experience."[39]

The CCC quickly drew the attention of social observers and educators. Its popularity was so great that some wanted to insure its continuance. As early as 1935, it was reported that "there is a widespread belief that a year of camp life would be a wholesome experience for American youth generally." Both the Society of American Foresters and the head of the U.S. Forestry Service urged "in the interest of our forests, the camps be made a permanent feature of American life." The head of the U.S. Army suggested that "military training be added to the present camp programs to the end of enlarging our reserve force."[40]

Educators were interested in the educational opportunities the camps afforded enrollees. Thus, George Coe wrote in the journal of the Progressive Education Association, *The Social Frontier,* that the CCC did provide much for which educators could be thankful.

> Any discerning eye, it is true, will delight in some features of CCC camp experience. To take part in making one's own habitation comfortable, sanitary, and neat; to build a playground and then use it oneself; to make the yard and the approaches to the camp attractive; to make flower-beds or rock gardens; to indulge such hobbies as photography, nature-study, and the building of radio receivers; to have regular hours; to adjust oneself to a cooperative group; to be in intimate contact with beauty in nature—all this means that important educational forces are already at work.

It must be remembered, too, that each of these young men actually earns $30 a month by self-respecting toil, that $25 of this amount is paid directly by the government to his parents or to his dependents, and that the remainder may be spent as one will. For all this no educator can fail to be thankful.[41]

While Coe was "thankful" for the educational experiences the CCC afforded the campers, he was not satisfied that the CCC experience was appropriate for furthering the education of young men. The basis of his dissatisfaction was that his conception of education was largely, if not solely, defined by formal public schooling. CCC camps were not comparable to schools. Campers spent "seven or more hours daily at road-building, erosion-prevention, fire-prevention, and the like." Such work was "educational," but, Coe argued, "to assume that effective cultural, civic, and vocational study requires only such left-over time and energy would be absurd." Enrollment in courses was not compulsory, even though "some camp commandants are willing to put pressure upon the young men, as by granting certain privileges only to those who attend educational classes."[42] Frank Ernest Hill reported that in June 1935, just a few months before the CCC reached its peak enrollment, about 175,000 campers were taking some type of class.[43]

CCC camps had neither sufficient libraries nor materials for laboratories. Reading rooms sometimes had nothing more than a few newspapers and a shelf or two of books. The camp buildings were for "feeding and sleeping" and were not suited for conducting conventional classes. Camp Badger in Fresno County, California, had a three-room school furnished with camper-made furniture. It was reported that the facilities for education at the Fresno site were "sufficiently rude," but they were nonetheless "above average for C.C.C. camps."[44] Coe emphasized the CCC's exclusion of girls and questioned the soundness of segregating young men from what was "wholesome" and conducive to preparing them for "normal family life." He also pointed out that the cost of improving the CCC facilities so they would be suitable for conventional schooling would be "crushingly expensive." Moreover, making the camps suitable would no more than "largely duplicate our high schools and junior colleges."[45]

Coe also questioned whether the organization and lines of authority in CCC camps were suitable for educational purposes. The camps were administered by military officers, and educational advisors were thus subordinate to men who had no formal training in school administration. If the camps were to become part of the nation's school systems, a decision about their administration would have to be made. Such a decision would be to "have either camps managed by military men for military purposes (even though educational phraseology be employed), or else school camps managed by educators for purposes of civil education, general and vocational." To make his point, he noted that Hitler's Germany required *Arbeitdienst* (a year of service), which was "intended to fuse the youth of Germany into a particular kind of national unity, namely, the kind that unquestionably and unanimously accepts political and economic orders from above just as a soldier accepts military orders." He further warned that "our own public education, to the extent that it becomes basically military, will promote the narrow virtues of the soldier not the virtues of a citizen of a democracy going freely about his daily duties."[46]

The criticism of the CCC by educators is significant. It shows that educators may have been, as Joel Spring has suggested, objecting to moving "part of the responsibility for the education of youth from the public schools."[47] However, more important than the possibility of a jurisdictional dispute over who is, or was, to have responsibility for youth is the belief that youth need to be especially prepared for adult society and that while being so prepared they need to be protected and isolated from it. When there were no, or few, places on the market-place for youth, attempts were made to remove them from adult society by providing them with something to do other than work at a job. The CCC camps, isolated from the cities, serve as a symbol of the removal. Schools are also places where students are removed from society when there is no work for them. Whether formal schooling is the best way to isolate and to prepare all youth for adult society and for work and whether youth should be so isolated are issues that have not yet been resolved.

The National Youth Administration

Soon after the founding of the CCC, educators met in Washington and noted that while the CCC was designed for young men who were not in school, no aid was being given to those who were either in school or trying to stay in school. The assembled educators recommended that financial aid be granted to college students. The rationale for such aid, according to Betty and Ernest K. Lindley, was that society would eventually benefit from such a modest investment in its youth.

> Until the unused capacity of the colleges was filled, it was obviously less expensive to keep youths in college than to put them in CCC camps. Indeed, there was no cheaper way to keep a larger number of people of college age off the labor market and usefully occupied. And for those capable of benefiting from a higher education, this way probably held the greatest promise of gain for society as a whole.[48]

That many students needed help was clear. Many colleges and universities tried to provide meals and shelters for students at the least possible cost. The University of Iowa converted a field house into a dormitory where students could live for a dollar a week. Some schools offered balanced meals for ten to twelve cents, but many students could not even afford that. As the Lindleys reported, school officials at one state university "found that one young man had been trying to feed himself on fifty cents a week and that another was sleeping during a cold winter in an old automobile parked on the edge of town."[49] Many students were "hanging on," but "these ambitious young people hung on grimly."[50]

Although the NYA was not formally established until June 26, 1935, when President Roosevelt issued Executive Order 7086, the Federal Emergency Relief Administration (FERA) granted funds to colleges and universities to employ up to 10 percent of their students, especially students who needed to work to remain in school. By early 1935, however, it was apparent that the 100,000 students who were earning an average of $15 a month in the FERA-sponsored programs and the youth who were enrolled in the CCC constituted only a small portion of the three million youth between ages sixteen and twenty-five who were on relief. A program of aid for college students served only a few of those who needed aid, for "of those on relief in cities, less than 40 percent had gone beyond the eighth grade and less than 3 percent had entered college."[51] To address that situation, the NYA not only expanded the student aid program to include high school and graduate students as well as undergraduates but also inaugurated a number of work projects for youth who were not in school and for whom the CCC was inappropriate.

NYA Student Aid. Consistent with the federal government's then traditional reluctance to become involved directly in educational matters, the NYA assigned responsibility for administering student aid programs and for selecting eligible students to the participating institutions (normal schools, junior colleges, colleges, and universities). Schools had to agree to the stipulation that "aid recipients shall be selected primarily on the basis of need; that they shall carry at least three-quarters of a normal course load of study, and that the work they perform shall be genuinely useful and not displace any of the school's regular employees."[52] High school students were allowed to work up to twenty hours a week and earn an average of $6 a month. College students and graduate students were allowed to work up to thirty hours a week and earn $15 and $25 a month, respectively. NYA student workers performed clerical duties in offices and libraries, worked on grounds and maintenance crews, assisted in museums or other civic institutions, or helped in educational programs. For college and graduate students, it was reported, a "special effort is made to assign them to tasks consistent with the courses of study being followed, thus giving practical application to the work of the classroom."[53]

NYA earnings usually were not sufficient to meet all student expenses, but in many instances, they made the difference between remaining in school or dropping out. In 1935, the Office of Education reported that in 20 percent of participating institutions, the $15 a month wage was enough to "cover the cost of a student's room and board."[54] Students who lived at home and commuted to school were frequently able to earn enough NYA wages to pay for most or all of their tuition, fees, and incidental expenses. For students who went away to school, NYA earnings usually covered between 25 and 60 percent of their total expenses. Many NYA students came from families who were unable to help them with their college expenses. Over half were from families with five or more people, and over a third were from families of six or more. Nearly 6 percent of the NYA students were from nonwhite minority groups.

Like the CCC, the NYA was soon successful. During its peak month of April 1936, "a total of 398,843 young people—216,611 of whom were male and 182,232 female—were receiving student aid benefits in 20,000 secondary schools and 1,600 colleges and universities."[55] Nearly 20,000, or 14 percent of the students who received academic and professional degrees in June 1936, had participated in the NYA student aid program. When the NYA was discontinued in 1943, Paul B. Jacobson reported that during its eight years, the NYA enabled 620,000 youths "to attend college or to continue in college without damage to their self-respect."[56] It also enabled more than 1.5 million youth to remain in high school. By providing assistance to students, the NYA "served as a safety valve to keep people out of the labor market."[57]

The NYA reached a greater cross section of the nation's youth than the CCC. While the CCC was restricted to males, the NYA was not. In 1938, 40 percent of NYA students were female. While the CCC maintained racial quotas and usually segregated blacks from whites, the NYA operated on the belief "that the general welfare would be best promoted by full integration and participation of Negro Youth in all phases of the program."[58] Blacks were appointed to all NYA advisory and planning committees. A Division of Negro Affairs was created in the Washington office of NYA. In late 1939, it was estimated that "of 591,000 young people employed by Student Aid and the Works Program of the N.Y.A., 63,000, or 10.8 percent, were Negroes," a percent that was equal to the percent of blacks then in the nation's population. About 57 percent of the black youth who participated in the NYA were in the Student Aid program. The other 43 percent participated in the Work Project Program. Besides allocating funds to 113 Negro colleges, the NYA also established "a special college and graduate aid fund of $100,000" that was distributed to black college and graduate students who would otherwise "have been excluded from the regular college and graduate quotas."[59]

NYA Work Projects. Youth for whom the CCC was not suitable and youth who were not able or not interested in remaining in school had few, if any, options during the 1930s. For such youth, the NYA devoted nearly 60 percent of its 1936–37 budget to its Work Projects Program. The program was designed to offer youth an opportunity to earn some money as well as acquire some "work experience" and "work discipline." The NYA accepted applications from local governments and public groups who wished to undertake some improvement in the public interest that could be completed successfully by youth. Once the NYA approved an application, it paid the wages of the youth while the local agency supplied necessary materials and supervision of the workers. Through NYA sponsored projects, youth helped to improve playgrounds, school facilities, and settlement houses, gathered statistics for police departments, and worked on some conservation projects similar to those performed by the CCC. For such work, youth were paid whatever the prevailing hourly wage was in their community. However, they were allowed to work only long enough to earn a third of whatever adults working on WPA projects earned. By June of 1936, a total of 183,477 youth were working on nearly 3,300 NYA projects and earning an average of $16.15 a month.

In 1935, the NYA assumed responsibility for supervision of resident camps for women that had been established in 1934 by the Workers' Education Section of the FERA's Division of Education. In 1936, it assumed financial responsibility for those camps. Usually situated in vacant schools, country hotels, or abandoned CCC camps, the camps accepted about twenty-five unemployed women between ages eighteen and twenty-five whose families were eligible for relief. During their three- to four-month term at the camps, their time was divided between work, education, and recreation. For their subsistence and a $5 a month payment, young women made "supplies for hospitals and State institutions, visual aids for the public schools, recreation equipment, [and] work[ed] the tree nurseries of the Forestry Service."[60] For recreation, there were athletic programs, arts, crafts, and dramatics. Educational programs included such "practical subjects as home economics, sewing, health education, English, and economics." In 1938, the camps for women were merged with camps for men that had been established a year earlier and became known as resident projects.

The establishment of resident centers allowed the NYA to assemble youth from sparsely populated areas in one place where they could be given assistance and an opportunity to secure some work experience. In 1937, resident projects were established for male youth. They typically enrolled about twenty-five young men who were put to work at farming crops that could be given to local welfare agencies for distribution to people who needed relief. When the NYA merged the female and male resident projects in 1938, it also initiated projects that were organized according to the industrial requirements of the nation rather than having males study agricultural occupations while females studied home economic and domestic sciences.

Industrial projects were located near enough to industrial sites to allow enrollees to see how industry functioned and to allow representatives from industry to "assist in planning production programs."[61] Resident-industrial projects enrolled as few as twenty-five youth or as many as 200. Youth worked and lived at the project site. With the wages they earned, they paid for their lodging in dormitories, purchased and prepared food under the supervision of NYA cooks and dietitians, and paid for their own medical care. All work performed by NYA workers "was cosponsored by some public agency, and all the products were disposed of through public agencies and institutions." NYA workers "produced playground equipment for public park boards, hospital supplies for public hospitals and clinics, radio apparatus for State and municipal police networks, and various metal and mechanical objects for city governments, State governments, and national and war agencies of the Federal Government."[62]

During its eight years of existence, the NYA works projects program aided and trained nearly 2.75 million youth. While earning wages and receiving training and work experience, they worked on many public service projects. However, by 1942, NYA opponents found it easy to argue that it was no longer necessary. It was created to provide relief, employment, and some training for youth. As the nation's war industries' demand for workers increased in the early 1940s, there seemed to be enough jobs for youth. As the Federal Security Administrator testified to the Senate's Committee on Education and Labor in March 1942, there was a need "for personnel, particularly trained personnel to fill special jobs in essential industry."[63] He reported that "youth training programs are accordingly needed for training as many as possible of the reservoir of 2,500,000 capable, but untrained, boys and girls of employable age." He emphasized that the NYA was then "the greatest single producer of trained workers for war industries." It had already established 38,800 work stations in 1,670 shops where "through full-time employment, under expert supervision," the NYA was readily training "operators of lathes, drill presses, milling machines, grinders, arc and spot welders, punch presses, and so forth." After youth were properly trained, they were sent by the NYA "to places where most needed in vital war work." He also related that besides training youth, the NYA shops had "manufactured for the military forces alone, more than 32,000 hand tools, 12,000 gun parts, 70,000 machine parts, 55,000 containers, and numerous miscellaneous items."[64] Congress, however, chose to terminate the NYA, as it saw no need to continue to provide opportunities for youth. The needs and problems of youth were not permanently solved by the war, however.

Opportunities for Youth: A Continuing Challenge

The need to find something useful, constructive, and meaningful for youth to do has persisted. World War II allowed the nation to postpone dealing with the issue, but it did not eliminate it. As Harold D. Carter of the University of California observed in the early 1940s, "manpower requirements of the war have eased some of the occupational problems of youth and immensely complicated others." He warned that "the return to peacetime occupations will bring new and rapidly changing conditions which will make heavy demands upon our resources for the vocational counseling of youth."[65]

Youth had many choices, but their ability to make those choices effectively was severely limited by ignorance and changing economic conditions. Through education, formal and informal, youth were "vaguely aware" of their "abilities, preferences, and ambitions," but they were "ignorant of the fundamental facts about most occupations" and did not know how to match their talents and interests with jobs. To complicate matters even more, it then seemed that occupations themselves had changing demands that contributed to the "insecurity of the young person." As new jobs appeared, others disappeared. For youth, "the world of jobs and the process of job orientation were disorderly and confused."[66] Neither youth nor their parents had the ability to make the right choices for the future. Expert counselors were needed for that.

After World War II, youth had little choice but to remain in school—at least through high school. As Morris Janowitz has so accurately observed, "the transformation and organization of the labor market under advanced industrialization restricted opportunities for youth and assigned a new role to the public schools." Before the depression, "the socialization of youngsters from European immigrant families and of migrants from rural areas was in good measure accomplished through work experiences—part time and full time."[67] After World War II, however, "high school graduation or its equivalent—not only in terms of social attitude, interpersonal competence, and maturity—[was] defined as a desirable and required goal, even for the lowest income groups."[68]

After World War II, "actual work requirements, changed standards of employment and trade unions, and new legislation about minimum wages" required the public schools to "accept responsibility for all youngsters who are not college bound until they develop levels of personal maturity sufficient for them to enter the labor market."[69] Educators welcomed the consequent expansion of public education. It seemed a true extension of equality of educational opportunity. The difficulty was that the schools, especially the high schools, attempted to do mainly what they had been accustomed to doing, but for a population that was in many instances and in many respects different from any they had previously served. Those who had previously dropped out of school to take jobs began to stay in school because there was no place else for them. What had once been a population seeking and exercising an opportunity became, in large measure, captive.

Once it was recognized that the schools were not totally successful in extending equality of opportunity to all, private and federal funds were invested in programs to reform the schools so they would be more effective. However, the funds were not usually devoted to developing new programs and practices for a population who would have to face a newly restructured economic order but rather to improving existing programs and practices. As an example, Janowitz cited the following:

> In Chicago, federal funds were actually used to increase the length of the school day. The educational procedures that produced a 40 percent dropout rate and massive academic retardation by third grade were extended, with only minor modifications, for another hour.[70]

The case of Chicago in the 1960s was not unique. The tendency to attempt to improve existing practices or simply to have more of the same rather than invent new programs, procedures, and educational arrangements is indeed strong. In the spring of 1983, for example, the National Commission on Excellence in Education, urged, after eighteen months of study, that school districts "strongly consider" increasing the six-hour school day to seven hours and increasing the 180-day school year to 200 to 220 days.[71]

A Persistent Problem

By the early 1960s, some recognized that the problems of youth employment had not been solved and had become a major national concern. Then, James B. Conant advised that the thousands of youth between ages sixteen and twenty-one who were both out of school and out of work constituted a social problem that he described as "social dynamite."[72] For black youth the problem was particularly acute. In the slums of large cities, both high school drop-outs and high school graduates had very high unemployment rates. In a slum section of one of the nation's largest cities populated mostly by blacks, Conant found that "of the boys who graduated from high school 48 percent were unemployed in contrast to 63 percent of the boys who had dropped out of school."[73] In another city with a slum area of 125,000 people, "mostly blacks," he found "roughly 70 percent of the boys and girls ages 16–21 . . . out of school and unemployed."[74] Completion of high school made a difference, but it was not great enough to encourage youth to remain in school. As Conant observed: "In such a situation, a pupil may well ask why bother to stay in school when graduation for half the boys opens onto a dead-end street?"[75]

For those who claimed that the United States had always had slums populated by poor people, that those poor found their way out of the slums to success through study and hard work, and that current slum residents could do the same, Conant had an answer. "Such a complacent projection of the past into the obscure future," he maintained, "is fallacious for several reasons."[76] The 1950s and 1960s were quite different from the 1900s, and the inhabitants of early twentieth century slums were quite different from the inhabitants of mid-twentieth century slums. The immigrants who populated the early slums believed, because their ancestors had done so, that they could work their way out of the slums into a better life. However, the blacks who were confined to the mid-twentieth century slums had no similar history to support such a belief. During the earlier part of the century, the United States had a shortage of workers and even a demand for unskilled laborers. When that demand disappeared during the Depression, the federal government intervened with relief programs to assist people and to maintain existing social structure. Blacks in the 1950s and 1960s had few parallels. Automation had greatly decreased the demand for unskilled labor and "racial discrimination" made "unemployment chronic for the Negro North and South."[77]

While Conant agreed that unemployment was "bad anywhere" and acknowledged that some would urge solving the unemployment problem of adults as top priority, he nonetheless insisted that "in the slums of the largest cities . . . the drastic reduction of unemployment of male youth under age 21 is a greater need."[78] In the slums, the unemployed youth were not only greater in absolute numbers than in other areas such as small towns or rural communities but also were more isolated from other members of the community and more densely concentrated. That peculiarity of geography made the problem especially dangerous. Dense concentrations of unemployed, disillusioned, and idle youth, he feared, could have "serious political consequences." Moreover, the obvious presence of "unemployed floaters on the street" served as "evidence to all the youth that nothing can be accomplished through education, that the door of the neighborhood schoolhouse indeed opens on a dead-end street."[79]

To counter the "demoralizing attitude" that youth acquired on the street required more than that which "lies within the province of the school authorities alone." It required the attention of all social agencies to many areas of concern:

> racial discrimination; employment practices of labor and management; Federal-State laws including insurance rates and wage scales; lack of jobs, as well as changing types of employment because of automation and the necessity for more highly skilled workers; the role of schools in preparing youth for employment, especially average and below-average youth, and in helping them make the transition from school to work; the coordination of the efforts of the schools, the

employers and labor unions, and the various community agencies that have a hand in promoting youth welfare; the role of the public sector of the economy at the local, state, and federal level in providing employment if the private sector of the economy is unable to do so.[80]

Conant did urge the public schools to offer programs deliberately designed to help students make a "smooth transition" from school to work. To do that, the schools needed to adjust to "the nature of the families being served, the vocational plans and aspirations of the students, and employment opportunities." They also needed to effect better relationships "between school, employers, and labor unions, as well as social agencies and employment offices." He further recommended that the school's obligation to students not end when the students either dropped out or were graduated. *"Guidance officers,"* he recommended, *"especially in the large cities, ought to be given the responsibility for following post-high school careers of youth from the time they leave school until they are 21 years of age."*[81]

The problem of youth, especially slum youth who were black, was in large measure a problem of racial discrimination. To the extent that it was not possible to enforce antidiscrimination laws, it was advisable, Conant urged, "for Congress to alleviate the problem of unemployment among youth 16 to 21 in the large cities."[82] He also acknowledged that "even if there were no discrimination, it might become necessary if the private sector of the economy is unable to provide sufficient jobs."[83]

While Conant was writing *Slums and Suburbs,* Congress was considering the Youth Opportunities Act of 1961. The three major provisions of the act included (1) federal subsidies for "on-the-job training programs" to be conducted by unions and private enterprises as well as educational institutions, (2) a program to hire youth to work in various public service jobs, and (3) a program designed to bring youth to residential centers where, in situations similar to those created a generation earlier by the CCC and the NYA, youth would "receive education and training, and work on conservation and forest projects." Conant then questioned "the relevance of the CCC proposal to the problem of unemployed youth in large cities" and argued that "what is needed are jobs in the big cities on a non-discriminatory basis." The other programs, he believed, "would be effective only if a non-discriminatory provision is included and enforced."[84]

By 1960, youth unemployment was a major problem. The causes of the problem were to be found in both the economic and the value structure of the society. Youth needed more education and training to secure a job than did their counterparts of earlier eras. For minorities, the problem was even more acute. They suffered, in many instances, not only from discrimination that made entry into the marketplace difficult but also from discrimination that frequently prevented them from securing the kind of preparation and training they needed to qualify for entry into the labor force.

During the 1970s, the federal government was spending nearly $14.5 billion annually for various work and training programs. Through the Job Corps, Youth Incentive Entitlement Pilot Projects, Youth Employment Training Programs, Youth Adult Conservation Corps, Youth Community Conservation and Improvement Programs, Summer Youth Employment Programs, and other programs, government was providing job training for more than three million people, mostly youth and young adults who had not completed high school. Yet, the problem persists. In the mid 1940s, the youth unemployment rate was about 9.5 percent and continued at or near that rate through the 1950s.[85] By 1980, it had just about doubled to 18 percent.[86] As Gordon I. Swanson has noted, "the period of transition from school to a full-time job in the adult work force, or if one prefers, the period of adolescence, is a mounting concern in the United States." He has further observed that "the high unemployment rate for youth, particularly of minorities, is a major cause of concern."[87] In fact, estimates for minority unemployment may be low, because "it has been estimated that as many as 700,000 minority youth have virtually 'disappeared' from the system because they are neither counted among the employed, nor among the unemployed, nor are they in school."[88]

By the time high school students reach the twelfth grade, about 75 percent work at a part-time job. However, how the mixture of schooling and part-time work experience is related to the ability of youth to secure full-time jobs is unknown. Two decades after Conant recommended that public school guidance counselors assume responsibility for monitoring the employment and unemployment experiences of youth, Swanson reported that:

> Virtually all of the employment is student initiated and unsupervised by school staff. . . . The extent to which various types of intensities of student employment may offer advantages or disadvantages to subsequent employment or education is unknown. Whether such part-time work opportunity is equally available to disadvantaged students and whether it compounds or alleviates their disadvantages are likewise unknown.[89]

What is known, according to Marcia Freedman, is that "all young workers encounter more difficulty now than in the past in becoming established in the labor market." Those who can afford to endure schooling through and beyond their teenage years seem to "gain a double advantage; they not only acquire important credentials for working, but they also achieve a postponement of the search for a first full-time job."[90] Because "age rationing" now seems to obtain on the labor market, it is to the advantage of youth to delay entry as long as possible, for "the better the job or its prospects, the less likely a young worker is to be hired."

Completion of high school and college seem to increase one's chances of securing employment. The advantages may not be as great as many have traditionally believed they were, however. Freedman reports that "it is likely that formal schooling will continue to outpace opportunity in an evolving occupational structure." The harsh reality seems to be that "jobs for dropouts have diminished faster than the dropout population, while jobs for college graduates have increased more slowly than the college graduate population."[91]

Employment Opportunities for Black Youth

The high rate of unemployment among black youth does not reflect failure of black youth to use the schools to prepare themselves for the labor force. Increased rates of enrollment among blacks since the mid 1960s indicate that they value education highly. While many may be in school because they cannot find work, "numerous researchers have reported on the high educational aspirations found among blacks and the conviction that schooling represents the best way to get ahead."[92] Between 1957 and 1977, there was "a marked narrowing of the school attainment gap between blacks and whites."[93] During that period, the median educational attainment among whites increased by .5 years, from 12.1 to 12.6 years. For blacks, the increase was 3.8 years, from 8.4 years to 12.2 years. In just two decades, a difference of 3.7 years in median educational attainment was reduced to .4 years.

Julia Wrigley has reported that "unemployment rates for all youth, male and female, white and black, have been high over the last twenty years," but the rate for blacks has been the highest. While unemployment rates for white teenage males are two to three times greater than those for white adult males, the rates for black teenage males are three to four times as great as for black adult males. While all youth suffer from business cycle variations, as do adults, "black employment-population ratios are estimated to be about 50 percent more sensitive to cyclic variations than are white youth employment-population rations."[94] Whether a youth comes from a "disadvantaged" background makes a difference but more so if the youth is black. In 1970, the unemployment rate for white disadvantaged youth between ages sixteen and twenty-four was 25.5 percent. For black disadvantaged youth, it was 40.8 percent. By the mid 1980s, it was still between 35 and 40 percent. Wages for black youth are now about the same as those for white youth, but that progress is not a sign that matters have improved for all youth. As Wrigley has suggested, "the relative wage equalization between blacks and whites may be due in part to the fact that the wages of young white workers have dropped relative to those of adult workers."[95] The surplus of youthful workers and the low demand for workers have depressed the wages youth earn.

Employment opportunities have not matched the increase in educational opportunities and attainment for blacks, but some evidence shows that it is advantageous to blacks to acquire education. In the 1960s and early 1970s, it appeared that blacks did not "gain greatly from high school graduation." In 1964, a high school diploma appeared to give white youth a distinct advantage in the labor market. Then, 13.6 percent of the white high school dropouts were jobless but "only 8.9 percent of the high school graduates." For blacks, the case was quite different. A high school diploma seemed to make little impact in acquiring a job. Then, according to Wrigley, "the unemployment rates of high school dropouts and high school graduates were almost identical (18.1 percent and 18.8 percent, respectively)."[96] By the mid 1970s, there was some indication that a high school diploma was an asset for black youth, but the diploma only helped them in relationship to high school dropouts. In 1977, the unemployment rate for black high school graduates had increased to 22 percent, but for dropouts it had increased to 31.7 percent. Data from 1978 show that the advantage of the high school diploma for black youth, especially black males, is not an immediate but a delayed advantage. For black high school graduates between ages sixteen and nineteen, the unemployment rate was only 5.6 percent less than for dropouts (28.1 percent versus 33.7 percent). However, for youth between ages twenty and twenty-four, the difference was greater. For that group, the difference was 11.4 percent (17.3 percent for high school graduates and 28.7 percent for dropouts). As Wrigley reports:

> The fact that more black youth are staying in school indicates that they are willing to take a long-range perspective for the most part. They are ultimately rewarded, in that young adult black men who have graduated not only have significantly lower unemployment rates than those who have not, but they also have higher earnings. High school graduation does pay off, but only in the context of unemployment rates that are far above those that occurred for black youth in the expansionary years of the mid-1960s.[97]

Neither Black Nor White

While unemployment for black women is greater than it is for black men, high school graduation seems to have a greater pay off for females even for those aged sixteen to nineteen.

While blacks constitute the largest minority group in the United States (between 11 and 12 percent), they are not the only minority group. The second largest minority group, about 4.5 percent of the population, is made up of people now frequently called "Hispanic." Among the membership of the Hispanic group are several distinct groups, each with its distinctive history and culture. Mexican-Americans comprise the largest group (57 percent). Others include Puerto Ricans (17 percent), Cubans (7 percent), Central and South Americans (6 percent), and others whose ancestry is Spanish (13 percent).

In the 1960s, the youth of the post–World War II generation of Mexican-Americans developed a new political awareness, began to articulate their pride in their cultural heritage in a forceful and effective manner, and began to call themselves Chicanos. They began to organize their efforts toward achieving full social and economic equality. Significantly, many of the efforts were directed toward public education, for they saw the lack of equal educational opportunity as a barrier to other opportunities. As Hershel D. Thornburg and Robert E. Grinder have reported:

> Chicano youth rallied in the 1960s to attack the highly visible educational system. It was the only course open to them that provided hope for meaningful citizenship. On the one hand, they could enter the agricultural or industrial labor force, but only jobs of marginal status were available. On the other hand, they could enter military service, but the highly professionalized system would relegate them disproportionately to foot-soldier status. The prospect of college was alluring, but the high schools which they attended were located in neighborhoods where curricula, facilities, and counseling were so deficient that few Chicano youth were being prepared for college-level work. The high schools serving them routinely administered 'culturally biased' intelligence and achievement tests; counselors traditionally advised Chicanos to pursue vocational courses and occupations.[98]

There is little wonder that Chicanos directed their attention to the nature and quality of school programs in the 1960s. The level of educational attainment for Mexican-Americans has lagged behind that of other Americans. The median years of schooling completed by Mexican-Americans in the early 1970s was significantly lower than for the total population. For people aged twenty-five years or older it was 12.1 years, but for Mexican-Americans it was 9.6 years (9.9 for men and 9.4 for women). The difference, 2.5 years, may not seem great, but it is the difference between being graduated from high school and dropping out. Perhaps as important is the 3.4 year difference among Mexican-Americans themselves, with a median as low as 7.2 years in Texas and as high as 10.6 years in California.[99]

The educational attainment of people with Spanish surnames in the five southwestern states—Arizona, California, Colorado, New Mexico, and Texas—is not as high as it is for the Anglo population in those states. For Anglos aged fourteen or over, it is 12.0 years but for those with a Spanish surname only 8.1 years. If the populations aged twenty-five or over are compared, the difference is even greater—12.1 years for Anglos and 7.1 years for Hispanics. The averages hide the wide ranges that exist within the region. In Texas, for example, people with Hispanic surnames who are twenty-five years old or over have an attainment level of only 4.8 years; for those between ages fourteen and twenty-four, it is 8.1 years. For the Texas Anglo population, the median level of educational attainment was 11.5 years for those aged twenty-five or older and 11.1 years for those between ages fourteen and twenty-four. In California, the Anglo population, aged twenty-five or older, was 3.6 years ahead of the Hispanic population (12.2 years and 8.6 years). California Hispanics between ages fourteen and twenty-four were only 1.2 years behind California Anglos (10.2 years and 11.4 years).[100] The higher attainment levels for the population between ages fourteen and twenty-four indicate that the younger group has had more opportunities to remain in school.

While the trend has been for Mexican-American youth to remain in school longer, it was still reported in 1975 that their dropout rate in southwestern states was higher than that for other minorities and Anglos.[101] One study, conducted in Dallas, revealed that 79 percent dropped out of school between the fifth grade and high school. Another study, conducted in California, showed that 50 percent of the Spanish-speaking students dropped out of school by the eighth grade and 25 percent of the remainder dropped out before reaching the end of the twelfth grade.[102] In 1972, 1.1 million of the 1.7 million Hispanic youth between the ages of sixteen and twenty-four were out of school. Of those 1.1 million, 500,000 had completed high school and 600,000 had dropped out. About 450,000 were in high school; 200,000 were in college.[103]

Nearly half of Mexican-American children do not speak English as well as Anglo children when they enter school. They do speak Spanish better than the Anglo children but that is not typically seen as an advantage. Rather, to improve the children's facility in the use of English, "Spanish is commonly discouraged or prohibited with punitive measures being applied to violators."[104] What is sometimes overlooked is that Mexican-American children are especially proud of their heritage and culture. Moreover, language is an integral part of heritage. Thus, "when the school or one of its teachers views the Mexican-American language as inferior, thus unacceptable, it creates immeasurable stress for the Mexican-American adolescent." One way such students alleviate the stress is by dropping out of school, "a phenomenon which is more common among Mexican-American than any other ethnic group in the southwestern United States." Youth who elect to maintain their loyalty to their cultural heritage "may find that they have minimal skills necessary for moving into the adult world."[105] One way to begin to remedy their difficulty is to maintain schools with teachers who encourage and respect bilingualism rather than punish it.

The high dropout rates of Mexican-Americans is reflected in their unemployment rates, which are about a third higher than those for blacks and whites. Even when Mexican-Americans, male or female, aged sixteen or over, secure employment, "their salaries are less than Anglo salaries in the same occupational areas."[106] At the beginning of the 1970s, the average annual income of Mexican-American males was $5,166, which was lower than the average annual income of several other groups: Japanese-American ($8,183), Chinese-Americans ($6,877), and Filipino-Americans ($5,710). Only black males, aged sixteen or over, had a lower average annual income ($4,572). There was then a close, but not perfect, relationship between the income levels and the percentage of people in each group who completed high school. According to William T. Liu and Elena S. H. Yu: "The 1970 Census showed that 69.9 percent of the Japanese, 62.2 percent of the Chinese, and 49.4 percent of the Filipinos completed high school. Whereas only 32.0 percent of the blacks and 28.1 percent of the Mexican-Americans attained a comparable level."[107] Out-of-school Mexican-American youth between the ages of sixteen and nineteen have greater difficulty in finding employment than those between nineteen and twenty-four, and out-of-school males have more difficulty than females.

A New View of An Old Problem

The support of President Carter's administration for the Youth Act of 1980 (passed in the House but allowed to die in the Senate) was not the first instance of an argument that federal funds had to be used to support youth. As Richard J. Becker has noted, however, the argument used by the Carter administration differed significantly from the traditional arguments. When the Commission on Vocational Education argued for federal support for vocational education in 1914, it emphasized that the support could properly be construed as a sound investment that would result in future economic prosperity. However, in neither the Vice President's Task Force Report on Youth Employment (*c.* 1980) nor in the year-long discussion and analysis of the youth employment/unemployment problem are there any significant discussions of the relationship between youth employment and the nation's prosperity. Rather, the Carter administration's support for the 1980 Youth Act was based on what Becker describes as a "genuine concern for this unfortunate segment of American society, and from a desire to satisfy certain political constituencies."[108]

That the Carter administration did not emphasize the importance of training youth to contribute to the economic prosperity of the nation is noteworthy. It may be a sign that children and youth are no longer viewed as the nation's most precious resource or most vital energy that must be conserved and properly developed for maximum economic advantages for society. It is not, however, necessarily a sign that children and youth are no longer seen as worthy and important, but rather that they may not be needed as workers. Economic changes in our society have created social changes, one of which is redefinition of the role of youth in our society. In the simplest of terms, youth are needed more as consumers than producers. They have been displaced from the labor force.

The Carter administration's failure to emphasize the economic benefits from finding ways to put youth to work is also consistent with the observations of the Panel on Youth of the President's Science Advisory Committee (the panel was appointed in 1972 and issued its report under the chairmanship of James S. Colemen in 1975). The panel noted that the nation's approach to youth could be described in terms of two phases. One was described as the "work phase," during which "young persons were brought as quickly as physical maturity would allow into economic productivity, to aid the economy of the family." The second, described as the "schooling phase," was one in which "young persons are being kept as long as possible in the school and out of the labor force, to increase their potential for productivity."[109] Some believe that the second phase has ended and that it may no longer be practical or even in the best interests of youth to continue to use the school to detain youth as long as they are marginal to the economy. As James Coleman wrote in the preface to the panel's report:

> As the labor of children has become unnecessary to society, school has been extended for them. With every decade, the length of schooling has increased, until a thoughtful person must ask whether society can conceive of no other way for youth to come into adulthood.[110]

The president's Panel on Youth concluded that "it is now time for a third phase in society's treatment of its young, including school but neither defined by nor limited to it."[111]

Conclusion

Depending on one's outlook and probably upon the resources to which one has access, the youth of today face either the best of times or the worst of times. A few generations ago, young people were pressed into work as soon as they were physically able. Educational opportunities were limited. Subsequently, educational opportunities were increased and opportunities for meaningful employment decreased. Today's youth probably are different from the youth of a generation or two ago. However, today's youth must contend with a social context different from that of their parents, certainly quite different from the one their grandparents knew. The president's Panel on Youth recognized that the settings in which youth are placed while they are marginal to the economy needed significant transformation.

> We think it is time to reappraise the contexts of youth, to question even the most accepted and ordinary aspects of their current institutional settings, and to consider the reformation of existing structures and if necessary the creation of new ones. We are proposing the establishment of alternative environments for the transition to adulthood, environments explicitly designed to develop not only cognitive learning but other aspects of maturation as well.[112]

The reformed or alternative environments need to be designed to achieve two classes of objectives. According to the panel, the first class consisted of those objectives "schools have traditionally focused upon" and was described as "essentially self-centered." The second class was described as one "in which youth is centered on others rather than self" and as one that focuses on "the opportunity for responsibilities affecting other persons."[113]

The panel recognized four major "self-centered" objectives. The first was the development of "those *cognitive and noncognitive skills necessary for economic independence and for occupational opportunities.*" Such skills include facility with language and numbers but also include a range of skills as wide "as the distribution of occupations within the labor force." The second objective was the development of the "capability of *effective management of one's own affairs.*" The panel noted that schools as then organized (and there has been little or no significant change since the mid 1970s) "provide little experience with self-management, in large part because, where there is little freedom of choice, there is little self-responsibility." In other words, students tend not to learn what they have no opportunity to learn. The third objective was the development of *"capabilities as a consumer, not only of goods, but more significantly, of the cultural riches of civilization."* In articulating this objective, the panel was affirming its belief that many derive pleasure from cultural pursuits, that such pleasure was good, that one could not do so unless one began to do so as a youth, and that all youth should have such preparation and experiences. The fourth objective was the development of those *"capabilities for engaging in intense concentrated involvement in an activity."* According to the panel, the most intense personal satisfaction and the greatest achievements of humankind issued not from "external pressure" but from "inner motivation which propels the person and focuses his or her attention." The panel further emphasized that the object to which the activity was directed was not as important as "the concentrated involvement itself."[114]

The second class of objectives consisted of three major objectives. The first showed the importance of creating opportunities for youth to enlarge their *"experience with persons differing in social class, subculture, and in age."* Some youth acquired such experiences through government service programs, such as the Peace Corps, or through enlistment in the armed services. However, for the majority of youth, life, especially life in school where students spend so much time, is effectively insulated from people who differ from themselves in any important respect. The significance of such an objective is that it would be extraordinarily difficult to realize in conventional public schools. The second objective focused on the need to give youth *"the experience of having others dependent on one's action."* That objective calls for experiences quite different from those acquired by most middle-class youth, who are usually cared for by others and learn how to be dependent rather than how to assume responsibility for the well-being of others. To obtain such experience, the panel noted, youth "would have to spend their time in a place different from the typical school." The third objective called attention to youth's need for *"involvement in interdependent activities directed toward collective goals"* so they learn how to serve "in the capacity of leader as well as follower." Youth are now typically subjected to authority but are rarely allowed to acquire or learn how to use it. Finally, the Panel noted that both classes of objectives were designed to allow youth to develop "a sense of identity and self esteem."[115]

Opportunities for youth to do something other than attend a conventional school, academic or vocational, while they make the transition to adulthood are very scarce. The federal government has sponsored several programs, mostly designed to equip youth with skills for the labor force or simply to employ them in order to keep unemployment rates low. Six major governmental programs with this design are the following:

1. The Young Adult Conservation Corps, which accepts youth between ages sixteen and twenty-four to work on conservation projects on public lands
2. Youth Community Conservation and Improvement Projects, which accepts youth who are economically disadvantaged between ages sixteen and nineteen to work on community and neighborhood projects
3. Youth Incentive Entitlement Pilot Project, which offers employment to youth from low-income families if they agree to remain in or return to school
4. Youth Employment and Training Programs, which accept youth between ages sixteen and twenty-one who are in school
5. Summer Youth Employment Program, which is designed for economically disadvantaged youth between ages fourteen and twenty-one
6. The Job Corps, which is a residential program for disadvantaged youth between ages fourteen and twenty-one.

Whether federal programs for youth can be deemed successful depends upon the criterion used to assess success. As political programs designed to reduce unemployment rates and the possible political and social problems attendant to unemployment, they may have been successful. Wrigley reports that they have "served as a means of reducing unemployment on a fairly large scale." It has been estimated, for example, that they reduced the unemployment rate for youth by nearly 4 percent in 1976. However, if the programs are judged in terms of how well they have helped youth make the transition into adulthood, the judgment may be less favorable. Even though the belief is widely held that "the employment problems of minority youth stem at one point or another from failures in work socialization, it is noteworthy

that there are almost no evaluations of the success or failures of government youth employment programs in socializing youth into good work values."[116] The absence of such evaluations leads to the conclusion that

> the socializing functions of these programs are subordinate to the income-transfer functions.
> The programs have been shaped, or misshaped, by political pressures to do something about
> youth employment and the perceived problems of crime and social disruption that it has brought
> in its wake. The most direct, easiest, and cheapest way to do something is simply to provide jobs
> for a segment of the most volatile youth during the period of their greatest hardship and social
> explosiveness—the teenage years and early twenties.[117]

Wrigley further observes that, unlike the federal projects of the 1930s such as the CCC
and NYA, "there are no recognizable projects of broad social scope or purpose identified with
the programs" of the 1960s and 1970s. During the 1930s, youth in government projects contributed to socially significant projects—the construction of zoos and parks, restoration of
historically significant buildings, and clearing of trails in woodlands. A generation later,
nothing comparable to the accomplishments of these projects was visible. Youth were not put
to work on socially significant projects but simply put to work "at unskilled or semiskilled
jobs for periods and received, in some cases, special but unevaluated services to help them adjust."[118]

While it may be difficult to find significant and useful projects for youth that would satisfy
the objectives set forth by Panel on Youth, it certainly is not impossible. In 1974, the National
Commission on Resources for Youth published a report—*New Roles for Youth in the School
and the Community*—which described seven types of programs designed to enable youth "to
participate more and more in adult activities and to assume an increasing degree of responsibility."[119] The chapter titles of the report indicate the kinds of programs described in the
report: "Youth as Curriculum Builders," "Youth as Teachers," "Youth as Community Manpower," "Youth as Entrepreneurs," "Youth as Community Problem-Solvers," "Youth as
Communicators," and "Youth as Resources for Youth." Within these categories are projects
that show how students participated in community service projects, tutorial projects, community service projects, drug counseling projects, developed a laboratory to produce films and
tapes of interest to them, and even organized and operated a restaurant for themselves and
their teachers.

Perhaps the most well known of the projects described by the National Youth Commission on Resources for Youth is *Foxfire*. It began when an English teacher in Rabun Gap, Georgia, suggested that his students consider publishing a magazine about their community. The
students accepted the suggestion. To secure material for their magazine, they decided to "go
into their mountain community with notebooks, cameras, and tape recorders to capture and
preserve, in words and pictures, a way of life that would otherwise disappear and leave no record."[120] *Foxfire* effectively required young people to interact and to learn from their elders. It
is an excellent example of what students can do, demonstrating how the efforts of youth can
contribute not just to their own immediate community but also the cultural life of the entire
nation. Through their efforts, the way of life of a distinctive people was preserved for all to
appreciate.

Foxfire however, is also an exception. There is no assurance that any project, no matter
how potentially significant, will endure. When the National Commission on Resources for

Youth presented its account of successful youth projects, it warned that "some of the projects described are no longer in existence." The Commission further related:

> It is important to bear in mind that in youth involvement programs, change is an inevitable and a desirable element. The concerns of one group of young people are not necessarily concerns of a succeeding group. Indeed, one of the values of youth participation projects is the acceptance of responsibility for identifying concerns and for devising means to deal with them.[121]

The nature and quality of the experiences that youth derive from an undertaking are at least as important as the nature of the undertaking itself. Youth must have the opportunity to make decisions and to assume responsibility for realizing those decisions. While the activity, or project, is a means for achieving that end, not an end in itself, a genuine activity is always better than a simulated one. Teachers and all others concerned with youth's successful transition into adulthood must focus their attention on the youth rather than on the search for a set of projects that are universally applicable and guaranteed to work. Activities that youth are expected to accept passively are not likely to help them make a successful transition into adulthood.

Notes

1. Charles E. Strickland and Charles Burgess, eds., *Health, Growth, and Heredity: G. Stanley Hall on Natural Education* (New York: Teachers College Press, 1965), 4.
2. Ibid., 19.
3. G. Stanley Hall, *Adolescence,* reprinted in Strickland and Burgess, eds., *Health, Growth and Heredity,* 106.
4. Ibid., 105.
5. Ibid., 113.
6. Ibid., 108.
7. Ibid., 109.
8. Ibid., 110–111.
9. Strickland and Burgess, *Health, Growth, and Heredity,* 161.
10. G. Stanley Hall, "The Needs and Methods of Educating Young People in the Hygiene of Sex," *The Pedagogical Seminary* 15 (March 1908), reprinted in Strickland and Burgess, eds., *Health, Growth, and Heredity,* 170.
11. Ibid., 170–171.
12. Ibid.
13. Ibid., 174.
14. Edwin G. Boring, *A History of Experimental Psychology,* 2d ed. (New York: Appleton-Century-Crofts, 1950), 522.
15. Strickland and Burgess, *Health, Growth, and Heredity,* 2.
16. Even though psychologists have tried to move away from G. Stanley Hall by employing different and more precise methodologies and by constructing theories on carefully collected data, they have had to acknowledge his influence. Even as they try to approach the subject in a manner different from Hall, the attempt to be different is recognition that Hall has been and continues to be an influence. For example, in 1925, when Leta S. Hollingsworth[a] tried to replace what Robert E. Grinder[b] described as "Hall's superficially plausible theory with an outlook based on clinical diagnoses" (p. 435), she made a point in her preface to warn Hall's students that they would "miss ex-

tensive reference to his voluminous pioneer works on adolescence." She explained that the ways psychologists approached the topic, as well as social conditions, had changed so much that references to Hall would be of "historic value primarily, rather than of scientific or practical value today" (p. ix). Twenty years later, George D. Stoddard[c] was still trying to show that the study of adolescence had gone beyond Hall, that it was no longer "the happy hunting ground of sentimentalists and fanatics." He acknowledged that "G. Stanley Hall knew that adolescence was important, and knew why" but also suggested that Hall's "followers were tainted with a sense of vicarious sin." Consequently, "they wallowed in subscience and sermons; the adolescent veered from evil to saintliness, without enough good, rational explorable territory in between" (p. 347). Grinder (see previous reference) noted that the field of adolescence had an "ignominious reputation" as a " 'happy hunting ground of sentimentalists and fanatics' " that "was born at the turn of the century with the publication of G. Stanley Hall's encyclopedic *Adolescence"* (p. 435).

[a]*The Psychology of the Adolescent.* New York: D. Appleton Century, 1925.

[b]"Epilogue: Two Models for the Study of Youth—1944 versus 1975," in Robert J. Havighurst and Philip H. Dreyer, eds., *Youth: The Seventy-fourth Yearbook of the National Society for the Study of Education, Part I.* Chicago: University of Chicago Press, 1975.

[c]"An Evaluation of the Yearbook," in Nelson B. Henry, ed., *Adolescence: The Forty-third Yearbook of the National Society for the Study of Education, Part I.* Chicago: University of Chicago Press, 1944.

17. David Fink, "Uncle Sam Takes on Teen Sex," *USA Today,* March 10, 1983.
18. Hall, "The Needs and Methods of Educating Young People in the Hygiene of Sex," reprinted in Strickland and Burgess, eds., *Health, Growth, and Heredity,* 173.
19. Randolph S. Bourne, "Youth," *Atlantic Monthly* 109 (1912), reprinted in Robert S. Bremner et al., eds., *Children and Youth in America: A Documentary History,* vol. 2 (Cambridge, Mass.: Harvard University Press, 1971), 85.
20. Ibid., 86.
21. Ibid., 86–87.
22. Ibid., 87.
23. Jane Addams, *The Spirit of Youth and the City Streets* (New York, 1910), reprinted in Bremner, ed., *Children and Youth,* vol. 2, 83–84.
24. Alain Locke, "Negro Youth Speaks," in Alain Locke, ed., *The New Negro* (New York: A. and C. Boni, 1925), reprinted in Bremner, ed., *Children and Youth,* vol. 2, 91.
25. Countee Cullen, "The League of Youth," *The Crisis,* 26 (1923), reprinted in Bremner, ed., *Children and Youth,* vol. 2., 90.
26. Ibid.
27. William James, "The Moral Equivalent of War," *Memories and Studies* (New York, 1911), reprinted in Bremner, ed., *Children and Youth,* vol. 2, 94.
28. U.S. National Youth Administration, *Final Report of the National Youth Administration, Fiscal Years 1936–1943* (Washington, D.C., 1944), reprinted in Robert S. Bremner et al., eds., *Children and Youth in America: A Documentary History,* vol. 3 (Cambridge, Mass.: Harvard University Press, 1974), 24–25.
29. Editorial note by Franklin D. Roosevelt accompanying Executive Order 7086 in Samuel I. Rosenman, comp., *The Public Papers and Addresses of Franklin D. Roosevelt,* vol. 4 (New York: Random House, 1938), reprinted in Bremner, ed., *Children and Youth,* vol. 3, 77.
30. Paul V. McNutt, U.S. Congress, Senate, Committee on Education and Labor, *Hearings on S. 2295, Termination of Civilian Conservation Corps and National Youth Administration, 77, Congress,* 2d sess., 1942, reprinted in Bremner, ed., *Children and Youth,* vol. 3, 74.
31. Quoted in Bremner, *Children and Youth,* vol. 3, 64.

32. "Radio Address on Third Anniversary of C.C.C. April 17, 1936," in Samuel I. Rosenman, comp., *The Public Papers and Addresses of Franklin D. Roosevelt,* vol. 5 (New York: Random House, 1938), reprinted in Bremner, ed., *Children and Youth,* vol. 3, 66.

33. Ibid., 67.

34. Roy Wilkins to Robert Fechner, June 6, 1934, Selection Division, Negro Selection, CCC records, National Archives, reprinted in Bremner, ed., *Children and Youth,* vol. 3, 70.

35. Robert Fechner to Roy Wilkins, June 7, 1934, Ibid., 71.

36. Luther C. Wandall, "A Negro in the CCC," *The Crisis,* 42 (1935), reprinted in Bremner, ed., *Children and Youth,* vol. 3, 72.

37. Kenneth Holland and Frank Ernest Hill, *Youth in the CCC* (Washington, D.C.: American Council on Education, 1942), reprinted in Bremner, ed., *Children and Youth,* vol. 3, 69.

38. Ibid., 70.

39. U.S. Congress, Senate, Committee on Education and Labor, *Hearings on S. 2295,* reprinted in Bremner, ed., *Children and Youth,* vol. 3, 76.

40. George Coe, "What Kind of a School Is a CCC Camp?" *Social Frontier,* vol. 1 (1935), reprinted in Sol Cohen, ed., *Education in the United States: A Documentary History* (New York: Random House, 1974), 2563.

41. Ibid., 2563–2564.

42. Ibid., 2565.

43. Frank Ernest Hill, *The School in the Camps: The Educational Program of the Civilian Conservation Corps* (New York, 1935), reprinted in Cohen, ed., *Education in the United States,* 2559.

44. Ibid., 2558–2559.

45. Coe, "What Kind of a School is a CCC Camp?" reprinted in Cohen, ed., *Education in the United States,* 2566.

46. Ibid., 2565–2566.

47. Joel Spring, *American Education: An Introduction to Social and Political Aspects* (New York: Longman, 1978), 85.

48. Betty and Ernest K. Lindley, *A New Deal for Youth: The Story of the National Youth Administration* (New York, 1938), reprinted in Cohen, ed., *Education in the United States,* 2556.

49. Ibid., 2555.

50. Ibid., 2557.

51. U.S. National Youth Administration. *Facing the Problems of Youth* (Washington, D.C., 1936), reprinted in Bremner, ed., *Children and Youth,* vol. 3, 78.

52. Ibid.

53. Ibid., 79.

54. Ibid.

55. Ibid.

56. Paul B. Jacobson, "The End of the N.Y.A.," *The School Review* 51 (1943), reprinted in Bremner, ed., *Children and Youth,* vol. 3, p. 91.

57. William E. Leuchtenburg, *Franklin D. Roosevelt and the New Deal* (New York: Harper Torchbook, 1963), 336.

58. "New Opportunities for Negro Youth," *Monthly Labor Review* 48 (June 1939), reprinted in Bremner, ed., *Children and Youth,* vol. 3, 85.

59. Ibid.

60. National Youth Administration, *Facing the Problems of Youth,* reprinted in Bremner, ed., *Children and Youth,* vol. 3, 80.

61. U.S. National Youth Administration, *Final Report,* reprinted in Bremner, ed., *Children and Youth,* vol. 3, 82.

62. Ibid., 83.
63. U.S. Congress, Senate, Committee on Education and Labor, *Hearings on S. 2295, Termination of Civilian Conservation Corps and National Youth Administration,* 77th Congress, 2d sess., 1942, reprinted in Bremner, ed., *Children and Youth,* vol. 3, 89.
64. Ibid., 90.
65. Harold D. Carter, "The Development of Interest in Vocations," in Nelson B. Henry, ed., *Adolescence: The Forty-third Yearbook of the National Society for the Study of Education, Part 1* (Chicago: University of Chicago Press, 1944), 185.
66. Ibid., 256.
67. Morris Janowitz, *Institution Building in Urban Education* (Russell Sage Foundation, 1969), 8–9.
68. Ibid., 9.
69. Ibid.
70. Ibid., 17.
71. National Commission on Excellence in Education, *A Nation at Risk: The Imperative for Educational Reform* (Washington, D.C., 1983), 21, 29.
72. James B. Conant, "Social Dynamite in Our Large Cities: Unemployed, Out-of-School Youth," reprinted in August Kerber and Barbara Bommarito, eds., *The Schools and the Urban Crisis* (New York: Holt, Rinehart & Winston, 1965), 170.
73. Ibid.
74. Ibid., 170–171.
75. Ibid., 170.
76. Ibid., 175.
77. Ibid.
78. Ibid., 172.
79. Ibid., 172–173.
80. Ibid., 181.
81. Ibid., 183. Conant's emphasis.
82. Ibid., 184.
83. Ibid., 185.
84. James B. Conant, *Slums and Suburbs* (New York: McGraw-Hill, 1961), 39.
85. Tim D. Kane, "The Emergence of the New Unemployed," *Intellect* 103(Fall 1975): 4.
86. Daniel H. Saks, *Distressed Workers in the 1980s* (Washington, D.C.: National Planning Association, Committee on New American Realities, 1983), 18.
87. Gordon I. Swanson, "Vocational Education Patterns in the United States," in Harry F. Silberman, ed., *Education and Work: Eighty-first Yearbook of the National Society for the Study of Education,* part 2 (Chicago: University of Chicago Press, 1982), 25.
88. Ibid., 26.
89. Ibid., 27.
90. Marcia Freedman, "The Structure of the Labor Market and Associated Training Patterns," in Silberman, ed., *Education and Work: Eighty-first Yearbook of the National Society for the Study of Education,* 235.
91. Ibid.
92. Julia Wrigley, "A Message of Marginality: Black Youth, Alienation, and Unemployment," in Silberman, ed., *Education and Work: Eighty-first Yearbook of the National Society for the Study of Education,* 235.
93. Ibid.
94. Ibid., 230.
95. Ibid., 234.

96. Ibid., 237.
97. Ibid., 238.
98. Hershel D. Thornburg and Robert E. Grinder, "Children of Aztlan: The Mexican-American Experience," in Robert J. Havighurst and Philip H. Dreyer, eds., *Youth: The Seventy-fourth Yearbook of the National Society for the Study of Education, Part I* (Chicago: University of Chicago Press, 1975), 347–348.
99. Ibid., 364.
100. Ibid., 358.
101. Ibid., 357.
102. Ibid., 357–359.
103. Ibid., 362–363.
104. Ibid., 359.
105. Ibid., 360.
106. Ibid., 364.
107. William T. Liu and Elena S. H. Yu, "Asian-American Youth," in Havighurst and Dreyer, eds., *Youth: The Seventy-fourth Yearbook of the National Society for the Study of Education,* 367.
108. Richard J. Becker, "Education and Work: A Historical Perspective," in Silberman, ed., *Education and Work: Eighty-first Yearbook of the National Society for the Study of Education,* 4–5.
109. Panel on Youth of the President's Science Advisory Committee, *Youth: Transition to Adulthood* (Chicago: University of Chicago Press, 1974), 2–3.
110. Ibid., vii.
111. Ibid., 3.
112. Ibid.
113. Ibid.
114. Ibid., 3–4.
115. Ibid., 4–5.
116. Wrigley, "A Message of Marginality," in Silberman, ed., *Education and Work: Eighty-first Yearbook of the National Society for the Study of Education,* 254.
117. Ibid., 255.
118. Ibid.
119. National Commission on Resources for Youth, *New Roles for Youth in the School and the Community* (New York: Citation Press, 1974), vii.
120. Ibid., 183.
121. Ibid., 7.

10
Teachers and Teaching

Doing More For Less

Since the end of World War II, both the public schools and the society they serve have been transformed by a multitude of economic, social, political, scientific, and technological developments. During the post–World War II era, when the nation enjoyed unprecedented political, military, and economic power, public education was seen as essential to the continuation and protection of that power and prosperity. Educators grew accustomed to bigger schools, bigger budgets, and a greater number of students. Theirs was truly a "growth industry." By 1950, 90 percent of the nation's youth between ages fourteen and seventeen were attending school. By the 1960s, reformers and educators agreed that public education was the best means for extending equality of opportunity and that expanded and improved educational opportunities would even eliminate poverty. Programs to serve those who had been previously excluded from school or ill-served by the public schools were funded and hastily implemented so that "full enrollment" could be finally achieved.

As prosperity gave many postwar Americans the wherewithal to adopt new values and to test new life-styles, some expected public schools to endorse and extend those new views and ways. Others expected the public schools to resist new values and life-styles and to strengthen adherence to traditional values. As the public attached greater importance to public education and increased the schools' budgets, teachers were assigned the responsibility for solving all sorts of social and personal problems: poverty, unemployment, drug abuse, juvenile delinquency, sexual promiscuity, teenage pregnancy, alcoholism, and even the high death rate on the nation's highways. When the problems seemed to persist, educators were blamed for not eliminating the problems and also for creating them.

Justly or unjustly, teachers have not been able to escape the problems of society. Schools have not and probably will not be sanctuaries from the troubles of society. More than most other professional groups, teachers have been required to confront nearly all of society's problems, changes, and controversies on a daily basis. At the same time, they have been paid less for the demands placed upon them and for their efforts. As the cost of living increased sharply during the 1970s and as the job of teaching became more difficult and, in some distances, even more dangerous, teachers' pay was effectively decreased.

In the 1960s, teachers' salaries were increasing faster than the consumer price index (CPI). Between the school years of 1960–61 and 1965–66, the average annual salary for teachers in-

265

creased 18.8 percent (from $5,264 to $6,253) and the CPI increased only 7.7 percent. Between 1965–66 and 1970–71, the average annual salary for teachers increased 48.1 percent (from $6,523 to $9,261) and the CPI increased 24.5 percent. By the mid 1970s, however, teachers began to see the purchasing power of their salaries decline sharply. Their salary increases were not as great as the increases in the cost of living. As the public lost faith and interest in its schools, teachers paid the price and suffered the loss.

In the early 1970s, the argument was even set forth that public education was no longer a sound investment. In 1972, Daniel Moynihan pointed out that public expenditures for public education during the 1960s rose faster than the gross national product (GNP). Expenditures for public elementary and secondary schools had been increasing an annual rate of 9.7 percent while the GNP was growing by only 6.8 percent per year. During the 1960s, the cost of public education had more than doubled, and, according to Moynihan, there was good reason to curtail the increasing educational expenditures. Recent social science research had shown that "once expenditure rises above a certain zone, money doesn't seem to matter that much in terms of what happens to students."[1] Increased expenditures would only benefit teachers, because two-thirds or more of a school system's operating budget was allocated to teachers' salaries. Teachers were, he admitted, deserving people, but increasing their pay would not increase student achievement. It would increase the inequality of income distribution in the society. Because the society's economic system was not working in a way to eliminate gross economic differentials, teachers would have to forego higher salaries.

Before the end of the 1970s, the conventional wisdom dictated that expenditures for public schools could not be increased and, if at all possible, should be reduced. Some had lost interest and confidence in public education. Others simply wanted their taxes, especially their local property taxes, reduced. The public's attitudes toward taxes were highly publicized during 1977–78 as the media reported extensively on the efforts of Howard A. Jarvis, Director of the United Organization of Taxpayers, to roll back property taxes in California. By the fall of 1977, Jarvis had assembled and organized a movement that had collected more than 1.2 million signatures on a petition to place what is now known as Proposition 13 before the California voters. On June 6, 1978, two-thirds of those who voted approved the measure which specified (1) that tax on property could not be greater than 1 percent of its fair market value, (2) that increases in property assessments could not be greater than 2 percent a year, and (3) that the state legislature could not increase other taxes to offset any loss of revenue at the local level unless a two-thirds majority voted in favor of a tax increase. The effect of Proposition 13 was twofold: (1) it moved the major responsibility for financing schools from the local to the state level and (2) it increased the public schools' vulnerability to fluctuations in the national economy.

Before Proposition 13, the state government in California provided between 40 and 50 percent of the schools' operating budgets. The remaining 50 to 60 percent came from locally levied property taxes. After Proposition 13 was approved, it was estimated that the local portion would fall somewhere between 21 and 28 percent. That estimate proved to be accurate. For 1981–82, the State of California provided the schools with 74.3 percent of their operating budgets. The federal government provided 6.8 percent and the remaining 18.9 percent came from local sources.[2]

The changing sources for school budgets in California are indicative of what has been happening throughout the nation. While the Education Commission of the States did report in 1983 that the decade-long trend of the states and the federal government to provide increased support for public schools was losing its earlier force, the states were still providing more of the schools' revenues than were local communities. During 1981–82, only eighteen states could claim that more than half the funds for public schools came from local sources. For the nation as a whole, 42.9 percent came from the states and 8.1 percent from the federal government.[3]

The longstanding practice of supporting schools with locally levied property taxes protected schools from fluctuations in the national economy. In California, for example, the proceeds from property taxes increased even faster than the rate of inflation. For over forty years—even during recessions—the revenues made available for schools from property taxes did not decline. However, the taxes upon which state governments mostly rely—sales and income taxes—fluctuate with the economy. As the states assume greater responsibility for financing public education and meet those obligations from revenues that are so sensitive to the economy, school budgets and teachers' salaries will be more vulnerable to changes in the economy than they have been since the Great Depression of the 1930s.

During the 1970s, teachers' salaries reflected the attitudes expressed by Moynihan and supporters of Proposition 13. The average annual salary for teachers increased between 1970–71 and 1975–76, but the increase was less than for the previous five-year interval and only about three-fourths as much as the increase in the CPI. The average annual salary increased by 43.3 percent (from $12,005 to $17,209) between 1975–76 and 1980–81, but the increase in the CPI was 57.4 percent. Thus, the average annual salary for a teacher in 1980–81 was 1.85 times as great at it was in 1970–71, but the cost of living was 2.2 times as great.[4]

The difference between the average annual salary for teachers and the CPI may be one reason that only 21.8 percent of teachers indicated in 1981 that they would choose teaching as a career again if they had a chance to do it over. In 1971, 44.9 percent of the teachers indicated they would choose teaching as a career again. The percent of those who indicated they would certainly not enter teaching again increased from 3.7 percent in 1971 to 12 percent in 1981.[5] Besides poor salaries, which ranked fourth among a list of factors contributing to job dissatisfaction among teachers in a 1980 survey, teachers listed lack of appreciation for schools by the public and media, students' lack of interest in learning, and the low status of teachers in their communities. Significantly, 49 percent of the teachers expressed dissatisfaction with student behavior.[6] Other reasons included feelings of insecurity or fear while in school. Teaching has not only become increasingly difficult but the school itself has in some instances become a place where teachers witness or are even subjected to violence or threats of violence.

Violence and Vandalism

According to the Department of Justice's National Institute of Law Enforcement and Criminal Justice, the incidence of school-based crime and disruption in schools reached a level high enough to warrant the creation of a new field of study in the 1970s. While "the field now referred to as school based crime and violence was largely unknown even as late as 1973,"[7] by 1979, the National Institute of Law Enforcement and Criminal Justice was able to assemble a four-part annotated bibliography of 124 selected entries to show how the new field was organized. The Institute's bibliography consisted of (1) "overview," which described the nature and extent of the problem in terms of its cost in dollars as well as in psychosociological terms,

(2) "The Students: Misbehavior and Traditional Discipline," which focused on the causes and signs of student disruptions, the effects of traditional methods of school discipline, and student rights, (3) "School Programs: Multiple Approaches," which included materials on programs schools established to curb school-based crime, and (4) "School Buildings: Physical Security," which described how school facilities could be better protected from vandalism.[8]

Senator Bayh's Subcommittee

The one person who probably did most to publicize violence and vandalism as major and daily problems in public schools was the former senator from Indiana, Birch Bayh. Writing in 1978, Bayh related that during his six-year tenure as chair of the Senate Subcommittee to Investigate Juvenile Delinquency, he "became increasingly concerned with reports from educators and others over the rising level of violence and vandalism in our Nation's Schools."[9] His subcommittee conducted a survey of 757 school systems that enrolled 10,000 or more students and accounted for nearly half (47 percent) of the nation's public school enrollment. In April 1975, it issued its findings—*A Report Card: 'A' in School Violence and Vandalism*. The subcommittee proceeded to conduct a "series of meetings and correspondence with over 70 prominent educational, governmental, and private organizations that have a particular interest and expertise in the solution to these problems," as well as a "series of public hearings with over 30 witnesses including teachers, administrators, students, parents, counselors, school security directors, superintendents, and several educational research groups."[10] In July 1976, the subcommittee issued two additional reports: *Nature, Extent and Cost of School Violence* and *Vandalism: Models and Strategies for Change*. In 1978, the National Institute of Education (NIE) published its report on the problem, *Violent Schools—Safe Schools*.

The Magnitude of The Problem

In 1975, the National Association of School Security Directors estimated that school-based violence and vandalism diverted more than $590 million from school budgets annually. Later NIE estimated that the annual cost of vandalism was only $200 million a year. The varying estimates reflect the difficulty in accounting for actual losses due to vandalism, the various ways of measuring the cost, and estimates made to compensate for unreported instances. A study of a West Coast school district revealed "that the true cost of vandalism . . . was about three times what was officially reported."[11] In that district only repairs made by outside contractors were recorded. Those made by school maintenance personnel were not counted as vandalism expenses. Another cost not always calculated is the increased insurance rates schools pay as vandalism claims increase. Some districts have even been forced to cancel their insurance as a result of high rates. However, as Bayh observed, "whatever the precise figure may be, the combination of rising vandalism costs and reduced budget resources cannot help but to have an effect on our overall educational effort."[12]

Costs for individual school districts were not insignificant. During 1974–75, the Los Angeles school system spent more than $7 million to prevent vandalism and to repair what could not be prevented. In 1974, the problem cost the Chicago schools nearly $10 million: $3.5 million to repair damages, $3.2 million for security programs, and $3 million for guards. During 1974–75, the per student cost of vandalism in Bellevue, Washington, an affluent suburban community, reached $55. There the schools incurred a $1 million loss when students set fire to a high school learning resources center and another $100,000 loss when arson was committed at an elementary school.

What is difficult to measure, yet difficult to deny, is the cost of school vandalism to students. It is certainly easy to agree with Bayh's claim that "school related crime has emotional, educational, and psychological impact far beyond the immediate victim of a particular incident."[13] As the Deputy Superintendent of the Chicago Schools testified, "When educational programs of schools are disrupted, when much needed educational funds are diverted to building upkeep and security personnel and devices, the children lose and society loses now and in the future."[14] Teachers are also denied the resources and equipment they need to do their jobs effectively.

Bayh's subcommittee sought to determine what the trend in school-based crime was. It learned that between 1970 and 1973 assaults on students had increased by 85.3 percent, assaults on teachers by 77.4 percent, and in-school robbery by 36.7 percent. A study published by the NEA in 1975 indicated that during the previous four years "assaults increased by 58 percent; sex offenses 62 percent; drug related crimes 81 percent and robbery 117 percent."[15] No matter how the statistics were reported, schools were clearly neither the most pleasant nor the safest places to spend a fourth of one's day. A study conducted in Philadelphia in 1974 showed that 44 percent of the boys surveyed believed schoolyards to be dangerous places and 21 percent even believed classrooms were dangerous.[16]

Schools have always been the sites of an occasional fight or two, and students have always been known to break school windows or scribble on some walls. However, as Bayh related, "What was once regarded as an unfortunate but tolerable fact of life for teachers and students has become a source of growing concern and even alarm for many members of the educational community."[17] Testimony heard by Bayh's subcommittee clearly indicated that the sense of alarm many parents and educators were expressing was well-founded. Albert Shanker, president of the American Federation of Teachers (AFT), testified that "violent crime has entered the school house, and the teachers and students are learning some bitter lessons."[18] Then president of the NEA, James A. Harris, told the subcommittee that "incidents of physical assault have increased dramatically; vandalism and destruction of property are even more awesome; and many schools are required to tax already strained resources to meet exorbitant costs of school insurance."[19] The executive secretary of the National Association of Secondary School Principals informed the subcommittee that "ten years ago . . . we would have a so-called 'blackboard jungle school,' but this was quite unique." What was once unique, however, had become common.

Students and teachers agreed with school officials and professional officers that there was indeed a serious problem in the schools. One student told the subcommittee:

> You would be surprised. You would not believe that some of the things could happen. You see somebody walking down the hall with a cane, if you unscrew the top and pull it out, it is a type of dagger—you would not believe something like that could go on in a school, but it does.[21]

Another student simply but clearly testified: "If you saw these people you would be shocked."[22] A teacher from Atlanta told of finding and confiscating a concealed weapon from an eighth grade girl. A teacher from a metropolitan high school explained that "the past few years have seen violence and vandalism become an almost daily occurrence on school grounds."[23]

NIE's *Violent Schools—Safe Schools* indicated that school-based crime seemed to be leveling off but certainly did not indicate that the problem had disappeared for either students or teachers. In a month's time, 2.4 million secondary school students could expect to be victimized by theft, and 282,000 could expect to suffer an assault. In a month's time, 5,200 teachers could expect to be assaulted and at least 1,000 would require medical attention. Theft would be experienced by 124,000 secondary school teachers, and another 6,000 would be robbed (personal confrontation) while at school.

While the crime rates were higher in metropolitan areas with populations of 500,000 or more, no place was free from school-based crime. The percent of teachers from cities with populations of 500,000 or more reporting theft in the previous month was 16.7 percent, or 1.76 times greater than those in rural areas where the percent was 9.5. Between those two extremes were teachers in smaller cities and suburban areas where the percents were 15.8 and 12, respectively. The percent of teachers from large cities reporting a robbery in the previous month was 1.3 or 3.25 times as great as in rural areas where 0.4 percent of the teachers reported experiencing a robbery. For smaller cities and suburban areas, the percents were 0.6 and 0.5. Teachers in large cities were experiencing physical assaults at a rate nine times as great as in rural areas (1.8 per cent for large cities and 0.2 percent for rural areas). In smaller cities and suburban areas, the percent of teachers reporting a physical assault in the previous month was 0.7 and 0.4.

Not suprisingly, teachers were, and probably still are, suffering more from the threat of violence than the actual incidence of violence. Government reports, the popular press, and professional literature all effectively reported how dangerous some schools were. The attention given to the problem indicated that the prevalence of weapons in the schools was greater and more serious than it was a decade or two earlier. Bayh, for example, observed that "while the gangs of the 1950s and early 1960s were satisfied with knives, chains, and an occasional homemade zip gun, the gangs of the 1970s are amply equipped with more sophisticated and powerful weaponry."[24] During 1974–75, the Los Angeles schools reported 187 incidents in which "knives and other forms of deadly but nonfirearm weapons on campus" were used. That was an increase of 73 percent over the previous year. During the first half of the 1974–75 school year, New York City had "31 incidents in the schools involving the use of handguns, including shootings and armed robberies."[25]

Just how many weapons students brought to school was and is difficult to determine, for students obviously attempt to conceal them. Moreover, in some schools the tendency is not to report their presence. As Albert Shanker testified:

> There is a tendency not to report school violence and school crime. There is pressure frequently brought to bear on the teachers—if this gets out it will hurt the reputation of our schools, and similar pressures are brought to bear on superintendents by school boards, up and down the line.[26]

Shanker further testified that school administrators had subtle ways to insure that teachers would not report all incidents.

> Teachers find that if they report to the principal an assault, the principal feels that his own reputation or her reputation or the schools' reputation is at stake here, will frequently turn around

and start harassing the teacher by saying, 'how come you are the one always complaining. You must have more observations or better planning, or this or that.' So the teachers soon find out that bringing these reports to the attention of the principal is not something that is wanted and [the principal] tends to suppress that information.[27]

Almost five years after Bayh's subcommittee conducted its hearings, underreporting of weapons' offenses in New York City schools was still common. Until May 1981, according to the *New York Times*, "the New York City public schools have left punishment of such offenses essentially at the discretion of principals, without even a firm requirement that the police be notified." However, School Chancellor Frank J. Marchiarola "decided to bite the bullet" and "announced new rules that require notification of the police when a student is caught with a dangerous weapon and that lift the five-day limit on the suspension that can be given to such a student."[28]

If teachers were not aware of the statistics that government and school officials were gathering and discussing, it is likely that reports in their own professional media and the popular media, as well as their own experiences, made them aware of the problem. Early in 1976, *U. S. News & World Report* published a special report, "Terror in the Schools." It began by informing readers that "violence and vandalism in the nation's public schools are approaching epidemic proportions—and nobody seems to know what to do about it." The magazine's staff conducted its own survey of twenty cities and discovered "numerous instances of gang warfare, stabbings and clubbings, extortion, abduction, destruction of school facilities and, in one case, the killing of all school pets in 25 classrooms in an elementary school."[29] In Atlanta, a fifteen-year old student shot an assistant principal soon after he had been paddled. In a year's time in Miami, "simple assaults jumped from 566 to 1830; robberies rose from 119 to 195; rapes, from 6 to 22" and there were 225 assaults on teachers and other school officials.[30] In Chicago, 25 percent were "worried about their physical safety." A representative of the Chicago Teachers Union related that teachers commonly refused to work in certain areas of schools because they feared "assault from students carrying guns and knives."[31] In 1965, Chicago had no security guards in its schools but by 1975 it had 700.

Doubtlessly, impressions of the situations in the schools differed from actual circumstances. For example, *U. S. News & World Report* indicated that one high school teacher said:

> I bet if you searched every kid in the city you'd find 60 percent of them with weapons. I know that teachers bring weapons to school—in fact, one had a gun stolen from his car.[32]

While no data support the claim that 60 percent of any student body is, or was, armed and no report has made on how many teachers held such beliefs, such conjectures do seem credible when presented in an article with pictures of a Los Angeles teacher wearing a wrist transmitter so she can signal for help from a security guard if and when needed, of teachers directing students through a metal detector at the entrance of a Boston school, and of security guards searching students for weapons at a New York City high school. Teachers, like others, develop their view of the world and act on what they believe is true even though it may not be.

In April 1976, *U. S. News & World Report* issued another special report, "Violence in Schools." While it did report a nationwide crackdown on violence in the schools, it left little doubt that the problem still persisted and was indeed serious. No part of the country was immune. All parts were subject to the wave of school-based crime rolling over the nation. When officials conducted drug crackdowns in "well-to-do" high schools in Houston, Texas, and in Westchester County, New York, students responded by breaking school windows and pelting police with rocks and apple cores. The worst drug abusers in Charlotte, North Carolina, were "the children of the most highly educated parents." In suburban San Mateo County, California, it was discovered "that more twelfth graders had tried marijuana than had smoked tobacco."[33]

As teachers acted to curb the violence, they frequently encountered either lawsuits or school officials who took little or no action. In 1976, in Georgia, twelve lawsuits were "pending against teachers accused of roughing up students."[34] Threats of lawsuits against educators had become so great that the National Association of Secondary School Principals began providing each of its members with a $300,000 liability insurance policy. In Kansas City, Missouri, the local Federation of Teachers offered to pay all legal fees and court costs for any teacher who took an assault case to court as well as a $100 prize for so doing. In Lancaster, Pennsylvania, the local education association "made a contractual discipline policy its number one priority in the bargaining" in 1979 because it was so dissatisfied with the way school officials handled the cases of eight teachers who had been assaulted by students. The contract it signed with the school district included reference to "a strong discipline policy included in a letter of understanding agreed to by both sides."[35]

While the president of the Kansas City, Missouri, Federation of Teachers was reporting that "there is no limit to the weapons students are using against teachers,"[36] *U. S. News & World Report* reported that some school boards "have reinstated wooden paddles or have given educators a freer hand in using them."[37] However, by then many teachers had concluded that physical punishment was ineffective and a form of violence that bred even more violence. In fact, in 1972, the NEA's Task Force on Corporal Punishment concluded that "physical punishment is an inefficient way to maintain order" and recommended that the NEA "propose and support the adoption of model state legislation for outlawing corporal punishment."[38] In 1975, Marilyn Whiteside of the University of Maine acknowledged that many teachers were victimized by student violence but reminded teachers that "violence and injustice live on both sides of the desk."[39] Moreover, just as the mass media were beginning to publicize the extent of school-based crime, teachers were reminding other teachers that "not only do too many teachers and administrators fail to see a difference between reasonable and unreasonable force, but abuse of any kind is too flagrant and widespread."[40]

Teachers Talk to Teachers

While teachers were learning that traditional methods of discipline were frequently ineffective, they were also telling each other of their experiences in the schools. For example, Nancy P. Wheeler, who taught English during 1977–78 in a Richmond, Virginia, middle school, wrote about her experiences and the reasons why she resigned at the end of the school year. Her year of teaching was not a satisfying one.

> In the single year I taught in Richmond, I would estimate conservatively that strangers and non-students entered my room 10 separate times. I was threatened with raised fists by students approximately 20 times, warned six times that my car would be vandalized, verbally threatened with beatings 15 times and cursed 12 times by outsiders I did not know. My family and children

were objects of threats 12 times. And my life was threatened in what certainly appeared to be serious ways 100 times (this, again is a conservative estimate).[41]

To Wheeler's dismay, her documented complaints to the school principal brought forth "not a single constructive answer."[42] More "baffling and distressing" than the violence teachers faced was the administrative refusal to acknowledge the problem and to begin to do something about it. Wheeler was not, however, the only teacher to claim that school principals failed to act to protect teachers against school-based crime. An Atlanta science teacher reported that:

> Students call you foul names every day. But sometimes I just ignore them because, if I take them to the office, nothing will be done. The principal usually can be found watching television.[43]

By 1980, educational researchers were claiming that violence and vandalism were no longer increasing. Then, Francis A. J. Ianni and Elizabeth Reuss-Ianni, who had worked on the Safe School Study for NIE, wrote that school-based crime had been increasing in the 1960s but was leveling off in the 1970s. They reported that "the studies do not indicate that the rates of the offenses we call violence and vandalism are currently growing worse."[44] In 1979, the director of the University of Chicago's Center for Criminal Justice reported that despite public perception, violent crime among youth may have begun to level off as early as 1970 and was perhaps even beginning to decline. According to a report in *USA Today*, "Arrest rates for homicide by offenders aged 13 to 20 years jumped by 84% during the 1960s, leveled off to a four per cent increase from 1970 to 1975, and then declined by eight per cent from 1975 to 1977."[45] However, "arrest rates for aggravated assault continued to climb during the first half of the 1970s and figures for 1975–77 remain close to the 1975 peak." Franklin Zimring of Chicago's Center reported that "aggravated assault is the single violent offense to display sharp increases during the 1970s that has not been counter-balanced by declines since 1975."[46] There was, he related, a "gap between symbol and substance that pervades public discussion."[47] One reason for the gap was that the absolute number of offenses commited by youth had increased because there were more young people than ever before.

The gap between "the symbol and the substance" may have been reflected in teachers' professional media by the late 1970s. By then, teachers were more aware of the problem than ever before. Their professional organizations were gathering data from teachers, reporting the results of surveys back to teachers, and discussing the severity of the problem in the professional literature. The action of the NEA Representative Assembly in 1979 certainly did not reflect any belief that the problem was subsiding. It passed a resolution expressing its conviction that "when school personnel are the victims of physical attack, verbal abuse, harassment, or theft, they should receive the full support of their employers in pursuing legal and other remedies." The Assembly also urged the NEA and its affiliates "to insist upon development and enforcement of laws that guarantee the safety of educators and other school personnel from physical attacks on their persons or property, and that provide reimbursement for loss." It futher recommended that "in no event shall time lost due to injury caused by such physical attacks be deducted from the teacher's accumulated sick leave."[48]

Teachers' power to contend with the problem of school-based crime was limited. As a junior high school teacher and a NEA vice-president, Willard McGuire suggested in 1975 that even though teachers did not have all the answers necessary to solve the problem, they could make a significant contribution by being honest about the problems confronting them and the schools. Teachers were too inclined to remain silent. It was easy for teachers to tell principals: "I didn't see anything." That, he explained, usually meant that the teachers did not want to risk having their heads or cars smashed or wanted to avoid a lecture from the principal about how better teaching would eliminate disturbances. Principals acted in much the same way as their teachers. They failed to report problems to their superintendents so they would avoid admonishments about not being able to control their schools. Teachers could not force others to "tell the truth" about the problems in schools but they could "start telling the truth about the problem" themselves.[49]

Four years later, as NEA president, McGuire was still writing about the "shocking incidents" that were daily occurrences in schools across the nation: "A high school student in Virginia bit off a third of his teachers' ear during a scuffle; a student in Oregon turned his teacher over in a chair during class; a third grader in rural Missouri twisted a teacher's thumb and tore several ligaments; students in California, angry over their low marks, set their teacher's hair on fire, and the teacher was criticized for leaving the classroom when she went to get help."[50] Teachers were not only still facing assaults and violence in schools but also were developing their own ways to reduce the level of school-based crime. McGuire reported that "police, parents, and legislators cannot solve the problems alone" and suggested that the NEA would "have to lead the way." Accordingly, *Today's Education* presented accounts of how teachers were working to solve the problem in the cities of San Antonio, Texas, and Portland, Oregon, and in the states of New Jersey and Hawaii—a sample that showed that no part of the nation was free from the problem.

Teachers' Responses

The Discipline Task Force of the San Antonio Teachers Council (SATC) prepared a "Classroom Survival Manual" for teachers. Its suggestions for preventing discipline problems were so well received and requested by so many that the NEA included it in its nationally distributed Discipline Kit. The SATC also sponsored after-school workshops on classroom management and discipline for teachers, began a parent volunteer aid program for the schools, and sent a checklist called "What Kind of Parent Are You?" to parents so they could assess how they influenced their children's attitudes toward school. The SATC also invited parents to use a checklist to evaluate the schools' programs before attending open house programs.[51]

The Portland Association of Teachers (PAT) negotiated a discipline clause into its contract with the school board that specified that teachers would "be reimbursed for losses caused by attack or vandalism," empowered teachers to "remove a disruptive student from the classroom and arrange a conference with the student's parents and principal," and allowed teachers to "grieve an administrative action if the administrator's handling of an incident is considered unsatisfactory."[52] PAT also conducted sessions for teachers to study the schools' discipline policies, to devise "standard ways to report violations of those policies," and to teach teachers how "to organize written records of their students' behavior"[53] Besides attending to measures teachers could take to protect themselves and their rights, PAT also used funds provided by the NEA's School Violence Grants Program to offer cash awards to students, teachers, school officials, and community groups who proposed plans to solve the schools' problems. At one school, "students surveyed staff and students on their attitudes toward vandalism; made and displayed photographs of examples of vandalism on their campus; held classroom discussions; and developed assembly programs, posters, and announcements in the school's daily bulletin." There students even "carried out a 'secret witness' program with rewards and fines."[54] At another school, students conducted a speech contest to select a "school Crime Stopper" who "served on the student council, chaired an anti-vandalism committee, and gave reports over the school's public address system."[55]

The New Jersey Education Association successfully worked for enactment of legislation requiring that acts of violence and vandalism in schools be reported systematically so that problem areas would be known. It also worked for a law that "requires immediate suspension of any student who assaults a school employee," as well as suspension of any student who commits a second offense "until all criminal charges have been settled, however long it takes."[56]

The Hawaii State Teachers Association (HSTA) used its own funds and those from the NEA's School Violence Grants Program, the U.S. Office of Education, and the Federal Law Enforcement Assistance Administration to work with the state law enforcement administration, community groups, students, politicians, and the media to support a program called "Hawaii Schools That Achieve." The program sent teachers, counselors, administrators, and parents to the Awareness House at Mills College in Oakland, California, to "develop communications and process skills" and "explore social and cultural issues, learn problem-solving techniques, and practice ways to develop coalitions of teams."[57] Program participants used their newly acquired skills to develop activities outside the classroom that would increase communication among students, teachers, and other school officers and to foster "school spirit." Early in the program, development of "school spirit" may have seemed "corny," but, according to Ray Sodetani of HSTA, "the incidence of disruptive behavior reported in several targeted schools has decreased by 64 percent."[58]

Even while the NEA was reporting the teachers' associations actions to combat violence in schools, it was continuing to report the dimensions of the problem to its membership. A survey completed in May 1980 revealed that "an estimated 113,000 of the nation's 2,184,000 public school teachers were physically attacked by a student during a recent 12 month period."[59] That was 50,000 more than the estimated reported in the NEA's survey for the 1975–76 school year.[60] Nearly two-thirds of those assaulted reported some form of subsequent suffering: "2,500 were seriously injured," "26,000 suffered minor injuries," 45,000 reported emotional suffering after experiencing an assualt, and "some 11,000 teachers missed an average of five days of school to recuperate from the attacks."[61] About 85 percent of the assaulted teachers reported the incidents to school authorities and about 15 percent reported the attacks to law enforcement officials but, from the teachers' viewpoint, disciplinary action was not taken frequently enough and was not sufficient when it was. In 25 percent of the incidents no disciplinary action was taken even though teachers believed some action was appropriate, and "in another 25 percent of the cases teachers thought the action taken was too little."[62] Charges were filed in about only 10 percent of the cases: 2 percent were filed by the school system, 2 percent by the police, and 6 percent by the teachers.

Blaming the Teachers

The mass media did bring the problem of violence in the schools to the public's attention, but did not present the problem as one-sided. Teachers were portrayed as perpetrators of violence as well as victims. The NEA Task Force on Corporal Punishment had recommended against its use in 1972, but that neither stopped its use or even its excessive use. While teachers were worrying about assaults on themselves in the schools, Nat Hentoff was telling readers of the *Ladies' Home Journal* "what every parent should know." He was telling them about "Child Abuse in the Schools." According to Hentoff, the United States

> is one of the last major nations (along with Germany and Great Britain) to permit corporal punishment in the schools. School children, moreover, are the only group of Americans who can legally be assaulted. Even prison inmates can no longer be beaten—and that includes youngsters confined in state correctional facilities. Yet any child in the "free world" of a public school is fair game for physical abuse.[63]

Corporal punishment had been banned in some major school districts—Baltimore, Chicago, New York, San Francisco, and Washington, D.C.—and in some small towns but it was "entirely legal" throughout most of the nation. Where it was permitted, it was routinely abused. Hentoff discovered that "in many school systems, children are routinely whacked for chewing gum, talking in class, being tardy, having their shirttails out or being noisy in the shower."[64] To illustrate his charge, he presented examples that were as gruesome as the reports of attacks on teachers. In Camden, Delaware, a fifth-grade boy "was beaten so severely that the welts and bruises on his back and buttocks were visible for days" because he was in the "bathroom too long." In Beggs, Oklahoma, learning disabled children were placed in regular classrooms and "if they can't keep up, they are whacked with a wooden paddle."[65] Even those who were not beaten were adversely influenced by the practice. An Illinois minister complained that his six-year-old daughter's "enthusiasm for school had been quickly dampened by warnings of physical punishment."[66]

The majority of teachers were not abusing students just as the majority of students were not assaulting teachers. However, the claims that many were at a time when the purchasing power of teachers' salaries was declining, when the public seemed disinterested in schools, and when teachers' working conditions seemed unsafe to them do show that teaching had become, in many instances, not only a very difficult undertaking but also one that the public did not fully appreciate. Under such circumstances, it seems not surprising that teachers often felt battered and suffered from burnout. By the summer of 1980, the NEA had conducted over 100 workshops in various parts of the nation to help teachers cope with job related stress.

Teacher Burnout

In 1977, Dr. Alfred M. Bloch, a clinical psychiatrist at the University of California at Los Angeles, reported that between 1971 and 1976 he had examined 250 Los Angeles classroom teachers—white, black, Mexican-American, and Asian-American—who "had symptoms of either physical trauma and/or prolonged psychic stress." All were suffering the consequences of "beatings, assaults with weapons, or continued harassment and threats of violence from students, parents, and vagrants" and were suffering from "anxiety, fear, and depression."[67]

Teachers were displaying the same kinds of symptoms found in military personnel who suffered from combat fatigue or neurosis. Their symptoms included cognitive impairment, phobias, nightmares, blurred vision, headaches, migraine headaches, hypertension, peptic ulcers, and respiratory problems. There was, however, a significant difference between teachers and military personnel. Military personnel "know that upon completion of a combat mission or upon surviving for a certain period of time in a war zone, they will be rotated to a nonstressful place for rest and recuperation before being returned." Teachers had no such assurance, Bloch explained, even though it was known that the rest and recuperation procedure "has a positive effect on their adverse symptoms."[68] Some teachers had to submit to psychiatric evaluations and engage counsel to secure workmen's compensation when they were so disabled that they were unable to return to the situations where they acquired their disabilities.

Some teachers responded to their stressful situations by leaving the profession. In 1982, Lois D. Spano reported that "last fall was the first time in 20 years that I did not return to my teaching job." When her friends asked why, she "simply said that I had burned out."[69] She readily admitted she was "lucky." Her spouse was a "successful professional," and she was "free to retire." However, that solution was not available to all teachers suffering from stress. Consequently, teacher stress, or burnout, became a problem the educational profession had to confront in the late 1970s and early 1980s.

Elaine G. Wangbert from the University of New Orleans who was among those who developed programs to help teachers cope with stress, indicated that "there can be no doubt that teacher stress, burnout, and job dissatisfaction are critical issues in education today."[70] Jeffrey S. Kaiser and James F. Polczynski reported that the teachers' need to "cope with an ever-growing number of social and environmental forces impinging on their time" was "becoming increasingly more difficult with the resultant stress taking its toll on physical and mental well-being."[71] They reported that the corporate-industrial sector of society was attending to the problem because premature deaths and illnesses were costing that sector billions of dollars. They suggested that if educators did not begin to address the problem, public education would soon experience similar losses.

Two other researchers, Fred C. Feitler and Edward Tokar, concluded that the problem of teacher stress was not as bad as some of media reports indicated, but they did not deny it was serious. Their survey of 3,300 public school teachers from kindergarten through senior high school revealed that 76 percent of the teachers rated their jobs as either "moderately" or "mildly" stressful. Only 16 percent reported that their jobs were "very" or "extremely" stressful; 7 percent reported their jobs "not at all stressful."[72] The amount of stress reported corresponded directly to grade level and size of community. Those most likely to report that their jobs were very stressful were high school teachers from urban areas. While 19 percent of high school teachers and 16 percent of junior high school teachers reported their jobs to be "extremely" or "very" stressful, only 13 percent of elementary school teachers so reported. In urban areas, 20 percent of teachers reported that their jobs were stressful "compared to 16 percent in suburban and only 14 percent in rural schools."[73]

Feitler and Tokar did find a relationship between the amount of stress teachers reported and their age but did not find that beginning teachers experienced the most stress. Rather, teachers between ages thirty one and forty-four reported more stress than those who were either younger or older and even less than that of first-year teachers. While 18 percent of the mid-career, experienced teachers reported that teaching had become either "very" or "extremely" stressful, 13 percent of those under age thirty and 17 percent of those over age forty five did so. Only 16 percent of the first-year teachers reported their jobs to be "very" or "extremely" stressful, and 7 percent reported no stress. The remaining 77 percent reported either "mild" or "moderate" stress. Teachers within five years of retirement constituted the group that revealed the greatest variation in stress. While 12 percent of that group described their jobs as "not at all stressful," 18 percent indicated that teaching had become "very" or "extremely" stressful.

Feitler and Tokar were unable to explain the high rate of stress among mid-career teachers who are "at the peak of their careers" but did offer their "hunch" that theirs were classrooms with "a high level of stress." The chief stress-causing factor reported by the teachers was "one or two students who chronically misbehave, rather than general lack of discipline or widespread student behavior problems in the school."[74] Spano reported that the trend away from ability grouping and toward mainstreaming, which began in the 1960s, often strained the energy and abilities of teachers. Introducing children with physical disabilities into regular classes did not present problems, "but," she reported, "if the disability is emotional or behavioral, the child can take half of the teacher's time and effort."[75] In such situations, she explained, teachers have little time for those who want to learn.

The pressure on teachers and school administrators to devote increasing amounts of time and energy to order-keeping functions, inside and outside the classroom, has heightened since the 1950s and 1960s. For some, it has taken the joy out of teaching. As Spano explained, "Being around young people is still stimulating and fun, but handling classes with behavior problems is much harder than just teaching 25 to 30 students five periods a day."[76] The claim that teachers spend significant portions of their time trying to control behavior problems is supported by the results of a study conducted in Maryland by Judith P. Ruchkin. She found that the number of "violent" students in the schools may not have been as great as media reports indicated, but that a "substantial minority" were "disruptive." In her study, she found that only 5 percent of the students were "violent" (having been sent to the office ten or more times or having committed a violent act) but 35 percent were "disruptive" (having been sent to the office an average of three times each). Disruptive students add to the teacher's "burden of maintaining order."[77]

Ruchkin's findings further indicate that the price for the attention paid to trying to control disruptive and violent students was less attention to "higher order achievement." A survey of school officials in 390 school districts conducted for the Law Enforcement Assistance Administration in 1972 to determine how school officials were responding to disruption and violence showed that "curricular response to school violence was most notable by its absence."[78] A subsequent survey conducted in 1976 by Research for Better Schools, showed that the school curriculum was not seen as having any significant relationship to the classroom disruption teachers were facing. Ruchkin reported that "rather than look at the basic and general issues of what shall be taught to whom, when, how, in what form, and how assessed, curricular responses tended to be specialized, course-addition focused."[79] It made no difference whether state school officials were from small or large districts. Their responses were basically the same. Curricular responses to discipline and behavior problems were less favored than the use of "ancillary services" (school counselors and security forces) and reliance on human relations activities to increase communication and understanding among various groups.

Conclusion

While school administrators were organizing human relations workshops for teachers and while teachers were being encouraged to join support groups to learn to manage their stress or to attend workshops on behavior management, both teachers and their supervisors were having their attention drawn away from what should be the most important concerns of teachers and principals: teaching and learning. In such a climate, it is indeed unlikely that principals had the opportunity to discharge effectively their most important duty—the supervision of instruction. Rather, they became managers of a variety of processes that often seem unrelated, especially to those who are more goal-oriented than order-oriented, to the primary goal of schooling. Spano, for example, related that when she quit teaching, school administrators were different from those who were school administrators when she began teaching. Principals were expected by their school boards "to run a tight ship and yet to be loved by all . . . to hire and keep happy a stable of master teachers, to deal with a leaky roof or vandalism without asking for an increase in the budget, and to administer the myriad programs and regulations that come down from on high with their legal clauses and subparagraphs."[80]

Rather than supervise instruction and assist teachers with their efforts, principals are now frequently obliged to evaluate teachers in a systematic and formal manner. The principal, according to Spano, had to contend with "a monster of an evaluation instrument" by spending three hours with each teacher so each could be evaluated "on some 50 qualifications and skills." For the teacher who was "conscientiously trying to do a good job with each student and who must, at the same time, worry about these 50-plus categories," such an evaluation was a "nightmare." When the principal came to conduct the evaluation, teachers had to "be sure not to over-look" any of the categories rather than focus on the achievement of the students. For Spano, "the days when the principal evaluated teachers informally, with a view toward helping them improve rather than with the objective of getting the evidence so that firing can take place if that seems advisable" were clearly better.[81] Whether new formal means of evaluation are better or worse than earlier forms of informal evaluation of teachers is debatable. What is not debatable, however, is that during the last generation, the job of teaching has changed and the relationship between the principal and the teacher has also changed.

As attention was drawn away from the school curriculum and student achievement, teachers were urged, if not required, to assume new roles and responsibilities and even new conceptions of themselves. Feitler and Tokar suggested that teachers be equipped with counselor skills so they could "diagnose causes, prescribe alternatives, and evaluate results for individuals who misbehave."[82] They did not note that public schools are organized to offer mass instruction and that such a recommendation could not be effected unless traditional school conventions were replaced with new ones. Besides advising that teachers be given opportunities for professional development, participate in support systems, and learn relaxation techniques, teachers were counseled that "the myth of the 'super teacher' " had to be destroyed. It was an "impossible standard to live up to." There was and is no way for teachers to do "perfectly" all that has been and continues to be asked of them.[83] Unfortunately, they are blamed for whatever behaviors youth display whether they are learned in school or not.

Notes

1. Daniel P. Moynihan, "Equalizing Education—In Whose Benefit?" *Public Interest,* no. 29 (Fall 1972): 71.

2. James W. Guthrie, "Proposition 13 and the Future of California's Schools," *Phi Delta Kappan* 60 (September 1978): 13.
3. "Trends in Federal, State, and Local Revenues for Public Schools," *Education Week* (June 9, 1982): 12.
4. Data on teachers' salaries and the CPI are from *The American Education Deskbook, 1982–83* (Washington, D.C.: Editorial Projects in Education, 1982), 246.
5. Ibid., 245.
6. "Teacher Opinion Pool: Job Satisfaction," *Today's Education* 69 (1980): 8, and "Teacher Opinion Poll: Attacks on Teachers," *Today's Education* 69 (1980): 21, cited in Richard A. Gorton, "Teacher Job Satisfaction," Harold E. Mitzel, ed., *Encyclopedia of Educational Research,* 5th ed. (Riverside, N. J.: Macmillan, 1983), 1905.
7. Robert Rubel et. al., comp., *Crime and Disruption in Schools,* prepared for the National Institute of Law Enforcement and Criminal Justice, Law Enforcement Administration, U.S. Department of Justice by Aspen Systems Corporation (Washington, D.C.: U.S. Government Printing Office, 1979), v.
8. Ibid., vi.
9. Birch Bayh, "School Violence and Vandalism: Problems and Solutions," *Journal of Research and Development in Education* 2 (Winter 1978): 4.
10. Ibid.
11. Birch Bayh, "Battered Schools: Violence and Vandalism in Public Education," *Viewpoints in Teaching and Learning* 55 (1979): 7.
12. Ibid., 6.
13. Ibid., 7.
14. Quoted in Bayh, "Battered Schools," 7–8.
15. Ibid., 4.
16. Bayh, "Battered Schools," 8.
17. Bayh, "School Violence and Vandalism," 4–5.
18. Quoted in Bayh, "Battered Schools," 2.
19. Ibid., 3.
20. Ibid.
21. Ibid.
22. Ibid.
23. Ibid.
24. Bayh, "Battered Schools," 4.
25. Ibid.
26. Quoted in Bayh, "Battered Schools," 7.
27. Quoted in John R. Ban and Lewis Ciminillo, *Violence and Vandalism in Public Education: Problems and Prospects* (Danville, Ill.: Interstate Printers & Publishers, 1977), 4.
28. "Disarmament Edict for City Schools," *New York Times*, May 10, 1981.
29. "Terror in Schools," *U.S. News & World Report*, January 26, 1976. 52.
30. Ibid., 54.
31. Ibid., 53.
32. Ibid., 54.
33. "Violence in Schools," *U.S. News & World Report*, April 14, 1976.
34. Ibid., 38.
35. "Lancaster Teachers Win #1 Priority—Discipline," *Voice*, November 5, 1979, reprinted in *Teacher* 97 (March 1980): 49.
36. "Violence in Schools," 38.
37. Ibid.

38. National Education Association, *Report of the Task Force on Corporal Punishment* (Washington, D.C.: NEA, 1972), 4, 7.
39. Marilyn Whiteside, "School Discipline: The Ongoing Crisis," *The Clearing House* 48 (December 1975): 160.
40. Vincent J. Hawkins, "The Negativism of Corporal Punishment," *The Clearing House* 49 (January 1976): 223.
41. Nancy P. Wheeler, "Violence in Schools: Paradox 1979," *Teacher* 96 (March 1979): 22.
42. Ibid., 24.
43. "Violence in Schools," 40.
44. Francis A. J. Ianni and Elizabeth Reuss-Ianni, "What Can Schools Do About Violence?" *Today's Education* 69 (April-May, 1980): 20G–21G.
45. "Violent Youth Crime May Be Declining," *USA Today* 108, (June 1979).
46. Ibid.
47. Ibid.
48. "NEA Resolution on Protection of School Personnel," *Today's Education* 69 (April-May 1980): 19G.
49. Willard McGuire, "What Can We Do About Violence?" *Today's Education* 64 (November-December 1975): 23.
50. Willard McGuire, "Violence in the Schools," *Today's Education* 69 (April-May 1980): 18G.
51. "How Education Associations Fight Violence: San Antonio, Texas," *Today's Education* 69 (April-May 1980): 30G–31G.
52. "How Education Associations Fight Violence: Portland, Oregon," *Today's Education* 69 (April-May 1980): 27G.
53. Ibid., 26G.
54. Ibid.
55. Ibid., 27G.
56. "How Education Associations Fight Violence: New Jersey," *Today's Education* 69 (April-May 1980): 24G.
57. "How Education Associations Fight Violence: Hawaii," *Today's Education* 69 (April-May 1980): 28G.
58. Ibid., 29G.
59. "Teacher Opinion Poll," *Today's Education* 69 (September-October 1980): 21GE.
60. Alfred M. Bloch, "The Battered Teacher," *Today's Education* 66 (March-April 1977): 58.
61. "Teacher Opinion Poll," 21GE.
62. Ibid.
63. Nat Hentoff, "Child Abuse in the Schools," *Ladies' Home Journal* (April 1980): 101,177.
64. Ibid., 177.
65. Ibid., 101.
66. Ibid., 177.
67. Bloch, "The Battered Teacher," 58.
68. Ibid., 61.
69. Lois D. Spano, "Why I Quit Teaching," *School and Community* 68 (February 1982): 7.
70. Elaine G. Wangberg, "Helping Teachers Cope With Stress," *Educational Leadership* 39 (March 1982): 453.
71. Jeffrey S. Kaiser and James J. Polczynski, "Educational Stress: Sources, Reactions, Preventions," *Peabody Journal of Education* 59 (January 1982): 127.
72. Fred C. Feitler and Edward Tokar, "Getting a Handle on Teacher Stress: How Bad is the Problem?" *Educational Leadership* 39 (March 1982) 457.

73. Ibid.
74. Ibid.
75. Spano, "Why I Quit Teaching," 7.
76. Ibid., 8.
77. Judith P. Ruchkin, "Does School Crime Need the Attention of Policeman or Educators?" *Teachers College Record* 79 (December 1977): 238.
78. Ibid., 230.
79. Ibid.
80. Spano, "Why I Quit Teaching," 8.
81. Ibid.
82. Feitler and Tokar, "Getting a Handle on Teacher Stress," 458.
83. Wangberg, "Helping Teachers Cope With Stress," 452–453.

11
New Developments for Teachers

Teachers' Competence

By the early 1980s, the popular media were reporting that public education had deteriorated so badly that the nation was faced with still another major educational crisis. Somehow, it was forgotten that for nearly two decades educators had been directed to expand educational opportunities for Americans, and that educational opportunities had indeed been extended to more than ever before. As Diane Ravitch noted in 1981:

> At mid-century, about 50 percent graduated from high school; the figure today is 85 percent. From 1968 to 1978, back enrollment grew from 6.4 percent to more than 10 percent of all college students, and the proportion of females increased from 39 percent to 48 percent. For the first time in our history, access to higher education is universal. . . . One-third of post-secondary institutions are "open door," accepting all applicants regardless of their academic credentials; more than half are "selective," accepting only those who meet their qualifications, but nonetheless accepting most or all of those who apply for admission; and just eight percent are "competitive," accepting only a portion of qualified applicants. [1]

As was reported in the *New York Times* in 1983, significant progress had been made in teaching basic skills to minority students, students from low-income families, and "those who were weakest academically." [2] As an official from the National Institute of Education observed, "We have made a big turn-around in teaching the most basic skills to the lowest quartile of kids . . . but in raising the floor we have at best kept the ceiling constant." [3] By the early 1980s, there was concern that the basic skills, which over two-thirds of the states had specified as minimum competencies in the 1970s, consisted only of "low order skills, such as the literal comprehension of a reading passage" and did not include "the abstract reasoning and problem-solving skills that are expected to become increasingly important in the emerging technological society." [4] "Literacy," a term much more difficult to define in a precise manner, became much more important than "basic skills" or "minimum competencies." "Quality" became more important to many than "equality," and some discussions seemed to indicate that "quality" and "equality" were somehow mutually exclusive.

What especially alarmed some observers were the dramatically falling SAT scores. Between 1963 and 1980, the median verbal score on the SAT fell from a high of 478 to 424, while the median score on the mathematical part of the test fell from 502 to 466. The immediate explanation for declining scores, once they were noted, was that more female and minority students and students from low-income families were taking the test and not performing as well as others who took the test. That explanation did not withstand inspection, however. Analysis of the composition of those who sat for the test showed that since 1970 the composition of the testtakers had not changed significantly, but the scores fell even more dramatically in the 1970s than they did in the 1960s. In fact, when the decline seemed to end in 1982, the College Board explained that the improved average scores could be attributed to the improved scores made by minority students. By 1984, the College Board was able to report that the 9-point increase in test scores (5 points on the verbal portion of the test and 4 points on the mathematical) was the largest single year gain since 1963. While the decrease in the number of black students taking the test was described as "disturbing," it was also noted that that decrease did not affect the average test scores.[5]

As significant to critics as the decline in the average SAT scores was the decline in the percent of students who scored between 600 and 800 on the SAT. Between 1972 and 1981, the percent of students scoring between 600 and 800 on the verbal part of the examination fell from 11.4 to 7, while the decline on the mathematical section was from 17.8 to 14.5 percent. In 1982, there were increases in the high scores, but they did not match the scores of the early 1970s. The percent of those who scored between 600 and 800 on the mathematical portion of the test increased from 14.5 to 15.2 percent, but the increase on the verbal portion was a modest 0.1 percent.[6] Claims that there was something peculiar about the SAT also failed to withstand inspection. Annegret Harnischfeger and David E. Wiley analyzed student performances on other tests (the ACT, the Iowa Test of Basic Skills, and the Minnesota Scholastic Aptitude Test) and found declines similar to those on the SAT.[7]

Even though Harnischfeger and Wiley's work showed that students who enrolled in the traditional college preparatory curriculum (though their number was declining) did well on tests and even though teachers are certainly not exclusively responsible for the curricular choices students and parents make, teachers were blamed for the crisis in education: for the poor enrollments and poor performance in mathematics and science, for declining enrollments in foreign language courses (from 24 percent in 1965 to 15 percent in the late 1970s), for the inability of students to write clearly, and for those who were functionally illiterate but nonetheless assigned respectable grades and awarded diplomas. The logic seemed clear and compelling. Students did not do well on tests that examined what they had not studied. Instead of teaching courses in death education, career education, drug education, environmental education, values clarification, and other electives that were neither academic nor vocational, teachers were to go back to teaching the traditional school subjects. Few bothered to note that many students had little reason to enroll in courses that colleges no longer required for admission. Even fewer noted that public school teachers control neither college entrance requirements nor public schools' graduation requirements. State legislatures typically do not allow teachers to decide what graduation requirements shall be.

Many explanations were offered for poor test performances: Vietnam, Watergate, "the rights revolutions," drugs, broken homes, the increased number of working mothers, television, computer games, busing, and programs designed to remedy historic social and economic injustices. The 1960s, the decade during which SAT scores began to decline, was a decade of extraordinary expansion of public secondary education. The number of high school teachers nearly doubled (from 575,000 to 1 million). However, teachers, rather than the problems attendant to expansion, were usually held accountable for the troubles with education.

Paul Copperman claimed that the expansion of secondary education set the stage "for an academic tragedy of historic proportions as the nation's high school faculty, about half of whom were young and immature, prepared to meet the largest generation of high school students in American history."[8] The problem of so many "young and immature" teachers was, according to *Time,* compounded by teachers who "had been radicalized by the 1960s" and "suspected that competition was immoral, grades undemocratic, and promotion based on merit and measurable accomplishment a likely way to discriminate against minorities and the poor."[9] The trouble was with the teachers, and as the mass media proclaimed, the teachers were in trouble.

Time's cover story for June 16, 1980, was "Help! Teacher Can't Teach!" About a year later, *Newsweek* proclaimed, "Teachers Are in Trouble." Teachers, "bewildered and beleaguered," were no longer "admired for selfless devotion," and no longer "pitied as overworked martyrs to an overburdened school system." They had become "the lone and very visible figure at the front of the classroom" being held responsible for what was wrong with public education.[10]

Time reported that some estimated that as many as 20 percent of the teachers "have not mastered the basic skills in reading, writing and arithmetic."[11] A 1977 survey of school superintendents and school personnel officers indicated that between 5 and 15 percent of the teachers' service was believed to be inadequate.[12] Many "horror stories" came from many places about how bad teachers were. A kindergarten teacher in Portland, Oregon, who had earned A and B grades in college was "found to be functionally illiterate." A third-grade teacher in Chicago could not spell "alphabet." Suburban Milwaukee teachers sent school board members "curriculum proposals riddled with bad grammar and spelling."[13] A teacher with six years' experience as an elementary teacher in Philadelphia submitted an application to the Dade County (Miami), Florida School District with the following statement: "Children is my lifes work, and to become a qualify educator has been my goal and ambition." Applicants' mistakes in grammar and punctuation were not "laughable." They were, according to a representative from the school district's personnel office, typical of most applicants. Dade County school officials were no longer turning down good applicants but having trouble finding them. According to the *Miami Herald's* Jeff Golden, the best teachers were quitting, and "the quality of teachers entering the profession gets worse," not just in Miami but throughout the nation.[14]

All deficiencies were not and are not confined to classroom teachers. In South Carolina, a judge ordered that a school board could not dismiss a teacher who failed to improve her grammar and who had failed a vocabulary test at a hearing. The judge pointed out that "her dismissal notice contained a misspelled word . . . the principal used faulty grammar in his deposition and that the official school-district policy manual had 77 grammatical errors in the first 82 pages."[15]

Some school districts and some states attempted to insure that their teachers would be minimally literate, if not demonstrably competent, by requiring teachers to pass competency or proficiency tests as a condition of employment. In the early 1980s, the American Federation of Teachers (AFT) agreed to the testing of new teachers but opposed the testing of veteran teachers. By 1985, the president of the AFT urged that an examination for teachers, comparable to those required for doctors and lawyers, be established and indicated that once the test was established, applicants to the AFT would have to make a satisfactory score on it.[16] The National Education Association (NEA) had been long opposed to the testing of all teachers, claiming that no paper and pencil test could predict how well or how poorly one will perform in the classroom as a teacher. At its 1985 national convention, however, the membership reversed itself and agreed with its president, Mary H. Futrell, who advised: "Let us tell America that just as no law graduate can practice law without passing the bar exam, no teaching graduate should be allowed to instruct America's children without first passing a valid exam that tests mastery of subject matter and professional skills."[17] It is likely that many, if not most, prospective teachers in the coming decades will have to sit for a competency test of some sort. A 1985 Gallup Poll commissioned by the NEA showed that 60 percent of those polled believed that testing of teachers would improve the quality of public education.[18] In May 1985, the executive committee of the American Association of Colleges for Teacher Education endorsed a resolution calling for all applicants to the teaching field "to pass a national professional examination, similar to those required by the medical and legal profession."[19]

It is extraordinarily difficult, if not foolhardy, to argue that teachers' proficiencies in basic skills—reading, writing, and arithmetic—and in the subjects they wish to teach should not be equal to the level ideally expected of a high school graduate. Indeed, the standards should be higher than that, but frequently not much more than that is required to pass such a test. Where competency testing of teachers has begun, the standards have not been unusually high. When Arizona was preparing to adopt a testing program for prospective teachers, a representative of the state legislature examined a sample copy and declared that anyone who did not know how many words should be capitalized in the sentence, "we live in the sunny state arizona," is "in pretty bad shape." His paperboy had no difficulty in passing it.[20] In the winter of 1985, it was reported that 45 percent of the 3,300 prospective teachers who sat for the three-part (reading, general mathematics, and English grammar) Arizona Teacher Proficiency Examination since August 1984 failed to earn a score of 80 percent or better on each of the three tests. Before August 1984, when candidates only had to have an average score of 80 percent rather than a minimum of 80 percent on each test, the failure rate was 35 percent.[21]

In 1975, the Prince Georges County, Maryland, School District began administering spelling and grammar tests to its applicants and added a mathematics test in 1977. It subsequently used those tests to disqualify nearly 20 percent of its applicants.[22] In 1976, the Pinellas County (Clearwater and St. Petersburg), Florida, School District began testing prospective teachers' abilities in reading comprehension and arithmetic, requiring applicants to score at the eighth-grade level on the reading test and at the sixth-grade level on the arithmetic test. By allowing applicants who failed the test to take it twice again, it cut the failure from nearly 30 percent to 15 percent.[23] In Mobile, Alabama, competency testing of high school seniors led to demands for testing of teachers. In 1978, after the seniors were tested and 53 percent failed, some parents demanded that the school board examine the teachers. After learning that Mobile had teachers "who could not write a grammatically correct sentence" and that the superintendent "wasn't shocked" by that, the president of the board urged competency tests for all teachers. Other board members did not agree but did agree that any new teacher must score at least 500 on the National Teacher Examination (NTE). Subsequently, about half the applicants of the Mobile schools passed the examination that tests general knowledge and ability in reading, writing, and arithmetic.[24]

The Dallas, Texas, Independent School District found that more than half its applicants failed to score at the tenth-grade level on tests of verbal and quantitative abilities.[25]

State Teacher Competency Testing

By 1983, 16 states—Alabama, Arizona, Arkansas, California, Colorado, Connecticut, Florida, Georgia, Hawaii, Mississippi, New Mexico, Oklahoma, South Carolina, Tennessee, Texas, and West Virginia—had adopted some form of a competency test for beginning teachers; nine states had their testing programs "in place," at least twenty-four others were either planning to initiate or were considering the adoption of some sort of teaching-licensing examination; and it was predicted that by 1985 at least twenty-five states would require all new teachers to pass a basic skills test of some sort.[26] As early as 1985, that prediction proved to be quite accurate.[27] By the winter of 1985, teacher certification in over half the states included either a test at the beginning of a teacher education program or a test at the end to determine eligibility for certification. While a few states were requiring teachers to sit for the NTE, many others were requiring that prospective teachers perform satisfactorily on basic skills, subject matter, and/or professional skills tests.

As the states administered the tests and released the results, confidence in teachers or the colleges and universities that awarded them their degrees was certainly not increased. The standards were not unusually rigorous, and the results were not very encouraging. Moreover, it was and is easy for the public to assume that the percent who fail such tests is indicative of the percent of incompetent teachers already in the classrooms. As the president of the Mobile, Alabama, school board observed, "If the current test-failure rate is, say 20 percent, then you have to figure that 20 percent of the people who would have failed in the past are still teaching in the system."[28] South Carolina began using the NTE in 1976, and 56 percent of its applicants failed. When Louisiana administered the NTE to its applicants in 1978, only 52 percent passed, even though the cut-off point was the twenty-fifth percentile. In 1979, the passing rate improved in Louisiana but over a third were still failing the examination.[29]

In 1982, the California Basic Education Skills Test, established by the state legislature and constructed by a panel of teachers and school officials, was administered to a trial group of 2,000 prospective teachers. It consisted of forty questions in reading and mathematics and two half-hour writing tests. After the performance of the trial group was evaluated, it was determined that about 23 percent would fail if applicants were required to answer 50 percent of the reading and 50 percent of the mathematics questions correctly.[30] Subsequently, the California State Superintendent of Public Instruction, William Honig, announced that to pass the test, applicants would have to score 65 percent in mathematics, 67 percent in writing, and 70 percent in reading. After the test was administered to 6,900 prospective teachers in December 1982, it was determined that the failure rate was not quite as high as had been predicted. Only 38 percent failed.[31]

When the twelfth grade edition of the California Achievement Test was administered to more than 600 prospective teachers—mostly college freshmen in Colorado colleges and universities—in 1983, 52 percent failed the mathematics portion of the examination, 39 percent failed the grammar portion, and 38 percent failed its spelling test. Teachers from other states who had already been awarded their college degrees and who were applying for positions in

Colorado schools did somewhat better than the college freshmen. More than 75 percent passed the grammar and spelling tests and 53 percent passed the mathematics test. Some students and even some faculty claimed that the seventy-fifth percentile was too high a cut-off point, but Rep. John Herzog, who sponsored the competency laws in the Colorado legislature, was not ruling out the possibility of making the tests mandatory for teachers who wanted to renew their teaching certificates.[32]

The success of prospective teachers on the Florida teacher certification examination, administered for the first time in October 1982, was greater than the success enjoyed by their counterparts in other states. In Florida, 83 percent of the prospective teachers passed each of the test's four parts: mathematics, reading, writing, and teaching skills. However, the administrator of the Florida testing program was reported to have indicated that "the skills tested by the mathematics test are usually learned at the 8th- or 9th-grade level" and "the reading and writing sections are 'not so difficult that a good high-school student couldn't pass them'."[33] To pass the mathematics portion of the test, Florida candidates only needed to answer 70 percent of the questions correctly and about half of the teaching skills test questions. The Florida standards may not have been very high but they were not atypical. In describing the mathematics questions on the Arizona test for teachers, the head of the certification department related that the "questions measure 8th, at best 9th, grade levels of difficulty."[34]

The Consequences of Teacher Testing

The elimination of minority students from the teaching profession may be among the possible "unintended consequences" of the movement to require teachers to pass written examinations before being granted a license to teach. In a review of testing programs "in place" in 1982, Thomas Toch wrote that "a disproportionately high percentage of black students are failing the tests and thus are being barred from becoming teachers."[35] After Alabama's teacher licensing test was administered in June 1982, it was found that while 28 percent of the white candidates failed the "basic professional studies" part of the test, 51 percent of the blacks failed it. In Arizona, where candidates were required to answer correctly 80 percent of the items on a 150-item, multiple-choice examination on reading, grammar, and mathematics, the failure rates were 74 percent for blacks and American Indians; 59 percent for Hispanics; and 25 percent for whites. Those failure rates, according to the head of the Arizona certification department, shrank the pool of potential minority teachers by two-thirds. In Florida, where 35 percent of the blacks failed the test, it was predicted that some school districts would not be able to satisfy court-ordered minority hiring quotas. In California, the failure rate for non-Asian minorities was 71 percent.[36]

Some argue that teacher tests are intentionally discriminatory. Others claim that they are culturally biased. Still others argue that the tests demonstrate that the vestiges of segregated education endure. In California, an attorney for the Mexican-American Legal Defense Fund questioned whether the state could justify using a test that had an "adverse impact" on minority candidates and asked whether the test would "actually predict who will be a better teacher." The California State Department of Education reported that its test had been reviewed by an independent panel to eliminate questions that have social, sexual, or ethnic biases.[37] In Alabama, the National Association for the Advancement of Colored People (NAACP) and the Alabama Education Association went to federal court to challenge the constitutionality of that state's teacher tests. The U.S. Justice Department decided to reopen an eight-year-old suit against the state of North Carolina, claiming that the state's use of the NTE was intentionally designed to exclude blacks from teaching positions. In 1985, fourteen black and Hispanic students from Texas and three civil rights organizations—the NAACP, the G.I. Forum, and the League of United Latin-American Citizens—went to federal court to try to stop the State of Texas from using students' performance on tests to exclude students from teacher training programs. The plaintiffs claimed that since the testing practice began in March 1984, too many blacks and Hispanics were denied admission to teacher training programs.[38]

It is not certain that the objections to teacher tests will either reverse or even significantly slow the teacher testing movement. It is likely, however, that the objections to the tests will be met with claims about the need for improved standards, that the tests will continue to be administered, and the criteria for passing them will be made even more difficult. It was reported in *Education Week* that those "familiar with the teacher testing movement agree that the tests are not very challenging," and some believe the standards should be raised.[39] The dean of the School of Education at the University of California at Long Beach, John A. Nelson, related that the passing score on his state's test was too low and should be raised rather than lowered.

> If we raise standards, students will work up to them. We're not doing minority groups any favor by implying that they are basically inferior; that is derogatory to them.[40]

In April 1983, Florida's governor, Robert Graham, approved an advisory panel's recommendation that the difficulty of his state's teachers' basic skills test be increased.[41] In 1985, Governor Graham vetoed a bill proposing new standards for teacher certification because it was not sufficiently rigorous.[42] Moreover, some objections to the tests have not been sustained. In 1978, the Supreme Court ruled that South Carolina's use of the NTE was permissible, even though the failure rate of black applicants was over four times as great as that of whites (83 percent and 18 percent, respectively). Subsequent to that decision, Louisiana, Tennessee, and West Virginia began to use the NTE in determining standards for eligibility for teaching certificates.[43]

The participation of nine predominantly black colleges in five states where prospective teachers must sit for the NTE—Benedict College in South Carolina, Bennet College in North Carolina, Hampton Institute in Virginia, Jackson State University in Mississippi, Norfolk State University in Virginia, North Carolina Central University, South Carolina State College, and Louisiana's Southern University and Grambling State College—in a program designed to increase students' abilities to answer the kinds of questions asked on the NTE indicates that some certainly believe the teacher-testing movement will not soon disappear. The program, sponsored by the Southern Regional Education Board, was designed to involve the nine schools' faculties in the writing of analytical questions and to provide them with a pool of 1,500 analytical questions to be used in their examinations so their students would have more experience with "analytical reasoning skills" required by the NTE.[44]

The Preparation of Teachers

As the public perceived that the performance of applicants for teaching credentials was unsatisfactory, attention was paid to possible causes and solutions. The obvious causes for poor teachers seemed to be working conditions and salaries that were not good enough to attract the best students to careers in public education. The obvious solution seemed to be better working conditions and better salaries so more of the best students would choose teaching as a career. Teacher education programs received, as usual, some criticism for accepting too many marginal students and for not offering sufficiently demanding courses but did not receive as much severe criticism as they have at other times when educational crises have been declared. However, the belief that no preparation for teaching is necessary has persisted and continues to be expressed. Early in the 1983 school year, New Jersey's governor, Thomas H. Kean, proposed a plan to allow people without any training in schools of education to teach in the state's schools.[45] The assumption underlying such proposals is that those who can pass a subject matter examination only need a few hours or days of practice teaching to be effective teachers. About a year after the governor's proposal, the New Jersey State Board of Education unanimously agreed that teachers could be trained by school boards and that teachers did not need to complete teacher preparation programs. Thus, if an applicant for teaching in New Jersey passes a subject-matter examination, he or she may be certified to teach after 100 hours of "preservice practice." However, if teachers are hired on "short notice," the practice "can occur simultaneously with the beginner's actual teaching." Martin Haberman was "so fascinated" with that provision that he

> checked on other New Jersey requirements for state licenses and discovered the following preservice requirements: manicurist, 200 hours of training; cosmetologist, 1,200 hours of study and clinical work; barber, 18 months (40 hours per week), private detective, five years of police experience; funeral director, two-year internship.[46]

The failure to assign most of the responsibility for the educational crisis to schools of education is probably due to a number of factors. The typical claim that teachers would be better if they completed more course work in the liberal arts and sciences and less in schools or colleges of education was probably muted by the general belief that there was a general decline, as seemingly illustrated by the SAT scores, in all of education. Between 1972 and 1982, every state showed a decline in SAT scores, but the District of Columbia showed a gain.[47] Charles R. Larson, a professor of literature at American University in Washington, D.C., claimed that during the late 1960s and the 1970s, the academic community "began graduating students from the university we wouldn't even have admitted a few years earlier." In his field, English, he noticed that by the mid 1970s, his "graduate students could not write a coherent paragraph, yet many of them were teaching assistants who regularly staffed our sections of freshman composition." Nonetheless those students were awarded advanced degrees and "were turned loose upon university communities across the nation."[48]

By the 1980s, there seemed to be some recognition that schools and colleges of education are not completely responsible for the total education of those students who elect to prepare themselves to teach or who elect to teach without any formal preparation for teaching. Typically, those preparing to teach in elementary schools complete about half their required course work outside colleges of education, and those preparing to teach in secondary schools typically are required to complete about three-fourths of their work outside colleges of education. The fact is that students who earn degrees in education are awarded passing grades not only by faculty in colleges of education but also by faculty in other university departments and colleges. Yet, alleged deficiencies in teachers are directed to the quality and quantity of work students complete in schools or colleges of education.

When the actual data do not support the claims that critics want to make, they sometimes turn to other data. For example, although *A Nation at Risk* was focused primarily on the nation's secondary schools, its authors saw fit to record that "the teacher preparation curriculum is weighted heavily with courses in 'educational methods' at the expense of courses in subjects to be taught." To support that claim, the authors related that "a survey of 1,350 institutions training teachers indicated that 41 percent of the time of elementary school teacher candidates is spent in education courses, which reduces the amount of time available for subject matter courses."[49] Such claims will continue to be meaningless until interested parties differentiate between those who are to teach in the elementary schools and those who are to teach in the secondary schools as well as define what they mean by "subject matter." To argue that one should not know his or her subject is certainly senseless. To argue that one can only acquire subject matter in some parts of an institution and not in others may be equally stupid.

Professional educators have received less criticism than at other times, but the belief persists that public education can only be improved if the professional educators charged with the responsibility for administering teacher preparation programs seek advice and approval of prestigious scholars and leaders of the traditional academic community. Yet, beginning teachers (those with one to three years of experience) are less critical of their training in subject matter areas and more critical of the preparation they receive in how to handle discipline problems, the needs of gifted students, parent-teacher relationships, classes consisting of culturally diverse students, and legal issues in education.[50]

That teachers and their students would benefit from better working relationships between students and experts in the subjects they teach seems too obvious to dispute, even though there is no evidence that improvement in those relationships would be enough to resolve all the alleged crises in the nation's schools. Such relationships are certainly essential for the construction and maintenance of curricula that accurately represent the processes whereby knowledge is discovered, organized, tested, and applied. Teachers need to know their subjects as well as professionals in other fields need to know theirs. Mastery of academic content that is to be taught is obviously indispensable. However, teachers must also know how those subjects relate to the purposes of the students they teach, the purposes of the schools in which they teach, and the purposes of their society. The faculties from colleges of arts and sciences and from colleges of education, who are sometimes portrayed as competing for the prospective teachers' time and energies, do not have contradictory interests. They do, however, have different interests. Faculty in the arts and sciences are typically most interested in advancing knowledge in the traditional academic disciplines. Faculty in colleges of education are most interested in determining how appreciation of the disciplines and ability to use them effectively for a variety of purposes can be inculcated in children and youth.

As long as the preparation of teachers is viewed as a problem of determining how little of one kind of study can be assigned to college students so they will be able to pursue that much more of the other, there will probably be no significant change in either their training or their subsequent performance as teachers. Adequate programs for teachers may require more time and study than the typical four-year baccalaureate program requires. To achieve parity with their counterparts in other fields and with the parents of many of the students they will teach, teachers may have to bear the burden of more study than they traditionally have. Requirements that were set over a generation ago may no longer be sufficient for the needs of a society that sends more children to school for longer periods than ever before. Noting that parents are now frequently as well educated or better educated than many teachers, the president of the AFT observed that "instead of looking up at teachers, they can now look straight at them or down on them."[51] A generation ago, and before that, teachers were frequently better schooled than the parents of the children they taught. Then, they could expect some respect for that schooling from the parents. Now, however, the educational gap between teachers and parents has been dramatically closed and may even be the reverse of what it once was. Possibly teachers are not worse than they once were, but their relative position has changed. Whatever the case, increased study and more rigorous requirements for teaching may be necessary to restore some of the respect and status teachers have lost.

The Prospect for Better Teacher Salaries

The media have dutifully reported that teachers' average pay is about $4,000 less than that of a plumber's, that the average starting salary for teachers is about $3,400 less than that for accountants and about $7,500 less than for computer scientists, and that the average salary for teachers in 1981, measured in "constant" dollars, was about 13 percent less than in 1971.[52] Yet, significantly improved salaries may not be soon forthcoming. The National Center for Educational Statistics projected that the average salary for teachers in the early 1990s would, if measured in "constant" dollars, still be a few dollars below the 1971 average salary.

Why no strong recommendations were made to grant significant raises to all teachers in the early 1980s can probably be explained by a number of factors. A study conducted for the National Institute of Education in 1981 concluded that the public "gets approximately what it pays for: The bottom one third of the college-going population is seeking positions paying salaries in the bottom one third of the economy."[53] It may be, media reports notwithstanding, that the public is relatively satisfied with the quality of its teachers. *Newsweek,* which proclaimed that "Teachers Are in Trouble" in 1981, commissioned the Gallup organization to conduct a poll, which showed that 29 percent of those interviewed believed their children's teachers were doing an excellent job, 45 percent thought they were doing a good job, and only 5 percent indicated that the teachers were doing a poor job.[54] Early in the 1983 school year, *USA Today* conducted a poll that revealed that 25 percent assigned an A to their children's teachers, 50 percent a B, and 22 percent a C.[55] In general, people tend to believe that the schools their children attend are better than the nation's average. By 1985, 49 percent of the public believed that the nation's schools had improved, and 64 percent of those with children in school believed that the schools had recently improved.[56]

Part of the explanation may be attributed to the "ill winds of Proposition 13." As Arthur Brown observed in his consideration of the effects of Proposition 13, "one thing is fairly certain: in the foreseeable future money for public education will be hard to come by as a consequence of tax spending limitations imposed by either the voting public or sensitized legislators."[57] It is not likely that educators will be able to cause those "ill winds" to subside. The focus of Proposition 13 and similar measures in about a dozen other states[58] has not been solely on education but also on increased government spending. According to Billy E. Ross,

Proposition 13 is "a symptom of a serious problem facing the American taxpayer and not . . . simply another attack on public education and/or educators."[59] When taxpayers experience declines in their disposable income, it is unlikely that they will be enthusiastic about taxing themselves still more to increase the salaries of others. During the 1970s, the nation's spendable income did not increase as it had in the 1960s, and housing costs (principal, interest, and property taxes) took 10 percent more of Americans' disposable income in 1976 than in 1966.[60] Moreover, while resistance to tax increases at the state and local levels was significant and successful, there was little reason to believe that the federal government's contribution to public education would increase, especially with the considerable concern about the size of growing federal deficits.

Whether failure to recommend significant salary increases for teachers is due to the relationships between the prospective demand and the prospective supply of teachers is difficult to assess, for various projections of the future differ. Some believe "that the lack of 'teacher turn-over' is hampering efforts to attract new talent into the profession."[61] In the early 1980s, Floretta D. McKenzie, superintendent of schools in the District of Columbia, reported that she was anticipating only a 2 percent turnover, and the New York Commissioner of Education was predicting less than a 2 percent turnover. School personnel officers used to assume an annual turnover rate of 8 percent, but the National Center for Education Statistics considers that high. While a rate of 6 percent is now generally considered the national average, regional variations are likely. The absolute minimum for the nation as a whole, which is calculated by estimating deaths, retirements, childbearing, and promotions to nonteaching positions is 4.8 percent.[62]

Projections of the future supply and demand for new teachers are basically attempts to apply what is known about the behavior of people in the past and the present to the behavior of people in the future who may or may not behave similarly. In general, people do not prepare themselves for careers in fields where projections indicate few future positions. As the enrollments in public schools grew in the 1960s, the number of people in teacher preparation programs increased to the point where a third of the undergraduates were majoring in education. As public school enrollments declined in the 1970s, the number of students in teacher preparation programs also declined. In fact, between 1973 and 1981, enrollments in education fell by 50 percent. While as many as 25 percent of beginning college students indicated they planned to be teachers in 1968, only 6 percent so indicated in 1980, a year after it was reported that half the new teachers who were looking for positions could not find any.[63]

Since the mid 1960s, the number of teachers with twenty or more years of experience has dropped in half. Thus, if teachers teaching in the 1970s and early 1980s continue to teach until retirement, the turnover rate could be low as could the demand for new teachers. However, if the four out of ten teachers who report that they plan to quit teaching before retirement do so,[64] the turnover rate would certainly be above the absolute minimum of 4.8 percent. Whether the turnover rate is high or low during the 1980s and 1990s, there will be some demand for new teachers. In the early 1980s, the National Center for Education Statistics projected that between 1982 and 1986, the supply of new teachers would be between 76.9 and 123.5 percent of demand. In other words, there would be either a shortage or a surplus of new teachers. Translated into numbers, the NCES projections indicated that the schools would need as many as 1,025,000 new teachers or as few as 816,000.[65] At the beginning of the 1985 school year, there were reports of 12,000 too few teachers and projections that by 1993 the need for new teachers would be 78,000 greater than the supply.[66]

Merit Pay

"Merit pay" and "master teacher" seem to be simple notions, but their simplicity is deceptive. In one sense, the two notions *are* simple and sometimes even used synonymously. Some teachers are obviously better than others, or at least common sense seems to dictate that conclusion to a good portion of the public, and therefore it makes good sense to give some the master teacher title as well as the pay their performances merit. Elected officials find it easy to be in favor of quality, merit, and excellence and to tell their constituents that government workers, including teachers, ought to be subject to the same kinds of performance reviews that exist in the private sector where one's position and rewards are supposedly related directly to how well the job is done. Elected officials also contend that teachers would only be granted salary increases if their performance warranted such, and that the opportunity to earn merit pay would enable school systems to attract and retain superior, or master, teachers. While it is argued that adoption of merit pay programs would serve as an incentive for better qualified people to become teachers, merit pay is different from "incentive pay." Merit pay plans usually require some kind of evaluation of teacher performance. Incentive pay is simply a bonus offered by a school district to teachers who will accept positions that are difficult to fill. For example, the Houston, Texas, Independent School District has paid $2,000 bonuses to teachers who agreed to teach in inner-city schools and to teachers qualified to teach in disciplines with shortages (mathematics, science, special education, and bilingual education).

Upon inspection it becomes clear that the adoption of merit pay and master teacher plans could be the beginning of significant changes in defining the job of teaching, assigning responsibilities, and devising criteria for promotion and compensation. Not all notions of the master teacher concept refer only to teachers who are somehow better than others. Such notions also refer to plans whereby some teachers, by virtue of their experience, performance, and training, are assigned either additional duties or duties that are different from those ordinarily assigned.

Merit pay was used by many school districts in the first quarter of the twentieth century, but in the 1920s, when attempts were made to eliminate the practice of paying high school teachers more than elementary school teachers, most school districts adopted the now familiar salary schedule by which all teachers are awarded salary increments for each year of experience or for completing either advanced degrees or a specified number of courses. Teachers' organizations have favored the single salary schedule for all teachers and have generally been opposed to merit pay plans. They have argued that in the absence of valid and reliable criteria for determining who is to be awarded merit pay, the pay is frequently awarded to those who have the "right" relationship to the evaluator, usually the principal, and that the right relationship may or may not be effectively related to effective teaching. Albert Shanker, president of the AFT, has claimed that "historically, people who received merit pay were those who got the paperwork in on time, people who didn't rock the boat, maybe people who were anti-union, faculty spies." Because so few ever received merit pay when such programs existed, most, Shanker noted, "viewed it as just a public relations stunt."[67]

Complaints have been made that the instruments and procedures used to evaluate teachers focus the evaluators' attention to superficial aspects of teaching and that the evaluators, usually principals, are not trained as assessers of curriculum and instruction but as institutional managers or public relations officers. Moreover, effective teaching is difficult to assess, especially if measured by student's performances on standardized tests. As has been discussed earlier, a strong and consistent relationship exists between the social setting in which children are reared and their academic achievement. Certainly that factor would have to be worked into whatever formula was devised for giving credit to teachers for either the students' achievement or lack thereof. If teachers were to be rewarded primarily or solely on the basis of the gains made by their students, a satisfactory procedure would have to be devised to equate the gains of children who have emotional or mental handicaps to those made by children who have been designated as "gifted." The problem becomes even more complex if the belief that schools are and should be responsible for outcomes that cannot be measured by achievement tests is not discarded. Measures of noncognitive outcomes are less reliable than those of cognitive outcomes, and there is controversy about what such outcomes are and how to measure them. It is easy to secure agreement that schools should teach students to be good citizens. It is not so easy to secure agreement about the behaviors, attitudes, and values that constitute good citizenship. What some believe to be disruptive behavior may be considered as effective and informed political expression by others. Still others may simply label such behavior a demonstration.

National interest was drawn to merit pay and master teacher plans in early 1983 when Tennessee's governor, Lamar Alexander, announced a master teacher proposal to insure that Tennessee schools would be able to increase the pay of its best teachers so they would not be lost to industry. The plan called for replacement of the customary two-tier certification system with the ranks of tenured and nontenured teachers with a four-tier system with four ranks: apprentice, professional, senior, and master teacher. Demonstrated ability as a teacher rather than experience or academic credentials would determine which teachers moved from one rank to the next. Alexander's plan promised to designate a third of the state's 46,000 teachers as either senior or master teachers and render them eligible for up to $8,900 in additional salary by the time of the plan's full implementation during 1986–87.

Besides changing the certification structure for teachers, the Tennessee plan was deliberately designed to change the nature of the duties assigned to teachers and to require a mandatory evaluation of every teacher every five years. As teachers move up the ranks from apprentice to master teacher, they assume responsibility for curriculum development, improvement of instructional strategies, and supervision of less experienced, or apprentice, teachers. Advocates of such plans emphasize that to retain good teachers the nature of teaching must be changed to provide a career ladder, an alternative to working year after year in classrooms, doing what they have always done and in isolation from their colleagues. As Philip C. Schlechty of the University of North Carolina has observed, "If we are going to attract those who wouldn't normally enter teaching and keep them in it, then we've got to give them status, career options, and control over these options, pride, and an opportunity to show off a bit."[68] Historically, the only way for teachers to assume different duties and acquire status and a position that would allow them to interact professionally with their colleagues was to move into administrative or other nonteaching positions that removed them from the classroom.

Even though Governor Alexander assembled a twelve-member task force to help him lobby for his plan, spent $75,000 for campaign expenses and publication of literature about the plan, "made an unprecedented appearance before a joint meeting of the state's House and Senate education committees in a hearing room packed with supporters of the master-teacher plan, many of whom sported buttons reading 'Master Teacher Now'," won the support of several groups—the Tennessee School Boards Association, the Tennessee Principals Study Council, the Tennessee Superintendents Study Council, the Memphis Board of Education, the Tennessee Children's Services Commission, and the state's manufacturers' association—and even modified the plan so that 87 percent of the teachers would be eligible for bonuses ranging from $1,000 to $7,000, the Senate Education Committee decided by a 5–4 vote to delay action on the bill for a year and the House Committee took no action on the bill.[69]

In large measure, the vote to delay action on the master teacher plan in Tennessee was indicative of how strongly the Tennessee Education Association (TEA) opposed it. When first introduced, it appeared to have strong support in both the House and Senate Education Committees. However, after its introduction, the Education Committees received "hundreds of letters and phone calls" that "ran about 75 to 80 percent against the bill." According to a Senate aide, "nearly 90 percent of the calls came from teachers, apparently prompted by the strong lobbying effort mounted by the Tennessee Education Association."[70] Opponents of the master teacher bill, who saw it as undermining teachers' job security by abandoning the traditional way of granting tenure and permanent teaching certificates, were happy with the decision to delay action. The NEA's president, Willard McGuire, described its defeat as "a great victory."[71]

The Tennessee plan was an important proposal for all teachers. Both the NEA and the AFT paid close attention to the bill, for, as the AFT's director of educational issues reported, "whatever happens in Tennessee will have implications for the rest of the country, so we are watching the situation very carefully."[72] The belief that developments in Tennessee were important for all teachers was warranted. While the TEA won a legislative victory, it was temporary and partial. It did not convince the public of the merit of its position. A poll of Tennesseans showed that 57 percent of those who responded "would support higher taxes to support salary increases for teachers meeting higher standards," while "only 13 percent said they would support tax increases for an across-the-board pay raise for teachers in the state."[73] Other polls indicated that Tennesseans reflected the attitudes of taxpayers in other states.

In making a counterproposal to Governor Alexander's master teacher pay proposal, the TEA essentially indicated a willingness to modify teacher certification procedures only for those who would be future members of the TEA. Besides recommending that teacher training programs develop more selective admission standards and increase the rigor of graduation requirements, the TEA also proposed that eligibility for permanent teaching certificates be determined by "a professional certification board that would be controlled by teacher members of the N.E.A."[74] The NEA gave TEA "technical assistance" in designing its counterproposal and, as was reported in *Education Week* in March 1983, "spent close to $200,000 in the past several months to promote the establishment of similar N.E.A.-dominated certification boards in nine other states—Virginia, Indiana, Michigan, Texas, Arizona, Montana, Kansas, Alabama, and Iowa."[75] In early 1984, the Tennessee legislature, after negotiating with the TEA, approved a modified form of Governor Alexander's proposal. TEA convinced the legislature that current teachers should have the right of protection under the tenure and certification laws that obtained when they entered the profession in Tennessee and that current teachers should have the right not only to try to climb the career ladder in a number of ways but also the right to step off the ladder.[76]

The NEA's interest in gaining control of, or at least participating in, how teachers are certified can be interpreted as a sign that teachers wish to assume responsibility for determining who shall be licensed to practice in their field just as other professionals exercise the right and the responsibility to determine the qualifications for applicants to their fields. It can also be interpreted as an attempt to move the power of determining certification standards from state departments of education and legislative bodies that now have and exercise that power. However the interests of teachers' association are interpreted, action to realize those interests will likely have consequences not only for how teachers must qualify themselves for their certificates but also for what they must do to maintain them. Colleges and universities also may find it necessary to secure approval of their programs from teachers' organizations as well as state departments of education.

Tennessee was not the only state to consider a revision of its teacher tenure and certification practices. In 1983, both houses of the North Carolina legislature passed, against the objections of teachers' organizations, a bill to exempt the Charlotte-Mecklenburg School district from the state's teacher tenure law so it could design and implement a more demanding and more complex tenure procedure.[77] The Charlotte-Mecklenburg Career Development Plan was designed to replace the traditional practice of either dismissing teachers or granting them tenure at the end of three years' service. It proposed to replace the traditional system with one that would not allow teachers to earn tenure until the end of six years of teaching. After two years as a "probationary" teacher, a teacher would either be terminated or become a "career nominee." At the end of their third, fourth, fifth, or sixth year, teachers would be eligible to become "career candidates." Before being awarded tenure, teachers would not have to earn a master's degree but would have to complete the equivalent of a set of professional skills equal to a master's degree, "such as course work provided by the district, some classroom teaching, and work with a master teacher on areas in which the teacher is weak."[78] Until they earned tenure, teachers would be subject to continual evaluation, which would be conducted by evaluators from schools other than the ones in which they teach.

Achievement of career candidate status and tenure would not place teachers at a level where they could expect to remain for the duration of their careers. Rather, it would be the beginning of a "three-tier career ladder." At each level of the ladder, teachers' duties would be divided between classroom teaching and other professional responsibilities. Teachers on the first step of the career ladder would be responsible for examination and testing of new instructional materials, evaluation of probationary teachers, and conducting in-service programs. For assuming those extra duties, they would receive a $2,000 salary supplement. Three years of service at level 1 and a satisfactory evaluation would qualify teachers for level 2 duties and an additional $2,000 supplement. Teachers who accepted level 2 positions would be required to move to schools that needed design of classroom research projects and/or development of in-service training programs. To be eligible for a level 3 position, teachers would not only have to pass evaluations but also be capable of designing, organizing, and managing research projects. However, like all other teachers, they would spend some time in the classroom. How much time would depend on their other duties, such as serving as a curriculum specialist, an area coordinator, or a specialist in in-service training.[79] It would, however, be possible for level 3 teachers to spend most of their time in the classroom if they so desired. Teachers could decide not to apply for level 2 or level 3 positions but they would still be subject to evaluations on a three- to five-year cycle. Successful evaluations would earn them a $2,000 bonus.

The Charlotte-Mecklenburg Plan would certainly make earning tenure more uncertain and difficult for teachers. It would also assure the public that teachers were evaluated periodically to determine their competence. Teachers would be given a number of career options that had not been traditionally available to them. While it would not increase the salaries of all teachers, some would eventually be able to earn as much as $40,000 a year, or about $15,000 more than the single-step salary schedule allowed in the early 1980s, though those teachers would have to accept a twelve-month contract in place of the customary ten-month contract. Even if teachers did not choose to compete for level 2 or level 3 positions, they could earn, if they taught in the system for 30 years, between $12,000 and $20,000 in bonuses for passing their evaluations.

The claim of North Carolina's state senator, W. Craig Lawing, that "other states are going to fall in like a bunch of dominoes" once the Charlotte-Mecklenburg plan was implemented[80] may have seemed overly sanguine to some. It may not, however, have been a complete exaggeration. Interest in merit pay and master teacher plans was not confined to Tennessee and North Carolina or to the South. While Governor Alexander was lobbying for his plan, the Southern Regional Education Board was preparing a follow-up to its 1981 report ("The Need for Quality") entitled "Meeting the Need for Quality: Action in the South." Among the actions recommended by the Board was merit pay, even though it warned that it was controversial and would not work unless teachers were allowed to participate in its development and execution.[81] Governor Alexander reported that, besides several other governors from the South, the governors from Utah and Kansas were interested in his master teacher plan. Moreover, the authors of *A Nation at Risk* urged that "school boards, administrators, and teachers should cooperate to *develop career ladders for teachers* that distinguish among the beginning instructor, the experienced teacher, and the *master teacher*." They also recommended that "master teachers should be involved in supervising teachers during their probationary years." The National Commission on Excellence further urged that "*salaries* for teaching *should be increased and should be* professionally competitive, market-sensitive, and *performance-based*." Traditional systems for promoting teachers, granting tenure, and determining their salaries seemed no longer adequate. In their place, the Commission maintained, there should be "an effective evaluation system that includes peer review so that superior teachers can be rewarded, average ones encouraged, and poor ones either improved or terminated."[82]

A Nation at Risk was but one of many reports that addressed the problems of the nation's public schools in the early 1980s.[83] About a month after the appearance of *A Nation at Risk,* the Twentieth Century Fund, a private foundation devoted to the study of social, political, and economic issues, released the report that it had commissioned a twelve-member panel of scholars and educators to assemble. While the National Commission on Excellence reported that "the educational foundations of our society are presently being eroded by a rising tide of mediocrity that threatens our very future as a nation and a people,"[84] the Fund's panel proclaimed that "the nation's public schools are in trouble." According to the panel, "by almost every measure—the commitment and competency of teachers, student test scores, truancy and dropout rates, crimes of violence—the performance of our schools falls far short of expectations."[85] Among the reasons for the "trouble" were teachers' organizations and the use of collective bargaining procedures that served to protect weak teachers rather than secure rewards for good teaching, severely limited the possibility of granting financial rewards to outstanding teachers, failed to dismiss poor teachers, and discouraged the best teachers. To remedy that situation, the Fund's panel proposed *"the establishment of a national Master Teacher's Program, funded by the federal government,* that recognizes and rewards teaching excellence."[86]

A report conducted by the National Task Force on Education for Economic Growth, sponsored by the Educational Commission of the States, echoed the concerns of the National Commission on Excellence. It noted that the nation had asked and therefore had received "too little of our schools over the past two decades." Consequently, schools were "not doing an adequate job of education for today's requirements in the workplace, much less tomorrow's."[87] So that schools could meet the challenge of international economic competition, they needed a "deep and lasting change." Among the necessary changes was a revision of the policies and practices governing how teachers were recruited, trained, granted tenure, and paid. The task force suggested that school officials "drastically overhaul" such procedures, that the practice of granting tenure "be examined and changed, where necessary, to insure more effective teaching in the public schools," and that merit pay plans be implemented.[88]

The calls for examination and evaluation of tenure and certification laws and the calls for the adoption of merit pay and master teacher plans were difficult to ignore. Merit pay became a national political issue.

If there were any doubts about whether the scheduling of twenty regional conferences for the discussion of *A Nation at Risk* would bring national attention to education, that doubt was quickly dispelled by the attention given to education by President Reagan after Tennessee's Governor Alexander failed to secure legislative approval for his master teacher plan. While students and teachers were beginning to plan for their summer vacations in 1983, proposals for creating merit pay programs and creating the rank of master teacher were becoming nationally discussed issues. As a White House aide is reported to have told a *Baltimore Sun* reporter, "merit pay is a mother issue." As a political issue, there was no doubt that it was a "winner."[89] In an address delivered on May 21, 1983, at Seton Hall University, President Reagan related his belief that "teachers should be paid and promoted on the basis of their merit and competence" and complained that "some of the heaviest hitters in the national educational lobby" were opposed to "rewarding excellence."[90] By June 1983, Gene I. Maeroff wrote in the *New York Times* that "Ronald Reagan is crisscrossing America charging that the schools have become 'just too soft and easy'." He believed the president's efforts were effective and that educational reform had become "a topic of political debate at the highest levels and teachers may no longer be able to escape the calls for reform." There was, he maintained, reason to believe that teachers would no longer be able to ignore criticism with their customary "confidence that there would be no disturbing changes."[91]

Before students and teachers returned to school for the beginning of the 1983–84 school year, President Reagan had, according to a report in *Education Week,* "been involved in more than ten major events in which education has been the major theme."[92] Besides two White House meetings with educators to discuss educational reforms, he addressed the national meetings of the PTA and the AFT, discussed educational reform during one of his weekly radio broadcasts, attended two of the regional conferences for the discussion of *A Nation at Risk,* conducted question-and-answer sessions with students in Kentucky, Tennessee, Kansas, and California, and attended the annual meeting of the presidents of the school principals' associations. While there were no signs that great numbers of teachers would be paid in accordance with a merit pay plan or that many would be designated as master teachers at the beginning of the 1983–84 school year, there were signs that the character of the discussions about teaching and the nature and role of teachers' organizations would be different from what they had been in the past. Teachers, it seemed, were accepting the merit pay notion. In August 1983, there were reports that the National School Boards Association had conducted a poll showing that 63 percent of the teachers agreed that "teachers who are more effective in the classroom should receive larger salary increases than teachers who are less effective."[93] Such agreement, however, does not constitute agreement about how effectiveness is to be ascertained.

Teachers' Organizations

Discussions of teachers' organizations have customarily emphasized the differences in the age and the origins of the NEA and the AFT, their positions on strikes and collective bargaining, their size and strength, and the possibility of a merger of the two organizations. If the trends of the 1980s continue, teachers organizations will have to pay special attention to merit pay and master teacher proposals, for such proposals have the potential not only to change the conditions of employment for teachers but also the nature of the collective bargaining process in the thirty-two states where it has been established. Changes in collective bargaining would have the potential for changing the working conditions for a significant number of teachers, because a majority of teachers work under some formal written agreement between their teachers' organization and the school board for which they work. Teachers' organizations will have to attend to proposals that specify classifications for teachers and that such classifications not be tied solely to seniority and academic credentials. Such proposals may force teachers' organizations to pay more attention to job security and less to teacher welfare issues and the rights of teachers to participate in educational decision making.

The NEA

Today's NEA was formed at the 1870 meeting of the National Teachers Association—an organization founded in Philadelphia in 1857—and at that time had a membership of less than 200. During the last decade of the nineteenth century, when the Report of the NEA's Committee of Ten dominated discussions of secondary education, its membership declined from 5,500 to just over 2,300 in 1900. When it issued its second major report on secondary education, *The Cardinal Principles of Secondary Education* (1918), its membership was about 10,000. By the eve of World War II, it had reached 203,000. During the 1950s and 1960s when public education was expanding and the number of teachers was increasing four times as fast as the population, its membership grew accordingly. By 1970, it had 1.1 million members, about five times as many as in 1940. By 1980, its membership was about 1.8 million. Of the 1.8 million, 1.4 million were classroom teachers and the others consisted of 275,000 school administrators, 75,000 college professors, and 50,000 students.[94]

Since the 1960s and 1970s, the image of the NEA as a professional organization made up primarily of classroom teachers but controlled by a minority of male school administrators and college professors concerned not with the welfare and rights of teachers but with maintaining a platform for the discussion of educational issues has been dispelled. When the NEA began a drive to win the right to participate in collective negotiations with school boards in the early 1960s, local NEA affiliates were transformed from agencies for the distribution of local board policy to organizations that communicated teachers' concerns, desires, and even demands to local school boards.

Even though teachers have traditionally been politically more conservative than liberal, many subscribed to "teacher militancy" in the 1960s, and many NEA members were among those who so subscribed. Surveys of NEA members have shown that in the mid 1960s about half the teachers believe strikes were appropriate. By 1970, 90 percent agreed that group action was sometimes necessary and 75 percent believed it was appropriate to strike to secure an agreement with the board of education, to improve schools' instructional programs, or to correct unsafe school conditions. As Ronald G. Corwin reported, "the previously timid National Education Association and its affiliates, representing over half of the nation's two million teachers, had not been involved in a single work stoppage between 1952 and 1963, but participated in one-third of the 1966 work stoppages; 80 percent of the striking teachers that year were NEA members."[95]

How long the NEA has endorsed the principle of collective bargaining is a matter of interpretation. Myron Lieberman claimed that the NEA endorsed the principle in 1947 when its Executive Committee issued the following statement:

> Group action is essential today. The former practice where teachers individually bargained the superintendent of schools or the board of education for their salaries is largely past. For years there has been a steady movement in the direction of salary schedules applying to all teachers.
>
> In the present crisis, it is especially important that there be professional group action on salary proposals. A salary committee composed of capable and trusted members of the group is necessary. This committee should be chosen by the entire teaching group and should have the authority to represent and act for the local education association."[96]

Once that policy was published and described by the media as collective bargaining, the executive secretary of the NEA indicated that it was not "collective bargaining" but "democratic persuasion."[97]

By the mid 1970s, the NEA could still maintain that, unlike the AFT, it was not affiliated with organized labor. However, it could no longer maintain that it was a professional organization that supported sanctions rather than strikes and professional negotiations rather than collective bargaining. NEA affiliates had and were calling strikes, and at its 1968 annual convention, it passed a resolution that maintained that strikes were sometimes necessary and that when necessary the NEA would assist the affiliate that found it necessary to strike. It had also joined the Coalition of American Public Employees, a nonprofit organization of several public employees' organizations devoted to securing legislation to permit collective bargaining for public employees. Moreover, in its 1975–76 goals statement, the NEA asserted that "the most effective vehicle to guarantee the economic and professional security of teachers within the capability of the NEA is the collective bargaining process."[98]

The NEA's size makes it the nation's largest public employees' organization, and, as a labor organization, it is second in size only to the Teamsters. Its size and presence in every state has contributed to its political power. Because there are schools and teachers in virtually all parts of the nation and because about half the teachers are represented by the NEA, there are about 4,000 NEA members in every congressional district. Through its political action committees, it has worked successfully to elect to public office candidates whose views and records are acceptable to the interests of its members. In 1976, it departed from its practice of not endorsing presidential candidates by supporting Jimmy Carter. It is generally believed that in exchange for that support Carter worked to secure congressional approval for adding a department of education to the presidential cabinet. At the 1980 Democratic convention, NEA members constituted the single largest block of delegates and alternates, and those delegates were credited with enabling Carter to turn back Sen. Edward Kennedy's bid for the nomination. One sign of the regard politicians have for its power in the Democratic party is the complaint in the spring of 1983 of California's Sen. Alan Cranston that the NEA was already working for Walter Mondale even before the NEA officially decided which person it would endorse for the Democratic party's presidential nomination.[99] Candidates who receive NEA endorsement can expect that the NEA will spend its funds to support their campaigns. Before the 1984 election, the executive secretary of the NEA reported that the association was planing to spend as much as $3 million to support its candidates' bids for office.[100]

The AFT

The AFT is smaller and younger than the NEA, has always been affiliated with the labor movement, and has traditionally been viewed as an organization primarily concerned with teacher welfare issues and the rights of teachers to participate in educational decision making. Although 1916—the year the president of the AFL, Samuel Gompers, gave the AFT its charter—marks the formal beginning of the AFT, its origins can be traced back to 1902 when two local teachers' organizations affiliated themselves with the labor movement. Then, a teachers' organization in San Antonio, Texas, affiliated with the AFL and the Chicago Teachers Federation, earlier organized by Catherine Coggin and Margaret Haley in 1897, affiliated with the Chicago Federation of Labor. While leaders of the Chicago Federation of Teachers were able to discuss educational issues with force and clarity, the issues they addressed were different from those addressed by the NEA. Besides trying to demonstrate how the interests of public education and labor were the same, they devoted their energies to fighting for pensions for female teachers, increasing teachers' salaries, lobbying for the enactment of the Illinois Child Labor Law (1903), and with the help of Illinois' highly reform-minded former governor, John Altgeld, instigated legal action that forced several Illinois utility companies to pay taxes they owed to the Chicago Board of Education. Its early efforts to improve the conditions of employment and to increase the rights of teachers have contributed to the view that the AFT is primarily concerned with teacher welfare issues, just as the early history of the NEA contributed to its longstanding image of an organization primarily concerned with other issues. In recent times, each organization has escaped the confines of its early history.

The first years of the AFT were difficult, but by 1919 it had 160 locals and a membership of nearly 11,000, and, according to Myron Lieberman, "for a short time, membership in the

AFT exceeded the membership of the NEA."[101] However, the success of the AFT was short-lived, for it alarmed many educational officials who viewed an alliance with labor as undignified and feared an organization that included only those who worked in the classroom and excluded school administrators and supervisors. Moreover, its initial success came when employers' organizations were campaigning for the "open shop" to combat the effective organization of labor in the private sector. Educators who feared that education would lose its traditional independence if it was allied with labor were able to take advantage of the anti-union sentiment reenforced by the publicity attendant to the Boston police strike and campaigned against the AFT. As Sterling D. Spero related:

> An antiunion campaign was launched directed by officials and influential members of the NEA, including prominent professors in the leading university schools of education. Deans, professors, state and local superintendents of schools toured the country, and with the prestige of their official connections and their relations with the NEA to add weight to their words, attacked the teachers' union movement before meetings of state associations and local and county teachers' institutions. They wrote articles in the educational journals deploring the unprofessional character of unionization. They roused the teachers prejudices, made effective appeals to their snobbery and played up the strike bogey. . . . The climax of the campaign came in March 1920, five months after the Boston strike, when the affiliation of teachers with the labor movement was attacked at the annual meeting of the Department of Superintendence of the NEA, the real policy-determining body of the Association.[102]

The campaign against the AFT was very effective. By 1925, its membership had fallen to just below 3,500 and was only about 6,000 in 1930. On the eve of World War II, it had almost 30,000 members and about 11,000 more by 1950. Its greatest increase in membership occurred between 1970 and 1980 when it almost tripled, increasing from 205,000 to 600,000. However, it also enjoyed a substantial growth in membership between 1960 and 1970 when it grew from 59,000 to 205,000. The increase in AFT membership is often associated with its decision in the late 1950s to concentrate its efforts on winning the right to represent teachers in New York City. In November 1960, the New York AFT local, the UFT, called a strike in an attempt to win improved working conditions, salaries, and benefits for teachers as well as the right to engage in collective bargaining with the school system. By the spring of 1961, it had secured a collective bargaining agreement and subsequently won the right to represent teachers in several other urban areas. Since then, the AFT has sometimes been viewed as the organization that represents mostly urban teachers, while the NEA has been seen as the organization representing suburban and rural teachers.

Policies On Strikes

The New York City strikes called by the UFT in the 1960s probably represent not only the beginning of a decade of "teacher militancy"—a phenomenon not confined to AFT members—but also a change of policy in the AFT. The conventional wisdom that the AFT was historically supportive of strikes while the NEA opposed them is, like most conventional wisdom, not completely accurate. The AFT did not include a "no-strike" clause in its constitution, but it did issue statements renouncing advocacy of strikes by teachers, and it did so with the support of the AFL. In 1942, the president of the AFL explained:

> The American Federation of Labor . . . has made it clear that those who are members of the American Federation of Teachers must secure redress for grievances and promote their economic welfare through the use of organizational methods other than resort to strike. Membership on the part of teachers in the American Federation of Labor means that the facilities of the American Federation of Labor, the concentration of organized effort and unity of action must be used in promotion of the economic status of teachers rather than the strike weapon. The American Federation of Labor could neither countenance nor endorse the exercise of the right to strike on the part of the American Federation of Teachers for the redress of grievances and the promotion of their economic welfare.[103]

Even as late as 1952, the AFT's Executive Council declared:

> The use of the strike is rejected as an instrument of policy of the American Federation of Teachers. The Executive Council and its national officers will not call a strike either nationally or in any local area jurisdiction, or in any way advise a local strike. The funds and facilities of the National Organization will not be used to support a strike.[104]

As late as the mid 1950s, however, the AFT was more explicit about its strike policy than was the NEA. When Myron Lieberman tried to ascertain what the NEA strike policy was in 1955 by writing to the NEA, the answer he received was a reference to a platform statement that emphasized that children and teachers required "salary schedules adequate to attract and hold men and women of marked ability and thorough preparation developed in a professional way through group discussion and action." From that Lieberman concluded that "a simple statement that teachers should be paid adequately is hardly a policy with respect to strikes."[105]

It should be emphasized that the policy of either of the national teachers' organizations may or may not coincide with the views and actions of teachers in a specific locality. Even though the NEA seemed to have a no-strike policy for years and even though the AFT did maintain a no-strike policy, some teachers did strike. For example, between 1940 and 1954, 97 local affiliates did strike and among them were 29 AFL affiliates, 22 NEA affiliates, and 14 CIO affiliates.[106] At times, the refusal of teachers to work was called something other than a strike and received the support of the national organization. At other times, aid and comfort were given to teachers who refused to work while formal approval of their refusal was withheld. However a refusal to work is named, Lieberman's observation is probably correct that "the distinction between 'professional' and 'trade union' methods is primarily semantic rather than substantive, at least insofar as educational organizations are concerned." However, more important than the semantic distinctions, according to Lieberman, is the fact that "virtually all codes of professional ethics require the practitioners to cease employment under certain circumstances."[107] It was and still is easier to claim that professionals have an obligation not to offer their services when conditions do not permit them to do so adequately than it is to specify what such conditions are. Such determinations probably cannot be made by organizations. Rather, each individual must make that decision.

An AFT-NEA Merger

For over a decade, there has been speculation about the possibility of a merger of the AFT and the NEA. The two organizations discussed the possibility in the early 1970s. Most, but certainly not all, who so speculate seem to favor the possibility because of the enormous political and economic power teachers would ostensibly have if they have all belonged to the same organization. Some assume that the million teachers who belong to neither organization would join the newly formed organization and thereby add even more power to the teachers' cause. There are, advocates of merger point out, similarities between the two organizations. Each now advocates collective bargaining, and neither is unalterably opposed to teacher strikes. Each has an interest in protecting the job security of teachers during a period when layoffs seem possible in some areas, in fighting for better salaries and fringe benefits when states and localities are strongly resisting budget and tax increases, and in maintaining and extending the teachers' right to engage in collective bargaining. Each is opposed to policies that would reduce federal aid to education, and each is concerned about tuition tax credit proposals that have the potential for increasing enrollment in private schools and decreasing it in public schools. Each is committed to influencing the legislative process at the national level with the aid of full-time lobbyists. Each has engaged in political activity by endorsing candidates and contributing to their campaigns through their political-action committees.

While the NEA and the AFT do share some common interests concerning teacher welfare and maintenance of public schools, the social and political positions taken by the two have differed from each other. The most longstanding and perhaps obvious difference between them is their position on affiliation with the labor movement. While the AFT appears steadfast in maintaining its relationship with labor because it believes labor has always supported education, the NEA remains equally steadfast in its refusal to merge as long as the AFT maintains that affiliation. While neither organization has been opposed to extending equality of opportunity, their positions on how to approach the problem of segregation in the 1950s were different, just as their positions on affirmative action have differed in the 1970s and 1980s. The AFT began to act against locals that practiced racial segregation *before* the Supreme Court handed down the Brown decision and "filed a brief, *amicus curiae,* seeking to strike down racial segregation in public education, whereas the NEA did not participate in any way in these cases."[108] While the NEA has a policy of specifying that a certain percentage of all committee membership would be from minority groups and insists that such a policy be continued if the two organizations merge, the AFT has refused to accept quotas.[109]

Each organization has taken different stands on the use of standardized tests. The NEA has maintained that standardized tests do not always adequately measure the achievements of many minority students, are therefore unfair, and should not be used. The AFT has maintained that they can be useful tools in determining how much progress students have made and does not object to their use.

A merger of the AFT and the NEA might create an organization more powerful than either and even give it sufficient power to resist many of the educational reforms that have been proposed in the 1980s. However, whether a merger would give teachers greater control over educational policy is not certain. A stronger teachers' organization could prompt legislatures to make clearer the distinctions between educational procedures and educational policy and thereby assign responsibility and authority in a way that would exclude teachers from participating in the formation of educational policy. Moreover, whether teachers should have increased power over educational policy is not a proposition on which there is universal agreement. As Joel Spring has pointed out, such increased power could come "at the expense of parental control of education."[110] If one believes that parents either have significant control over public education or that they do in fact want such control, that is a significant observation. It should, however, also be noted that there is no evidence to indicate that either of the two organizations wish to accrue power to implement educational systems different from what the public wants. There is simply no evidence to indicate that the aims of teachers are significantly different from those of the public, though teachers do seem to be more insistent about expressing the need for the conditions and resources that would make realization of those aims less difficult.

Conclusion

The attention paid to merit pay and master teacher proposals since they were reintroduced in the 1980s indicates that those who secure teaching positions in the late 1980s and early 1990s may be taking jobs very different from those of their own teachers. The nature of that difference is still unclear, however; while some apparently believe that teaching should be different from what it has been, others believe that changes are necessary to render schools and teaching more like they believe they used to be. Some believe better salaries will attract better teachers, and conditions will be like they imagine they used to be. However, some recognize that schools could be more effective and even more interesting places for both students and teachers if, as Robert Joseph Schaefer urged in the late 1960s, the workaday world of the school was restructured to make teachers something other than cogs in a vast machine designed to dispense skills and information to students according to a schedule not made by either students or teachers.[111] Schaefer proposed that modular scheduling, paraprofessionals, and differentiated staffing all be used to enable some teachers to become scholar-teachers. The scholar-teacher, freed from spending virtually every minute of every day in a classroom with thirty, forty, or even more students would have the opportunity to inquire into the nature of the teaching-learning process. Teachers would be able to focus on tasks related to the purposes and the functioning of schools. Changing the workaday world of the teacher is receiving renewed attention in the 1980s.

In his comments on merit pay and master teacher proposals, Fred M. Hechinger of the *New York Times* observed that because the salary schedules of teachers cannot be adjusted dramatically enough to attract better teachers, it was necessary "to offer young people the carrot of high pay, not for doing the same things longer, but for doing different things."[112] Included in "different things" was assigning master teachers responsibility for clinical training of new teachers. However, all advocates of the master teacher and merit pay proposals do not believe they necessarily entail any significant changes in the teacher's workaday world. While there are forces for change, there are also contrary forces. For example, in an interview with Thomas Toch, the assistant editor of *Education Week,* then Secretary of Education Terrel H. Bell indicated that his support for master teacher projects was based on the belief that good teachers needed better rewards. He emphasized that higher education had ranks—assistant professor, associate professor, full professor, and even distinguished professor—"to recognize and reward outstanding performance . . . based on peer review" and that his hope was "that the master teachers will be for elementary and secondary education what the full professor is to higher education."[113] He emphasized that there was "a big difference" between differentiated staffing and "adapting the concept of academic rank to the elementary and secondary schools." After an interview with President Reagan about education, Hugh Sidey concluded that the president was quite satisfied with his own schooling and was supporting reforms because he wanted all American children to have the opportunity to attend the kinds of schools he attended and have the kinds of teachers he had.[114]

The 1960s and 1970s were neither the easiest nor the most uneventful times for teachers. Earlier improvements in salaries vanished, and the public seemd to have lost some of its confidence in teachers. In many instances, teachers were confronted with an unprecedented level of disruptive behavior. While schools apparently will be safer in the 1980s and 1990s than they were in the 1960s and 1970s, teaching will be no less demanding. To the extent that the disruptions in public education were largely symptoms of a largely successful national effort to extend equality of educational opportunity to more people than ever before, it is likely they will subside. As Joan Newman has noted, "History has shown that school disorder and violence have often increased when education has been extended to many children who, for a variety of reasons, did not or could not share the goals of the school."[115] In the post–World War II era, and especially in the 1960s, public schools were trying to serve students they previously either had not served or had not served very well. In large measure, the schools met the challenge presented to them. Between 1947 and 1977, the percent of high school graduates in the adult population nearly doubled, increasing from 33 to 65 percent.[116] However, the schools' difficulties were attributed to social problems, to curricula that were either too far removed from the immediate interests and experiences of students or too closely defined by their interests and experiences, and to disciplinary methods that were either too permissive or too oppressive. While none of these factors can be positively related to the difficulties teachers encountered in the schools, the inability to show that relationship does not mean that the schools did not confront profound difficulties or, on the other hand, that they did not necessarily merit some criticism. There were failures as well as successes.

Ironically, some of the criticism of the schools can be attributed to the schools' efforts to do what they were asked to do. As Patricia Albjerg Graham has observed, "Whenever schools take on the task of educating 'out groups'—those that society has ostensibly, but perhaps reluctantly, asked them to educate—we find the schools severely criticized and the public confidence in them diminished."[117]

While it can be argued that the schools have accepted the challenges offered them in the post–World War II era and while statistics can be cited to support those claims, it cannot be argued that there will be no problems in the future. As has been already noted, more youth are expected to remain in school longer than ever before. The retention of so many more adolescents in school is a relatively new condition that still requires the attention of political leaders and educators, for there is no reason to believe that all youth will subscribe to the values that dictate the conventions and purposes of traditional schooling. As Newman has observed:

> While academic achievement may be a goal of some adolescents most of the time, and most adolescents some of the time, it will not be the goal of all adolescents ever. . . . As more and more

adolescents are kept in school, more of them will be unprepared, unsuccessful, and unmotivated. Members of this captive, failing class are likely to become bitter and hostile to the authority and values of the school. They may well feel a need to assert their importance in ways that are detrimental to the functioning of the school.[118]

As schools change and expand to satisfy new clientele or to satisfy the requirements of new social and economic conditions, they will be subject to scrutiny and criticism. Teachers should recognize that criticism of schools and even of themselves during such periods is not simply a consequence of the schools' inability to adapt immediately to new clientele with different needs, experiences, expectations, aspirations, and interests. It is also a sign that all do not agree with the social philosophy that directs schools to extend opportunity to all. As Graham has related:

> The schools are the stage on which our implicit social dramas are made explicit, and the dramas are played to audiences that are sometimes filled with hostile critics. The schools are easier targets than the more abstract social goals they are implementing. Thus, in the last decade, when the schools followed the law by enrolling blacks with whites and by providing special services for the poor, the lack of social consensus for such equitable treatment became apparent and took the form of criticism of the schools.[119]

To the extent that the schools are required to respond to new social developments, especially developments about which there is neither social nor educational consensus, schools and their teachers will be subject to criticism. Teachers can inform themselves about the nature of their society so they can understand and evaluate such criticism, but it is unlikely that they can eliminate it, for schools are more than dispensaries for handing out skills and knowledge to children and youth. Schools are the stages on which we act out our social and political aspirations. Debates about schools are debates about the kind of society we want for ourselves and our children. Better ways to instruct youth and to manage schools are always in order but in themselves are not the final answer to school problems. Our history dictated that we make a better society for our children, and, as long as that dream—the American dream—obtains, Americans will never be completely satisfied with their schools. Such is the nature of American society and its public schools.

Notes

1. Diane Ravitch. "The Schools We Deserve," *The New Republic* (April 18, 1981): 24.
2. Edward B. Fiske, "Students Gain in Basic Skills But High School Scores Fall," *The New York Times,* April 10, 1983.
3. Quoted in Fiske, "Students Gain in Basic Skills."
4. Fiske, "Students Gain in Basic Skills."
5. Cindy Currence, "Reforms Could Increase Dropouts, Dilute Curriculum, Study Says," *Education Week* 5 (October 7, 1985): 4.
6. Fiske, "Students Gain in Basic Skills."
7. Ravitch, "The Schools We Deserve," 25.
8. Quoted in "Help! Teacher Can't Teach!," *Time,* June 16, 1980, 58.
9. "Help! Teacher Can't Teach!," 58.

10. Ibid., 55.
11. Ibid.
12. *Staff Dismissal: Problems and Solutions* (Arlington, Virginia: American School Boards Association, 1978), cited in Allan C. Ornstein and Daniel U. Levine, *An Introduction to the Foundations of Education,* 2d. ed. (Boston: Houghton Mifflin 1981), 97.
13. "Help! Teacher Can't Teach!," 55.
14. Jeff Golden, "Teaching's Low Pay and Hassels Help Scare off Best and Rightest," *The Miami Herald,* November 15, 1981.
15. "Teachers Are In Trouble," *Newsweek,* April 27, 1981, 79, 81.
16. Cindy Currence, "Shanker Urges National Test for New Teachers," *Education Week* 4 (February 6, 1985): 1, 34, and Blake Rodman, "Shanker Recommends 'Super Certification'," *Education Week* 4 (August 21, 1985): S–1, S–18.
17. Blake Rodman, "N.E.A. Endorses Teacher Testing," *Education Week* 4 (August 21, 1985): S–15.
18. Blake Rodman, "Public Favors Pay Raises, Competency Testing for Teachers, N.E.A./Gallup Polls Indicates," *Education Week* 4 (August 21, 1985): S–2.
19. Cindy Currence, "AACTE Endorses Tougher Standards, Teachers' Exam," *Education Week* 4 (May 8, 1985): 1.
20. "Teachers Are in Trouble," 83.
21. "Forty-Five Percent of Teacher Trainees Fail Arizona Exam," *Education Week,* 4 (February 6, 1985): 3.
22. Ornstein and Levine. *An Introduction to the Foundations of Education,* 97.
23. Thomas S. Tocco and Jane K. Elliget, "On the Cutting Edge: The Pinellas County Teacher Applicant Screen Program," *The Board* (Winter 1980): 5, cited in Ornstein and Levine, *An Introduction to the Foundations of Education,* 98.
24. "Help! Teacher Can't Teach!," 57.
25. Ornstein and Levine, *An Introduction to the Foundations of Education,* 98.
26. "School-Improvement Initiatives, State by State," *Education Week* 2 (September 22, 1982): 11; Thomas Toch, "Tests Exclude Blacks from Teaching Profession," *Education Week* 2 (January 19, 1983): 1; and "What's Wrong With Our Teachers," *U.S. News & World Report,* March 14, 1983, 40.
27. "Changing Course: A 50-State Survey of Reform Measures," *Education Week* 4 (February 6, 1985): 11–29.
28. "What's Wrong With Our Teachers," 38.
29. "Help! Teacher Can't Teach!," 58.
30. David G. Savage, "State Will Begin Testing of New Teachers: Many Expected to Fail," *Los Angeles Times,* December 15, 1982.
31. Alex Heard, "California Joins States Screening Teachers With Skills Test," *Education Week* 2 (January 26, 1983): 6.
32. John Chaffe, Jr., "Many Prospective Teachers Fail Colorado Test," *Education Week* 2 (March 2, 1983): 9.
33. Toch, "Tests Exclude Blacks from Teaching Profession," 18.
34. Ibid.
35. Ibid., 1.
36. Heard, "California Joins States Screening Teachers With Skills Test," 6.
37. Ibid.
38. "Civil-Rights Groups, Minority Students in Texas File Suit to Block Teacher Test," *Education Week* 4 (Aug. 21, 1985): S–9.
39. Heard, "California Joins States Screening Teachers With Skills Tests," 18.
40. Ibid., 6.
41. "Florida to Upgrade Test Requirements for State's Teachers," *Education Week* 2 (April 20, 1983): 3.

42. Lynn Olson and Anne Bridgman, "Teacher-Quality Policies Stirring Widening Disputes in the States," *Education Week* 4 (Aug. 21, 1985): S–1.
43. Ornstein and Levine, *An Introduction to the Foundations of Education*, 97.
44. Hope Aldrich, "Black Colleges Seek to Boost Test Skills," *Education Week* 2 (April 6, 1983): 1, 17.
45. Charlie Euchner, "N.J. Gov. Offers Plan to Waive Education Courses for Teachers," *Education Week* 3 (September 14, 1983): 1, 19.
46. "Update," *Education Week* 4 (September 1984): 4, and Martin Haberman, "Backtalk," *Phi Delta Kappan* 67 (October 1985): 167.
47. "50-State Rating of Our Schools, Students," *USA Today,* January 6–8, 1984.
48. Charles R. Larson, "Competency Tests for Everyone," *Newsweek,* June 8, 1981.
49. The National Commission on Excellence in Education, *A Nation at Risk: The Imperative for Educational Reform* (Washington, D.C.: U.S. Government Printing Office, 1983), 1.
50. John Chaffe, Jr., "Colorado Teachers Report Training Inadequate," *Education Week* 2 (April 6, 1983): 1, 17.
51. "Teachers Are in Trouble," 78.
52. "What's Wrong With Our Teachers," 38.
53. Ibid., 40.
54. "Teachers Are in Trouble," 79.
55. Pat Ordovensky, "Hometown Teachers Beat USA Average," *USA Today,* September 13, 1983.
56. Jack Kelley, "Public Schools Get High Marks," *USA Today,* May 6, 1985.
57. Arthur Brown, "Michigan's 'Proposition 13'," in Society of Professors of Education, *The Ill Winds of Proposition 13* (printed and distributed by the Society, 1979), 17.
58. Ibid.
59. Billy E. Ross, "Proposition 13 and the Taxpayers Revolt," in *The Ill Winds of Proposition 13,* 40.
60. John Shannon, "Tax Revolt Issues," in *The Ill Winds of Proposition 13,* 40.
61. Sheppard Ranbom, "Educators Seek Solutions to 'Crisis' in Teaching," *Education Week* 2 (March 2, 1983): 16.
62. Martin M. Frankel, ed., *Projections of Education Statistics to 1986–87* (Washington, D.C.: National Center for Education Statistics, 1978), 51.
63. "Teachers Are in Trouble," 79.
64. "Help! Teacher Can't Teach!," 59.
65. Franke, *Projections of Education Statistics,* 64.
66. Barbara Zigli, "Teacher Supply: From Boom to Bust," *USA Today,* May 6, 1985.
67. Quoted in Thomas Toch, "Merit-Pay Issue Dominates School-Reform Debate," *Education Week* 2 (June 15, 1983): 14.
68. Quoted in Toch, "Merit-Pay Issue Dominates School-Reform Debate," 14.
69. Peggy Caldwell, "Tennessee Governor Urges Merit Pay for Teachers," *Education Week* 2 (February 9, 1983): 1, 17; Thomas Toch, "Tennessee Governor Presses Master-Teacher Proposal," *Education Week* 2 (March 16, 1983): 1, 16; and Hope Aldrich, "Tennessee Governor's Master-Teacher Pay Plan Voided," Education Week 2 (April 20, 1983): 1, 17.
70. Aldrich, "Tennessee Governor's Master-Teacher Pay Plan Voided," 17.
71. Ibid.
72. Toch, "Tennessee Governor Presses Master-Teacher Proposal," 16.
73. Toch, "Merit-Pay Issue Dominates School-Reform Debate," 15.
74. Toch, "Tennessee Governor Presses Master-Teacher Proposal," 16.
75. Ibid.
76. Jim O'Hara, "Tennessee Legislature Passes Master-Teacher Bill," *Education Week* 3 (February 29, 1984): 6, 18.

77. Hope Aldrich, "Charlotte Plans 3-Level Track for Teachers," *Education Week* 2 (June 15, 1983): 1, 15.
78. Ibid., 15.
79. Ibid.
80. Ibid.
81. Susan Walton, "Panel Urges Changes in South's Schools," *Education Week* 2 (June 15, 1983), 1, 16.
82. *A Nation at Risk,* 30.
83. As earlier indicated (Chapter 2, note 10), lists of what is and what is not one of the "national reports" vary, but nearly all include, besides *A Nation at Risk,* the following: Ernest L. Boyer, *High School: A Report on Secondary Education in America* (New York: Harper & Row, 1983); College Board, *Academic Preparation for College: What Students Need to Know and Be Able to Do* (New York: College Entrance Examination Board, 1983); Philip A. Cusick, *The Egalitarian Ideal and the American High School* (New York: Longman, 1983); Linda Darling-Hammon. *Beyond the Commission Reports: The Coming Crisis in Teaching* (Washington, D.C.: Rand Corporation, 1984); Emily C. Feistritzer, *The Condition of Teaching: A State by State Analysis* (Princeton, N.J.: Carnegie Foundation for the Advancement of Teaching, 1983); John I. Goodland, *A Place Called School: Prospects for the Future* (New York: McGraw-Hill, 1983); Sara Lawrence Lightfoot, *The Good High School: Portraits of Culture and Character* (New York: Basic Books, 1983); The National Science Board Commission on Precollege Education in Mathematics, Science and Technology, *Educating Americans for the 21st Century.* 2 vols. (Washington, D.C.: National Science Board, 1983); Task Force on the Business–Higher Education Forum, *America's Competitive Challenge: The Need for a National Response* (Washington, D.C.: Business–Higher Education Forum, 1983); Task Force on Education for Economic Growth, *Action for Excellence: A Comprehensive Plan to Improve Our Nation's Schools* (Washington, D.C.: Education Commission of the States, 1983); The Twentieth Century Fund Task Force on Federal Elementary and Secondary Education Policy, *Making the Grade* (New York: Twentieth Century Fund, 1983); and Theodore Sizer, *Horace's Compromise: The Dilemma of the American High School* (Boston: Houghton Mifflin, 1984).

    Mortimer Adler's works on the paideia proposal are also sometimes included in the lists of national reports: Mortimer Adler, *The Paideia Proposal: An Educational Manifesto* (New York: Macmillan, 1982), and *Paideia Problems and Possibilities: A Consideration of Questions Raised by the Paideia Proposal* (New York: Macmillan, 1983).

    For a discussion of some of the "national reports," see "Symposium on the Year of the Reports: Responses from the Education Community," *Harvard Educational Review* 54 (February 1984).
84. *A Nation at Risk,* 5.
85. *Making the Grade,* reprinted in *Education Week* 2 (May 11, 1983), 14.
86. Ibid. Emphasis in the original.
87. Ann Green, "Schools, Businesses Should be 'Partners' in Economic Push," *Education Week* 2 (May 11, 1983), 1.
88. Ibid.
89. Toch, "Merit-Pay Issue Dominates School-Reform Debates," 1.
90. Eileen White, "Education Seen Emerging as 1984 Presidential Campaign Issue," *Education Week* 2 (June 8, 1983), 15.
91. Gene I. Maeroff, "Teachers Unions Are Courted and Castigated," *The New York Times,* June 26, 1983.
92. Tom Mirga, "Reagan Continues to Court Leading Education Groups," *Education Week* 2 (July 27, 1983), 9.
93. Eileen White, "Poll Finds Public Endorsement of School Reforms," *Education Week* 2 (August 31, 1983), 1.
94. Ornstein and Levine, *An Introduction to the Foundations of Education,* 49–50.

95. Ronald B. Corwin, "The New Teaching Profession," in Kevin Ryan, ed., *Teacher Education: The Seventy-fourth Yearbook of the National Society of the Study of Education, Part II* (Chicago: University of Chicago Press, 1975), 232.

96. NEA Executive Committee, "The Professional Way to Meet the Educational Crisis," *NEA Journal* 36 (February 1947), quoted in Myron Lieberman, *Education as a Profession* (Englewood Cliffs, N.J.: Prentice-Hall, 1956), 335.

97. Lieberman, *Education as a Profession*, 335.

98. Quoted in Joel Spring, *American Education: An Introducton to Social and Political Aspects* (New York: Longman, 1978), 174.

99. Pat Ordovensky, "Mondale Leads NEA Race, But Not Winner Yet," *USA Today*, July 15, 1983.

100. Maeroff, "Teachers Unions Are Courted and Castigated."

101. Lieberman, *Education as a Profession*, 301.

102. Sterling D. Spero, *Government as Employer* (New York: Emsen Press, 1948), quoted in Lieberman, *Education as a Profession*, 301–302.

103. American Federation of Teachers, *Can Teachers' Unions Be Called Out on Strike?* (Chicago: American Federation of Teachers, 1943), quoted in Lieberman, *Education as a Profession*, 318.

104. *American Teacher* 36 (February 1952), quoted in Lieberman, *Education as a Profession*, 309.

105. Lieberman, *Education as a Profession*, 309.

106. Ibid., 310.

107. Ibid., 310–311.

108. Ibid., 312.

109. Ornstein and Levine, *An Introduction to the Foundations of Education*, 57.

110. Spring, *American Education*, 187.

111. Robert Joseph Schaefer, *The School as a Center of Inquiry* (New York: Harper & Row, 1967), 27–44.

112. Fred M. Hechinger, "Teachers Should be Open to Pay Reform," *The Tampa Tribune*, June 28, 1983.

113. "Secretary Bell Would Fund Model 'Master-Teacher' Projects," *Education Week* 2 (July 1983): 13.

114. Hugh Sidey, "School Days, Then and Now," *Time*, July 11, 1983, 16.

115. Joan Newman, "From Past to Future: School Violence in a Broad View," *Contemporary Education* 52 (Fall 1980): 10.

116. Patricia Albjerg Graham, "Whither Equality of Educational Opportunity?" Daedalus (Summer 1980): 121.

117. Ibid.

118. Newman, "From Past to Future," 10.

119. Graham, "Wither Equality of Educational Opportunity?," 121.

Appendix:

An Educational Research Guide

This guide has been designed to assist further investigation of topics presented in the text or other educational topics of interest. It includes references to standard works that are usually available in most public libraries as well as in college and university libraries.

Good accounts of the issues and problems attendant to teaching in general and to the teaching of the various school subjects, as well as a review of the research related to those issues and problems, can be found in the third edition of *Handbook of Research on Teaching,* edited by Merlin C. Wittrock (New York: Macmillan, 1985). Still very useful are the earlier editions: *Second Handbook of Research on Teaching,* edited by Robert M. W. Travers (Chicago: Rand McNally, 1973) and *Handbook of Research on Teaching,* edited by Nathaniel L. Gage (Chicago: Rand McNally, 1963).

Information and bibliography on teaching as well as other educational topics, such as school surveys, school libraries, reading, school transportation (busing), and testing, can be found in one of the five editions of the *Encyclopedia of Educational Research,* completed under the auspices of the American Educational Research Association. The complete citations for these are: *Encyclopedia of Educational Research,* edited by Walter S. Monroe (New York: Macmillan 1941); the revised edition, also edited by Walter S. Monroe (New York: Macmillan, 1950); the third edition, edited by Chester W. Harris (New York: Macmillan, 1960); the fourth edition, edited by Robert L. Ebel (New York: Macmillan, 1970); and a four-volume edition edited by Harold E. Mitzel (New York: Macmillan, 1982). Comparison of articles on the same topics in the several editions can provide an overview of the topic's development over several decades. A selected bibliography of the best work on a topic usually follows each article. The American Educational Research Association has also established an annual *Review of Research in Education.* The first issue in this series appeared in 1973. In these reviews the reader can find information and bibliography on a variety of educational topics.

Those interested in comparing the development of public education in their states to the development of public education in the nation or to other states may want to begin with the first volume of *Education in the United States: Historical Development and Outlook,* edited by Jim B. Pearson and Edgar Fuller (Washington, D.C.: National Education Association, 1969). The second volume, *Education in the United States: Nationwide Development Since 1900,* is a good beginning for more recent developments. Together these two volumes provide good summaries of the organization and development of public education in the states. They also include references to the standard histories of education in each of the fifty states.

313

Less compact than the references already cited are the *Yearbooks* of the National Society for the Study of Education (NSSE), which have been published since 1902, and as a series, cover just about every topic imaginable; the *Yearbook of Education,* which began in 1932 and became the *World Yearbook of Education* in 1965; and the Teachers College, Columbia University Contributions to Education—a set that now contains nearly one thousand volumes.

Other useful works are *The Educator's Encyclopedia* edited by Edward W. Smith and others (Englewood Cliffs, N.J.: Prentice-Hall, 1961); the ten volumes of *The Encyclopedia of Education,* edited by Lee C. Deighton (New York: Crowell-Collier, 1971); and the five volumes of *A Cyclopedia of Education,* edited by Paul Monroe (New York: Macmillan, 1911). Monroe's *Cyclopedia* is over half a century old but is still interesting and useful. From it one can see how education, as a field, was conceptualized and organized at the turn of the century and how that basic conceptualization and organization has endured.

For handy lists of references to educational topics, one should consult Marda L. Woodbury, *A Guide to Sources of Educational Information* (Arlington, Va.: Information Resources Press, 1982); Dorothea M. Barry, *A Bibliographic Guide to Educational Research* (Metuchen, N.J.: Scarecrow Press, 1975); Arvid J. Burke, *Documentation in Education* (New York: Teachers College Press, 1967); and Theodore Manheim, *Sources in Educational Research: A Selected and Annotated Bibliography* (Detroit: Wayne State University Press, 1969).

For material on recent developments in education and studies related to policy questions, two weekly newspapers, *Education Week* and the *Chronicle of Higher Education* are useful. The Rand Corporation of Santa Monica, California, periodically publishes annotated bibliographies of its publications. For its bibliography of materials on education see Rand Publication No. SB-1026.

Many libraries now offer nonprint data bases. Computer data bases that are useful and likely to be available in most college and university libraries are *Child Abuse and Neglect,* which is available from DIALOG Information Retrieval Service, and *Family Resources,* which is available from Bibliographic Retrieval Service. Students should also consult with their reference librarian about ERIC for materials on virtually all educational topics.

Biographical sources for leaders in American education, past and present, are plentiful. Two that are readily available are *Who's Who in American Education* and the three-volume *Biographical Dictionary of American Educators,* edited by John F. Ohles (Westport, Conn.: Greenwood Press, 1978). For material on those in the field of education and related areas, one or more of the following should be consulted: Maxine Block, ed., *Current Biography: Who's Who and Why* (New York: H. W. Wilson, 1942); the supplementary Yearbooks, *Who Was Who in America,* which covers historical figures from 1607 to the present; *Who's Who in America,* which has been in existence for more than a hundred and thirty years; *Who Was Who,* a companion to *Who's Who;* and the original *Dictionary of American Biography* and its more recent supplements.

In recent years, many directories to works by and about "special populations" have appeared. Compilations of materials on women and women's studies and issues are increasing in number rapidly. Relatively recent guides to the literature on women's studies include Hasia R. Diner, *Women and Urban Society: A Guide to Information Sources* (Detroit: Gale Research, 1979); Elizabeth H. Oakes and Kathleen E. Sheldon, *Guide to Social Science Resources in Women's Studies* (Santa Barbara, Calif. Clio Books, 1978); Virginia R. Terris, *Women in*

America: A Guide to Information Sources (Detroit: Gale Research, 1980); and Mary Anne Warren, *The Nature of Women: An Encyclopedia and Guide to the Literature* (Inverness, Calif.: Edgepress, 1980). Also useful are the three volumes of *Notable American Women, 1607–1950: A Biographical Dictionary* (Cambridge, Mass.: Belknap Press, 1971) and its more recent companion volume, *Notable American Women, The Modern Period: A Biographical Dictionary* (Cambridge, Mass.: Belknap, 1980); Esther Stineman, *American Political Women: Contemporary and Historical Profiles* (Littleton, Colo.: Libraries Unlimited, 1980); and *Women: A Selected Bibliography,* edited by Patricia O'Connor (Springfield, Ohio: Wittenberg University, 1973), which lists books and articles under several categories: anthropology and biology, psychology, economics, social conditions and theory, law and political science, history, biographies and autobiographies, and education.

Good beginnings for literature on minority groups is the fourth edition of Jack F. Kinton's *American Ethnic Groups and the Revival of Cultural Pluralism* (Aurora, Ill.: Social Science and Sociological Resources, 1974), which includes direction to materials on various ethnic groups in the United States, as well as references to works on race relations and ethnic group theory. Also see Meyer Weinberg's *The Education of the Minority Child: A Comprehensive Bibliography of 10,000 Selected Entries* (Chicago: Integrated Education Association, 1970).

For bibliographies on the Afro-American and Afro-American experience in America see Elizabeth W. Miller and Mary L. Fisher, *The Negro in America: A Bibliography* (Cambridge, Mass.: Harvard University Press, 1970); Dennis C. Bakewell, *The Black Experience in the United States* (Northridge, Calif.: San Fernando Valley State College Foundation, 1970); and Lenwood G. Davis, *The Black Woman in American Society* (Boston: G. K. Hall, 1975).

For those who like to examine documents from the period they are studying as well as earlier periods, there are many good collections. A very ambitious collection is the five-volume *Education in the United States: A Documentary History,* edited by Sol Cohen (New York: Random House, 1974). Cohen provides an extensive collection that covers the last four centuries and also some very useful and thorough introductory essays. The standard collection devoted to education in the South is *A Documentary History of Education in the South Before 1860,* five volumes edited by Edgar W. Knight (Chapel Hill, N.C.: University of North Carolina Press, 1949–1953).

An outstanding collection on American children and youth is *Children and Youth in America,* three volumes edited by Robert H. Bremner and others (Cambridge, Mass.: Harvard University Press, 1970).

Periodical literature on education is more than abundant. Direction to articles either by topic or by author can be found in the *Education Index,* which has been published continuously since 1929. Hundreds of journals and periodicals may be of interest and use. The following is a selected list of generally available journals with the year of their first issue: *Educational Forum* (1936); *Educational Record* (1920); *Educational Research* (1958); *Educational Review* (1948); *Educational Studies* (1970); *Educational Theory* (1951); *Elementary School Journal* (1900); *History of Childhood Quarterly* (1973), which became the *Journal of Psychohistory* in 1964; *History of Education Quarterly* (1961); *Journal of Education* (1875); *Journal of Educational Psychology* (1910); *Journal of Educational Research* (1920); *Phi Delta Kappan* (1915); *Review of Education* (1975); *Review of Educational Research* (1931); *Women's Studies Abstracts* (1972); and *Women's Studies Newsletter* (1972).

Index